Suriname

el Guide

edition
I

www.bradtguides.com

Bradt Travel Guides Ltd, UK
The Globe Pequot Press Inc, USA

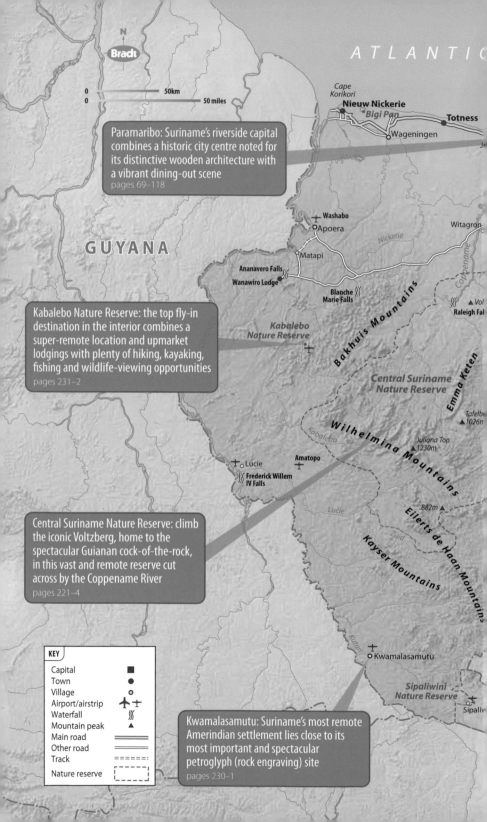

ATLANTIC

Cape Korikori

Nieuw Nickerie
Bigi Pan
● Wageningen
Totness

Paramaribo: Suriname's riverside capital combines a historic city centre noted for its distinctive wooden architecture with a vibrant dining-out scene
pages 69–118

Washabo
○ Apoera
Matapi
Witagron

GUYANA

Nickerie

Coppename

Ananavero Falls
Wanawiro Lodge

Blanche Marie Falls

▲ Vol
Raleigh Fal

Bakhuis Mountains

Kabalebo Nature Reserve: the top fly-in destination in the interior combines a super-remote location and upmarket lodgings with plenty of hiking, kayaking, fishing and wildlife-viewing opportunities
pages 231–2

Kabalebo Nature Reserve

Central Suriname Nature Reserve

Emma Keten

Tafelbe ▲1026m

Wilhelmina Mountains

Kabalebo

Juliana Top ▲1230m

+ ○ Lucie
Amatopo
Frederick Willem IV Falls

882m ▲

Central Suriname Nature Reserve: climb the iconic Voltzberg, home to the spectacular Guianan cock-of-the-rock, in this vast and remote reserve cut across by the Coppename River
pages 221–4

Lucie

Zuid

Eilerts de Haan Mountains

Kayser Mountains

Kutari

○ Kwamalasamutu

Sipaliwini Nature Reserve

○ Sipaliw

KEY

Capital	■
Town	●
Village	○
Airport/airstrip	✈ +
Waterfall	⌇⌇
Mountain peak	▲
Main road	═══
Other road	═══
Track	======
Nature reserve	⌐ ¬

Kwamalasamutu: Suriname's most remote Amerindian settlement lies close to its most important and spectacular petroglyph (rock engraving) site
pages 230–1

N

Bradt

0   50km
0   50 miles

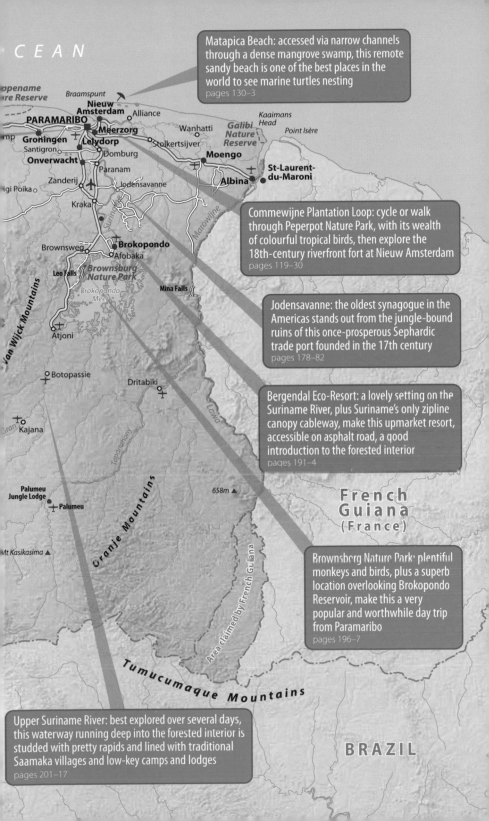

Matapica Beach: accessed via narrow channels through a dense mangrove swamp, this remote sandy beach is one of the best places in the world to see marine turtles nesting
pages 130–3

Commewijne Plantation Loop: cycle or walk through Peperpot Nature Park, with its wealth of colourful tropical birds, then explore the 18th-century riverfront fort at Nieuw Amsterdam
pages 119–30

Jodensavanne: the oldest synagogue in the Americas stands out from the jungle-bound ruins of this once-prosperous Sephardic trade port founded in the 17th century
pages 178–82

Bergendal Eco-Resort: a lovely setting on the Suriname River, plus Suriname's only zipline canopy cableway, make this upmarket resort, accessible on asphalt road, a good introduction to the forested interior
pages 191–4

Brownsberg Nature Park: plentiful monkeys and birds, plus a superb location overlooking Brokopondo Reservoir, make this a very popular and worthwhile day trip from Paramaribo
pages 196–7

Upper Suriname River: best explored over several days, this waterway running deep into the forested interior is studded with pretty rapids and lined with traditional Saamaka villages and low-key camps and lodges
pages 201–17

Suriname
Don't
miss...

Wildlife
Seek out colourful birds and monkeys
in the Central Suriname Nature
Reserve (AZ) pages 221–4

Architecture
Be enchanted by the Dutch-Creole
architecture of the Historic Inner City
of Paramaribo (AZ) pages 101–14

Turtles
The beaches of
Matapica and Galibi
are the ideal spots
for turtle viewing
(AZ) pages 130–3
and 143–7

**Rapids and
remote villages**
Take a boat up the river
and pass the isolated
villages of the
Upper Suriname
(AZ) pages 201–17

Ziplining
Speed along the
zipline cableway at the
top-notch Berg en Dal
Adventure Centre
(AZ) page 194

Suriname in colour

above In the suburb of Weg-na-Zee, the Tirat Sthaan Rameswarem Temple is one of the country's largest Hindu shrines (AZ) page 116

below left A statue of Johan Pengel, Prime Minister from 1963 to 1969, stands in front of the Ministry of Finance on Paramaribo's Independence Square (AZ) page 104

below right The distinctive wooden architecture associated with Paramaribo is largely a product of the city's location – Suriname possesses an almost unparalleled natural supply of timber (AZ) pages 101–14

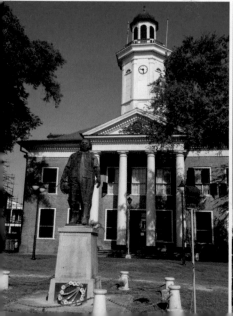

above   The Commewijne Plantation Loop covers a 60km road loop that runs past several of the more popular sites (AZ) pages 119–30

right   Albina, situated on the Marowijne River, is the springboard for boat trips to the Galibi Nature Reserve (AZ) pages 139–42

below left   The large, covered central market at Nieuw Nickerie (AZ) page 166

below right   The second-largest settlement in Upper Suriname, the alleys of New Aurora are lined with stilted wooden palm-roofed houses, some of them still adorned with elaborate traditionally carved façades (AZ) pages 208–11

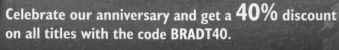

AUTHOR

Philip Briggs (e *philip.briggs@bradtguides.com*) has been writing for Bradt Travel Guides since 1991, when he authored the first guidebook to South Africa to be published internationally after the release of Nelson Mandela. During the rest of the 1990s, Philip wrote a series of pioneering Bradt guides to destinations that were then – and in some cases still are – otherwise practically uncharted by the travel publishing industry. These included the first dedicated guidebooks to Tanzania, Uganda, Ethiopia, Malawi, Mozambique, Ghana and Rwanda, all of which are  still regularly updated for ongoing new editions. More recently, he has authored the first guidebook to Somaliland and a new guide to The Gambia, both for Bradt. Philip still spends several months on the road every year, usually accompanied by his wife, the travel photographer Ariadne Van Zandbergen, and spends the rest of his time battering away at a keyboard in Plettenberg Bay, South Africa.

CONTRIBUTOR

From Macedonia to Mozambique, as a writer and tourism consultant, **Kirk Smock** (*www.kirksmock.com*) has worked in and written about numerous countries. The one that has held his attention the longest is Guyana, Suriname's neighbour and near biodiversity twin. Kirk is the author of the Bradt guide to Guyana and his writings have appeared in numerous publications.

ACKNOWLEDGEMENTS

My first and biggest debt is to my wife Ariadne Van Zandbergen for her company in Suriname and support at home. While on the road, and while writing the book up afterwards, I received a massive amount of support, assistance and other input both from within the tourist industry and from other travellers I met along the way. This wouldn't be the book it is without the input of the following people, and my ongoing gratitude goes out to them all: Amichand Jhauw, Avinash Radjkoemar, Bill Mauk, Bjorn de Jager, Brigitte Küchler, Bryan van 't Kruys, Chapeau Siesa, Charlotte Merckaert, Claire Antell, Claudia Langer, Dale Battistoli, Dara Lipton, Donovan Waterberg, Egon von Foidl, Emma Thomson, Etto Paulus, Evan Delahanty, Fabienne and Yayo of Un Pied-à-Terre, Fokke Kooistra, Frans 'Jangjanman' Dinge, Frans van Beersum, Iris Van de Vijver, Jan Van Charante, Jan van Swaaij, Jeewan Viera, Jenny Kornelis, Joan Lieuw, Jolijn Geels, Joyce Dawson, Judith Luijken, Karel Dawson, Karen Van Eyndhoven, Katie Fahrland, Kirk Smock, Kitty Verheul, Leonoor Wagenaar, Liesbeth Gummels, Lizet Van Velzen, Marco Becker, Monique Pool, Natascha de Randamie, Natascha Verbij, Nelson Tiapoe, Nigel Redman, Raghenie Radjkoemar, Rea Karijoredjo, René Segerius, Roché Wong A Fa, Ronny Bhoelai, Safora Hermelijn, Steffi Robberecht, Stephanie Kramawitana, Thomas Laurens, Vincent Van Twuijver, Wouter Vergeer, Yves Tjon and Zeudi Dawson.

PUBLISHER'S FOREWORD   *Adrian Phillips, Managing Director*

Bradt and Philip Briggs have a very long and happy partnership – Philip has been writing Bradt guides for nearly 25 years. He's best known for his unrivalled coverage of Africa, but once in a while Philip fancies a change of scenery. And so he jumped at the chance to write the first English-language guide to Suriname. It's a perfect 'Philip' place: wildlife-rich and with lots of exciting opportunities for the adventurous independent traveller. Suriname remains under-developed as a tourist destination but Philip's meticulously researched book charts the way for those travellers who recognise its enormous potential.

First edition published February 2015
Bradt Travel Guides Ltd
IDC House, The Vale, Chalfont St Peter, Bucks SL9 9RZ, England
www.bradtguides.com
Print edition published in the USA by The Globe Pequot Press Inc,
PO Box 480, Guilford, Connecticut 06437-0480

Text copyright © 2015 Philip Briggs
Text in Chapter 2, Wildlife copyright © 2011 Kirk Smock and Philip Briggs
Maps copyright © 2015 Bradt Travel Guides Ltd
Photographs copyright © 2015 Individual photographers (see below)
Project Managers: Claire Strange, Katie Wilding
Cover research: Pepi Bluck, Perfect Picture

ISBN: 978 1 84162 910 0 (print)
e-ISBN: 978 1 78477 111 3 (e-pub)
e-ISBN: 978 1 78477 213 0 (mobi)

British Library Cataloguing in Publication Data
A catalogue record for this book is available from the British Library

Photographs
Ariadne Van Zandbergen (AZ); Suriname Tourism Foundation (STF)
Front cover Sloth (AZ)
Back cover Saramacca River (AZ)
Title page Channel-billed toucan (AZ); fishing on the Upper Suriname River (AZ); traditional woodcarving (AZ)

Maps David McCutcheon FBCart.S; colour map relief base by Nick Rowland FRGS
Base mapping modified by Bradt Travel Guides, provided by ITMB Publishing Ltd
(www.itmb.com) 2014.

Typeset from the author's disc by Ian Spick, Bradt Travel Guides
Production managed by Jellyfish Print Solutions; printed in India
Digital conversion by the Firsty Group

Contents

Introduction

Suriname is an odd little place. Geographically, it forms part of South America, and though quite large by European standards, it is actually the smallest country on that immense continent. Politically, it looks more towards the Caribbean, or even to the Netherlands, than to the rest of South America. Indeed, as the only Dutch-speaking country on the American mainland, supporting an ethnically diverse population of predominantly West African, Indonesian and Asian descent, Suriname is emphatically not Latin American in character, nor does it seem to sway to a calypso beat. It is just, well, odd – a real one-off kind of place, individualistic, singular, and utterly intriguing.

Suriname has three main attractions. The first is its characterful multi-ethnic capital Paramaribo, whose historic inner city has been inscribed as a UNESCO World Heritage Site on account of its unique Dutch-Creole architecture, a style epitomised by the spectacular Cathedral of Saint Peter and Paul, which is reputedly the largest wooden structure in the western hemisphere. This wealth of colonial architectural gems aside, Paramaribo, set on the west bank of the Suriname River, is also a very relaxed, safe and enjoyable city, noted for its lively waterfront bars and cosmopolitan culinary scene.

Suriname's second key attraction is the coastal hinterland around Paramaribo. True, this murky-watered, mangrove-lined stretch of Atlantic coastline is somewhat deficient when it comes to conventional beach resorts but it has a lot to offer wildlife enthusiasts. The Surinamese coast includes some of the world's finest and most reliable marine turtle-viewing sites, particularly at Matapica and Galibi, while the likes of Bigi Pan and Warappa Creek offer superlative aquatic and marine birdwatching, and dolphins are regularly encountered in the Suriname Estuary downriver of Paramaribo. There are also some fascinating cultural and historic sites within easy day-tripping distance of the capital, ranging from the brooding ruins of the old Sephardic settlement of Jodensavanne and the solid bastions of Fort Nieuw Amsterdam to isolated Marron villages such as Santigron and Berlijn.

Last but by no means least among Suriname's attractions is the immense tract of pristine rainforest that swathes the interior. This vast and thinly inhabited wilderness, a northern extension of the Amazon jungle, is home to an untold wealth of wildlife, ranging from secretive, solitary jaguars to inquisitive and sociable squirrel monkeys, from the outsized psychedelic macaws that screech overhead to the iridescent *Morpho* butterflies that flutter beguilingly along the forest tails. The interior is also home to a small number of astonishingly remote villages. Some, such as Palumeu and Kwamalasamutu, are inhabited by Amerindian peoples whose tenancy stretches back to the pre-Columbian era. Others, most notably along the Upper Suriname, were established by the Saamaka, Paramacca and other 'Marron' descendants of escaped slaves who still retain a strong West African cultural identity.

Largely untrammelled by roads but penetrated by a series of long, wide navigable rivers, the jungle of the deep interior is accessible only by light aircraft or by motorised dugout boat. Flying in is the more efficient approach, and though relatively costly, it does provide passengers with a magnificent grandstand aerial view over an endless canopy tinged a hundred shades of green. But exploring the interior by boat – whether it's the three-hour approach to Raleigh Falls up the Coppename River, or a longer lodge-hopping excursion up the Upper Suriname and Gran Rio – is the stealthier and more adventurous option, leading to a feeling of total immersion in this mesmerising landscape.

Although few visitors to Suriname would want to miss out on at least one excursion into the deep interior, those with limited time, money or tolerance for basic travel conditions will find plenty of opportunities to explore slightly tamer tracts of jungle closer to Paramaribo. At the most luxurious end of the scale, the superb Bergendal Eco-Resort lies on the Suriname River little more than an hour's drive from the capital on a good, surfaced road. More affordably, Peperpot Nature Park and Brownsberg Nature Park provide equally alluring but very different opportunities to see colourful forest birds and monkeys in their natural habitat. Suriname is in fact so thinly populated that almost every settlement or resort outside the capital in fringed by some unexpectedly wild forest and/or swamp habitats.

Despite all this, tourism to Suriname is still in its infancy. True, there is no shortage of midrange to upmarket hotels in the capital, which also has a lively restaurant scene, but mostly these cater towards business travellers and Dutch-based visitors with strong family connections to Suriname. Further afield, facilities are generally rather basic (a few notable exceptions such as the Bergendal and Kabalebo resorts notwithstanding) and exploration is almost always in the form of day or overnight trips out of the capital to a specific site in the hinterland of Paramaribo or the deep interior. But much of the country is also open to independent travel, whether it be cycling, bussing or self driving through the developed coastal belt, or lodge-hopping with the taxi-boats that service the remote villages of the Upper Suriname. Indeed, like so many countries with a small nascent tourist industry, Suriname makes for a fabulously rewarding travel destination – safe, relaxed, unaffected, friendly and easy to get around!

LIST OF MAPS

AUTHOR'S FAVOURITES

Finding genuinely characterful accommodation or that unmissable off-the-beaten-track café can be difficult, so the author has chosen a few of his favourite places throughout the country to point you in the right direction. These 'author's favourites' are marked with a ✳.

MAPS

Keys and symbols

Maps include alphabetical keys covering the locations of those places to stay, eat or drink that are featured in the book. Note that regional maps may not show all hotels and restaurants in the area: other establishments may be located in towns shown on the map.

Grids and grid references

Several maps use gridlines to allow easy location of sites. Map grid references are listed in square brackets after the name of the place or sight of interest in the text, with page number followed by grid number, eg: [80 C3].

On occasion, hotels or restaurants that are not listed in the guide (but which might serve as alternative options if required or serve as useful landmarks to aid navigation) are also included on the maps; these are marked with accommodation (🏠) or restaurant (✗) symbols.

Road names

To improve clarity on the maps, the Dutch words such as 'street', 'lane', 'way' have not been used, so while the text may typically say Hajary Straat, Letitia Vriesde Laan and Grote Combe Weg, the maps will show Hajary, Letitia Vriesde and Grote Combe.

Administered by author Philip Briggs, Bradt's Suriname update website www.bradtupdates.com/suriname is an online forum where travellers can post and read the latest travel news, trip reports and factual updates from Suriname. The website is a free service to readers, or to anybody else who cares to drop by, and travellers to Suriname and people in the tourist industry are encouraged to use it share their comments, grumbles, insights, news or other feedback. These can be posted directly on the website, or emailed to Philip (e philip.briggs@bradtguides.com).

It's easy to keep up to date with the latest posts by following Philip on Twitter (@philipbriggs) and/or liking his Facebook page: www.facebook.com/pb.travel.updates.

You can also add a review of the book to www.bradtguides.com or Amazon.

Part One

GENERAL INFORMATION

Location Northeast Atlantic coast of South America

Neighbouring countries Bordered by Guyana to the west, French Guiana to the east and Brazil to the south

Size 163,821km² (63,251 square miles)

Population 550,000 (2014 estimate)

Climate Topical: hot and moist all year, with the main rainy seasons falling from late April–August and November–February.

Status Republic

Capital Paramaribo

Economy Major earners are mining, forestry, agriculture and tourism

GDP US$5.23 billion (2013)

Gross National Income per capita US$4,650 (2013)

Languages Dutch is the official language. Sranan Tongo is a widely used Creole street language. Many other minority languages are also spoken.

Religion Around 48% Christian, 22% Hindu, 14% Muslim (2012). The remainder follow traditional or unspecified faiths, or none at all.

Currency Suriname dollar (SRD), divided into 100 cents

Exchange rate £1 = SRD 5.15, US$1 = SRD 3.28, €1 = SRD 4.09 (November 2014); for up-to-date rates, go to www.xe.com

International telephone code +597

Time GMT/UTC -3 hours

Electricity 110/127V AC at 60 cycles per second

Weights and measures Metric

Flag Three horizontal stripes – green top and bottom, red in the middle, each colour separated by a narrow white stripe. The red strip is the widest and incorporates a yellow star.

National anthem 'God zij met ons Suriname' ('God be with our Suriname')

National motto 'Justitia – Pietas – Fides' (Latin for 'Justice – Piety – Trust')

Public holidays 1 January, 25 February, 1 May, 1 July, 9 August, 10 October, 25 November, 25 December, 26 December (for details of public holidays where dates vary, see pages 51–2)

1

Background Information

GEOGRAPHY AND LOCATION

Extending over 163,821km², Suriname is the smallest country in South America, though not the smallest distinct territory (neighbouring French Guiana, an overseas *département* of France, is only half the size). By global standards, however, Suriname is a medium-sized territory, ranked 92nd in the world, with a total area almost identical to that of the United Kingdom excluding Scotland, slightly smaller than the US state of Georgia, and four times larger than the Netherlands, its former coloniser. Bordered by the Atlantic to the north, French Guiana to the east, Brazil to the south and Guyana to the west, it lies between approximate latitudes of 3°35 and 4°10 W and longitudes of 1°50 and 6°30 N.

Suriname (formerly Dutch Guiana) forms part of a geographic region often referred to as the Guianas, which also comprises the state of Guyana (formerly British Guiana), the French *département* of Guiana and (depending on one's exact definition) the Brazilian state of Amapá (formerly Portuguese and then Brazilian Guiana) and the Venezuelan region of Guayana (formerly Spanish Guyana). All five of these Guianan components extend southwards from South America's northeast Atlantic coastline to the Amazon Basin, and they share a very similar geography, flora and fauna.

Like the other territories in the Guianas, Suriname is underlain by the Guiana Shield, a geologically stable Precambrian formation of predominantly crystalline rocks (such as granite and gneiss) that extends over some 1,500,000km² bounded by the Orinoco River to the northwest, the Rio Negro to the southwest and the Amazon River to the south. The Guiana Shield supports the world's largest expanse of undisturbed tropical rainforest, with a broadly similar floral and faunal composition to the Amazon Basin, of which it is essentially a northern extension. Unsurprisingly, the Guianan rainforest is recognised as one of the world's most important centres of biodiversity, supporting an estimated 15,000 vascular plant species (around 5% of the global total) and an ever-growing checklist of more than 2,000 vertebrate species, including 282 mammals, 1,004 birds (including around 50 regional endemics), 295 reptiles and 269 amphibians.

Most of Suriname is quite flat and densely forested. Indeed, some estimates place the total forest cover as high as 147,760km², accounting for 90% of Suriname's surface area, the highest of any country in the world. Average elevations are low throughout but increase in the south, which is studded with quartzite protrusions and the table-like mountains of the Guiana Highlands. The most extensive of Surinamese ranges is the Wilhelmina Mountains, which run for about 115km from east to west, and include the country's highest peak, the 1,280m Juliana Top, along with another well-known formation, the 1,026m Tafelberg (Table Mountain).

Suriname's most prominent geographic features are the rivers that flow through the country in a broadly northerly direction before emptying into the Atlantic.

The most important of these in human terms is undoubtedly the 480km-long Suriname River, the banks of which support the capital Paramaribo and several smaller towns. It is also an important shipping conduit and site of the hydro-electric Afobaka Dam and associated Brokopondo Reservoir. Other important rivers, most of them navigable deep inland, running from east to west, are the Marowijne (bordering French Guinea), Cottica and Commewijne (both of which ultimately flow into the Suriname mouth), Saramacca, Coppename, Nickerie and Corantijn (on the border with Guyana).

ADMINISTRATIVE DIVISIONS Suriname was first divided into administrative areas by royal Dutch decree in 1834, at which point the colony essentially consisted of the coastal belt and plantations along the various rivers. Nickerie and Coronie were declared full districts largely because of how remote they were, while the area closer to Paramaribo was divided into eight: Upper Suriname and Torarica, Lower Commewijne, Upper Commewijne, Matapica, Lower Cottica, Upper Cottica and Perica, Saramacca and Para.

In 1927, the colony was reorganised into seven districts. Three of these closely resembled their modern namesakes: Paramaribo, Commewijne (capital Nieuw Amsterdam) and Coronie (capital Totness). The other four, namely Marowijne (capital Albina), Nickerie (capital Nieuw Nickerie), Saramacca (capital Groningen) and Suriname (administered from Paramaribo) were much larger, stretching inland along the rivers for which they were named towards the Brazilian border.

Brokopondo and Para districts were split from Suriname District in 1958 and 1966 respectively. The ten modern districts of Suriname (see box below) date to 1985, when the remote southern reaches of Marowijne, Nickerie, Saramacca and Suriname were amalgamated into the vast but thinly populated district of Sipaliwini, which now accounts for 80% of the country's surface area but supports a mere 7% of the population.

Below district level, the country is divided into 62 *ressorts*, whose names often have a strong significance locally. As with districts, ressorts vary greatly in area and population. Most of the 12 ressorts in Paramaribo District are less than 10km^2 and each one typically supports 15,000–30,000 people. Elsewhere, however, there are several ressorts that support fewer than 500 people, while the Tapahony Ressort in Sipaliwini at 42,199km^2 covers a significantly larger area than that of the nine other districts combined.

DISTRICTS OF SURINAME (LARGEST TO SMALLEST)

	Capital	Area (km^2)	Population (2012)
Sipaliwini	None	130,567	37,065
Brokopondo	Brokopondo	7,364	15,909
Para	Onverwacht	5,393	24,700
Nickerie	Nieuw Nickerie	5,353	34,233
Marowijne	Albina	4,627	18,294
Coronie	Totness	3,902	3,391
Saramacca	Groningen	3,636	17,480
Commewijne	Nieuw Amsterdam	2,353	31,420
Wanica	Lelydorp	443	118,222
Paramaribo	Paramaribo	182	240,924

CLIMATE

Its equatorial location and low altitudes ensure that Suriname has a typically hot, sunny and moist tropical climate. Temperatures are fairly consistent throughout the year and countrywide, typically hitting a daily maximum of around 30°C, exacerbated by a high relative humidity (typically more than 80%) but tempered in many areas by a river or sea breeze. Average annual rainfall in most parts of the country is around 2,000mm. It rains year-round, mostly in the form of short dramatic cloudbursts, but rainfall peaks during the two wet seasons, which run from late April to August and from November to February. There is still quite a bit of rain in the intervening dry seasons, as indicated in the weather charts below, with Paramaribo being typical of the coastal belt and Brokopondo of sites further inland.

Paramaribo (coast)

	Jan	Feb	Mar	Apr	May	Jun	Jul	Aug	Sep	Oct	Nov	Dec
Max (°C)	29	29	29	30	29	29	30	31	31	31	29	29
Min (°C)	22	22	22	23	23	23	22	23	23	23	23	22
Rain (mm)	180	125	110	175	290	310	230	180	100	110	120	190

Brokopondo (interior)

	Jan	Feb	Mar	Apr	May	Jun	Jul	Aug	Sep	Oct	Nov	Dec
Max (°C)	30	30	30	31	30	30	31	32	33	33	32	31
Min (°C)	22	22	22	23	23	23	23	23	23	23	22	22
Rain (mm)	220	160	180	230	320	320	230	160	90	70	115	190

GOVERNMENT

The Republic of Suriname is a multi-party democracy whose current constitution was adopted in September 1987 following a national referendum. This constitution superseded a 1975 constitution that was suspended five years later in the wake of the coup of 25 February 1980, but resembles its predecessor in several respects. It allows for a unicameral National Assembly whose 51 members are elected democratically every five years along lines of proportional representation. The National Assembly must elect the president, who also serves a five-year term, by a two-thirds majority, and the vice president by a simple 51% majority. A cabinet comprising 16 ministers is appointed by the president. The president must forfeit any additional posts in politics or business for the duration of his term, but there is no constitutional provision to remove or replace a president unless he resigns. Since the adoption of the new constitution, six general elections have been held, interrupted by a bloodless coup in 1990, resulting in five legitimate changes of president. Recent elections have typically attracted a voter turnout of around 70% and the last two resulted in coalition governments, with no party winning an outright majority. The next election is due in May 2015. The judiciary is headed by a Supreme Court, members of which are appointed for life by the president in consultation with the National Assembly and two other judicial bodies.

As might be expected of such a sparsely populated country, Suriname has a modest economy, with a gross domestic product (GDP) estimated at US$5.23 billion in 2013 placing it around 150th in the world. However, the picture appears far healthier when you look at the per capita PPP (GDP at purchasing power parity), where the World Bank placed Suriname 68th in the world between 2011 and 2013. The country also fares reasonably well (marginally better than the global average) in terms of other quality-of-life indicators such as average life expectancy (74.5 years), child mortality rates (21.1 deaths per 1,000 births), intentional homicide rates (6.1 per 100,000 inhabitants) and adult literacy rate (90%). Anecdotally, Suriname also seems far less blighted by economic inequality than most so-called developing nations, and it seems to be almost entirely free of the gross poverty frequently encountered in many parts of Africa and Asia.

The traditional mainstay of the Surinamese economy is mining. And throughout most of the 20th century, mining in Suriname was practically synonymous with the extraction of the alumina-bearing ore **bauxite** (see box, opposite page). The colony's first bauxite mine was established in 1920 at Moengo, to the east of Paramaribo, by the Aluminium Company of America (Alcoa), which soon after also established mines at Paranam and Onverwacht to the south of the capital. In 1957, the Suriname government and Alcoa joined forces to form the Suriname Aluminium Company (Suralco), which still dominates the local industry today. As recently as 2001, alumina exports accounted for 72% of Suriname's export earnings, and while that figure has since dropped to around 35% today, partly due to the closure of the smelter in Paranam, there is plenty of scope for future development at as yet unexploited sites such as Bakhuis.

Bauxite mining has been the primary or sole impetus for much of the country's subsequent infrastructural development, often aided by Dutch or US funding. The international airport at Zanderij owes its existence to the bauxite industry, as does the Afobaka hydro-electric dam and the associated Brokopondo Reservoir (see box, pages 198–9), and the airstrips, roads, ports and yet-to-be-used railway constructed as part of Operation Grasshopper and the West Suriname Plan in the 1960s and 1970s (see box, page 220).

The 21st century has seen a resurgence in Suriname's long-dormant **gold**-mining industry, and the country is now ranked as the world's 26th largest producer of this commodity. Low-key gold mining first took place in Suriname following the discovery of deposits in the vicinity of Brokopondo and the Lawa River in the late 19th century. It was the presence of gold in these areas that led to the construction of the railway connecting Paramaribo to Brownsweg between 1902 and 1913, and the associated development of Lelydorp as the country's second-largest town. However, it was only in 2004 that the first modern gold mine opened, in the form of the 170km² Rosebel concession north of Brokopondo. A joint venture between the Canadian IAMGOLD Corporation (70%) and the Government of Suriname (30%), Rosebel employs more than 1,000 people and is the country's main supplier of gold, which now accounts for about 24% of export revenue. This is supplemented by gold supplied by an estimated 20,000 small-scale operators, known derogatively as *porknokkers*, many of whom are illegal immigrants from China, Brazil and elsewhere, and fewer than 5% of which are government registered. In June 2013, it was announced that a second large-scale gold mine would be opened at Merian, 65km south of Moengo. No date for the opening has been announced, but when it does happen, it will most likely boost gold production.

Another growing industry is offshore oil extraction and petroleum production. In 2013, the state-owned oil company Staatsolie extracted around 16,000 barrels of crude oil per day, while the refinery in Wanica produced 7,500 barrels of petroleum daily. Petroleum exports current account for about 10% of export revenue. Other important export industries are timber production, agriculture (in particular rice and bananas, which together account for 10% of export revenue) and fishing. Major imports are mostly related to the motor industry and include cars, construction vehicles, trucks and rubber tyres. The manufacturing industry is limited to small-scale enterprise producing processed foods, clothing, cigarettes, alcohol and import-substitution goods almost entirely aimed at the small domestic market. Service industries are also generally quite low-key and localised, but nevertheless account for around 40% of jobs, a larger proportion of the labour force than is

BAUXITE

The world's main source of aluminium, bauxite is a naturally occurring ore composed of aluminium-based minerals such as gibbsite, boehmite and diaspore, along with iron oxides such as goethite and haematite, the clayey mineral kaolinite, silica, titania and various trace elements. It is named after the Provençal village of Les Baux, where its aluminium content was first identified in 1821 by the French geologist Pierre Berthier. The rock in Les Baux is categorised as a karst or carbonate bauxite, formed by a combination of weathering and residual accumulation in clay strata above a soft limestone and dolomite base, and mainly occurring in Europe. The bauxite deposits in Suriname, as well as in certain other parts of South and Central America, Australia, Asia and West Africa, are lateritic bauxites, which means that they were formed by the lateritisation of granite, gneiss and other silicate bedrocks.

Because bauxite is almost always a surface rock, it is usually strip mined. In the 19th century, aluminium was extracted from the ore by a complicated process that involved heating it until molten, together with pure sodium or potassium, in a vacuum. This made aluminium among the most expensive of all natural materials, costlier even than gold. That changed in the 1880s when two 22-year-old scientists, the American student Charles Martin Hall and the Frenchman Paul Héroult, independently developed the more cost-efficient Hall–Héroult smelting process. The resultant reduction in the production cost of this lightweight but durable metal had a profound effect on the global economy, paving the way, for instance, for the modern aviation industry, which depends on aircraft made almost entirely from aluminium alloys. Hall would go on to found the Aluminium Company of America (Alcoa), which was largely responsible for opening Suriname up to bauxite mining.

Today, Australia is the world's main supplier of bauxite, accounting for around 30% of the global total of approximately 220 million tonnes. Other key producers include China, Brazil, India and Guinea. Suriname is one of the world's top ten bauxite suppliers, producing around five million tonnes annually, despite the dwindling reserves at the only active mine at Paranam and the inactivity of the smelter there since its closure in 1999. Fortunately, the long-term future of bauxite mining in Suriname looks good, with the global demand for aluminium now higher than ever, and known reserves of around 6,000 million tonnes scattered around the country, much of it in the vicinity of the Bakhuis Mountains.

employed by any other sector. The tourist industry, though still in its infancy, is rapidly growing and has enormous potential both to create employment and to encourage the conservation of protected areas and wildlife.

HISTORY

TIMELINE

8000BC	First human settlers arrive from North America
AD500	First agricultural societies in Suriname
1595	Spanish navigators land close to the mouth of the Suriname River
1630	Sephardic Jews found Torarica upriver of present-day Paramaribo
1651	The English colony of Willoughbyland, centred on Paramaribo, opens the first plantations in Suriname and imports the first slaves
1663	Fort Willoughby is captured by the Dutch and renamed Fort Zeelandia
1670s	Jodensavanne is established on the east bank of the Suriname River
1683	Amsterdam's Sociëteit van Suriname is ceded control of Paramaribo
1735–47	Fort Nieuw Amsterdam is built at the Commewijne–Suriname confluence
1740	The agricultural economy peaks with around 400 plantations operating. Tens of thousand of slaves are employed by these plantations, but several escape into the jungle to form Marron communities.
1762	Treaty signed between the colonial government and Saamaka Marrons
1776	Cordon Path opens to protect plantations along the Commewijne and Suriname rivers
1790	Fort Groningen is constructed at the site of the modern-day town of Groningen
1797	Scottish settlers establish the first two plantations in the Nickerie area
1799–1816	Suriname occupied by Britain for all but two years of the Napoleonic Wars
1807	Britain abolishes the slave trade throughout its empire, followed by the Dutch in 1814
1832	Jodensavanne is abandoned after being destroyed by fire
1834	Nickerie and Coronie districts created
1848	Paramaribo declared a free port
1863	Suriname abolishes slavery, offering freedom to its 33,000 slaves
1866	Suriname granted its own parliament by the Dutch
1876	Albina founded as capital of Marowijne District
1870s	Gold discovered in the vicinity of Lawa and Brokopondo
1879	Nieuw Nickerie established to replace the flooded New Rotterdam as capital of Nickerie District
1902	24 striking workers are shot dead by police at Mariënburg Plantation
1913	Lawa Railway from Paramaribo reaches its most southerly terminus near Brownsweg
1920	First bauxite mined at Moengo
1920s	Zanderij Airport opens as a stop for Pan Am flights to South America
1922	All Surinamers qualify for Dutch citizenship as Suriname is declared part of the Netherlands
1931	A year into the Great Depression, hunger riots break out in Paramaribo
1941	3,000 troops are flown into Suriname to protect US bauxite interests
1949	Wageningen built to service a US-funded rice production scheme
1954	Suriname is granted self-government

1959	Airstrips cut at seven remote sites to map the interior's unexplored natural resources under Operation Grasshopper
1960	Construction of the Afobaka Dam commences, with Brokopondo Reservoir first filling up in 1971
1975	Suriname attains full independence under President Henri Ferrier and Prime Minister Henck Arron.
1975–80	West Suriname Plan results in construction of Apoera port and a 300km road running west of Zanderij to service a planned bauxite mine at Bakhuis
1980	Arron and Ferrier are deposed in a bloodless coup that initiates seven years of *ipso facto* military dictatorship under Dési Bouterse
1982	15 prominent critics of the regime are executed by Bouterse in Fort Zeelandia
1985	Ten districts of Suriname created in their present form
1986	Outbreak of civil war in eastern Suriname results in the Moiwana Massacre near Albina
1987	New democratic constitution enacted after a public referendum. Civilian rule restored after the November election.
1990	Bouterse leads a second bloodless coup and installs another military backed government
1991	Civilian rule restored after an election brings Ronald Venetiaan to power. Venetiaan serves as president for all but four of the next 19 years (he is replaced by Jules Albert Wijdenbosch between 1996 and 2000).
2004	Rosebel gold mine opened north of Brokopondo
2010	The controversial former military dictator Dési Bouterse is elected president for a five-year term

PRE-COLUMBIAN ERA (UP TO 1498) Little is known about the prehistory of Suriname, which effectively covers the entire period prior to the arrival of Europeans. What can be ascertained is that the area was first settled around 10,000 years ago by the descendants of northeast Asian migrants who had crossed to Alaska perhaps 2,000 years earlier along a temporary land bridge formed at the end of the last Ice Age. Skilled hunters, these early Stone Age settlers left behind ample traces of their presence in the form of arrowheads, axes and other tools, as well as several petroglyph (rock engraving) sites, and intriguing one-off relicts such as a beautiful stone mask unearthed near Albina and now on display in the Suriname Museum in Paramaribo.

The earliest agriculture was introduced to present-day Suriname in around AD500, probably by Arawak migrants from the Amazon Basin. The Arawak mostly settled along the coastal plain, where they cultivated crops such as cassava, pineapple, tobacco and cotton in areas prone to seasonal flooding. Many Arawak people were driven inland along the rivers, and forced to adopt a slash-and-burn planting culture, following the arrival of the territorially expansive Carib people from the south circa AD1200. By the early 17th century, it is thought that Suriname was inhabited by around 20 different ethnic groups, each with its own distinct culture and language. Tragically, however, exposure to the first European settlers or more specifically to the guns and exotic diseases these intruders carried with them, led to the swift extinction of many such indigenous ethnic groups.

EUROPEAN CONTACT AND SETTLEMENT (1498–1674) The first documented sighting of the Surinamese coast was made by Christopher Columbus on his historic third voyage of 1498. However, the best part of a century would pass before the first recorded landing there, which took place in 1593, when a Spanish fleet explored the area around the Suriname River mouth, named it after the local Surinen people and staked a loose claim to the territory, one that was evidently never followed up by the Spanish crown. The first half of the 17th century saw several European attempts to establish a permanent settlement on the Suriname River, most of which were foiled by the resistance of the indigenous people, by disease or by the intervention of other foreign powers. These included short-lived Dutch and French encampments on the site of present-day Paramaribo, the closest point to the estuary and where the shore is not impeded by shallow sandbars.

The most substantial settlement in Suriname for much of the 17th century was Torarica (also spelled Thorarica), which was situated on the west bank of the Suriname about 50km upriver of Paramaribo (close to the present-day Overbridge River Resort). Torarica was established in around 1630 by Sephardic Jews, and its name is most likely from the Portuguese for 'Rich Torah' (the latter a Hebrew word that means 'teaching', but also refers to the five Old Testament books known to Christians as the Pentateuch). It could also derive from the Arawak phrase Toraraharariraca, meaning 'Place of White People'. Torarica was strategically located on a wide bend of the river where several ships could dock at one time. It was also relatively impregnable to naval attacks, and lay close to a good supply of drinking water.

The precursor for a more enduring European presence in Suriname came in 1651 when Governor Willoughby of Barbados established the more-or-less unofficial English colony of Willoughbyland, centred on Fort Willoughby, on the site of present-day Paramaribo. By 1663, Willoughbyland had expanded to comprise around 50 sugar plantations, covering a total area of 125km^2, and it was home to around 1,000 English and Sephardic settlers, as well as several thousand slaves, mostly from West Africa but also some of Amerindian descent. Fort Willoughby was captured by the Dutch and renamed Fort Zeelandia in February 1667. This arrangement was rendered official by the Treaty of Westminster of 1674, wherein England surrendered all claims to Willoughbyland in exchange for the North American Dutch colony of New Amsterdam (today's New York).

In 1682, Suriname was placed under the control of the Geoctrooieerde West-Indische Compagnie (GWIC; Chartered West India Company), an early multinational heavily involved in the slave trade between West Africa and the Americas. In 1683, the colony was taken over by the Sociëteit van Suriname (Society of Suriname), a private company with three equal shareholders: the GWIC, the City of Amsterdam, and the Lord of Sommelsdijck, Cornelis van Aerssen, who served as governor of the territory for five years prior to his death in 1688. Although Sommelsdijck played a huge role in the development of Paramaribo during his tenure as governor, the largest colonial settlements in Suriname in the late 1680s were still Torarica and Jodensavanne, which comprised 100 and 60 houses respectively, as compared with around 25 in the nascent capital.

EARLY DUTCH COLONISATION (1674–1799) Under settled Dutch governance, Suriname emerged as a prosperous producer and exporter of sugar and other crops, including cacao, coffee and cotton. By 1740, at least 400 different plantations had been established along the Suriname, Commewijne and Cottica rivers, as well as in a hinterland irrigated by a vast network of natural creeks and artificial canals. The emergent town and port of Paramaribo was protected by the vastly expanded Fort Zeelandia, while the main buttress against attacks on more remote plantations was Fort Sommelsdijck, built on the confluence of the Commewijne and Cottica

in the 1680s. Both of these older forts were eventually superseded by Fort Nieuw Amsterdam, constructed at the confluence of the Suriname and Commewijne between 1735 and 1747. And while the Dutch administration centre at Paramaribo slowly emerged as Suriname's main port, the Sephardic towns of Torarica and Jodensavanne, centrally located among the earliest plantations further inland along the Suriname River, remained thriving hubs of agricultural based commerce until the mid 18th century.

WRECK OF THE *LEUSDEN*

On 19 November 1737, the *Leusden*, a 34m-long slave ship owned by the Chartered West India Company (GWIC), set sail from the port of Elmina (in present-day Ghana) with a cargo of approximately 700 African captives, on what would be its tenth and last transatlantic voyage to the Americas. Six weeks later, on 1 January 1738, whilst sailing off the Guianan coast, the ship ran into a fierce tropical storm and its Swedish captain Joachim Outjes decided to take shelter in the Marowijne estuary, probably under the erroneous impression that it was the mouth of the Suriname River. As the *Leusden* entered the estuary, however, it was dragged off course by a strong outgoing tide, causing it to run aground on a sandbar. Hoping that his ship would be dislodged with the next rising tide, Captain Outjes decided not to evacuate but to wait out the storm, and he allowed his prisoners to leave their quarters and have a meal on deck.

Tragically, as dusk descended, the ship's rudder cracked open, allowing sea water to flood below decks, and the captain, fearing that panic might trigger a revolt, sent the slaves back to their quarters and ordered his crew to seal the shutters and sit on them through the night. The next morning, the captain and his 72 crew members escaped the flooded ship in two lifeboats, together with a booty of 16 captives (which they later sold in Paramaribo) and a casket of gold. Crew accounts indicate that 664 Africans were entombed below the decks of the *Leusden*; those who had not already died during the night would have suffocated or drowned before the storm ended a few days later.

The *Leusden* incident was the greatest documented mass murder to take place during the slave trading era. It claimed almost five times as many victims as the infamous *Zong* Massacre of 1781, wherein 132 slaves were thrown overboard from a British-owned boat as part of an insurance scam. And although the captain and crew of the *Leusden* freely admitted to orchestrating the massacre, nobody associated with the incident was punished – on the contrary, the GWIC rewarded several survivors for their efforts in rescuing a casket of gold from the wreck.

The Surinamese historian Leo Balai has written a detailed book about the *Leusden* Massacre (see page 236) and is also the main mover behind recent attempts to locate the wreck. Its probable location near the Marowijne mouth has been determined by a team that includes students from Plymouth University and a specialist underwater search company from Norwich. While the current makes the water too dangerous for divers, a sonar scan from a boat is planned for 2015. If the wreck is located, it would not only be a find of great historical significance, but, as Balai has noted, an opportunity to hold a belated proper funeral for the 664 men, women and children who died tragically below the decks of the *Leusden*.

The plantation economy of Suriname was built almost entirely on slave labour. Many indigenous Amerindians were enslaved by the plantation owners, but their numbers were insufficient to feed the industry, so the colonists looked to Africa as a primary source of forced labour. Precise figures are not available, but over the course of the 17th and 18th centuries at least 300,000 captives were shipped to Suriname from the coast of West and Central Africa. This figure is all the more chilling when you consider that their descendants, assuming they had any, would almost invariably have been born into a life of slavery, yet the total population of the colony never exceeded 50,000. This is because the harsh working conditions and prevalence of tropical diseases on the plantations ensured a very high mortality rate. In addition, the law regarded slaves as a form of property, with no legal rights, and their owners had a free hand to mistreat them as whimsy dictated. As a result, many plantation owners routinely meted out cruel and often fatal punishments – cutting off the nose or limbs of slaves, burning them alive, or whipping them to death – for minor or imagined transgressions or acts of disobedience.

Ultimately, the biggest threat to the plantation economy of Suriname came not from outside attackers but from within. Over the course of the 18th century, thousands of angry slaves fled the plantations for the surrounding jungle and found the freedom they desired, but also faced a fresh struggle to survive in wild and unfamiliar conditions. Initially known as Bakabusi Nengre (Back-to-the-Bush Negroes) and then as Marrons or Maroons, these escapees organised themselves into small bands and started raiding the plantations to acquire food, other goods and women. Many plantations collapsed under the strain of repeated Marron raids, or were abandoned by their owners.

In 1762, the beleaguered colonial government signed a peace treaty with the notorious Saamaka Marrons (see box, pages 204–5). However, this concession seems only to have intensified the attacks led by other Marron groups, plunging the colony into a state of virtual revolt that was partially curbed by the construction in 1776 of the Cordon Path (a 94km defensive line dotted with military outposts) enclosing most active plantations between Jodensavanne and the coast. By this time, however, some 5,000–6,000 Marrons lived in the jungle outside the cordon, and the economy was in clear decline. It is also likely that the Marron threat was an important factor in the 18th-century decline of Torarica, no trace of which appears to survive today, and it certainly contributed to the gradual abandonment of Jodensavanne in the late 18th century, a process completed when it was razed by fire in 1832.

SURINAME IN THE 19TH CENTURY The chartered administration of Suriname and other Dutch colonies unravelled in the late 18th century. In 1792, the GWIC was bought out by the Dutch government, which took over the administration of its territories. Three years later, the Society of Suriname was nationalised by the Batavian Republic. Soon after, Suriname's three centuries of Dutch rule were interrupted by two short British occupations (1799–1802 and 1804–16) associated with the Napoleonic Wars. These British interludes may have been brief, but they were not without consequences, among them the opening up of the coastal belt of Paramaribo following the establishment of the first (mostly Scottish- and English-owned) plantations in what are now Coronie and Nickerie districts, and the opening of the Saramacca Canal in 1808. A more significant change, enacted by the British government in 1807 and its Dutch counterpart in 1814, was the abolition of the slave trade. An illicit slave trade still persisted in Suriname until the mid-1820s, but even so, when Dutch rule resumed in 1816, the colony's plantations were no longer guaranteed a limitless supply of West African labour.

In the early days, the Dutch colony centred on Paramaribo and the plantations of the Suriname, Commewijne and Cottica rivers, but its extent further afield was poorly defined. Following the return of Dutch in 1816, however, Suriname formally consisted of the entire coastal belt between the Marowijne and Corantijn rivers (though the inland borders would remain vague until the 20th century). In 1834, the administration of the remote plantations in the far west was decentralised with the creation of Nickerie and Coronie districts. In 1848, Paramaribo was declared a free port, and in 1866 the Dutch granted Suriname a parliament of its own.

The outlawing of the slave trade had no immediate effect on the status of Suriname's tens of thousands of existing slaves. Nor did it do much to ease the ongoing guerrilla attacks on slave-owning plantations that were waged by Marron groups based in the remote jungles of Cottica and elsewhere. When Britain passed the Abolition of Slavery Act in 1835 however, granting immediate freedom to some 700,000 slaves in its Caribbean colonies, including the neighbouring territory then known as British Guiana, it did not go unnoticed in Suriname. Several South American states followed suit in the 1850s, notably Argentina, Peru and Venezuela and finally, in 1863 (two years before the USA), the Dutch administration of Suriname bowed to the trend, granting freedom to the colony's 33,000 slaves, with the proviso that they had to continue working on the same plantation for another ten years, but on a paid basis.

Abolition imposed radical changes on the already struggling plantation economy. The most consequential of these, at least in terms of the peopling of Suriname, was the introduction of an indentured labour system wherein migrants from India and the Dutch East Indies were brought into the country, usually on a five-year contract. Although they were not slaves, the indentured Asians were frequently forced to work under harsh conditions, and they enjoyed very little or no legal protection. Dissatisfaction among the migrant workers culminated in the Mariënburg Massacre of July 1902 (see box, page 128), wherein 24 striking workers were shot dead and another 32 injured by the colonial military forces. In total, around 75,000 contract workers were shipped into the plantations in the late 19th and early 20th centuries, around 45% each from India and the Dutch East Indies, and most of the remainder from China or various Caribbean islands. Despite the hardships, many of these contract workers stayed on in Suriname after their five-year term expired, seeking other work or establishing small businesses. A large proportion of the country's modern Hindustani and Javan population is descended from this wave of immigrants.

THE EARLY 20TH CENTURY As the 19th century drew to a close, many of Suriname's struggling plantations had long ceased operations. And while a few of the larger plantations still continued to produce sugar and other crops for export (indeed, some still do today), the early 20th century is when the economy started to shift towards the mining and service industries. Gold was the main natural resource exploited at the turn of the century, but a more important development was the establishment of the Alcoa bauxite mines at Moengo and Paranam (see page 6). While the economy was boosted in the 1920s by income and work associated with the newly established mines, so too was the standing of the colony's residents when Suriname was declared an integral part of the Kingdom of the Netherlands in 1922 – meaning that all Surinamers automatically qualified for Dutch citizenship.

Suriname was particularly hard hit by the Great Depression of 1930, which led to the return of large numbers of unemployed Surinamese workers from Curaçao and the other islands of the Dutch Antilles. In 1931, hunger riots broke out in

Paramaribo. An important leader of the festering anti-colonial resistance of the 1930s was Anton de Kom, a Surinamese-born son of a former slave who spent most of the 1920s in the Netherlands before returning to Paramaribo in January 1933. A committed and vocal socialist, de Kom was arrested on 1 February after leading a demonstration against Governor Kielstra. Six days later, an angry crowd gathered in front of Kielstra's office (on what is now Onafhankelijkheids Plein) to demand de Kom's release, and police opened fire, killing two protesters and wounding at least 30 more. In May 1933, de Kom was exiled to the Netherlands, where he completed his book *Wij slaven van Suriname* (We Slaves of Suriname) and continued to agitate against colonial policies.

During World War II, whilst the Netherlands was occupied from May 1940 onwards, a government-in-exile was established in Suriname, which refused to recognise the dummy administration installed by the Germans. The colony was also secured by some 3,000 US troops from September 1941 onwards, stationed there by President Roosevelt with the blessing of the government-in-exile in order to protect the interest of Alcoa and to ensure the supply of bauxite remained unbroken. After the war, the status of Suriname and other Dutch colonies changed rapidly. Indonesia (formerly the Dutch East Indies) was granted independence in 1949, while a statute passed in 1954 redefined the status of its other colonies, including Suriname, and they became overseas territories. Other post-war developments included the introduction of universal suffrage in 1948, the emergence of several home-grown political parties in the early 1950s, and most important of all, self-government in 1954.

INDEPENDENCE AND BEYOND The key figure in Surinamese politics during the build-up to independence was Johan Henri Ferrier, a mixed-race former teacher who was the first prime minister elected in the self-government era, serving from 1955 until 1958, and also the last colonial governor of Suriname from 1968 to 1975. Ferrier, together with Prime Minister Henck Arron, was a pivotal figure in the negotiations between the Nationale Partij Suriname (NPS; National Party of Suriname) and the Dutch government that led to Suriname attaining full independence on 25 November 1975. The NPS automatically retained power for two years after independence, with Arron continuing as prime minister and Ferrier as the country's first president. By October 1977, when the first post-independence election was held, Surinamese politics had started to fragment along ethnic lines. Arron and Ferrier were narrowly returned to power, but accusations of NPS corruption were rife, some probably justified (for instance that Dutch aid was being used for partisan purposes), others perhaps less so (that the electoral victory was rigged). It is some indication of the political unease of the era, as well as the economic situation, that around 130,000 Suriname residents – a third of the population at the time – took advantage of their Dutch citizenship to emigrate to the Netherlands in the mid- to late 1970s.

On 25 February 1980, Prime Minister Henck Arron was ousted in the bloodless Sergeants' Coup initiated by a group of 16 military sergeants led by Sergeant-Major Dési Bouterse. Bouterse's seven-year military dictatorship was marked by strict evening curfews in Paramaribo, limited press freedom, a ban on political parties, overt government corruption and the killing of political opponents. Henri Ferrier retained the presidency for six months after the coup, resigning in August 1980, after which Hendrick Chin A Sen (1980–82) and Fred Misier (1982–88) were installed as puppet presidents to front the military regime. The most notorious of many excesses committed by the post-coup military dictatorship was the torture and execution of 15 prominent journalists, lawyers, university lecturers and other critics of the regime in Fort Zeelandia on December 1982 (see box, page 103).

In the wake of the December killings, several countries, among them the Netherlands and USA, announced the suspension of all aid to Suriname until democracy was restored. The resultant economic crisis gave Bouterse little option but to start working towards the reintroduction of democracy, which he did in 1985 by lifting the ban on opposition parties and starting to draft a new constitution. Meanwhile, dissatisfaction with the Bouterse regime's treatment of the Marron population (not to mention an ongoing dispute over control of the lucrative cocaine trade that had emerged to fill the vacuum left by US and Dutch aid) led to the outbreak of civil war in eastern Suriname in 1986. The main protagonists of this conflict were Ronnie Brunswijk, leader of the so-called Jungle Commando, a Marron guerrilla force based mainly in Marowijne and Brokopondo districts, and the national army under the command of Dési Bouterse. A notorious early casualty of the fighting was Brunswijk's home village of Moiwana (see page 142), where at least 38 civilians were killed by the national army in November 1986. Although subsequent conflict was sporadic, the scorched earth policy adopted by the national army resulted in several towns in the northeast, including Albina and Moengo, being all but abandoned in the late 1980s as their terrified residents took up temporary exile in French Guiana.

Back in Paramaribo, a new constitution was adopted on the back of a public referendum in 1987, and an election was held on 25 November, attracting a turnout of 87.5%. The result was an overwhelming victory for the Front for Democracy and Development (a three-party alliance), which took 40 of the 51 seats in the National Assembly. Ramsewak Shankar of the Progressive Reform Party (PRP) was elected president by the National Assembly in January 1988. Superficially, the election marginalised Bouterse, since his National Democratic Party (NDP) accrued a mere three seats in the National Assembly. However, the new constitution allowed for Bouterse to remain in charge of the army, and it wasn't long before he demonstrated his behind-the-scenes power, dismissing Shankar by telephone, probably due to his handling of the civil war in the northeast, in November 1990. Following this so-called 'telephone coup', Bouterse installed another military-backed government, with Johan Kraag appointed acting president. Fortunately, a peace agreement between Brunswijk and the government was negotiated less than six months after this second coup, paving the way for another democratic election which was held, in accordance with the 1987 constitution, in May 1991.

The 1991 election attracted a rather low voter turnout of 64% (presumably a reflection of widespread disillusionment in the wake of the 1990 coup), but it did result in the resumption of democratic civilian rule in Suriname. The New Front for Democracy and Development (NFDD; by then an alliance of four parties) claimed 30 of 51 seats, while only 12 went to Bouterse's NDP. The National Assembly elected Ronald Venetiaan of the National Party of Suriname (NPS) as president. The NFDD still dominated the 1996 elections, taking 24 seats to the NDP's 16, but it was Jules Albert Wijdenbosch of the NDP who became president in what was probably a compromise vote. The next elections, held in 2000, were dominated by the NFDD, which also attracted sufficient votes in 2005 to ensure Ronald Venetiaan served another two terms as president.

This trend was reversed in 2010, with the NFDD taking just 15 seats, a poor second to the 23 won by the oddly named Mega Combinatie (Mega Combination), a coalition dominated by the NDP. As a result, the National Assembly voted in the former dictator Dési Bouterse as president in 2010. Since then, a controversial amnesty law passed in 2012 has granted Bouterse full immunity for any crimes committed under his military dictatorship, including the 15 executions that took place at Fort Zeelandia in December 1982, and the Moiwana Massacre of 1986. The incumbent president's alleged involvement in the drug trade also remains controversial. Surinamese extradition laws have prevented Europol from enacting a 1999 warrant for Bouterse's arrest on drug-related charges, as well as ensuring that he has yet to serve a day of the 11-year prison sentence imposed by a Dutch court in 2000 when he was found guilty *in absentia* of trafficking 474 kilos of cocaine. Still, while the elevation of Bouterse to the presidency in 2010 came as surprise to many, Suriname, two decades since the resumption of civilian rule, is in many respects a model democracy. It has transformed itself into one of the most stable, safe, progressive and economically viable countries in the region.

PEOPLE

The national population of Suriname stood at 541,000 in the 2012 census and is estimated at more than 550,000 today. This gives Suriname the sixth-lowest population density of the world's 206 sovereign states, ahead only of Iceland, Australia, Namibia, Western Sahara and Mongolia, and the lowest population density of any country that isn't dominated by desert or icy habitats. Most of Suriname's population is confined to the coastal plain, with some 45% centred on the capital Paramaribo and another 33% split across the small but relatively urbanised neighbouring districts of Wanica, Para and Commewijne. The rest of the country is very thinly populated, with the only other towns of any stature outside a 50km radius of the capital being Nieuw Nickerie and at a stretch Moengo, Albina, Apoera and Wageningen.

Although Suriname has a small population, ethnic diversity is high, reflecting several waves of forced and voluntary migration since the post-Columbian era. The oldest inhabitants of the country are the indigenous Amerindians; the major population groups are Hindustanis, Marrons, Creoles and Javanese, while the country also supports small numbers of Europeans, Chinese, Sephardic Jews and Brazilians.

AMERINDIANS   Although Amerindians comprise a mere 3.7% of Suriname's modern population, they are the only ethnic and cultural relict of pre-Columbian times. They are also known as *Indiaan, Inheemsen* (Dutch for 'Indigenous People') or *Ingi* (a derogatory Sranan Tongo name), but the preferred term used to refer to them collectively is Amerindian (partially to distinguish them from latter-day Hindustani migrants from India). In practice, far from being a collective entity, the Amerindians of Suriname are represented by as many as eight distinct cultural groups, most of whom live in relatively remote villages and small towns scattered along the rivers of the interior. Running roughly from north to south, these are the Karina (or Carib), Lokono (or Arawak), Tiriyó (or Trio), Akurio, Wayana (or Wajana), Sikiyana, Tunayana (or Katwena) and Mawayana. None of these groups number more than a few thousand today, and some are represented by fewer than 100 individuals. The Karina and Lokono, both relatively large groups associated with the coastal belt, are now mostly Christian, schooled in Dutch, and otherwise quite exposed and integrated into modern Surinamese culture, though traditionalists who speak the Karina language still exist in some areas, for instance the village of Galibi.

Though some of the Amerindians of the sparsely populated interior have converted to Christianity, most still adhere to traditional animist beliefs, which typically treat the jungle as a potentially dangerous spiritual realm wherein all living creatures have a dualistic nature, possessing both a physical body and a soul, which may or may not be in mutual accord. Here, many people still subsist largely as their ancestors did, fishing in the rivers and collecting edible vegetables or hunting (in particular monkeys and iguana lizards) in the jungle. The characteristically soft-spoken Tiriyó are numerically the largest Amerindian group in the interior, followed by the more culturally outgoing Wayana. Minority groups are the Akurio, some 50 of whom live in a few family units alongside the Tiriyó in Tëpu, Palumeu and Kwamalasamutu; the Mawayana (Frog People) who are represented in Suriname by a few elders (mostly Christian converts) integrated into the Tiriyó community at Kwamalasamutu; the 80-strong Sikiyana, also now based at Kwamalasamutu, who are renowned for their knowledge of medicinal plants and are also regarded as highly spiritual, even shamanistic; and the Tunayana (Water People), around 120 of whom are divided between Kwamalasamutu and Alalapadu.

Though many Amerindian tongues are mutually unintelligible, which is hastening the death of minority languages, elements of the vocabulary have made their way into several European languages: familiar words with Amerindian roots include canoe, potato, jaguar, maize and iguana.

ASIANS Around half of Suriname's population is of Asian descent. The country's largest single ethnic group, accounting for 27% of the population, are the Hindustani or Indo-Surinamese descendants from Indian contract labourers who landed in Suriname to work on the plantations in the late 19th and early 20th centuries. Most of these workers originated from the northern states of Bihar and Uttar Pradesh, near the border with Nepal. Their descendants are still mostly practising Hindus, with about 25% following the late 19th-century Arya Samaj reform movement and the remainder a more traditional form known locally as Sanatan Dharm.

The second main Asian population group in Suriname, representing 14% of the total, are the Javanese-Surinamese descendants of contract workers brought over from Java (an island in the former Dutch East Indies, now Indonesia) at around the same time as their Indo-Surinamese counterparts. Mostly Islamic and Dutch-speaking, the Javanese community is a highly visible component of modern Surinamese society, and the primary influence on the local cuisine.

In addition, around 40,000 people of Chinese descent or birth are resident in Suriname, comprising some 7% of the population. About a third of these are 'old' Chinese, descendants of the earliest contract workers to reach Suriname in the mid 19th century. The remainder are so-called 'new' Chinese, who have come to dominate the retail industry to such an extent that supermarkets throughout Suriname are now routinely referred to as *Chinees*. Many illegal Chinese migrants are reputedly involved in illicit gold mining in the interior.

CREOLES AND MARRONS Although both are primarily of West or Central African descent, Creoles and Marrons are best treated as distinct cultural groups. Creoles, some of whom have mixed Dutch or other European blood, make up 14.5% of the Surinamese population and are mostly descendants of slaves who gained their liberty at the time of abolition. Most Surinamese Creoles live in Paramaribo or other large towns, are practising Christians and are strongly integrated into the broader Surinamese community, both linguistically and culturally. Marrons, by contrast, are the descendants of the many slaves who escaped from the plantations over the course of the two centuries prior to abolition and made their home along the rivers of the interior, where they often displaced Amerindian communities and adopted much of the inherited wisdom of their indigenous predecessors when it came to surviving in the unfamiliar jungles of South America. Comprising around 23% of the Surinamese population, the Marrons are divided into five distinct main subgroups: Ndyuka, Kwinti, Matawai, Saamaka (Saramacca) and Paramacca. Most Marrons these days prefer to be referred to by the name of their subgroup, as the term Marron, from Spanish-American *cimarrón*, meaning 'feral or runaway', is regarded as derogatory by some. By far the largest of these subgroups, representing around 10% of the national population, and the one tourists are most likely to interact with, are the Saamaka (see box, pages 204–5), who are the main inhabitants of the Upper Suriname, Gran Rio and Brokopondo areas. Although some Saamaka and other Marron villages are now Christian, many adhere to the traditional Winti religion, which is of clear West African origin. The Marrons of the Surinamese interior remain somewhat apart from the rest of the country culturally, and had to fight long and hard for the full recognition of their right to occupy their traditional lands granted by the Inter-American Court of Human Rights in 2007. They still tend to be slightly distrustful of outsiders, and understandably so given their history.

OTHERS Suriname still supports a small number of people of **European** origin. Many old Surinamese residents of Dutch descent returned to the Netherlands in the tumultuous period immediately after independence, but some have since returned. Paramaribo also supports a significant number of Dutch and other European residents who have settled there in recent years or are working in the capital on a semi-permanent basis. A distinct subgroup of European origin is the thousand or so **Boeroes** (literally, 'Farmers') whose ancestors arrived as farmers in the 19th century and who still play an important role in the agricultural sector, particularly in Saramacca and Commewijne districts. Small numbers of **Sephardic Jews** (many with Portuguese names) and **Ashkenazi Jews** live in Paramaribo, though the Jewish population has declined significantly since the heyday of Torarica and Jodensavanne (see pages 178–80). The country is also home to quite a few **Brazilians**, many of them gold miners, along with significant numbers of immigrants from across the border in Guyana and French Guiana.

LANGUAGE

Dutch is the only official language in Suriname. It is also the mother tongue of around 60% of the population, and the second language of most other people. Education, business and official matters are all conducted in the official language, which makes it a very easy country for Dutch and Flemish travellers. In 2009, Surinaamse Nederlands was recognised as a distinct dialect, one characterised by several quirks in vocabulary and somewhat more guttural consonants than the Dutch spoken in Holland or Belgium. It also has a rising intonation rather reminiscent of the form of Afrikaans spoken by Cape Coloureds in South Africa's Western Cape region.

The other main national language – although it has no official status – is Sranan Tongo (literally 'Surinamese Tongue'). Sranan Tongo started life as a Creole language during the time of slavery but it is now widely used as an informal street language, particularly between those who wouldn't speak Dutch at home. It incorporates a large number of words from English (indeed, the Dutch used to refer to Sranan Tongo as Negerengels ('Negro English'), though often in a barely recognisable form, along with bastardised elements of Portuguese, Dutch and certain African languages.

Close to, but far from interchangeable with, Sranan Tongo are several Marron languages, such as Saamaka Tongo. These are generally only spoken locally, for instance in areas such as the Upper Suriname. Other minority languages, usually only spoken between people of the ethnic group with which they are associated, include Hindi, Javanese, Cantonese, Mandarin, Spanish, Portuguese and various Amerindian tongues such as Carib and Arawak.

English is spoken far more widely than might be expected. This is in part because it is the second language of choice for many school-goers, but also because so many Surinamese have been raised outside the country. It also reflects the influence of neighbouring Guyana and of American television and movies. Within the tourist industry, almost everybody speaks passable English, and you will also find it is widely spoken in Paramaribo and the surrounding area, and in the likes of Nickerie and Apoera on the Guyana border.

RELIGION

Suriname is as diverse in terms of religion as it is ethnically. The country is also characterised by high levels of religious tolerance, with many neighbourhoods supporting a mixture of denominations living harmoniously in close proximity. According to the 2012 census, around 48% of the population is Christian, with the Roman Catholic, Methodist and Moravian churches being particularly well established. Another 22% is Hindu, while 14% is Muslim. The remainder mostly adhere to traditional Winti or indigenous Amerindian animism belief structures. There are around 1,500 (mostly Sephardic) Jews in Paramaribo, along with small numbers of Buddhists.

2

Natural History

Adapted from the corresponding chapter in Bradt's guide to Guyana, by Kirk Smock

Boasting a rare wealth of wetland habitats, the highest proportion of forest cover of any country in the world, and one of the lowest human population densities, Suriname packs a remarkable amount of biodiversity into a relatively modest area. It is home to at least 192 mammal, 720 bird, 175 reptile, 102 amphibian and 370 freshwater fish species, along with hundreds of thousands of invertebrates. Furthermore, since scientific exploration of its vast jungles and swamps has been rather patchy, it seems likely that a great many species still await discovery. Indeed, a three-week Conservation International expedition in 2012 discovered 11 previously undescribed fish species, one new snake, six new amphibians (including a unique cocoa-coloured tree frog) and several dozen types of insect to the remote southeast. This chapter can thus provide the reader with only the briefest overview of Suriname's flora and fauna; for a list of sources that provide more thorough coverage, see pages 236–7.

Suriname currently has 16 established protected areas, covering a total of 21,383km² (13.5% of the country's territory), as well as four proposed reserves comprising another 1,320km². The 15,920km² Central Suriname Nature Reserve in the western interior is by far the largest of these protected areas. The other reserves all lie along or within 100km of the coast, and none is larger than 1,000km².

FLORA

According to a 2005 assessment by the UN's Food and Agriculture Organization, Suriname has the highest percentage of forest cover of any country in the world, estimated at almost 95%, the vast majority of which is still pristine. Around 90% of this comprises well-drained multi-storey dryland forest dominated by mesophytic trees, while the remainder mostly consists of seasonal or perennial swamp forest, and coastal and estuarine tidal mangroves dominated by Avicenniaceae and Rhizophoraceae trees. Small patches of ridge and savannah forest together constitute less than 0.5% of the surface area. The country's vegetation can be divided into four main eco-zones, running from north to south. The estuarine zone follows the Atlantic coastline and typically runs up to 10km further inland. The greater coastal plains lie immediately south of that, giving way further inland to a narrow belt of northern savannah forest that grows on white sandy soil. Further south still is the vast tract of lowland forest that comprises around 90% of the country's surface area, running all the way to the Brazilian border. This last zone is interspersed with patches of highland forest on isolated hills and mountains whose altitudes exceed 400m.

As Suriname is tropical, plants flourish everywhere. More than 5,000 plant species have so far been identified, many of which are put to use as food or medicine, or to meet other requirements. Orchids, helliconias and flowering trees coveted in other parts of the world abound, but perhaps the most celebrated plant is the giant water lily *Victoria amazonica*, which grows on the canals in several towns, as well as the moats at Fort Nieuw Amsterdam. The world's largest water lily, its leaves can attain a diameter of 3m and support the weight of a baby, while the stalks can reach a length of 7–8m. At dusk the lily's flowers open slowly, eventually blooming a brilliant white. At the same time they emit a strong odour and increase their temperature, attracting the beetle that pollinates them. Roughly 24 hours later, when the flower blooms again, it is a pinkish-red colour.

MEDICINAL USES Many plant species found in Suriname's tropical forests have been used to make medicines, both by large pharmaceutical companies and by locals in need of bush medicine. If you suffer an ailment while in the forest and are with a local guide, chances are they'll know of a local remedy that will alleviate pain, cure you of the malady or, in worst-case scenarios, greatly increase your chances of making it to mainstream medical care.

One of the many local contributions to modern-day science comes from curare, a paralytic plant-derived poison that Amerindians have used for centuries when fishing and hunting. It's produced through a varying combination of plants, barks and leaves, and in strong enough quantities it will cause death by asphyxiation, by paralysing the muscles needed to breathe. Curare was first recorded by early explorers to the Guianas, who brought back samples to Europe, where it eventually became used in muscle relaxants and anaesthetics.

LOGGING There are about 1,000 tree species in Suriname and many of these are highly coveted species of hardwoods with exotic names like greenheart, purpleheart, bulletwood, crabwood, iteballi, locust, mora, wallaba, wamara and tonka bean. Many of these hardwood species are in demand from countries overseas and the timber industry is growing. Thankfully, Suriname has a reasonably good system in place that oversees the forestry sector in an attempt to ensure that forests are managed sustainably through a process of selective and reduced impact logging, and directional felling.

Suriname is also in the process of formulating a Low Carbon Development Strategy in collaboration with neighbouring Guyana, which already has one in place. If this goes ahead, the rigorous supervision it requires will help Suriname's abundant rainforests avoid the same fate as those in certain other countries. That said, mining, rather than logging for timber, is probably the main cause of deforestation in Suriname, a phenomenon easily observed when you fly over the vicinity of Brownsberg and Brokopondo Dam.

MAMMALS

Based on information provided by Guyana's Iwokrama International Centre for Rainforest Conservation and Development, www.iwokrama.org

Among the species of mammals documented in Suriname are some of the largest in their family or genus, including the capybara (the world's bulkiest rodent), giant anteater, giant river otter, false vampire bat (largest bat in Central and South America) and jaguar (largest cat in the western hemisphere).

Other mammals that don't get to claim a record but are still much sought after include five additional cat species, as well as the manatee, tapir and eight species of monkey.

Information on some key mammal species is provided below. Average statistics are given in parentheses as body length/tail length/weight or body size/weight.

CARNIVORES Even though these mammals are often associated with large canines perfect for tearing flesh, many will still supplement their diet with fruits, nuts or other vegetable matter.

Jaguar (*Panthera onca*) This big cat (1.25m/55cm/70kg), which looks rather like a heftier version of the Old World leopard and ranks as the world's third-largest felid, is often call a *tijger* by locals, the Dutch for tiger. Aside from its girth, the jaguar can be identified by the beautiful black markings on its golden coat, which consist of rosette-like spots forming a broken circle around a small central spot. Also look for the large head and short, stocky legs. Jaguars are both nocturnal and diurnal, and while they are mainly terrestrial they climb low trees and are excellent swimmers.

Solitary and secretive, jaguars are occasionally spotted along trails or gaps along the forest edge, where roads or rivers run. Their size is used to take down large prey, including peccaries (a pig-like mammal, see pages 27–8), capybara and deer, but jaguars are also known to attack livestock, dogs and horses. Chances are you'll see one before hearing one, but you may hear a roar or series of loud grunts.

Their preferred habitat is primary forest. Adult jaguar tracks, which are much more likely to see than the animal itself, are 120mm wide on the front paw and 95mm wide on the rear. They have four toes with rounded pads; there are no claw marks. The footpad is also wide and has a rounded top.

Puma (*Puma concolor*) Known as *poema* in Dutch, and sometimes also called a cougar, the puma is slightly smaller, and much slimmer, than a jaguar (1m/60cm/45kg). Its body is outfitted with a small head flanked by large pointed ears, long legs and a long black-tipped tail; colours are sandy to reddish brown on the top and cream or white on the underparts. Only young pumas have brown spots.

Pumas are nocturnal and diurnal and mainly stick to the ground, although they are good climbers. They rarely enter the water. Sightings of the solitary animals are rare, and while they're found in all types of forest and savannahs they prefer higher-level rocky terrain to wetlands. The puma's main prey is deer, paca and agouti (both rodent species, see page 29), but they also attack livestock.

Tracks are about 80mm wide with four toe pads that are more pointed than rounded. The top of the footpad has a small indentation (which the jaguar lacks).

Jaguarundi (*Herpailurus yaguarondi*) This medium-sized cat has a long body (75cm/50cm/7kg) with shorter legs and a long narrow tail, which distinguishes it from the similar-looking, but bushy-tailed tayra (see page 24). They have no spots and their colours can be dark grey (more common) or reddish.

Jaguarundis are mainly diurnal and are good climbers. They favour dense brush near water but are found in forests, savannahs and cultivated areas; they may be seen crossing roads. Their diet consists mainly of small rodents, birds and occasional lizards.

Their tracks are roughly 40mm wide, with the front toe and footpads being more spread out.

Ocelot (*Leopardus pardalis*) Ocelots are medium-sized (75cm/35cm/10kg) spotted cats. They are much smaller, and not as stocky, as jaguars and their spots typically form rows. Ocelots have a heavier build than the other two smaller spotted cats, margay and oncilla.

Ocelots are mainly nocturnal and usually terrestrial, climbing and swimming only occasionally. They can be found in all forest types and are solitary cats that

23

travel at night; during the day they rest in trees or among buttresses or tree fall. Their diet consists of small terrestrial mammals, iguanas, land crabs and birds.

Tracks have four toe pads and the front tracks (60mm) are noticeably wider than the hind tracks (50mm).

Oncilla (*Leopardus tigrinus*) Roughly the size of a domestic cat, this is the smallest of the spotted cats (50cm/30cm/2.25kg). Its slim body, with long bushy tail, is yellowish brown with black spots that form stripes on the neck. Usually found in mature forest, it is a nocturnal animal that feeds on mice and small birds. Front tracks (27mm) are broader than the hind (22mm) and there is a large gap between the front footpad and toe pad.

Margay (*Leopardus wiedii*) Margays are small and slim spotted cats (60cm/40cm/ 3.5kg) with long bushy tails and long legs with large feet. Typically found in mature forest, margays are nocturnal and arboreal, and they hunt mostly in trees (they can rotate their hind legs and descend a tree head first). They eat small arboreal mammals, including mice, opossums and squirrels, as well as birds. Tracks, which are rarely seen, are roughly 35mm wide.

Kinkajou (*Potos flavus*) Sometimes called honey bear or night monkey by locals, this medium-sized carnivore (55cm/50cm/3kg) has a golden-brown body and prehensile tail that darkens at the tip. It has a short, wide face with round ears and large eyes.

Common in all types of forest, kinkajous are nocturnal and arboreal and usually solitary. Because they move noisily through the trees and often freeze when caught in light, the kinkajou is one of the most commonly seen nocturnal arboreal mammals. Mainly a fruit eater, its diet also includes nectar, insects, mice and bats.

Coati (*Nasua nasua*) Also known as coatimundi, this relative of the raccoon has an orange-brown to dark brown coat with a pale yellow belly, and a bushy and banded tail that often stands straight up. The short legs have long claws on the front feet and the brown face has white spots. Its most distinctive feature is the very long snout, alluded to in its Dutch name *neusbeer* ('nose bear'), and which it uses to probe the forest litter.

Seen in all forest types and scrub, the diurnal coatis are both terrestrial and arboreal. Females live with their young in large groups, while the males are solitary outside of the breeding season. They eat fruits, worms, insects and small rodents. The roughly 45mm-wide tracks are five-toed with large footpads and long claw markings.

Tayra (*Eira barbara*) These are long-legged and weasel-like animals (75cm/40cm/4kg). The body is typically black with a pale yellow or grey-brown head and neck; tails are long and bushy. The arched back is long and the large feet are tipped with strong claws.

Most common in evergreen and deciduous forest and second growth, they are mainly diurnal and semi-arboreal, often moving rapidly through the trees or on the ground. Tayras eat insects, fruit and vertebrates, including lizards, monkeys and agoutis.

Tracks are five-toed and wide (55mm) with noticeable claw marks.

Bush dog (*Speothos venaticus*) This rarely seen and strange canid has a short and squat body (65cm/12cm/6kg) with a stubby tail and light brown to dark brown colourings. It is so inconspicuous in the wild that it was first described on the basis of a fossil found in a Brazilian cave and was believed to be extinct. It prefers swampy areas of mature forest and feeds on agouti, paca and fish. It sounds much like the common dog.

Tracks have small footpads and four toe pads with claw marks; the front is 45mm wide, and at 42mm the hind is narrower and longer.

Neotropical river otter (*Lontra longicaudis*) These aquatic carnivores have low streamlined bodies (65cm/40cm/6.5kg), brown upperparts, and pale grey or whitish underparts. The feet are webbed and the thick tail tapers towards the tip.

Diurnal river otters are terrestrial and semi-aquatic, moving with agility in the water and awkwardness on land.

They are typically found along larger forested rivers, streams and lagoons and eat fish and aquatic invertebrates. Their burrows can be seen on banks along rivers or streams.

Tracks, often found on sandy banks, are fairly broad (60–80mm) with visible webbing between the toes; the tail also leaves drag marks.

Giant otter (*Pteronura brasiliensis*) Most often called a *waterhond* ('water dog') in Suriname, the largest member of the Mustelidae (weasels and relatives) family has a low streamlined body and is mainly rich brown in colour with white markings on the throat and chin. Its feet are webbed and it has a thick tail that flattens into a paddle at the tip.

Diurnal and semi-aquatic, giant otters are often seen in groups of five or more along remote large rivers, lakes and flooded areas. Groups sleep in burrows on the riverbank and eat fish and caiman (crocodilians, see page 33). Their social lifestyle and diurnal habits have made them easy prey for hunters, who kill them for their fur.

Tracks are larger and wider (95–105mm) than river otters', with the same drag marks.

PRIMATES The most conspicuous large mammals in Suriname are primates, of which eight species are present. All have dextrous, grasping hands and feet suited to arboreal living, and some larger species also have long prehensile tails used for grabbing onto tree trunks and branches.

Squirrel monkey (*Saimiri sciureus*) Far and away the most conspicuous primate in Suriname, the squirrel monkey, known locally as *monki monki*, is often seen in and around Paramaribo, and is common at most other forested locales countrywide. Small and slender (30cm/40cm/800g), it has beautiful colouration. The sides, shoulders and rump are pale grey with an olive tinge, the mid-back is a dark rusty hue, and the forelimbs, hands and feet are a bright golden orange. The squirrel monkey also has a white mask around its eyes and forehead, alluded to in its Dutch name of *doodskopapje* (literally 'deadhead', or 'skull ape').

These diurnal and arboreal monkeys are commonly found in primary and secondary forest and along the river's edge. Very social, they are usually seen foraging in the sub-canopy in chirruping troops of ten to 20 animals led by a dominant male, but group sizes of up to 75 have been recorded. They are mainly insectivorous, but also eat ripe fruits and small vertebrates. The male has, proportionately, the largest penis of any primate, and often displays it non-sexually to assert his dominance.

Brown capuchin (*Cebus apella*) Another common inhabitant of primary or secondary forest, this small to medium-sized monkey (45cm/50cm/3kg) is known locally as *keskesi* and in Dutch as a *gekuifde* (fringed) *kapucijnaap*, in reference to the cap of black hairs on its head and black sideburns. The general colour is light to dark brown, but the hands and feet are black, and the prehensile tail is black at the tip.

Diurnal and strongly arboreal, the brown capuchin lives in troops of eight to 14 individuals, and is very inquisitive. It mainly eats fruit, but will also dine on insects, eggs, reptiles and small mammals. Researchers regard brown capuchins to be the most individualistic in appearance of Suriname's monkeys, and even casual visitors who spend time in one place will come to recognise different troop members.

Wedge-capped capuchin (*Cebus olivaceus*) This medium-sized monkey (45cm/50cm/3kg) has a predominantly brown body with a long, prehensile tail. The top of its head has a wedge-shaped black cap that comes to a point on the forehead. Pink around its mouth, nose and eyes, the rest of its head is a greyish white.

Resident in primary or secondary forest, favouring higher elevations, it is social and usually moves in groups of ten to 40 individuals, but is rather uncommon and difficult to locate. It is omnivorous, feeding on fruits, seeds and insects. It is known locally as *bergi keskesi*, and the Dutch name is *grijze* (grey) *kapucijnaap*.

Red-handed tamarin (*Saguinus midas*) Also known as the golden-handed tamarin (or as *saguwenke* locally or *roodjhandtamarin* in Dutch), this is Suriname's smallest primate (25cm/35cm/450g) and one of the less regularly seen, perhaps because it spends up to 60% of its time sleeping in a discreet roost. It is entirely black in colour except for yellow markings on the back and bright orange-yellow hands and feet.

Diurnal and arboreal, it is found in primary and secondary forest, especially in edge habitats such as along roads and streams. It is most likely to be seen in groups of two to six, feeding on insects and fruits in vines and tangles at least 5m above the ground.

White-faced saki (*Pithecia pithecia*) These shaggy monkeys are medium-sized (40cm/40cm/2kg) with long hair covering their entire bodies, including their tails. Males are all black except for a striking pale white face circling the dark nose, mouth and eyes. Females are dirty grey, with the sparsely haired belly and throat a rusty colour.

Diurnal and arboreal, the white-faced saki is most common in primary forest, where it is typically seen in or below the sub-canopy feeding on fruits, seeds, leaves and insects. It is among the less conspicuous of Suriname's moneys. The local name is *wanaku* and the Dutch name *witkopsaki*.

Bearded saki (*Chiropotes satanas*) Similar in size to the white-faced saki (40cm/40cm/3kg), and just as shaggy, this closely related monkey lacks the white face patch but does have a long brownish beard extending down from the jaw to the top of the chest.

It is diurnal and arboreal, lives in family groups of 18 to 30 animals, and can sometimes be seen in the sub-canopy with other primates, including squirrel and capuchin monkeys.

Red howler monkey (*Alouatta seniculus*) The communal calling of howler monkeys is one of the most distinctive sounds of the Surinamese forest, typically heard around dusk or dawn but also often through the night. It is a prehistoric-sounding melange of snorts, grunts, roars and howls that can be heard from several kilometres away. Known locally as *babun* (baboon), and in Dutch as *rode brulaap*, it is a large monkey (55cm/55cm/7kg) with dark, red-orange fur, a large head, a furry beard (larger in males) and a prehensile tail. Diurnal and strictly arboreal, troops of three to nine are often found in the forest near tree gaps or along rivers, where they feed on leaves and fruit. Howler monkeys are seen far more often than they are heard, and even when calling quite close by they can be surprisingly difficult to locate.

Black spider monkey (*Ateles paniscus*) Suriname's largest (50cm/75cm/10kg) and most spectacular monkey has a small head, long gangly limbs and a long, strong prehensile tail it uses as a fifth limb. In addition to being incredibly agile in the trees, often hanging for long periods just from its tail or one limb, it is surprisingly adept at walking upright for short periods, when it looks rather like a streamlined chimpanzee. Its entire body is covered in long black hair except for a bare pink face. Determining the sex of a spider monkey can be confusing to the uninitiated, since the female's clitoris, which grows up to 6cm long, is far larger and more conspicuous than the male's penis.

Common in primary or secondary forest, black spider monkeys live in large troops but are often seen in groups of two to five. They feed on fruit, flowers and leaves. They are highly vocal monkeys, sometimes emitting a series of low grunts, barks, whistles and screams. The black spider monkey can be inquisitive about human observers, but it will also sometimes threaten those watching by shaking branches, calling or dropping items to the ground. It is known locally as *kwatta*, and the Dutch name is *zwarte spinaap*.

UNGULATES The animals in this group are large herbivores that walk on toes tipped with one, two or three hooves.

Lowland tapir (*Tapirus terrestris*) South America's largest native mammal (2m/250kg), Suriname's only tapir is a peculiar-looking creature with short grey hair and an elongated, trunk-like snout that curves downwards. It also has a dark crest of hair that runs from its forehead and along its neck. Although rather swine-like in general appearance, tapirs are odd-toed ungulates most closely related to rhinos and more distantly to horses.

Tapirs are nocturnal and diurnal and have a wide range of habitat in the forest, but they are good swimmers and are typically seen near streams, creek beds and swamps. They are shy and quiet solitary creatures but can make a racket when travelling through the bush. They communicate using a loud, long whistle. Their tracks (170–175mm wide) are three-toed, with a fourth toe sometimes showing on the front foot. Sightings are uncommon except at Kabalebo Nature Reserve, where they are quite often seen crossing the airstrip.

White-lipped peccary (*Tayassu pecari*) These bush hogs are medium-sized (1.2m/35kg) pig-like beasts, have stocky bodies and slim legs, and are all black or dark brown except for a white patch on their lower jaw and throat.

Found predominantly in mature evergreen forests that have little human disturbance, they are very social and live in herds ranging from 40 to more than 200 individuals. They travel walking single file on forest paths, turning up the soil for fruit, roots, vegetation, invertebrates and palm nuts along the way. They are very aggressive and are one of the more dangerous mammals in the forest. They often make a clicking sound with their canine teeth when surprised, although you are likely to smell them before you see them. A foul musty odour is a good sign of their presence. If you come across a herd, climb the nearest tree.

Their tracks have two triangular hooves with a slightly rounded tip, about 55mm wide.

Collared peccary (*Pecari tajacu*) Small and very pig-like (90cm/20kg), collared peccary have stocky bodies and slim legs. They are grey-brown in colour with a pale collar along their shoulders and chest, and their heads are large and triangular.

These social animals are usually seen in groups of five to 15 in all forest types, savannah and agricultural areas. They dine mostly on palm nuts and other fruits, and the occasional vegetables, roots and invertebrates. They have the same dirty-sock odour as white-lipped peccaries.

Tracks are two triangular hooves with a slightly rounded tip, about 35mm wide.

Red brocket deer (*Mazama americana*) Commonly called bush deer, red brocket deer are medium-sized (90cm/22kg) with rounded bodies and arched backs; the rump is higher than the shoulders or head. They are reddish brown with white along the throat, chest and underneath their small tails. Males have short, straight antlers and the young have white spots.

They are common in primary and secondary forest, and are usually seen alone in the morning, at dusk or at night while foraging for fungi, fruit, flowers and vegetation.

Tracks are 25mm wide and are split hoof prints that taper to narrow tips; together they form a triangle.

Grey brocket deer (*Mazama gouazoupira*) Aside from being shorter, slimmer (80cm/15kg) and a greyish-brown colour – and having longer ears and legs – the bodies of grey brocket deer are similar to those of red brocket deer and their young also have white spots.

Grey brocket deer are mainly diurnal and usually seen alone near streams in primary and secondary forest, feeding mainly on fruit.

Tracks are similar to, but slightly smaller than, those of the red brocket deer.

White-tailed deer (*Odocoileus virginianus*) One of the most widespread New World ungulates, with a range that extends from Canada to Peru, this is also the largest deer (up to 120cm/50kg) found in Suriname. It has a distinctive white under-tail that it raises when alarmed. It is a versatile eater and unusually habitat tolerant, but it generally avoids dense forest interiors.

LARGE RODENTS These mammals are important to the forest because they use their chisel teeth to crack hard nuts and feed on the seeds, thereby dispersing them throughout the forest.

Capybara (*Hydrochaeris hydrochaeris*) The capybara is the world's largest (90cm/30kg), and certainly strangest-looking, rodent. It's stocky with a large, rectangular head and an arched, rounded rear. Its fur is dark reddish-brown and it has large webbed feet.

Capybaras are always seen near water in lowland forest, swamp, gallery forest and flooded savannah. They are diurnal or nocturnal and semi-aquatic, and are usually found in family groups of between two to six. They feed mainly on grass and aquatic vegetation.

Their webbed tracks are very broad (105–110mm) with four toes visible on the front foot and three on the hind foot.

Paca (*Agouti paca*) Most often called *labba* locally (or *Surinaamse haas*, meaning 'Surinamese rabbit'), paca are often hunted for their meat. They have large, stocky bodies (70cm/8kg) with reddish-brown fur and four stripes of white spots on each side. Found in forest and secondary brush, they are terrestrial, nocturnal and usually solitary or in male–female pairs. They eat fruit and nuts and are often seen along creeks, streams and rivers.

Their broad tracks (40–45mm) have four toes at the front and three at the rear.

Red-rumped agouti (*Dasyprocta leporina*) Commonly referred to as *akuri*, this is a medium-sized (50cm/3.5kg) rodent with long legs and a large rectangular head; it is said to look like a short-eared rabbit on stilts. Its head, back and shoulders are grey-black while its rump is orange-red.

Red-rumped agouti are commonly found throughout primary or secondary forest and are diurnal and terrestrial. A good place to see them is around the camp at Brownsberg Nature Park. They feed on nuts, seeds and fruit and are most commonly seen at dawn or dusk.

Their forefront tracks are 25mm wide at the front and 30mm wide at the rear. The hind foot has three elongated toes and pointed claws, while the front foot shows three or four toes.

Brazilian porcupine (*Coendou prehensilis*) This oddball member of the porcupine family is notable for its strong prehensile tail and long-clawed toes, both of which reflect an almost exclusively arboreal lifestyle. It is large for a rodent (100cm/5kg) but almost half its body length is composed of its tail. The torso is covered with short pale spines, but these do not extend to the tail. Nocturnal, solitary and secretive, it spends the day resting in a tree hollow or the canopy, and often rolls into a ball when threatened.

XENARTHRANS Unique to the Americas, the superorder Xenarthra is today represented by three distinct groups of mammals, the anteaters and sloths of the order Pilosa, and the armadillos of the order Cingulata. Though superficially very different, these creatures all share several common features, notably the extra articulations and ischiosacral fusion of their vertebral joints (the name Xenarthra derives from two Greek words meaning strange-jointed), the presence of internal testicles between the male's bladder and rectum, and a much lower metabolic rate than other placental mammals. The superorder originated in South America around 60 million years ago, when the continent was isolated from other landmasses, and spread to Central and North America around nine million years ago. Until humans arrived in the Americas some 10,000 years ago, giant ground sloths such as *Megatherium* were widespread in both North and South America. Today, however, most of the 29 recognised species are confined to South America, and all but one has a range confined to southern Mexico, or further south. The only exception is the nine-banded armadillo, the state animal of Texas.

Anteaters This group of mammals have long snouts and no teeth. They tear open ant and termite nests with their powerful front legs and long claws and then use their long, sticky tongues to feast on the bugs. When on the ground, anteaters twist their feet and walk on the sides, or on the knuckles.

Giant anteater (*Myrmecophaga tridactyla*) This large creature is unmistakable, as its lengthy nose and bushy tail make it appear incredibly long (1.2m/75cm/30kg). It is mostly black, with white forelegs and a distinctive white stripe running from its ears to its mid-back. It is found in forest and savannah, especially in open areas with large termite mounds. It is terrestrial and active day or night. Outside of breeding season, it is solitary but the female also carries the young on her back for up to nine months. The giant anteater moves with a shuffling gait or rolling gallop and will rear up and slash at predators when cornered.

Tracks have front claws pointing backwards or sideways and are 100mm wide at the front and 80mm wide at the back.

Tamandua (*Tamandua tetradactyla*) This is a medium-sized (60cm/50cm/6kg) anteater with a long prehensile tail. It is usually blonde on its head, upper back and legs with a black vest but can also appear as entirely blonde.

Tamandua are semi-arboreal, nocturnal or diurnal and are found in primary and secondary forest and savannah. They are solitary creatures that feed on ants, termites and bees. Tracks have front claws pointing backward and are 55mm wide at the front and 40mm wide at the back.

Pygmy anteater (*Cyclopes didactylus*) This tiny anteater (15cm/20cm/225g) is golden brown with black stripes down the middle of its back and belly. The furry

THE GREEN HERITAGE FUND

Established in October 2005 by the naturalist Monique Pool and friends, the Green Heritage Fund Suriname (GHFS) is a non-profit trust inspired partly by the work of the late Wangari Maathai, who won the 2004 Nobel Peace Prize for her grassroots approach to combating deforestation and other environmental concerns in Kenya. The broad aim of the GHFS is to promote the sustainable development of Suriname's natural resources and biodiversity in a manner that includes and benefits local communities, partially though the development of ecotourism.

GHFS has developed two main programmes since its inception. The first has been the ongoing research into, and monitoring of, the Guiana dolphin at the mouth of the Suriname River, and other cetaceans further out at sea. Since 2005, the GHFS has conducted regular research and monitoring trips, and when a popular local magazine wrote an article about the project in 2006, it generated so much interest that GHFS decided to allow visitors to experience its research up-close. Community-based dolphin-watching tours were started, which benefit the local boatmen the most (see pages 116–17). Today, it is estimated that almost 6,000 tourists visit Suriname's dolphins annually, a threefold increase since 2006. Dolphin tourism also helps generate income for five different local communities living along the Suriname or Commewijne rivers.

In 2014, a marine mammal baseline study was under way as part of the Suriname Coastal Protected Areas Programme for which GHFS co-operates with French NGO Association Kwata, CAR-SPAW-RAC, regional scientists and WWF Guianas. It is partially funded by the Global Environment Facility.

The other, perhaps more important, project overseen by the GHFS and its chairman Monique Pool is the Xenarthra Rehabilitation Program (XRP). The primary goal of this programme is to rescue and shelter wounded, orphaned or otherwise debilitated sloths, anteaters and armadillos (all of which belong to the tail is prehensile and there are two large claws on the front foot and four on the hind foot.Pygmy anteaters live in mature and tall secondary forest, and are nocturnal and strictly arboreal. They are solitary creatures that feed on ants in hollow stems of trees.

Sloths
These sedentary creatures spend most of their lives in trees, hanging upside down from hooked claws and eating leaves. Only rarely do they descend to the ground.

Pale-throated three-toed sloth (*Bradypus tridactylus*) The more striking of the two different species of sloth, this one has a predominantly yellow head with a dark nose and crown. Its furry body (60cm/6kg) is dark grey-brown with off-white blotches. Its forelegs are longer than its hind legs, and it has three long claws on each foot.

Found in mature and secondary forest these sloths are nocturnal, diurnal and arboreal. They descend to the ground roughly once a week to dig a hole with their stubby tail and defecate. On the ground they move by dragging themselves. They are good swimmers. Pale-throated three-toed sloths are solitary, silent and very easily overlooked. To spot them look for a furry grey ball on or under a branch.

Linnaeus's two-toed sloth (*Choloepus didactylus*) This sloth has similar habits and body size and shape to the three-toed sloth. It has long brownish fur that is

superorder Xenarthra; see pages 29–32), and to rehabilitate them for eventual release back into their natural habitat.

Typically, the XRP acquires and releases about one sloth every week. However, in October 2012, it was asked to assist with the removal of an estimated 14 sloths from a soon-to-be-cleared forest patch near Paramaribo. What occurred was referred to by Pool as a 'slothageddon'. As the trees were felled one by one, the sloths would fall to the ground as expected, and they were picked up and placed in cages by a group of XRP volunteers – but they came down much faster rate than anybody had anticipated. After a month of clearing, nearly 100 sloths had been recovered and the final tally was over 200. At one point, more than 50 sloths, including 17 babies that required dropper feeding, were clustered in Pool's house and garden, hanging from the trees, the window bars, the television stand, and pretty much anything else they could lay their amply clawed hands on. Between rescuing sloths and releasing them, an overwhelmed Pool coined the term 'slothified' to describe her state. And yet despite the daunting nature of the task, all but three of the animals rescued during 'slothageddon' have since been released back into the forest – the exception being a trio of young babies unready to fend for themselves in the wild.

Despite the success of 'slothageddon', sloths, and other wounded or orphaned animals, continue to need rescuing and therefore GHFS is in the process of building a new Xenarthra Rehabilitation Centre at Cola Creek near Zanderij (see page 183). It is hoped that this facility will be able to care for up to 100 animals per year, rehabilitating and preparing them for release back into the forest. It will also be able to generate revenue through tourist visits. For further details, visit the GHFS website www.greenfundsuriname.org or their Facebook page https://www.facebook.com/pages/Green-Heritage-Fund-Suriname/129859957040929.

darker on its limbs. There are two claws on its front foot and three on its hind foot. This sloth has no tail, and has a pig-like snout.

Two-toed sloths are mainly nocturnal and arboreal. Like the three-toed sloth they come down once a week to do their business, and they are also good swimmers.

Armadillos These creatures are easily identified by their protective bony shell.

Giant armadillo (*Priodontes maximus*) Another unmistakable animal, the giant armadillo has a large body (90cm/50cm/30kg) covered in a greyish shell with yellow edges, although its pink underbelly remains exposed. It has large feet and a tail covered in scales.

Found in rainforest and savannah, this armadillo is nocturnal, terrestrial, subterranean and solitary. With the assistance of its massive front claws, it feeds on the nests of ants and termites.

Great long-nosed armadillo (*Dasypus kappleri*) This medium-sized mammal (55cm/45cm/10kg) has a snout that isn't as long as you'd expect from its name. Its bony shell has seven to nine moveable scales on its mid-back, much like an accordion.

Found on the forest floor near swamps and streams, it is nocturnal, terrestrial and solitary. Its three-toed tracks appear bird-like.

BATS Bats account for more than half of Suriname's mammal diversity, and around 100 different species have been documented. In the forest they are important seed dispersers and pollinators, in addition to consuming tonnes of mosquitoes every night. There are also fruit-, frog-, nectar- and small-mammal-eating species.

Suriname is home to two of the world's three species of vampire bat, the only mammals regarded to be parasitic, feeding solely on blood, mostly sourced from livestock and birds. Humans are very, very occasionally bitten by vampire bats.

REPTILES AND AMPHIBIANS

At least 175 reptile and 102 amphibian species are present in Suriname. Highlights include **poison dart frogs** (*Dendrobatidae*), which come in a range of colours including orange, black, blue and yellow, and are used by some Amerindian tribes to poison their arrows and blow-gun darts. Another striking species is the **Suriname** or **star-fingered toad** (*Pipa pipa*), a very flat, almost leaf-like forest dweller that can grow up to 20cm long, has tiny eyes, neither tongue nor teeth, and is notable for being incubated through to tadpole stage in honeycomb-like pockets on the female's back.

Besides the four species of **sea turtles** that nest on the coast (see pages 36–7), there are a few other chelonians of note. Probably the most common, and most likely to be seen by tourists, is the hulking **yellow-footed tortoise** (*Chelonoidis denticulata*), which is the world's third-largest mainland tortoise, and easily recognised both by its yellow feet and the pale yellowish patches on its shell. The endangered **giant river turtle** (*Podocnemis expansa*) is found in the interior, but like the marine turtles its population is endangered because its meat and eggs have long been considered delicacies. The female turtle, which typically weighs around 23kg and measures 60cm in length, is easy prey for hunters because it nests in large colonies.

The **matamata turtle** (*Chelus fimbriatus*) is certainly one of the more bizarre turtle species. Its shell is covered with horny plates that make it look like a rough dead leaf, but it's the head that's really strange. Its large and flat head and neck are covered with ridges, warts and numerous other bumps. It has a very wide mouth and long snout used to breathe while submerged, and it sucks prey into its mouth like a vacuum. Its head also has flap-like appendages that allow it to sense fish swimming by, which is necessary due to its poor eyesight.

Suriname is also home to the world's largest alligator, the **black caiman** (*Melanosuchus niger*), which can reach a length of more than 5m. Far from common in Suriname, this nocturnal creature is generally associated with slow-moving rivers, wetlands and flooded savannahs. Its diet consists of fish, turtles, large rodents and sometimes deer. Other (much smaller) crocodilians include the **spectacled caiman** (*Caiman crocodiles*), **Schneider's dwarf caiman** (*Paleosuchus trigonatus*) and the world's smallest caiman, **Cuvier's dwarf caiman** (*Paleosuchus palpebrosus*).

As for snakes, there are highly poisonous species including the **labaria** (*Bothrops atrox*), the **bushmaster** (*Lachesis muta*), the largest venomous snake in the Americas, the **rattlesnake** (*Crotalus durissus*) and the **himeralli coral snake** (*Micrurus surinamensis*), but visitors are unlikely to see any of these. There are also several species of tree boas, such as the **emerald tree boa**, that can be spotted at night along the riverbanks. The most famous boa constrictor is the **anaconda** (*Eunectes murinus*), which grows throughout its life and can reach lengths of more than 10m. These nocturnal carnivores spend most of their time in swamps and near rivers and eat just about anything, including peccary, deer, caiman, birds, fish, capybara and agouti.

Visitors are likely to see green iguanas, geckos and several other species of lizards scampering around.

BIRDS

Although Suriname is somewhat overlooked as a birdwatching destination, at least compared with certain other South American countries, the national checklist of around 720 species is very impressive given its relatively small size. And you don't need to be a dedicated birdwatcher to appreciate some of the country's more spectacular feathered creatures. Almost anywhere outside central Paramaribo, visitors will encounter colourful **parrots** and **macaws** screeching overhead, gaudier bill-heavy **toucans** and **aracaris** perched in the treetops, raptors such as the striking **swallow-tailed kite** soaring in the skies, and **herons**, **ibises** and other shorebirds picking along the river margins.

For more serious birdwatchers, Suriname's avifauna is well documented. Some of the most useful printed resources include WWF Guiana's *Annotated Checklist of the Birds of Suriname*, the hefty Vaco-published *Birds of Suriname* and Helm Field Guides' comprehensive two-volume *Birds of Northern South America* (see also pages 236–7). Excellent websites written partly or totally in English include Birds in Suriname (*www.surinamebirds.nl*) and Birding in Suriname (*www.planktonik. com/birdingsuriname*), the latter being run personally by the country's only resident professional ornithologist, Otte Ottema, who also leads or can arrange birding tours.

Of particular interest to serious birders are the 50 or so Surinamese species whose global range is centred on, or restricted to, the Guiana Shield. This list includes one species thought to be endemic to Suriname, the **arrowhead piculet**, as well as several near endemics, notably **sulphur-breasted parakeet**, **blood-coloured woodpecker** and **Palzeln's tody-tyrant**, as well as several distinct subspecies. Other localised species of high interest to visiting birdwatchers include **rufous** crab-hawk, green-throated mango, crimson topaz, grey-winged trumpeter, red-fan parrot, Guianan tucanet, boat-billed tody-tyrant, Finsch's euphonia, Guianan red-cotinga and white-fronted manikin.

Almost anywhere in Suriname will offer rewarding birdwatching for first-time visitors, and several important sites are covered in greater detail in Part Two of this guide. Outstanding sites in and around the capital are Peperpot Nature Park, Paramaribo Zoo and the adjoining Cultuurtuin, Chocopot and nearby Weg-na-Zee, and the mangrove-lined Suriname River itself. Key sites further afield include Brownsberg Nature Park, Raleigh Falls and the Voltzberg (the last is famed as the best site for the stunning **Guianan cock-of-the-rock**, see box, page 224), Bigi Pan near Nieuw Nickerie, and riverside resorts further inland such as Overbridge, Babunhol and Berg en Dal. The prevalence of forest and water throughout Suriname, however, really does mean that interesting birds can be seen almost everywhere you travel, even in relatively urban settings such as Groningen, Apoera and Nieuw Nickerie.

INVERTEBRATES

Although rainforest accounts for little more than 10% of the world's surface area, it is thought to support around two-thirds of its insect species. This means that Suriname, with its wealth of tropical rainforest and wetland habitats, is home to an immensely diverse range of insects and other invertebrates. And it is these (mostly very small) critters – ants, millipedes, centipedes, spiders, butterflies, beetles, ticks, flies, gnats, bees, roaches, scorpions, etc – that tourists to Suriname will generally see the most. This is, however, perhaps a mixed blessing. Some invertebrates, such as mosquitoes or ticks, are notable mostly for their nuisance value, while others are too secretive or small to catch the attention. Equally though, some of the most amazing creatures present in Suriname are invertebrates, and while it wouldn't be realistic to attempt a complete inventory in a book like this, a few examples are discussed below.

BUTTERFLIES AND MOTHS Suriname supports around 1,500 species of butterfly (more than 5% of the global total) and a far greater number of moths, both of which belong to the order Lepidoptera. One of the most conspicuous butterflies is the **blue morpho** (*Morpho menelaus*), a spectacular iridescent blue frugivore with a wingspan of up to 15cm, often seen flitting through forest interiors in the likes of Brownsberg Nature Park. Also very striking and hard to miss are the 30-odd **swallowtail species** – most black and yellow with prominent wing extensions – of the Papilionidae family.

The **silk moths** of the Saturniidae family include the massive *Eacles Penelope*, which is orange-yellow with an 18cm wingspan, and the smaller *Copiopteryx semiramis* and *C. jehovahi* which are trailed by remarkable wing pennants up to 8cm long.

The largest Lepidoptera species found in Suriname (and possibly anywhere in the world) is the **ghost moth** or great owlet *Thysania agrippina*, whose spectral white wings have a span of 27–30cm. Nectar-feeding **hawk moths**, though far smaller, are notable for their hummingbird-like ability to hover in mid-air while they feed using a long narrow proboscis that reaches its extreme (15–20cm) in the giant sphinxes *Cocytius antaeus and C. cluentius*.

ANTS Conspicuous rainforest residents, often seen marching in military fashion across footpaths, the ants of the Formicidae family represent possibly the world's most successful and prolific life form. Some estimates suggest that for every single person on earth, there are up to 1.5 million ants, and they are thought to represent more than 10% of the entire biomass created by animals in the rainforest. In common with the closely related honeybees, they also have the most advanced social structure of all insects, wherein sterile female workers construct large, usually subterranean, 'cities' to protect their queen and males. Ants also play an important role in cleaning up the forest of dead animals and forest plants in a cycle that creates new matter for plants to feed on. Still, it is wise to be very wary of ants when they are on the march – which means always looking carefully before putting your foot down on the forest floor. Probably the most vicious species in Suriname is the **lesser giant hunting ant** (*Paraponera clavata*). This is the second-largest ant in the world, measuring up to 3cm long, and has a sting to match its size. It is also known as the bullet ant. Some say this is because the pain of a bite is like being hit by a bullet. Another explanation is that bite victims shoot off as quickly as a bullet!

BEETLES Distinguished by their hard protective shells – a modification of the front wings – beetles are placed in the order Coleoptera, which constitutes around 25% of the world's described species. One of the most impressive specimens found in Suriname is the **Actaeon rhinoceros beetle** (*Megasoma actaeon*), which can grow to almost 15cm long and has a thick, black, matt armoured coat and large horn-like head appendages that strongly resemble a rhino form. Almost as large, but less formidable, is the **giant longhorn beetle** (*Enoplocerus armillatus*), named for its curving black antennae which are often longer than the rest of its body.

OTHER INSECTS Stick insects of the order Phasmatodea are wonderfully camouflaged creatures, shaped like sticks and capable of rocking their elongated bodies – in some cases up to 10cm long – to imitate a twig in the wind. **Damselflies** will be familiar to European readers, but in Suriname they often take on extreme forms and sizes, most notably perhaps the so-called 'helicopters' of the Neotropical genus *Mecistogaster*, whose impressive wings (in some cases with a span of almost 20cm) are outdone by their exaggeratedly long narrow torsos. Another distinctive order of large insects is the Mantodea, often known as **praying mantises**, which can be distinguished by their triangular heads and the unusual posture dictated by their long serrated forelegs.

ARACHNIDS Suriname supports a huge number of arachnids, a class of invertebrates that includes spiders and scorpions, and is distinguished from insects by having eight legs as opposed to six.

Tarantulas The best known arachnids are tarantulas, a group of hairy predatory spiders belonging to the Theraphosidae family. Despite their large size (in some cases they can have a leg span of up to 30cm), fearsome appearance, notorious reputation and venomous fangs, tarantulas generally only bite people when provoked. The bite can be very painful, with side effects lasting for several days depending on the species and the severity of the bite, but no human fatality has ever been recorded. Most species of tarantula will also display before biting, and the first-line defence of many New World tarantulas is to fire off the row of barbed urticating bristles laced with skin irritants that line their abdomen. Most tarantulas live in underground burrows and feed on large insects, which they hunt down rather than trap in their webs.

SEA TURTLES *(Based on information provided by Michelle Kalamandeen, Guyana Marine Turtle Conservation Project)*
From March to August, the sandy beaches of Suriname, particularly Galibi and Matapica, serve as nesting grounds for four of the world's seven species of marine turtle, all of which appear on the IUCN Red List of Threatened Species. Most common are the green turtle and leatherback, but the beaches also attract small numbers of olive ridley and hawksbill turtles.

The decline in turtle populations has several causes: the first is direct hunting and egg collection, for while Amerindian and other beachside communities have long relied on sustainable turtle harvesting as a dietary staple because these massive creatures provide large amounts of meat, as well as numerous eggs (and beautiful shells), this has become increasingly unsustainable in recent decades; and while climate change also plays a role, the bigger culprits are the trawling nets used by fishermen, which often trap and accidentally kill turtles.

Marine turtles range from around 35–500kg at maturity, and all species have forelimbs modified into paddle-like flippers, which typically have one claw instead of distinct digits. Unlike their terrestrial and freshwater counterparts, marine turtles cannot pull their heads into their shell for protection. Instead, the skull is topped with a very strong bone that acts much like a shell.

In all sea turtle species, breeding females must crawl ashore on a beach to nest (males typically never leave the sea). Once on shore the females excavate a broad 'body pit' and a deep narrow hole into which the eggs will be deposited. Sea turtles usually lay a clutch of around 100 soft-shelled eggs. The eggs are then covered and the female lumbers back to the sea.

Sea turtles normally mate more than once in a season, and often close to the same spot. Green turtles and leatherbacks have been known to nest eight or nine times in one season. These species also tend to take a year or two off before nesting again.

Leatherback *(Dermochelys coriacea)* With a shell that can reach about 2m in length and an overall body mass that can be more than 500kg, the leatherback is the largest of the sea turtle species. It is a prehistoric beast that is a marvel to see in its natural environment. The giant size of the leatherback doesn't impede its mobility in water; it can rapidly descend to below 300m and has been known to travel thousands of kilometres in a matter of a few months. Its diet consists mainly of jellyfish. It has the largest range of any turtle species, occurring in all tropical and subtropical oceans as far north as Alaska and Norway and as far south as the southernmost tips of South Africa and New Zealand. At least 25,000 females annually are estimated to nest globally, a dramatic decline from the 1980 estimate of more than 100,000. The leatherback was formerly IUCN listed as Critically Endangered, but its status was downgraded to Vulnerable in a new 2013 assessment. The local name is *aitkantie*.

Green turtle *(Chelonia mydas)* Green turtles can have a shell length of roughly 1.5m and weigh upwards of 300kg. They are easily identified by their small head tipped by a short, rounded snout and their smooth shell, which has four scutes, or horny plates, on each side.

Colour is one aspect that does not work well in identification. The 'green' in their name actually refers to the colour of their fat; outer colouring varies from black above and white below in hatchlings to brown streaks, spots or a uniform grey colour in adults. The green turtles that nest in the Guianas are amongst the largest in the world, and can be twice the weight of some Caribbean green turtles found nesting in Costa Rica.

Green turtles eat mainly seagrasses and seaweeds that are typically found growing in calm waters, but the ideal nesting grounds occur where there is strong wave action. As a result, the turtles must migrate hundreds of kilometres from feeding to nesting grounds. Many of those that nest in the Guianas come from Brazil.

After years of slaughter, green turtle populations in the Guianas dwindled to a very low level, but they have been on the increase recently and are the most commonly seen species in Suriname. Nevertheless, green turtles are listed by IUCN as Endangered. The local name is *krape* and the Dutch name, rather tellingly, is *soepschildpad* ('soup turtle').

Hawksbill (*Eretmochelys imbricata*) The average shell length of an adult hawksbill is about 1m, and they weigh around 75kg. A hawksbill's head is narrow with a straight, pointed, protruding beak (strangely it does not resemble a hawk's bill, which curves down).

The hawksbill is found throughout the tropics, predominantly around coral reefs where they mainly feed on sponges. They have been hunted for many years for their thick, decorative shells, often called 'tortoiseshell', which used to fetch high prices on international jewellery markets (they are currently banned internationally).

Only small numbers of hawksbills nest in Suriname. Hawksbill turtles are listed by IUCN as Critically Endangered.

Olive ridley (*Lepidochelys olivacea*) With an average length of about 65cm and a weight of 30–50kg, the olive ridley is the smallest sea turtle species. It has a short, nearly circular shell that is yellowish-olive in colour. When seen from above, the head is triangular and the shell has five to nine plates along each side.

The olive ridley is a tropical species that nests in large groups on remote beaches in locations such as Mexico, Costa Rica and India. Nesting in Suriname is a rare occurrence, and years can pass between recorded instances. The olive ridley is listed by IUCN as Vulnerable.

WEST INDIAN MANATEE (*Trichechus manatus*) This large aquatic mammal, known locally as the *zeekooi* ('sea cow'), is grey or brown in colour with an average length of 3m and a weight of up to 400kg. It has a split upper lip for feeding and is typically found in shallow coastal areas and rivers. You're most likely to see it in the Saramacca River around Groningen.

WHALES AND DOLPHINS Thanks partly to the activities of the GHFS (see box, pages 30–1), it is now known that at least 16 cetacean (whale and dolphin) species have been recorded off the coast of Suriname, of which four are baleen whales and 12 are toothed whales. This checklist includes the world's second-largest mammal, the fin whale (*Balaenoptera physalus*), which can grow to be almost 30m long. However, the only cetacean likely to be seen by tourists is the **Guiana dolphin** (*Sotalia guianensis*), which is common at the mouth of the Suriname River close to Paramaribo. It is a relatively small species, usually around 2m in length, and otherwise resembles the well-known common bottlenose dolphin due to its longish beak and blue-grey colouring.

Other cetacean species confirmed for Suriname are Bryde's whale (*Balaenoptera brydei*), sei whale (*Balaenoptera borealis*), minke whale (*Balaenoptera acutorostrata*), sperm whale (*Physeter macrocephalus*), melon-headed whale (*Peponocephala electra*), false killer whale (*Pseudorca crassidens*), short-finned pilot whale (*Globicephala macrorhynchus*), rough-toothed dolphin (*Steno bredanensis*), Fraser's dolphin (*Lagenodelphis hosei*), common bottlenose dolphin (*Tursiops truncatus*), Atlantic spotted dolphin (*Stenella frontalis*), pan-tropical spotted dolphin (*Stenella attenuata*), spinner dolphin (*Stenella longirostris*) and long-beaked common dolphin (*Delphinus capensis*).

FISH Suriname supports a diverse range of fish, with at least 370 freshwater species present, and countless marine ones. Fish thrive in a range of wetland habitats, including rivers, creeks, ponds, oxbow lakes and flooded forests and savannahs. Fishing is a very popular activity among Surinamese men in particular, and the low human densities along the country's many rivers mean that no licence is required to fish at any time of the year.

3

Practical information

WHEN TO VISIT

Suriname can be visited at any time of year. Being close to the Equator, temperatures are not strongly seasonal, with daily averages in Paramaribo ranging from 27–29°C throughout the year. The low-key nature of tourism means that seasonal overcrowding is not really a concern either. In most respects, however, the best time to visit Suriname is during the relatively dry months of February to March and August to November, and the worst time is during the wettest months of May to August, when the interior in particular is prone to flooding and the already limited road network becomes even more so. For wildlife enthusiasts, turtle viewing, a very popular activity, is best from late February until May, although leatherbacks keep laying until August. Migrant shorebirds are most prolific from mid-August to late April.

ITINERARIES AND HIGHLIGHTS

Suriname has developed a rather unusual tourist industry, wherein most visitors base themselves in Paramaribo for the duration of their stay and use it as a springboard from which to join several short (mostly one- to three-day) modular tours to individual sites of interest, returning to the capital between excursions. We assume that this system has developed partly as a result of the limited all-roads-lead-to-Paramaribo nature of the transport infrastructure. It also reflects the fact that most visitors to Suriname – whether they be Dutch or Belgian interns, holidaying emigrants, or family of one or the other – typically stay for months rather than weeks, and slot in a few short trips during weekends. As a result of this, few tours follow a long itinerary countrywide, and opportunities for independent travel without returning to the capital are somewhat restricted. It also means that you are usually best off taking a mix-'n'-match approach to setting up a trip, checking what tours are available to your first priority destinations, booking those, and then slotting in other short tours or independent day and overnight trips around them.

As for highlights, these are detailed at the start of the two main parts of the regional guide (see pages 66–7 and 189–90), with an indication of the minimum or ideal time to dedicate to the place, as well as whether it can be visited independently, on a tour, or both. Broadly, however, we would recommend that visitors dedicate at least three days to Paramaribo, Commewijne District and their immediate environs, as well as slotting in a tour to one of the two recognised turtle-viewing sites (Matapica and Galibi), and at least one expedition deeper into the interior, whether it be a day trip to Brownsberg, lodge-hopping along the Upper Suriname, a no-frills organised tour to Raleigh Falls (Central Suriname Nature Reserve), an adventurous kayak excursion on the Upper Coesewijne, or a more upmarket package to the likes of Bergendal Eco-Resort, Kabalebo Nature Reserve or Palumeu.

SURINAME
Administrative districts & nature reserves

Atlantic Ocean

GUYANA

French
Guiana
(France)

GUYANA

N

Bradt

0 ━━━ 50km
0 ━━━ 50 miles

Area claimed by
French Guiana

BRAZIL

KEY TO ADMINISTRATIVE DISTRICTS	
1 Nickerie	6 Commewijne
2 Coronie	7 Marowijne
3 Saramacca	8 Para
4 Wanica	9 Brokopondo
5 Paramaribo	10 Sipaliwini

KEY TO NATURE RESERVES			
A Kabalebo	F Brinckheuvel	K Central Suriname
B Hertenrits	G Brownsberg	L Sipaliwini
C Peruvia	H Copi	
D Coppename	I Wanekreek	
E Boven-Coesewijne	J Galibi	

Backpacker-style independent travel is still in its infancy in Suriname, but it can be done. A rewarding loop from Paramaribo would be to follow the coast west to Nieuw Nickerie, then catch the twice-weekly passenger boat up the Corantijn River to Apoera, and bus back to Paramaribo from there. Another area well suited to backpacking is the Upper Suriname River, which could be explored over several days, first bussing to Atjoni, then hopping by taxi-boat between different lodges, with the possibility of returning to Atjoni by boat or flying directly to Paramaribo. The Upper Suriname could be combined with Brownsberg Nature Park and Stoneiland, both of which are accessed from Brownsweg on the main road between Paramaribo and Atjoni. Finally, to the east of the Suriname River, the plantations of Commewijne District are easily explored by bicycle from Paramaribo itself, while the village of Galibi, bordering the turtle-viewing reserve of the same name, can also be reached by bus and then boat via Albina.

TOUR OPERATORS

As noted above, most visitors to Suriname arrive independently and book all their tours (whether in advance or on the spot) through various local operators, as listed on pages 78–9. It is more unusual to book a full package in advance through an international operator, not least because few such trips exist. However, international operators specialising in Suriname include the following:

UK

Explore Worldwide Adventure Holidays
\+44 (0)845 013 1537; e res@explore.co.uk;
www.explore.co.uk
Wilderness Explorers \+44 (0)20 8417 1585;
e suriname@wilderness-explorers.com; www.
wilderness-explorers.com. See ad, page 38.

HOLLAND

Fox Vakanties \+31 (0)252 660000;
e info@fox.nl; www.fox.nl
Sawadee \+31 (0)20 4202220;
www.sawadee.nl

RED TAPE

All visitors must produce a passport on arrival. Check well in advance that your passport hasn't expired and will not do so within six months of your date of arrival, or you risk being refused entry to the country. Most visitors require either a visa or a tourist card, the only exceptions being nationals of Argentina, Aruba, Bonaire, Brazil, Curaçao, Israel, Japan, Malaysia, the Philippines, Saba, St Eustacius, St Maarten, South Korea and Singapore, who may enter the country freely (in some cases for up to 30 days only without a visa). Be aware that visa requirements frequently change, so it's advisable to check for up-to-date information before you travel and the best source of clear and detailed current information (in English or Dutch) is the website of the Suriname Consulate in the Netherlands (*www.consulaatsuriname.nl*).

TOURIST CARD As of November 2011, nationals of the USA, UK and other EU member states no longer require a visa to enter Suriname, provided that they are there as tourists and not on business. Instead, they can buy a tourist card, valid for one entry only, at a cost of US$25 (or €20). No paperwork is involved (other than showing your passport) and the card can be bought prior to departure at the tourist card counter at Amsterdam's Schiphol Airport, or upon arrival at Johan Adolf Pengel International Airport, at a desk signposted immediately before the immigration queues. People of Surinamese origin can stay for up to six months on a tourist card, but other visitors are only allowed 90 days. Note, however, that you will only be stamped for 30 days on arrival. If you wish to stay for longer, you need to report to the Immigration Department in Paramaribo (see page 100) with your passport and air ticket to obtain an extension.

VISAS All nationalities not listed above require a visa, which must be obtained in advance through a Surinamese consulate or embassy. This can be quite a laborious and bureaucratic process, so leave yourself plenty of time. The Suriname Consulate in the Netherlands website (see below) maintains an exhaustive list of all Surinamese embassies, consulates and honorary consuls abroad (look under 'Government' then 'Addresses'). These include the following:

Belgium 200 Franklin Roosevelt Laan, Brussels;
\+32 26401172; e sur.amb.bru@online.be

France 94 Rue du Ranelagh, Paris; \+33 145
259 300; e info@ambassadesurinamefr.org

French Guiana 3 Leopold Heder Av, Cayenne; ☎+594 594282160; e cg-sme-cay@wanadoo.fr
Guyana 54 New Garden & Anira St, Georgetown; ☎+592 2267844; e amb.guyana@foreignaffairs.gov.sr
Netherlands 11 De Cuser Straat, Amsterdam; ☎+31 20 6426137/6426717/6465311; www.consulaatsuriname.nl
UK Flat 89, Pier Hse, 31 Cheyne Walk, London SW3 5HN; ☎+44 (0)20 308 7143; m +44 (0)7768 196 326; www.honoraryconsul.info
USA 866 UN Plaza, New York; ☎212 8260660 or 4301 Connecticut Av, Washington DC; www.surinameembassy.org

GETTING THERE AND AWAY

BY AIR Most visitors to Suriname fly from Europe, the USA or the Caribbean. However, only four international carriers fly to Paramaribo, as detailed below, and while there are direct flights from Miami and Amsterdam, there are none from elsewhere in Europe. Flights from the UK tend to be quite costly, with Caribbean Airlines usually the cheapest option.

Caribbean Airlines www.caribbean-airlines.com. To/from Port of Spain, with connections to London, Toronto & several cities in the USA.
Fly AllWays www.flyallways.com. New airline that will start operating flights from São Luís, Cayenne, Belém, Georgetown, Boa Vista & Barbados in Jan 2015.

InselAir www.fly-inselair.com. To/from Curaçao only.
KLM www.klm.com. Daily to/from Amsterdam with worldwide connections.
Suriname Airways www.flyslm.com. To/from Aruba, Amsterdam, Belem, Cayenne, Curaçao, Georgetown, Port of Spain & Miami.

All international flights land at **Johan Adolf Pengel International Airport** (JAPI; *IATA code PBM;* ☎*325200;* e *smjp@japi-airport.com; www.japi-airport.com*) which lies in Zanderij, about 45km south of Paramaribo. Usually referred to as Zanderij Airport, JAPI is serviced by a few unremarkable cafés and shops, most of which only kick into action to coincide with incoming or outgoing flights, and a branch of the DSB Bank (⊕ *10.30–17.30 Mon–Fri*) which has a 24-hour ATM where local currency can be drawn against a Master or Maestro card. There is also a Digicell shop (where you can buy a local SIM card), and kiosks for the main car rental companies: Avis, Budget and Ross.

Most people arriving at JAPI book a shuttle transfer to the city through their hotel. This typically costs around SRD 35–50 per person in an air-conditioned bus, including drinking water, and takes up to two hours depending on traffic. If you don't have a transfer booked, several kiosks in the airport lobby represent various shuttle companies, among them Garage Ashruf (☎*450102/454451/458485;* e *ashruf@sr.net; www.garage-ashruf.com*), Le Grand Baldew (☎ *474713; www.legrandbaldew.com*) and Garage Paarl (☎ *403600/403610;* m *8808277;* e *info@garagedepaarl.com; www. garagedepaarl.com*).

Private taxis from JAPI to Paramaribo are also available, but these are quite pricey at around SRD 125–175 one-way. At the other end of the price scale, the Nationaal Vervoer Bedrijf (NVB) transport company operates four buses daily between Zanderij and the Heiligen Weg terminus in central Paramaribo. These cost SRD 1.15 per person, leave in either direction at 05.30 (Monday to Saturday only), 06.30 (Sunday only), 08.00, 15.30 and 17.00, and are scheduled to take 80 minutes, though up to two hours is more likely. More regular private Lijn POZ (Paramaribo–Onverwacht–Zanderij) buses connect Zanderij to Maagden Straat in central Paramaribo.

Note that most domestic flights leave Paramaribo from the more central **Zorg en Hoop Airport** (see page 74). This means that if you are planning on transferring between a domestic and international flight on the same day, you should leave at least two hours, preferably longer, between the first flight landing and check-in for the second flight.

BY VEHICULAR FERRY You can cross into Suriname from neighbouring Guyana and French Guiana (the latter actually a *département* of France and thus part of the European Union). In both cases, the border crossing is by boat or motor ferry and details are given elsewhere in this guide (Nieuw Nickerie for Guyana, see page 163, and Albina for French Guiana, see page 143). Both crossing are quite straightforward in terms of bureaucracy as long as your papers are in order. EU passport holders do not need a visa to cross into French Guiana. Visas for Guyana, if required, can be bought at the consulate in Nieuw Nickerie.

SAFETY

Suriname is generally a very safe country for travel, judged by almost any standards. Indeed, the biggest concerns for most travellers should probably be insect-borne diseases such as dengue fever (see page 59) and road accidents, particularly for cyclists. It should also be pointed out that, as is the case almost anywhere in the world, breaking the law – in particular by using or handling illegal drugs – could land you in trouble.

THEFT The only place where crime is a slight concern is the capital Paramaribo (see page 79), but probably no more so than in most European cities of comparable size. In smaller towns and thinly populated villages, crime levels are very low, not least because communities are small and tightly knit. Nevertheless, the basic common-sense precautions appropriate to most parts of the developing world are worth repeating:

- Casual thieves are often associated with busy markets and bus stations. Keep a close eye on your possessions in such places, and avoid carrying loose valuables or large amounts of money.
- Keep all your valuables and the bulk of your money in a hidden money belt. Never show this money-belt in public. Keep any spare cash you need elsewhere on your person.
- Where the choice exists between carrying valuables on your person or leaving them in a locked room, we would tend to favour the latter, particularly after dark, but obviously you should use your judgement and be sure the room is secure.
- When in doubt, don't walk around after dark but take a taxi instead.
- Leave any jewellery of financial or sentimental value at home.
- Avoid quiet or deserted places at night, such as unlit alleys.

MARINE AND AQUATIC DANGERS Opportunities to swim in the sea in Suriname are limited, as most of the coastline is rather inaccessible. However, if you do end up staying at the coast, for instance at Matapica or Galibi Nature Reserve, be cautious. The sea can be very rough, and there are no lifeguards or display flags indicating when or whether conditions are unsafe. As a result swimmers risk being dragged away from shore by riptides and strong undertows, the presence of which may not always be apparent until you are actually in the water. If you do decide to swim and sense a strong undertow, get out immediately. If you are caught in a riptide, it is generally advisable not to fight the current by trying to swim directly to shore, but rather to save your strength by floating on your back or swimming parallel to shore until the tide weakens, and only then to try and reach land.

There are plenty of opportunities to swim in the rapids and rivers of Suriname. Indeed, swimming is an integral activity in many tours to the interior. As far as we can ascertain, this is safe enough in most places, though you should always check with your guide before taking the plunge. One submarine threat that most visitors are aware of is piranhas, but in practice these are not nearly as ferocious as the popular media would have you believe, and the very occasional attacks that do occur usually only result in the loss of a fingertip or similar (which should be enough to discourage most men from skinny dipping!). The general consensus locally is that these rare attacks usually only happen where piranhas are used to being fed, deliberately or inadvertently, by edible waste dumped into the water at lodges or villages. Follow local advice and avoid swimming at such hotspots.

GAY TRAVELLERS Homosexuality, though legal, has a much lower profile than in most European countries. Nevertheless, while Suriname is probably not suited to anyone seeking an active gay scene, gay couples are unlikely to encounter any problems with discrimination in hotels and other tourist institutions. The homosexual age of consent is 18, two years higher than the heterosexual age, but this is seldom enforced. The law does not recognise homosexual marriages, civil unions or domestic partnerships, nor does it actively protect gays and lesbians from discrimination. Since 2011, the country's most prominent gay and lesbian organisation LGBT Platform Suriname (*www.lgbtplatformsuriname.com*) has held an annual Gay Pride march called OUT@SU every 11 October to coincide with International Coming Out Day.

WOMEN TRAVELLERS Suriname is probably as safe as anywhere for women travellers. That being said, women travelling alone are frequently subjected to high levels of hassle in the form of staring, whistling, flirtatious behaviour and lewd propositions. Paramaribo is particularly bad for this sort of thing, though it might happen anywhere. Generally, make it clear that you are not interested, firmly but without being openly unfriendly, and you'll soon be left alone. If hassle is persistent, it may sometimes help to pretend you have a husband at home or waiting for you (in which case wearing a wedding ring is accepted as 'proof'). It would also be prudent to dress more conservatively than you might at home, not so much to avoid offending local sensibilities but because it will help deter unwanted male attention. And while this attention can become cumulatively annoying, and some women travellers find it disrespectful or upsetting or both, we have heard nothing to suggest it might tip over into genuinely threatening behaviour.

More mundanely, if you're travelling into the jungle for a few days, it's advisable to carry enough tampons and/or sanitary pads to see you through until you return to the city, just in case your period starts unexpectedly (bearing mind that travelling in the tropics can sometimes instigate heavier or more irregular periods than normal).

TRAVELLERS WITH DISABILITIES Suriname, in particular the deep interior, is not generally well suited travellers with mobility problems. Transport and accommodation away from the few main roads tends to be basic, often involving boat rides that would be risky to anybody who cannot swim. Travellers with disabilities wanting to visit Suriname are pointed to the following specialist websites, and should also liaise closely with an upmarket local operator who is aware of the exact nature of their disabilities and what limits these might impose on them.

www.apparelyzed.com A site dedicated to spinal injury, & hosting a hugely popular forum. **www.globalaccessnews.com** A searchable database of disability travel information. **www.rollingrains.com** A searchable website advocating disability travel. **www.youreable.com** A UK-based general resource for disability information, with an active forum.

WHAT TO TAKE

When packing for a country such as Suriname, many travellers devote considerable thought and effort to finding the right balance between bringing everything they might possibly need and keeping down weight and bulk. The following are a few general points worth bearing in mind. Firstly, almost all genuine necessities are easy to get hold of in Paramaribo (less so elsewhere in the country), so no need to over-pack. Secondly, the vast majority of those ingenious outdoor gadgets sold to neophyte tropical travellers in camping shops turn out to be gimmicky deadweight once on the road. Thirdly, however and whenever you travel, except perhaps in Paramaribo itself, the 'rain' in rainforest tends to trump the 'dry' in dry season, so expect to be caught in the occasional tropical downpour at all times of year, and try to bring plenty of light quick-dry clothing as well as waterproofing for your luggage and electronic gear.

CARRYING LUGGAGE Unless you plan on using a lot of public transport, any solid suitcase or duffel bag should suffice. Ideally, it should be waterproof to protect against tropical downpours and splashes when travelling on the rivers. If it isn't, a large rubbish bag or two should be effective protection against a dousing. For those expecting to use public transport or to walk a lot, a rucksack, or other bag that can be carried on the back, would be the best choice. Either way, make sure your bag is designed in such a way that it can easily be padlocked; this won't prevent a determined thief from slashing it open, but it will be a real deterrent to more casual theft. For regular travellers, an excellent option, pre-empting most climatic and other travel conditions, is the Base Camp series of duffel-bags-with-back-straps produced by North Face (the only disadvantage of these rugged, waterproof and easily padlocked bags being that they have only one single compartment).

CLOTHES Suriname's sweaty and often stormy tropical climate is ideally suited to light summery clothing that dries quickly. Minimum requirements might be two pairs of long trousers or long skirts, two sets of shorts, half a dozen T-shirts, one (very light) jumper, a poncho or similar waterproof windbreaker, a bathing costume, enough socks and underwear to last a week, one solid pair of walking shoes with decent ankle support, and one pair of sandals, thongs or other lightweight shoes. Socks and underwear should ideally be made from natural fabrics, as these are less likely to encourage fungal infections such as athlete's foot, or prickly heat in the groin region. Socks and underwear are light and compact enough that it's worth bringing a week's supply. With enough clothes to last a week, it should be easy enough to arrange laundry at any decent hotel, but if you do run short you can top up by buying a few cheap supplementary items in Paramaribo.

CAMPING GEAR AND OTHER USEFUL ITEMS There is almost no reason to bring camping equipment to Suriname. If you want to sleep out, a hammock and net is a far better option than a tent, and can be bought cheaply in Paramaribo (see page 98). On organised tours where a hammock or camping gear is required, it is almost invariably supplied by the operator.

If you're interested in natural history, it's difficult to imagine anything that will give you such value-for-weight entertainment as a pair of binoculars, which these days needn't be much heavier or bulkier than a pack of cards. Binoculars are essential if you want to get a good look at birds, or monkeys and other wildlife high in the trees. For most purposes, 7x or 8x magnification will be fine, but serious birdwatchers will find a 10x magnification more useful.

All the toilet bag basics (soap, shampoo, conditioner, toothpaste, toothbrush, deodorant, basic razors) are very easy to replace as you go along – so there's no need to bring family-sized packs – but women planning on longer stays might want to stock up on some heavy-duty, leave-in hair conditioner to minimise sun damage. If you wear contact lenses, be aware that many people find the intense sun and dry climate irritates their eyes, so you might consider reverting to glasses. Most budget hotels provide toilet paper and many also provide towels, but it is worth bringing your own to make sure you don't get caught short.

You should carry a small medical kit (see page 58), as well as a mosquito net. Two other important items of tropical toiletry are mosquito repellent of a type suitable for skin application, and high-factor sunscreen. A pack of wet or facial cleansing wipes can help maintain a semblance of cleanliness on long journeys into the jungle, and anti-bacterial gel is a good way of ensuring you don't make yourself ill if you're eating on the move with grimy hands.

Other useful items include a padlock for your bag, a torch, a penknife and (if you don't have one on your phone) a compact alarm clock. A twisted no-peg washing line is great for hanging clothes out. Some people won't travel without a good pair of earplugs to help them sleep at night, and a travel pillow to make long journeys that bit easier to endure.

ELECTRICITY The mains supply is 110/127V AC at 60 cycles per second. If you travel with a device that doesn't accept this, you will need a voltage converter. The standard electric socket in Suriname is European Type C with two round pins. If you have appliances with a different plug shape, bring a universal adaptor.

MONEY

The unit of currency is the Suriname dollar (SRD), which was introduced in 2004 in response to long-standing inflation, with one SRD being equal to 1,000 of the now obsolete Suriname guilder. The SRD is divided into 100 cents. Banknotes are printed in denominations of SRD 100, 50, 20, 5, 2.50 and 1, while 250, 100, 25, 10, 5 and 1 cent coins are also issued. It is a reasonably stable currency, trading at around £1 = SRD 5.15, US$1 = SRD 3.28 and €1 = SRD 4.09 in November 2014.

ORGANISING YOUR FINANCES The easiest way to obtain local currency in Suriname is from an ATM that accepts international credit or debit cards. The most useful cards are Maestro or MasterCard, which are accepted at most ATMs. Visa is generally accepted only at ATMs affiliated to the Royal Bank of Canada (RBC), which also takes Cirrus, Maestro and Plus cards. ATMs are dotted all over Paramaribo but most smaller towns only have one or two, most of which will take MasterCard only. There are no ATMs at all in the likes of Apoera, Brokopondo or Brownsweg, in the Upper Suriname region or in nature reserves and other remote destinations accessible only by air or boat. It is thus advisable to withdraw all the local currency you are likely to need for any given excursion whilst still in Paramaribo. Note, too, that opportunities to pay directly by credit card are limited in the capital and almost non-existent elsewhere in the country, except at a few upmarket lodges.

Those who rely primarily on a credit or debit card should be aware that an individual or group with only one such card can be faced with real complications if the card is stolen, swallowed by an ATM, or otherwise rendered useless. It is best to carry a second card as a back-up, keeping it apart from the rest of your funds. It is also worth carrying some hard currency cash, ideally euros or US dollars, perhaps to a total value of around €500. This can be changed into SRD at numerous banks and private *cambios* (bureaux des change) in Paramaribo. There are also foreign exchange facilities in most other relatively substantial towns. In the worst instance, should your card let you down and your cash run out, Western Union is widely represented and can be used for quick cash transfers from anywhere in the world.

Carry your hard currency and cards (plus passport and other important documentation) in a money-belt, ideally one that can be hidden beneath your clothing. The money-belt should be made of cotton or another natural fabric, and everything inside it should be wrapped in plastic to protect it against sweat.

PRICES IN THIS BOOK In Suriname, most prices are quoted in the local currency and it is best to pay that way. Many smarter hotels countrywide and a few restaurants in Paramaribo quote prices in euros or more occasionally in US dollars, but they will all accept payment in SRD. For the sake of consistency and in order to facilitate comparison, we have opted to quote all prices in this book in local currency, using the current conversion rate at the time of writing. This may result in slight inconsistencies as exchange rates fluctuate, but with the SRD being reasonably stable, it seemed less confusing on the whole than quoting rates in three different currencies.

BUDGETING

Suriname isn't a cheap country, certainly not by comparison with parts of Asia, but generally things are reasonably priced and represent fair to good value for money. For many visitors, travel costs are exaggerated by doing all excursions from the capital on organised tours, which tend to be costlier than the do-it-yourself approach.

So far as travel basics go, the cheapest accommodation for one or two people will probably average out at under SRD 100 per day. You're looking at more like SRD 200–250 per day for a moderate self-contained double with air conditioning, and upwards of SRD 300 for something more upmarket. For food, expect to spend around SRD 15–20 per head for a one-course meal at a cheap local eatery, and upwards of SRD 60 per head for a main course with drink at a superior restaurant in Paramaribo. Depending on how often and how far you travel, public transport shouldn't come to more than around SRD 10 per person per day, while a charter taxi ride in most towns costs no more than SRD 15.

Other sample prices are as follows:

local beer (1l 'djogo')	SRD 12–18	wine (750ml bottle)	SRD 25+ (supermarket
mineral water (1l)	SRD 2–4		price)
loaf of bread	SRD 3–4	soft drink (330ml)	SRD 3–6
petrol (1l)	SRD 4.70	street/local food	SRD 10–15
apple	SRD 2.50		

Paramaribo is the point of departure for all domestic flights, as well as being the hub for the country's road network and most associated public transport. This road network is very limited, consisting as it does of around 4,000km of surfaced and unsurfaced roads. These include the surfaced east–west link running along the coastal belt east and west of Paramaribo to Albina (on the border with French Guiana) and Nieuw Nickerie (on the border with Guyana), a small grid of mostly surfaced roads through the plantations of Commewijne District, a network of surfaced roads running south from Paramaribo through Wanica and Para to Zanderij (site of Johan Adolf Pengel International Airport), a surfaced road running north from Zanderij to Brokopondo and the small port of Atjoni on the Upper Suriname, and a long rough dirt road running west through the interior from Zanderij to Apoera. Most other parts of the country are accessible only by boat or by light aircraft, or are effectively inaccessible to tourists.

SELF-DRIVE This is an excellent way for flexible and confident travellers to explore the coastal districts and the vicinity of the Suriname River as far south as Brokopondo. Cars or 4x4s can be rented affordably through a few companies in Paramaribo (see pages 74–5) and most sites of interest are within easy driving distance on well-maintained surfaced or dirt roads. Traffic densities are relatively low, except in the capital itself, and driving styles are not as wild as in many developing countries. The good news for visitors from the UK and many other former British colonies is that Suriname and neighbouring Guyana are the only two countries on the American mainland where you drive on the left side of the road. Some say that this is because the first cars in Suriname were imported from England, others that it is a hangover from before the 18th century when wagon traffic in the Netherlands converted from the left to the right side of the road.

Note, too, that a recent change in the Road Traffic Act means that visitors who wish to drive in Suriname must possess an international driver's licence. In most countries this can be bought through the local AA (*www.theaa.com*); Dutch people should contact the ANWB (*www.anwb.nl*). If you haven't organised an international driver's licence in advance, a Surinamese driver's permit, valid for one year, can be obtained for SRD 150 at Nieuwe Haven Police Station, on Van 't Hogerhuys Straat in Paramaribo, close to the new harbour. You'll need to show a valid foreign driver's licence, an official Dutch translation thereof and a passport, with proof of legal stay in Suriname.

BUSES Most roads in Suriname are covered by some form of public transport. This includes the cheap, extensive and reliable bus network operated by the parastatal National Transport Company or Nationaal Vervoer Bedrijf (NVB; ℡ 472450/473591; e *nvbnv@sr.net; www.nvbnvsuriname.com*). Current schedules are included in the relevant regional sections of this guide and can be checked online at www.nvbnvsuriname.com/Nvb/Fof/Rou/Rou001Php.php or at the Heiligen Weg depot in central Paramaribo (see page 75). There are private vehicles that also cover most routes in Suriname, including a few beyond the reach of the NVB, for instance the road west from Witagron to Apoera. These private buses tend to depart more regularly, but can be slightly less reliable. Again, details are provided in the relevant regional sections of this guide. Traffic volumes reflect the low population densities outside Paramaribo and the surrounding area, so it is generally a good idea to check details of onward transport locally the day before you plan to travel. Paramaribo is serviced by a good network of urban buses, plus plenty of taxis (see page 77).

BOAT Boat transport is a big part of travel in Suriname. Affordable waterborne public transport connects Paramaribo to several sites on the east bank of Commewijne, as well as servicing the Upper Suriname and Gran Rio from Atjoni south to Kajana, the Corantijn River from Nieuw Nickerie south to Apoera, and the Cottica River near Moengo. Ferries or taxi-boats are also the only way to cross between Suriname and its Guianan neighbours (Guiana and Guyana). Several other sites visited by organised tours are also most easily accessed by boat, ranging from the remote Raleigh Falls to the north bank plantations of Commewijn, the turtle-nesting beaches at Matapica and Galibi, and birding sites such as Bigi Pan. As with road transport, details of local boat transport options are provided in the relevant regional sections of this guide.

AIR The hub of Suriname's limited domestic flight network is Paramaribo's Zorg en Hoop Airport (see page 74). Scheduled and unscheduled light aircraft flights leave from here to airstrips all around the country, including Laduani, Botopassie and Djumu in the Upper Suriname, Kajana on the Gran Rio, and Palumeu, Kabalebo, Washabo (for Apoera), Fungu Island (Raleigh Falls), Amatopo and Kwamalasamutu. Given how remote these destinations are, both custom and common sense dictate that most tourists book their domestic flights through an operator or lodge in conjunction with associated accommodation.

BICYCLE Characteristic of Paramaribo is the (at first somewhat incongruous) sight of small groups of (mostly young female) Dutch and Belgian interns weaving serenely through the traffic on bicycles. It is tempting to recommend that tourists emulate this affordable and eco-friendly way of getting around the city, but before doing so it should be pointed out that most Dutch city dwellers are so used to cycling that they look like they were born to it, whereas travellers from many other countries may find cycling to be quite stressful in the crowded roads of the city centre, and considerably more dangerous than bussing or walking. For reasonably experienced cyclists, bicycles really come into their own as a means of exploring suburban sites such as Peperpot Nature Park, Fort Nieuw Amsterdam and most of Wanica and Para. For bicycle rentals in Paramaribo and details of cycling tours further afield, contact Fietsen In Suriname (*www.fietseninsuriname.nl*) or Cardy Adventures (*www.cardyadventures.com*), see page 76.

ACCOMMODATION

Accommodation in Suriname tends to be of fair to high quality and quite reasonably priced. However, the hotel industry is clustered in the capital, which probably has more tourist-quality accommodation than the rest of the country combined. A fair range of accommodation is also available in the districts close to the capital, such as Commewijne, Saramacca, Wanica and Para. Elsewhere, urban accommodation tends to be quite basic. However, the country is also dotted with a large number of more rustic camps and lodges, most of which lie on one of Suriname's many rivers, and these range from superb upmarket lodges such as Bergendal, Kabalebo and Palumeu, to more basic hutted camps catering to backpackers and other budget travellers. There are also simple hammock camps aimed mainly at the local weekender market.

Accommodation entries for this guide have been categorised under five main headings: exclusive/luxury (**$$$$$**), upmarket (**$$$$**), moderate (**$$$**), budget (**$$**) and shoestring (**$**). Broadly speaking, exclusive or luxury hotels are truly world-class institutions that meet the highest standards or come close to it, while upmarket hotels also meet international standards but with slightly less flair. Moderate hotels are generally decent lodgings that don't quite make the upmarket grade but are still comfortable enough for most tourists, offering facilities such as air conditioning, satellite TV, and en-suite hot showers and toilet. Budget accommodation is typically aimed at the local or backpacker market, but is still reasonably comfortable and in many cases has air conditioning and en-suite facilities. Shoestring accommodation consists of the cheapest rooms around.

In order to help travellers isolate the establishment that best suits their taste and budget, the above categorisation is not based rigidly on absolute prices but has been evaluated taking into account both the feel of the hotel and its price, and it is often relative to other options in the same town or location. Intended as a quick visual aid to help navigate the options, the dollar symbols **$–$$$$$** are included next to the category header for longer listings, and are added at hotel level for shorter listings without category headers. If this sounds confusing, a full rate breakdown is included in italics at the end of every accommodation entry.

One quirk to watch out for, particularly if you are travelling as a couple, is that a room advertised as single will often have a double bed, while one advertised as double might actually be a twin (ie: with two beds). In this situation, you're less likely to be misunderstood if you ask for a room with one big bed as opposed to asking for a double. Note, too, that for room prices quoted in this book's listings, we list a room as what it actually is, rather than repeating what the hotel refers to it as: for instance, if the 'single' at any given hotel is in fact a double, then we list it as a double.

Something of a Surinamese institution is the hammock hut, which typically comprises an open-sided wooden shelter designed for hanging anything from six to 20 hammocks (known locally as a *hangmat*) and nets in the open air but with protection from the rain. These are often the cheapest option around, but usually require you to have your own hammock (and ideally net), which can be bought in Paramaribo. Note that when a lodge or camp refers to a 'hut', they almost invariably mean somewhere to hang a hammock as opposed to proper hutted accommodation.

EATING AND DRINKING

Paramaribo, like most capital cities, has a varied and cosmopolitan culinary scene, with enough restaurants in most price brackets to keep you busy for weeks. Elsewhere, local eateries predominate, serving a range of Surinamese dishes reflecting the country's diverse cultural heritage (see box, pages 52–3) typically for around SRD 10–15 per plate. Most common is the ubiquitous Javan-style *warung* or *eethuis* (literally eat house), but these are supplemented in some towns by Chinese restaurants (which usually serve a mix of Javan-Surinamese staples and bona fide Chinese food) and Hindustani roti shops.

Vegetarians and more so vegans are quite poorly catered for outside Paramaribo (indeed, even within the capital, many prominent restaurants have a rather limited selection of vegetarian dishes by contemporary Western standards). Vegetarians and other travellers with specific dietary requirements will need to communicate these very clearly to the operator before they join any organised tour.

You'll most likely drink a lot more in Suriname than at home, thanks to the hot sticky climate. It's fine to drink tap water in Paramaribo and its environs, but probably not in more remote areas. Bottled mineral water is available in 1.5-litre and 500ml bottles in most supermarkets and shops, but independent travellers might need to stock up before heading out to very remote areas such as the Upper Suriname, Blanche Marie or Raleigh Falls (most organised tours include all the bottled water clients are likely to need). The usual brand-name soft drinks are also widely available, and most supermarkets will sell a range of fruit juice in cans and cartons.

The most widespread alcoholic drink is Parbo Bier, an affordable and tasty locally brewed lager (made partly with rice) sold in one litre 'djogo' bottles and 500ml cans in most supermarkets, restaurants and hotels. Heineken is also produced locally, along with Chiller, which comprises lager beer flavoured with passion fruit or lime, and is generally perceived to be a woman's drink. For more dedicated imbibers, Suriname is renowned for its strong high-quality rum, which is most usually drunk with Coca-Cola or other soft drinks. The best known brands, all produced by Suriname Alcoholic Beverages (*www.sabrum.com*), are Borgoe, Black Cat and Mariënburg. For connoisseurs, the prestigious Jubilee Reserve and Borgoe '82 are oak-fermented premium rums designed to be drunk pure or with ice. Many supermarkets also stock a range of imported beers, wines and spirits.

PUBLIC HOLIDAYS AND FESTIVALS

In addition to the fixed dates listed below, several variable religious dates are taken as public holidays (see table below for dates for 2015 to 2018). Chinese Lunar New Year was recognised as a one-off public holiday in 2014 and 2015, but it's unclear whether this will be an ongoing arrangement,

FIXED DATE PUBLIC HOLIDAYS

1 January	New Year's Day
25 February	Liberation Day (anniversary of the 1980 revolution)
1 May	Labour Day
1 July	Emancipation Day (abolition of slavery)
9 August	Indigenous People's Day
10 October	Marron Day
25 November	Republic Day
25 December	Christmas Day
26 December	Second Day of Christmas

Surinamese cuisine reflects the country's diverse cultural heritage and includes many unique or hybrid dishes similar to but not quite the same as their Javan, Chinese, Dutch, Indian, African, Jewish or Portuguese antecedents. Local food is usually very tasty, though the menus offered at the typical warung do tend to become a bit repetitive after a while. A great place to diversify with some more unusual local dishes is Blauwgrond, a suburb of Paramaribo famed for the dozen or so Javan-Surinamese restaurants clustered on one block of JS Green Straat. Surinamese cooking tends to be quite spicy, but if a meal isn't hot enough to your taste, ask for *sambal* (hot pepper) on the side. A brief overview of some popular staple and fusion dishes follows:

baka kesaba	Literally 'baked cassava', and also known as *khali* or cassava bread, this traditional Amerindian and Marron staple is a flat, hard loaf baked on a griddle and best dipped in water or soup to soften it
bakabana	Traditional dessert made with overripe plantains that are battered and deep-fried, then served with a peanut dip
bakkeljauw	Of Portuguese origin, this is a dried and salted fish, usually cod, also spelled *bakalhau*
bami	Ubiquitous fried noodle dish (similar to the Chinese *bakmi*) usually served with chicken (*kip*)
bara	Savoury skillet-fried Hindustani cake made with flour and *tajer* or spinach leaves, plus plenty of spices
bojo	Rich spongy cake made from grated coconut and cassava, often spiced with rum
broodje pom	Cold *pom* (see below) sandwich, usually on a bread roll
dhal	A lentil-based Indian-influenced curry-like stew, served at most roti shops, usually as a side dish but also as an alternative to meat during religious holidays or festivals
goedangan	Cabbage, bean sprout and *kousenban* (a type of green bean) salad served with a piquant coconut dressing, and optionally hard boiled eggs or peanut sauce
her'heri	West African in origin, this hearty stew is made with *bakkeljauw*, vegetables and usually a mix of cassava, plantain and sweet potato
loempia	Javan-Surinamese equivalent of spring roll
lontong tahu	Vegetarian dish of Indonesian origin containing fried tofu blocks, bean sprouts and small rice cakes

PUBLIC HOLIDAYS WITH VARYING DATES

	2015	2016	2017	2018
Phagwa (Holi)	6 Mar	23 Mar	13 Mar	2 Mar
Good Friday	3 Apr	25 Mar	14 Apr	30 Mar
Easter Monday	6 Apr	28 Mar	17 Apr	2 Apr
Eid al-Fitr (End of Ramadan)	17 Jul	6 Jul	25 Jun	15 Jun
Eid al-Adha	24 Sep	13 Sep	2 Sep	22 Aug
Diwali	11 Nov	30 Oct	10 Oct	7 Nov

FESTIVALS The biggest annual festival in Suriname is probably Phagwa (see above), the Hindu festival of colours, which is celebrated throughout the country (at least where Hindus are present) but is particularly colourful and inclusive in Paramaribo,

moksi alesi	A Creole dish, originally a kind of pot luck mixture of leftovers, now usually boiled rice mixed risotto-like with salted meat or fish
moksi meti	Literally mixed meat, comprising several kinds of roasted meat and Chinese sausage
nasi	This popular fried rice dish, similar to the Indonesian *nasi goreng*, is served at almost all warungs, usually with chicken (*kip*)
pastei	Chicken pot pie, made with carrots and peas, introduced by the earliest Jewish settlers
patat	Literally potatoes, but in practice usually chips (French fries), a recent Western introduction usually served as a standalone dish or with greasy fried chicken
pepre watra	Literally 'pepper water', this spicy fish soup is an Amerindian dish also known as *adjupo*
petjil	Javanese vegetables topped with a peanut sauce and served in a leaf
phulauri	Spicy deep-fried ball made with split peas or chickpeas and often served as a snack at Hindustani restaurants and celebrations
pinda soep	Named after the peanuts that dominate its taste, this thick spicy soup usually also contains chicken and various vegetables
pom	A unique Surinamese dish of Jewish origin, often served on festive days, the name *pom* derives from the Portuguese word for potato but it actually consists of an oven-baked pie made of grated *pomtajer* (the tuber of the indigenous arrowleaf elephant ear), chicken, onion, tomato, bitter citrus juice and various spices
roti	Flat, round Indian-style bread usually eaten with *masalakip* (spicy chicken curry)
samosa	Well-known Indian snack made by wrapping a spicy filling (vegetable or meat) in a thin dough triangle, then deep frying it
satao	Spicy thin soup of Indonesian origin, usually containing shredded fried potatoes, bean sprouts and shredded chicken. Also known as Blauwgrond soup (after the warung-rich suburb of Paramaribo) it is a very common dish and a good light lunch.
teloh	Deep-fried cassava wedges usually eaten as a side dish
tjauw min	Local variation of *chow mein*, comprising stir-fried noodles, usually served with vegetables, chicken or shrimp

where the centre of activity is Independence Square. Other key annual festivals in Paramaribo are the Brazilian Carnival (early February), the International Film Festival (*Apr; www.thebacklot.sr*), the Staatsolie Swim Marathon on the Suriname River between Domburg and Paramaribo (*18km; Jul; www.staatsolie.com*), the Suriname Jazz Festival (*Oct; www.jazzfestivalsuriname.com*), the National Art Exhibition (*Oct*) and ebullient New Year festivities associated with a local festival called the Pagara Estafette (*31 Dec*).

SHOPPING

Paramaribo is the only place in Suriname with much shopping variety, and this is covered in detail in *Chapter 5* (see pages 96–8). Elsewhere, almost every settlement has at least one supermarket, almost invariably managed by 'new' Chinese (who may well speak more English than Dutch, or very little of either), and usually open seven days a week from around 08.00 to 22.00. Most supermarkets stock a fair range of imported and local packaged goods, chilled soft drinks and Parbo and Heineken beers, a limited selection of fresh(ish) goods (apples, vegetables, bread) and in some cases imported wine, spirits and fruit juices. In smaller towns, supermarkets are closer in style to old-fashioned general stores, and may also sell a limited selection of clothes and hardware items. In general, however, shopping opportunities are very limited except in Paramaribo and to a much lesser extent largish towns such as Lelydorp and Nieuw Nickerie.

PHOTOGRAPHIC TIPS   *Ariadne Van Zandbergen*

EQUIPMENT Although with some thought and an eye for composition you can take reasonable photos with a 'point-and-shoot' camera, you need an SLR camera if you are at all serious about photography. Modern SLRs tend to be very clever, with automatic programmes for almost every possible situation, but remember that these programmes are limited in the sense that the camera cannot think, but only makes calculations. Every starting amateur photographer should read a photographic manual for beginners and get to grips with such basics as the relationship between aperture and shutter speed.

Digital SLRs come in different formats, which refer to the size of the sensor. The format of the future is the full-size sensor, but at present all full-size sensor cameras are in the higher price bracket. Different lenses are designed to accommodate the camera sensor sizes.

Always buy the best lens you can afford. The lens determines the quality of your photo more than the camera body. Fixed fast lenses are ideal, but very costly. A zoom lens makes it easier to change composition without changing lenses the whole time. If you carry only one lens with a full size sensor camera, a 28–70mm or similar zoom should be ideal. This corresponds to a 17–55mm or similar for a camera with a smaller sensor. For a second lens, a lightweight telephoto zoom will be excellent for candid shots and varying your composition.

Modern dedicated flash units are easy to use; aside from the obvious need to flash when you photograph at night, you can improve a lot of photos in difficult 'high contrast' or very dull light with some fill-in flash. It pays to have a proper flash unit as opposed to a built-in camera flash.

The resolution of digital cameras is improving the whole time and even the most basic digital SLRs are more than adequate for ordinary prints and enlargements. For professional reproduction cameras with a resolution up to 24 megapixels are available.

Memory space is important. The number of pictures you can fit on a memory card depends on the quality you choose. Calculate in advance how many pictures you can fit on a card and either take enough cards to last for your trip, or take a storage drive onto which you can download the content. A laptop gives the advantage that you can see your pictures properly at the end of each day and edit and delete rejects, but a storage device is lighter and less bulky.

Bear in mind that digital camera batteries, computers and other storage devices need charging, so make sure you have all the chargers, cables and converters with you.

NEWSPAPERS Several Dutch and Chinese daily newspapers are published in Paramaribo. The best known of these is the *Times of Suriname* (*www.surinametimes. com*), which despite its name is not published in English but Dutch. Imported English-language newspapers are difficult to come by in Suriname, so you will be dependent on internet and television for news.

TELEVISION AND RADIO The Surinaamse Televisie Stichting (STVS; *www.stvs.sr*), a government television network founded in 1965, broadcasts in the Dutch language

DUST, HEAT AND WATER Exposure to dust, heat and water can damage sensitive camera gear. Keep your equipment in a sealed bag whilst driving on dirt roads, and avoid excessive exposure to the sun. Digital cameras are prone to collecting dust particles on the sensor, which results in spots on the image. The dirt mostly enters the camera when changing lenses, so be careful when doing this. To some extent photos can be 'cleaned' up afterwards in Photoshop, but this is time-consuming. In Suriname, a far bigger concern than dust and heat is exposure to water, either in the form of sudden tropical storms, or splashes and leaks whilst travelling on boats. Sea and estuarine water is particularly problematic, as the salt is corrosive. It is advisable to travel with a waterproof camera bag that fits all your gear, and to keep your camera in the bag on boat trips, taking it out only when you want to photograph something. Thick black rubbish bags provide good additional protection for your camera bag assuming they are properly sealed.

LIGHT The most striking outdoor photographs are often taken during the hour or two of 'golden light', after dawn and before sunset. Shooting in low light may enforce the use of very low shutter speeds, in which case a tripod might be required to avoid camera shake. Some top digital SLRs now give good results with minimal grain when shooting at very high ISO settings which makes low-light photography a lot easier and reduces the need of a tripod in many situations.

With careful handling, side lighting and back lighting can produce stunning effects, especially in soft light and at sunrise or sunset. Generally, however, it is best to shoot with the sun behind you. When photographing animals or people in the harsh midday sun, images taken in light but even shade are likely to be more effective than those taken in direct sunlight or patchy shade, since the latter conditions create too much contrast.

PROTOCOL In Marron and Amerindian villages it is totally unacceptable to photograph people without permission, which will generally be refused. In such circumstances, don't try to sneak photographs, as you might get yourself into trouble.

Ariadne Van Zandbergen is a professional travel and wildlife photographer. She runs 'The Travel Image Library'. For a good selection of Suriname images, visit www.travelimagelibrary.photodeck.com or contact her by email at e *info@ africaimagelibrary.com.*

only. A number of radio stations operate out of Paramaribo but most are also in Dutch or Sranan Tongo only. However, almost all hotels and many restaurants have satellite TV showing various news and sports channels in English.

TELEPHONE Suriname has a reliable terrestrial phone network, operated by the national phone supplier Telesur (*www.telesur.sr*). All landline numbers are six digits long, with no area codes, though a leading '2' indicates that the number is located in the west, a leading '3' that it is located in the central or eastern part of the country outside of Paramaribo, and a leading '4' or '5' that it is in Paramaribo.

The terrestrial network is supplemented, and outside of Paramaribo surpassed, by a very efficient mobile network with three main providers: Telesur (*www.telesur.sr*), Digicel (*www.digicelsuriname.com*) and Uniqa (*www.uniqa.sr*). Mobile numbers are seven digits long. Those starting with 71, 81 or 82 are with Digicel, those starting with 83 or 84 are with Uniqa, and those starting with a 6, 75, 85, 86, 87, 88 and 89 are with Telesur.

If you're going to be in Suriname for any length of time, rather than roaming on your home number, which can be very costly, it is worth buying a SIM card from a local provider and inserting it in your phone. This is a simple and inexpensive procedure that also allows you to link other facilities on your phone (text messages, internet access, emails, etc) to a local network. The provider of preference is probably Digicel, if only because it has the best network of customer service centres (all listed on their website) that can help you set up a SIM card, buy airtime, order data bundles and so on.

Note that there is no mobile reception in more remote and unpopulated parts of Suriname, a category that covers most of the vast Sipaliwini District. One exception is the Upper Suriname and Gran Rio, where most villages do have good reception, though not sufficient to handle internet or email.

Dialling overseas, the country code should be preceded by 00. Dialling into Suriname, the international code is +597.

POST Suriname's international post service is cheap and reasonably reliable, but often quite slow. To help speed things up, best send all post from the main post office in Paramaribo (see page 101).

INTERNET The easiest way to access internet and emails on a regular basis is on a smartphone or tablet with a local SIM card. Most hotels in Paramaribo and some further afield now offer free Wi-Fi to guests. There are internet cafés in Paramaribo and Nieuw Nickerie, but not elsewhere in the country.

4

Health

With Dr Felicity Nicholson

Suriname, like most tropical countries, is home to several diseases unfamiliar to people living in more temperate and sanitary climates. However, with adequate preparation, the chances of serious mishap are small. To put this in perspective, your greatest concern should not be the combined exotica of venomous snakes, stampeding wildlife, gun-happy soldiers or killer viruses, but something altogether more mundane: a road accident.

Within Suriname, a range of adequate (but well short of world-class) clinics, hospitals and pharmacies can be found in and around Paramaribo. Facilities are far more limited and basic in the interior. Wherever you go, however, doctors and pharmacists will generally speak fluent Dutch and some English, and consultation and laboratory fees are relatively inexpensive – so if in doubt, seek medical help.

BEFORE YOU GO

Sensible preparation will go a long way to ensuring your trip goes smoothly. Particularly for first-time visitors to the tropics, this includes a visit to a travel clinic to discuss matters such as vaccinations and malaria prevention.

A full list of current travel clinic websites worldwide is available on www.istm. org. For other journey preparation information, consult www.nathnac.org/ds/map_world.aspx (UK) or http://wwwnc.cdc.gov/travel/ (US). Information about various medications may be found on www.netdoctor.co.uk/travel. All advice found online should be used in conjunction with expert advice received prior to or during travel.

The Bradt website now has a Suriname health section (*www.bradtguides.com/C&SAmericahealth*) to help travellers prepare for their trip, elaborating on most of the points raised below. The following summary points are worth emphasising:

- Don't travel without comprehensive medical **travel insurance** that will fly you home in an emergency.
- Make sure all your **immunisations** are up to date. A yellow fever vaccination is advised for health as there is risk of the disease, and immigration officials may require you to show proof of immunisation upon entry if you are entering Suriname from another yellow fever endemic area (a requirement that excludes visitors from North America and Europe). A valid yellow fever vaccination certificate (currently within the preceding ten years but this will be for life from mid-2016) will then be required on entry. If the vaccine is not suitable for you then you would be wise not to travel. Yellow fever is prevalent throughout Suriname and has around a 50% mortality rate in those who are non-immune to the disease. It's also unwise to travel in the tropics without being up to date

on tetanus, polio and diphtheria (now given as an all-in-one vaccine, Revaxis), hepatitis A and typhoid. Immunisation against rabies, hepatitis B, and possibly tuberculosis (TB) may also be recommended.

- Despite recent efforts, malaria remains a problem in the more remote parts of Suriname. For more information about precautions to take before travelling to Suriname, see page 60.

- Though advised for everyone, a **pre-exposure course of rabies vaccination**, involving three doses taken over a minimum of 21 days, is particularly important if you intend to have contact with animals, or are likely to be 24 hours away from medical help. If you have not had this then you may need to evacuate for medical treatment, as local hospitals almost certainly will not have all the necessary treatment (see pages 60–1).

- Anybody travelling away from major centres should carry a **personal first-aid kit**. Contents might include a good drying antiseptic (eg: iodine or potassium permanganate), Band-Aids, suncream, insect repellent, aspirin or paracetamol, antifungal cream (eg: Canesten), an antibiotic to treat severe diarrhoea, antibiotic eye drops, tweezers, condoms or femidoms, a digital thermometer and a needle-and-syringe kit with accompanying letter from a healthcare professional.

- Bring any **drugs or devices relating to known medical conditions** with you. That applies both to those who are on medication prior to departure, and those who are, for instance, allergic to bee stings, or are prone to attacks of asthma. Carry a copy of your prescription and a letter from your doctor explaining why you need the medication.

- Prolonged immobility on long-haul flights can result in **deep vein thrombosis** (DVT), which can be dangerous if the clot travels to the lungs to cause pulmonary embolus. The risk increases with age, and is higher in obese or pregnant travellers, heavy smokers, those taller than 6ft/1.8m or shorter than 5ft/1.5m, and anybody with a history of clots, recent major operation or varicose veins surgery, cancer, a stroke or heart disease. If any of these criteria apply, consult a doctor before you travel.

POTENTIAL MEDICAL PROBLEMS

COMMON MEDICAL PROBLEMS

Travellers' Diarrhoea Many visitors to unfamiliar destinations suffer a dose of travellers' diarrhoea, usually as a result of imbibing contaminated food or water. Rule one in avoiding diarrhoea and other sanitation-related diseases is to wash your hands regularly, particularly before snacks and meals. As for what food you can safely eat, a useful maxim is: PEEL IT, BOIL IT, COOK IT OR FORGET IT. This means that fruit you have washed and peeled yourself should be safe, as should hot cooked foods. However, raw foods, cold cooked foods, salads, fruit salads prepared by others, ice cream and ice are all risky. It is rarer to get ill from drinking contaminated water but it happens, so stick to bottled water, which is widely available.

If you suffer a bout of diarrhoea, it is dehydration that makes you feel awful, so drink lots of water and other clear fluids. These can be infused with sachets of oral rehydration salts, though any dilute mixture of sugar and salt in water will do you good, for instance a bottled fizzy drink with a pinch of salt. If diarrhoea persists beyond a couple of days, it is possible it is a symptom of a more serious sanitation-related illness (typhoid, cholera, hepatitis, dysentery, worms, etc), so get to a doctor. If the diarrhoea is greasy and bulky, and is accompanied by sulphurous (eggy) burps, one likely cause is giardia, which is best treated with tinidazole (four x 500mg in one dose, repeated seven days later if symptoms persist).

Dengue fever Often referred to as 'breakbone fever' because of the symptoms of joint and muscle pain, dengue fever and dengue haemorrhagic fever are viral diseases transmitted by mosquitoes and are quite common in Suriname. The mosquitoes that transmit the illness are most frequently found in or around human habitations and bite during the day, particularly in the morning for a couple of hours after sunrise and in the late afternoon for a couple of hours until sunset. Symptoms tend to occur three to 14 days after being bitten by an infected mosquito and include high fevers, headaches, joint and muscle pain, nausea, vomiting and a rash. Severe manifestations of dengue can present with haemorrhagic fevers and can be fatal. No vaccine is available, so travellers should take precautions against mosquito bites. Acetaminophen should be used for treating fever, while aspirin and ibuprofen should be avoided. If infected, rest, drink plenty of fluids and closely monitor your vital signs.

Tick bites Like an endless host of other insects, ticks are common in Suriname, especially during the dry season. Most visitors won't have any major problems with the parasites, but caution should always be exercised, especially when you're climbing over or around dead trees. Wear cover-up clothing including long trousers tucked into boots, and hats. Insect repellents may be of benefit too, so apply to exposed skin. If a tick attaches itself to you, it should ideally be removed complete as soon as possible to reduce the chance of infection. The best way to do this is to grasp the tick with your fingernails as close to your body as possible, and pull it away steadily and firmly at right angles to your skin (do not jerk or twist it). If possible douse the wound with alcohol (any spirit will do) or iodine. If you are travelling with small children, remember to check their heads, and particularly behind the ears, for ticks. Spreading redness around the bite and/or fever and/or aching joints after a tick bite imply that you have an infection that requires antibiotic treatment, so seek advice.

Skin infections Any mosquito bite or small nick is an opportunity for a skin infection in warm humid climates, so clean and cover the slightest wound in a good drying antiseptic such as dilute iodine, potassium permanganate or crystal (or gentian) violet. Prickly heat, most likely to be contracted on the humid coast, is a fine pimply rash that can be alleviated by cool showers, dabbing (not rubbing) dry, applying talc and sleeping naked under a fan or in an air-conditioned room. Fungal infections also get a hold easily in hot, moist climates so wear 100%-cotton socks and underwear and shower frequently.

Eye problems Bacterial conjunctivitis (pink eye) is a common tropical infection, particularly for contact-lens wearers. Symptoms are sore, gritty eyelids that often stick closed in the morning. They will need treatment with antibiotic drops or ointment. Lesser eye irritation should settle with bathing in salt water and keeping the eyes shaded. If an insect flies into your eye, extract it with great care, ensuring you do not crush or damage it, as otherwise you may get a nastily inflamed eye from toxins secreted by the creature.

Sunstroke and dehydration Overexposure to the sun can lead to short-term sunburn or sunstroke, and increases the long-term risk of skin cancer. Wear a T-shirt and waterproof sunscreen when swimming. When walking in the direct sun, cover up with long, loose clothes, wear a hat and use sunscreen that is at least a factor 25 and with a UVA rating of four stars or more.

The glare and the dust can be hard on the eyes, so bring UV-protecting sunglasses. A less direct effect of the tropical heat is dehydration, so drink more fluids than you would at home.

LESS COMMON BUT SERIOUS PROBLEMS

Malaria Suriname was once regarded to be a high-risk malaria area, but a five-year malaria control programme introduced in 2005 has eliminated this mosquito-borne disease from most of the country. According to the Suriname Tourism Foundation, Paramaribo and the coastal belt are now entirely free of malaria though this should be considered as low risk rather than no risk. However, parts of the interior do have malaria, with occasional outbreaks occurring in the gold-mining camps of the Upper Marowijne, Brokopondo and Apoera regions. This means that if your travels are restricted to Paramaribo and the coastal belt, the risk is sufficiently low that you need not take malaria prophylaxis. For the rest of Suriname malaria prophylaxis is advisable, especially if you intend to visit Apoera, Upper Marowijne or the gold mines of Brokopondo. For more up-to-date information on endemic malarial areas in Suriname, check www.nathnac.org/travel/.

No vaccine against malaria exists, but several prophylactic drugs are available. To decide which anti-malarial is most suitable to your situation, visit your doctor or a specialist travel clinic at least three weeks before you travel. Since no prophylactic is 100% effective, those spending a long time in South America may also want to carry a cure.

Malaria usually manifests within two weeks of transmission, but it can take anything from seven days to a year. Symptoms include a rapid rise in temperature (over 38°C), and any combination of a headache, flu-like aches and pains, a general sense of disorientation, and possibly nausea and diarrhoea. The earlier malaria is diagnosed, the better it usually responds to treatment, so if you display symptoms, visit a doctor or clinic immediately, and ask to be tested.

Bilharzia Also known as schistosomiasis, bilharzia is an unpleasant parasitic disease transmitted by freshwater snails and is most often associated with reedy shores where there is lots of waterweed. It cannot be caught in hotel swimming pools or the ocean, and fast-moving water such as rivers should be free of the parasite. It is unlikely to be present in the rivers where travellers often swim. However, travellers should avoid swimming in stagnant water or close to reedy shores where there is lots of weed. If you do swim, you'll reduce the risk by applying DEET insect repellent first, staying in the water for under ten minutes, and drying off vigorously with a towel. Bilharzia is often asymptomatic in its early stages, but some people experience an intense immune reaction, including fever, cough, abdominal pain and an itching rash, around four to six weeks after infection. Later symptoms vary but often include a general feeling of tiredness and lethargy. Bilharzia is difficult to diagnose, but it can be tested for at specialist travel clinics, ideally at least six weeks after likely exposure. Fortunately, it is easy to treat at present.

Rabies This deadly disease can be carried by any mammal and is usually transmitted to humans via a bite or a scratch that breaks the skin. In particular, beware of village dogs and of monkeys habituated to people, but assume that *any* mammal that bites or scratches you (or even licks an open wound) might be rabid even if it looks healthy. First, scrub the wound with soap under a running tap for a good ten to 15 minutes, or while pouring water from a jug, then pour on a strong iodine or alcohol solution, which will guard against infections and might reduce the risk of the rabies virus entering the body. Whether or not you underwent pre-exposure vaccination, it is vital to obtain post-exposure prophylaxis as soon as possible after the incident. If you have had the pre-exposure course you will no longer need Rabies Immunoglobulin (RIG), which is expensive and very unlikely to be available in Suriname. If you have not had a pre-exposure course of the vaccine, you will need to evacuate as soon as you can. Death from rabies is probably one of the worst ways to go, and once you show symptoms it is too late to do anything – the mortality rate is almost 100%.

Tetanus Tetanus is contracted through deep dirty wounds, including animal bites, so ensure that such wounds are thoroughly cleaned. Immunisation protects for ten years, provided you don't have an overwhelming number of tetanus bacteria on board. If you haven't had a tetanus shot in ten years, or you are unsure, get a booster immediately.

HIV/AIDS Rates of HIV/AIDS infection stand at around 1% in Suriname, and other sexually transmitted diseases are present. Condoms (or femidoms) greatly reduce the risk of transmission.

OTHER INSECT-BORNE DISEASES Although malaria and dengue fever are the insect-borne diseases that attract the most attention in the tropics, there are others, but most are too uncommon to be of significant concern to short-stay travellers. Bearing this in mind, however, it is sensible and makes for a more pleasant trip if you avoid insect bites as far as possible (see box, page 62).

Lymphatic filariasis Lymphatic filariasis is an infection caused by threadlike worms that are spread through mosquito bites. The worms can live in the bloodstream and the body for many years without a person showing any signs of infection. In some cases, however, symptoms include fever and swelling of the lymph nodes in the groin, armpits, arms, legs, scrotum or breast. For those visiting Suriname long term or living in the country, filariasis can be prevented by using salt fortified with diethylcarbamazine citrate (DEC) regularly when preparing food. DEC kills the filaria worm and stops the disease before signs and symptoms can develop.

Leishmaniasis Leishmaniasis is a parasitic disease caused by the bite of a sand fly and presents in two forms: cutaneous (skin) or visceral (internal organ). The cutaneous form is distinguished by a skin sore(s) that develops weeks to months after being bitten by an infected sand fly. The sores can last from weeks to years and will eventually develop a raised edge with a crater-like centre. Signs and symptoms of visceral leishmaniasis (also called kala azar) include fever, weight loss, enlargement of the spleen or liver, and anaemia, and develop months to years after infection. If left untreated, visceral leishmaniasis is typically fatal. Travellers should avoid sand fly bites by using insect sprays and wearing protective clothing, and should sleep under a bed net.

Chagas disease Chagas disease or American trypanosomiasis is a potentially serious disease caused by the protozoan *Trypanosoma cruzi* and is spread through the bite of a type of reduviid bug called the 'kissing bug' (*Panstrongylus megistus*), which is endemic in Central and South America. The disease is most prevalent in rural areas where the bugs live in mud walls and only come out at night. Avoidance is the best

4

The *Anopheles* mosquitoes that spread malaria and the *Culex* mosquitoes that spread filariasis are active at dusk and after dark, while those that spread dengue fever are essentially diurnal (ie: day biting). Most bites can be avoided by covering up in the afternoon and at night. This means donning a long-sleeved shirt, trousers and socks, and applying a DEET-based insect repellent to any exposed flesh. It is best to sleep under a net, or in an air-conditioned room, though burning a mosquito coil and/or sleeping under a fan will also reduce (though not entirely eliminate) bites. Travel clinics usually sell a good range of nets and repellents, as well as permethrin treatment kits, which will render even the tattiest nets a lot more protective, and help prevents mosquitoes from biting through a net when you roll against it. These measures will also do much to reduce exposure to other nocturnal biters. Bear in mind, too, that most flying insects are attracted to light: leaving a lamp standing near a tent opening or a light on in a poorly screened hotel room will greatly increase the insect presence in your sleeping quarters.

When walking in the countryside by day, especially in wetland habitats (which often teem with diurnal mosquitoes), wear a long loose shirt and trousers, preferably 100% cotton, as well as proper walking or hiking shoes with heavy socks (the ankle is particularly vulnerable to bites), and apply a DEET-based insect repellent to any exposed skin. Clothing can also be treated with permethrin for maximum protection.

method, so when travelling through an endemic region try not to sleep in adobe huts where the locals sleep, keep away from walls when sleeping and use mosquito nets. Spraying the insides of rooms with an insecticide spray is also a good idea. Symptoms include swelling around the site of the bite followed by enlargement of the lymph glands and fever. Long-term symptoms include damage to the heart causing sudden death, and paralysis of the gut causing difficulty in swallowing and severe constipation. There is no preventative vaccine or medication for Chagas disease and treatment is difficult as agents toxic to the trypanosomes are also toxic to humans.

OTHER SAFETY CONCERNS

SNAKE AND OTHER BITES Snakes are very secretive and bites are a genuine rarity, but certain spiders and scorpions can also deliver nasty bites. In all cases, the risk is minimised by wearing closed-toe shoes and trousers when walking in the bush, and watching where you put your hands and feet, especially in rocky areas or when gathering firewood. Only a small fraction of snakebites deliver enough venom to be life-threatening, but it is important to keep the victim calm and inactive, and to seek urgent medical attention immediately.

CAR ACCIDENTS Dangerous driving is possibly the biggest threat to life and limb in Suriname. On a self-drive visit, drive defensively, being especially wary of bullying overtaking manoeuvres. Avoid driving at night and pull over in heavy storms. On a chauffeured tour, don't be afraid to tell the driver to slow or calm down if you think he is being too fast or reckless. Always wear a seatbelt and refuse to be driven by anyone who has been drinking.

64

Part Two

PARAMARIBO AND THE COASTAL BELT

The five chapters that follow cover the Surinamese capital of Paramaribo and the administrative districts of Commewijne, Marowijne, Saramacca, Coronie, Nickerie, Wanica and Para, all but the last of which partially incorporate a section of Suriname's 385km Atlantic coastline. This is the most densely populated part of the country and the most ecologically varied, with a range of habitats that includes saline mangrove swamps, wide freshwater rivers, dense primary rainforest and lush tropical plantations. Paramaribo, with its equable atmosphere and historic riverfront city centre, makes a great base for exploring the coastal belt, whether you go on a series of organised tours, use public transport or travel under your own steam with a rented car or bicycle. There are some very varied sites of interest, ranging from sandy turtle-viewing beaches and forested plantations teeming with birds, to historic old forts and the brooding ruins at Jodensavanne. The highlights that really stand out are described below.

HIGHLIGHTS

(Normal duration of journey from Paramaribo given in parentheses)

INNER CITY OF PARAMARIBO A UNESCO World Heritage Site due to its trademark colonial architecture, central Paramaribo incorporates the largest wooden building in the Americas in the form of the Saint Peter and Paul Cathedral. Historic Fort Zeelandia is now an excellent museum, while the lively Waterkant is dotted with riverside bars and restaurants. See pages 101–14. (*Day trip, independent or tour*)

DOLPHIN CRUISES Scour the mangrove-lined mouth of the Suriname River for Guianan dolphins and marine birds such as the beautiful scarlet ibis and bulky greater frigate bird. See pages 116–17. (*Half-day trip, tour only*)

PEPERPOT NATURE PARK Easily reached from Paramaribo by bicycle or public transport, this WWF-affiliated private reserve is renowned for its wealth of forest birds and monkeys. See pages 124–6. (*Half-day trip, independent or tour*)

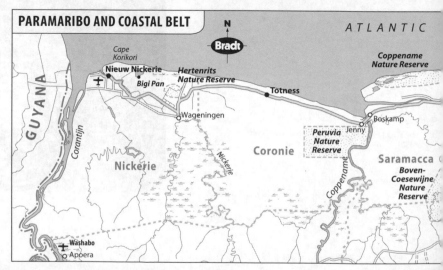

FORT NIEUW AMSTERDAM Situated opposite the capital at the confluence of the Suriname and Commewijne rivers, this strategically located 18th-century fort is now an informative open-air museum. See pages 127–8. (*Half-day trip, or full day combined with Peperpot, independent or tour*)

MATAPICA BEACH The top turtle-viewing site in Suriname, this remote sandy beach is reached via a labyrinthine mangrove swamp alive with birds and caimans. See pages 130–3. (*Day trip possible, 1 night more normal & better, tour only*)

GALIBI Another recommended base for turtle-viewing, this sprawling village on the Marowijne River is also a good place for uncontrived interaction with the Amerindian community. See pages 146–7. (*1 or 2 nights, best on tour but independent possible*)

GRONINGEN One of the best urban wildlife-viewing sites in Suriname, this small town resounds with the calls of howler monkeys. Boat trips on the Saramacca River here offer a good chance of spotting monkeys, sloths and manatees. See pages 149–54. (*1 or 2 nights, independent*)

NIEUW NICKERIE AND BIGI PAN The country's third-largest town has a relaxed riverside vibe and no shortage of affordable lodges and eateries serving Javanese influenced local staples. It is also the base for popular day and overnight trips to the bird-rich Bigi Pan. See pages 160–8. (*Overnight tour or 2-plus nights independently*)

NEOTROPICAL BUTTERFLY PARK Found in Lelydorp, a short bus ride south of Paramaribo, this excellent educational facility provides a fascinating introduction to Neotropical butterflies and other creepier-crawlier invertebrates. See page 172. (*Half-day trip, independent or tour*)

JODENSAVANNE These compelling ruins on the east bank of the Suriname River are all that remain of a once prosperous town founded by Sephardic Jews in the 17th century, and now home to what is left of the oldest synagogue in the Americas. See pages 181–2. (*Day tour or overnight independent*)

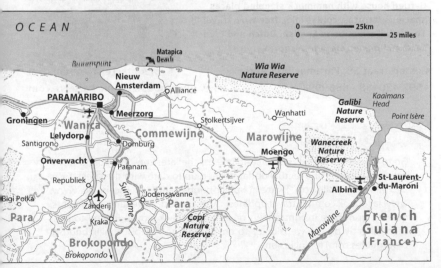

UPDATES WEBSITE

Go to www.bradtupdates.com/suriname for the latest on-the-ground travel news, trip reports and factual updates. Keep up to date with the latest posts by following Philip on Twitter (@philipbriggs) and via Facebook: www. www.facebook.com/pb.travel.updates. And, if you have any comments, queries, grumbles, insights, news or other feedback, you're invited to post them directly on the website, or to email them to Philip (e philip.briggs@ bradtguides.com) for inclusion.

5

Paramaribo

Paramaribo is not only the capital of Suriname, it is also the country's largest population centre and its main transport hub. Often referred to as Parbo, it's a safe, welcoming and decidedly beguiling city, steeped in history and strong on character. Founded in the early 17th century on the west bank of the Suriname River, the inner city is renowned for its unique and thoroughly attractive Dutch-Creole wooden architecture, which earned it recognition as a UNESCO World Heritage Site in 2002. Yet despite this Dutch architectural heritage, Paramaribo today is a strikingly multi-ethnic city, one whose diverse population of 250,000 primarily reflects successive waves of forced and voluntary migration from Europe, West Africa, Indonesia, India and China, but also includes a small number of indigenous Amerindians. The Surinamese capital is also justifiably proud of its reputation for religious and ethnic tolerance, epitomised by its grandest mosque and oldest synagogue rubbing shoulders on Keizer Straat, a block west of a historic Dutch Reformed Church.

It is fortunate that Paramaribo is such a gem of a city, as anybody planning a trip to Suriname will quickly recognise that almost all the country's roads converge on the capital, as does pretty much every last bus service, domestic flight and organised tour. As a result, visitors tend to end up planning around several one- and two-night stays in Paramaribo between upcountry excursions. This, it must be said, is no hardship. The UNESCO-endorsed inner city warrants a full day's exploration, starting with historic Fort Zeelandia and its excellent national museum. Further afield, Paramaribo offers rich pickings for day trippers: a leisurely stroll through the forested Peperpot Nature Park to look for colourful parrots and toucans, a relaxed cycling excursion to historic Fort Nieuw Amsterdam and the old plantations of Commewijne, a boat trip in search of the dolphins and marine birds that frequent the mouth of the Suriname River, an all-day organised tour to beautiful Brownsberg Nature Park or a bus trip to Lelydorp's underrated Neotropical Butterfly Park. And after the day's adventures, it is a genuine pleasure to while away the balmy tropical evening over a few chilled drinks on the breezy riverside Waterkant, or to work through a few of the city's countless eateries, which range from cheap and cheerful Javan-style warungs and Indian-style roti shops to a surprisingly cosmopolitan but still mostly affordable selection of smarter restaurants.

HISTORY

Paramaribo probably started life in pre-Columbian times as an Amerindian village on the west bank of the Suriname River. Strategically located 15km from the Atlantic Ocean at the first place upstream where boat access is unimpeded by shallow sandbars, the village was chosen as the site of a short-lived Dutch settlement in 1614. A quarter of a century later, French traders settled briefly at Paramaribo,

Paramaribo's modern ethnic diversity might unwittingly have been presaged in the name given to it by the first settlers. Although the suffix 'bo' (meaning 'place') indicates a clear Amerindian origin, more than 20 different interpretations of the city's full name have been put forward. The situation is further confused by the many different spellings used over the years (one early document, for instance, refers to the city as Permeriba). Paramaribo might thus derive from the Tupi-Guarani phrase *para maribo* (literally 'people of the large river'), or from the Carib-Karina *paramuru* (a type of tree'), or from *parmur* or *panari* (respectively meaning 'flower' and 'friends' in an unspecified Amerindian tongue). However, the most likely derivation is Paramuru-bo, from *paramuru*, the Indian word for rainbow, which also happens to be what the original inhabitants called the small creek that now runs past the Palm Garden in the form of Sommelsdijck Canal.

building a simple wooden precursor to Fort Zeelandia. The English arrived next in the form of the then Governor of Barbados, Baron Francis Willoughby, who established the private fiefdom of Willoughbyland at the site in 1651. Willoughby also expanded the original French fort and encouraged the first permanent settlers to establish sugar plantations along the Suriname River.

In February of the final year of the Second Anglo Dutch War of 1665–67, Fort Willoughby was captured by a Dutch fleet commanded by Abraham Crijnssen. Crijnssen re-christened the settlement Nieuw-Middelburg, an appellation that never took hold, and left a garrison at the fort, which he renamed Zeelandia after his home province. Paramaribo was formally ceded to the Dutch in July 1667 under the Treaty of Breda, but when Crijnssen returned in April 1668, he had to drive out the English again as they had reoccupied it the previous October. The town would remain a Dutch possession for the next three centuries, interrupted only by two short periods of British rule, 1799–1802 and 1804–15.

A pivotal figure in the early development of Paramaribo was Cornelis van Aerssen, Lord of Sommelsdijck. Sommelsdijck was appointed governor of Suriname in 1683, months after the formation of the Societeit van Suriname, a private company of which he was a one-third shareholder. He established a governor's residence on the site of the present Presidential Palace, founded a vegetable garden at what is now the Palm Garden, and oversaw many extensions to Fort Zeelandia. Never popular with those stationed under him, however, Sommelsdijck was murdered in July 1688 by mutinous soldiers who reputedly emptied more than 50 shots into his body.

By 1710, Paramaribo was a thriving small town. The original port, which ran along the Waterkant between Fort Zeelandia and Steenbakkersgracht (now Dr Sophie Redmond) Straat, was the main export centre for sugar and other crops produced by an ever-growing number of plantations along the Commewijne and Suriname rivers. Immediately inland, bounded by Graven (now Henck Arron) Straat to the east, Klipstenen Straat to the northwest and Heiligen Weg to the west, a small town of around 500 houses and slave quarters was laid out along a road grid and the modern town plan broadly corresponds to this. The town hall and court were situated on present-day Kerkplein, in a building that doubled as a place of Christian worship on Sundays. Much of this land was inherently marshy, but the colonists constructed a system of canals – many of which still exist in subterranean form – that drained into the main Sommelsdijck Canal.

Paramaribo expanded rapidly in the latter half of the 18th century. One reason for this is that many of the colony's wealthiest farmers retired to the relative safety and comfort of the city after employing managers to handle to day-to-day operations on their plantations. Another is that Paramaribo was naturally impervious to land attacks, which meant that it could grow unimpeded by city walls or moats. The city was also perceived to be largely safe from naval attacks following the construction of Fort Nieuw Amsterdam at the confluence of the Suriname and Commewijne rivers, the latter 10km nearer to the Suriname Estuary. By 1800, Paramaribo, thriving on the produce of more than 600 plantations, comprised around 2,000 houses, running inland as far as present-day van Idsinga Straat and west to Willem Campange Straat. A 1790s extension of the city east of Fort Zeelandia was bounded by Grote Combe Weg and Mahony Laan.

Central Paramaribo, with its many fine houses built along wide tree-lined avenues, experienced two destructive fires in the early 19th century. The first, in January 1821, was probably the result of a kitchen accident. The second, in September 1832, started when three runaway slaves decided to take revenge on their master by setting fire to his home. An estimated 400 wooden properties were razed in the fires, including most of the old inner city. And while this had little long-term effect on the overall street plan, it does mean that most extant buildings in the oldest quarter of Paramaribo were built after 1832.

Paramaribo's export-based economy suffered in the mid 19th century as a result of the declining productivity of the surrounding plantations. The rot had started in the late 18th century, when many plantations ceased to function properly while their absentee owners were living it up in Paramaribo. By the late 1860s, following the abolition of slavery in 1863, fewer than 100 plantations survived. Abolition also had a dramatic effect on the growth and social composition of Paramaribo. Directly, and most immediately, it resulted in a huge influx of former plantation owners, freed slaves and one-time runaways.

Less dramatic but of no less long-term significance was the influx of Indian, Chinese and Javanese labourers, tens of thousands of whom were imported to work on the remaining plantations from 1863 onwards. Many of these immigrants settled in the city after their contracts expired. This influx of Asian settlers between 1873 and 1939 not only helped to forge the diverse multi-ethnic cultural identity that characterises Paramaribo today, but it was also the main impetus for its gradual transformation from a glorified and somewhat ailing colonial port into a multi-faceted modern city with a diverse service economy. Another important boost to Paramaribo's export-based economy was provided in the early 20th century by the gold-mining industry around Brownsberg and US-funded bauxite mines at Moengo and Paranam. By 1945, the city was made up of 13,000 houses and the total population was 75,000. Following an administrative reorganisation in 1987, Paramaribo now consists of 12 jurisdictions with a total area of 183km², and it supports a population of around 260,000, more than half the national total.

GETTING THERE AND AWAY

BY AIR All international flights to Suriname land at **Johan Adolf Pengel International Airport** (JAPI; IATA code PBM; *www.japi-airport.com*), which lies 45km south of Paramaribo in the small junction town of Zanderij, and is normally referred to as Zanderij Airport (see page 42 for details of facilities at the airport and transport to and from Paramaribo).

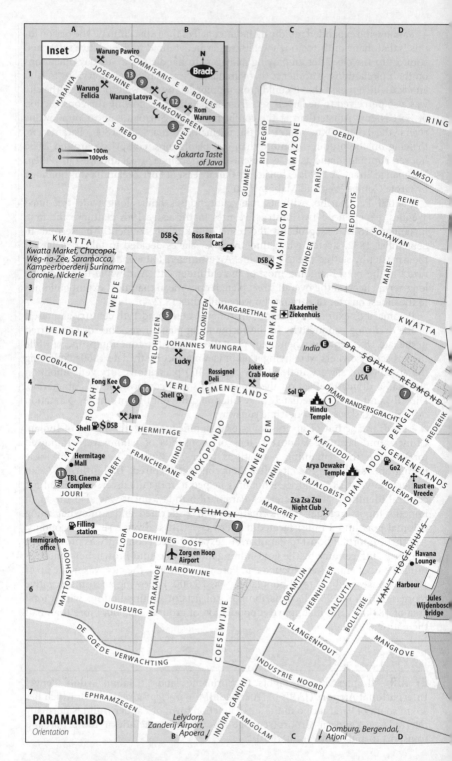

Inset

Warung Pawiro

COMMISARIS E B ROBLES

N

Bradt

NARAINA

JOSEPHINE

13   9

Warung
Felicia

Warung Latoya   12

SAMSONGREEN

Rom
Warung

J S REBO

GOVEA

3

0 ———— 100m
0 ———— 100yds

*Jakarta Taste
of Java*

RING

OERDI

AMAZONE

RIO NEGRO

AMSOI

PARIJS

REINE

REDIDOTIS

WASHINGTON

SOHAWAN

GUMMEL

KWATTA

DSB $ Ross Rental
Cars

MUNDER

MARIE

*Kwatta Market, Chacopot,
Weg-na-Zee, Saramacca,
Kampeerboerderij Suriname,
Coronie, Nickerie*

DSB $

TWEDE

MARGARETHAL

KERNKAMP

Akademie
Ziekenhuis

KWATTA

5

KOLONISTEN

India E

DR SOPHIE REDMOND

HENDRIK

VELDHUIZEN

JOHANNES MUNGRA

USA E

COCOBIACO

Lucky

Rossignol
Deli

Joke's
Crab House

Sol

DRAMBRANDERSGRACHT

7

Fong Kee 4

VERL

GEMENELANDS

1

Hindu
Temple

PENGEL

FREDERIK

10

Shell

6

ROOKH

Java

S KAFILUDDI

ZONNEBLOEM

JOHAN ADOLF

GEMENELANDS

Go2

Shell $ DSB

L HERMITAGE

BINDA

BROKOPONDO

ZINNIA

Arya Dewaker
Temple

MOLENPAD

Rust en
Vreede

LALLA

FRANCHEPANE

ALBERT

FAJALOBIST

Zsa Zsa Zsu
Night Club

11   TBL Cinema
Complex

JOURI

J LACHMON

MARGRIET

7

Filling
station

FLORA

DOEKHIWEG OOST

CORANTIJN

HERNHUTTER

CALCUTTA

VAN 'T HOGERHUYS

Havana
Lounge

MATTONSHOOP

Immigration
office

Zorg en Hoop
Airport

MAROWIJNE

Harbour

Jules
Wijdenbosch
bridge

DUISBURG

WATRAKANOE

COESEWIJNE

BOLLETRIE

MANGROVE

DE GOEDE VERWACHTING

SLANGENHOUT

INDUSTRIE NOORD

7

EPHRAMZEGEN

PARAMARIBO
Orientation

*Lelydorp,
Zanderij Airport,
Apoera*

INDIRA GANDHI

RAMGOLAM

*Domburg, Bergendal,
Atjoni*

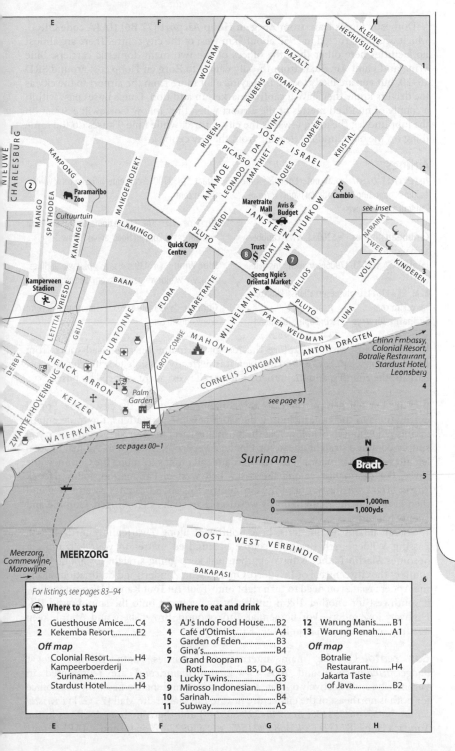

see inset

see page 91

see pages 80–1

Suriname

Bradt

N

0 — 1,000m
0 — 1,000yds

Meerzorg,
Commewijne,
Marowijne

MEERZORG

OOST - WEST VERBINDIG

BAKAPASI

For listings, see pages 83–94

🏠 **Where to stay**

1 Guesthouse Amice...... C4
2 Kekemba Resort............E2

Off map
    Colonial Resort............H4
    Kampeerboerderij
        Suriname...................A3
    Stardust Hotel..............H4

❌ **Where to eat and drink**

3 AJ's Indo Food House...... B2
4 Café d'Otimist....................A4
5 Garden of Eden.................B3
6 Gina's..................................B4
7 Grand Roopram
        Roti...................B5, D4, G3
8 Lucky Twins........................G3
9 Mirosso Indonesian..........B1
10 Sarinah..............................B4
11 Subway..............................A5

12 Warung Manis........ B1
13 Warung Renah....... A1

Off map
    Botralie
        Restaurant...........H4
    Jakarta Taste
        of Java..................B2

Domestic flights leave from **Zorg en Hoop Airport** [72 B6] (IATA code ORG), which was constructed in 1952 about 5km west of the city centre. There are almost no facilities here other than the offices of the two main domestic carriers: Blue Wing and Gum Air. Taxis from the city centre to Zorg en Hoop cost around SRD 15–20, but you are likely to end up paying a lot more from the airport to the city as the drivers know they have a captive market. In addition, Line 8 buses pass within a couple of hundred metres of the airport when they follow Coesewijne Straat on the inbound leg (heading towards the city centre), while Line 9 buses do the same thing on the outbound leg (leaving from the city centre).

Airlines

International Local contact details for the 4 airlines operating international flights to/from Zanderij are as follows:

Caribbean Airlines ✎520034; www.caribbean-airlines.com
InselAir ✎479043/479066; www.fly-inselair.com
KLM ✎411811; e pbmreservations@klm.com; www.klm.com
Suriname Airways 219 Dr Sophie Redmond

Straat; ✎432700; e callcenter@flyslm.com; www.flyslm.com

Domestic The 2 main domestic carriers, both with offices at Zorg en Hoop, are as follows:

Blue Wing ✎434393; e sales@bluewingairlines.com; www.bluewingairlines.com. See ad, page 218.
Gum Air ✎498760/432057; e info@gumair.com; www.gumair.com

BY ROAD Most visitors explore the rest of Suriname on organised tours from Paramaribo (see pages 78–9). However, it is perfectly possible to self-drive to most parts of the country, and main roads, such as they exist, are serviced by buses.

By car For self-drivers, there are three main routes out of the city centre. For all destinations to the east, including the Commewijne plantations, the route entails taking Wijdenbosch Bridge across the Suriname River to Meerzorg, from where you simply continue straight ahead for Plantage Peperpot, Moengo or Albina, or turn left after around 5km for Nieuw Amsterdam and other sites along the Commewijne River. For destinations along the costal belt west of Paramaribo, follow Henck Arron Straat northwest out of the city centre; this soon becomes Kwatta Weg and then eventually the main highway west to places such as Groningen, Coronie and Nieuw Nickerie.

For all inland destinations, head southwest along Zwartenhovenbrug Straat, passing Wijdenbosch Bridge a couple of hundred metres to your left, until it becomes Martin Luther King Weg, then just keep going straight for about 10km south of the city centre. For Lelydorp, Onverwacht, Zanderij and destinations along the Apoera road, you need to turn right onto Tout Tui Faut Kanaal Weg, and follow it southwest for another 10km until it brings you out onto the southbound JFK Highway to Zanderij. For Bergendal, Brokopondo, Brownsberg and Atjoni, keep heading south along Martin Luther King Weg.

Car rental Of the main international agencies, both **Budget** (*www.budgetsuriname.com*) and **Avis** (*www.avissuriname.com*) are represented in Paramaribo and effectively operate as one company and share offices. The head office for both is northeast of the city centre next to the Maretraite Mall [73 G3] (*1 Kristal Straat;* ✎ *457636/551158;* m *8748439/8805144*) and there are branch offices in the Torarica Hotel [87 G2] (✎*473686/421567;* m *8650923/8775644)* and at JAPI airport

(\457363; m 8775645/8748439). Rentals start at around SRD 125 per day, including insurance.

A reliable local operator, established in 1996, **Ross Rental Cars** (*264 Kwatta Weg;* m *7620212/8822140;* e *info@rossrentalcars.com; www.rossrentalcars.com*) also has an airport branch and operates a 24-hour phone hotline. See ad, page 64.

By bus Most bus routes out of Paramaribo are covered by the parastatal National Transport Company or Nationaal Vervoer Bedrijf (NVB; \ *472450/473591;* e *nvbnv@sr.net; www.nvbnvsuriname.com*), whose main depot, and information and booking office, is centrally located off the Waterkant at Heiligen Weg [80 D6]. The buses are reliable and fares very reasonable. The NVB operates at least one bus daily to the likes of Zanderij, Santigron, Brownsweg, Atjoni, Groningen, Wageningen, Nieuw Nickerie, Moengo and Albina. Most NVB buses depart from the Heiligen Weg depot, but buses to Brokopondo District leave from nearby Saramacca Straat and those for Atjoni leave from the margarine factory on Indira Gandhi Weg. Current schedules are included in the relevant regional sections of this guide. In all cases, however, it is advisable to check departure points and times, and for longer journeys, to book a seat a day in advance. You can check times online at www.nvbnvsuriname.com/Nvb/Fof/Rou/Rou001Php.php or (perhaps more reliably) at the Heiligen Weg office.

BY BOAT For cyclists or pedestrians heading to Fort Nieuw Amsterdam or Plantage Peperpot, the easiest way to cross the Suriname River into Commewijne is by boat. Public taxi-boats cross from Plattebrug [81 E7] (on the Waterkant, opposite the junction with Heiligen Weg) to Meerzorg on the east bank every few minutes between 06.00 and 18.00, and cost SRD 1.20 per person. Taxi-boats between Leonsberg (the northern terminus for Line 4 buses out of Paramaribo) and Fort Nieuw Amsterdam charge about the same but are rather more infrequent, so you might consider chartering one, which should only cost around SRD 20 per group for the ten-minute crossing.

GETTING AROUND

Central Paramaribo is easy to get around on foot but for travel further afield, the two main options are buses and taxis.

ORIENTATION Paramaribo is a relatively small city with a compact centre, so it is quite easy to orientate yourself. The historic centre is roughly triangular, bounded by the Suriname River to the south, Sommelsdijck Canal to the northeast and Zwartenhovenbrug Straat to the northwest. The historic Fort Zeelandia, the Palm Garden, the Presidential Palace and Independence Square are clustered at the southeastern tip of this triangle. Running west from this, the riverfront Waterkant (literally 'Waterside') and Saramacca Straat are flanked by some of the city's most popular eateries, as well as the main bus station (at the junction with Heiligen Weg), Plattebrug (the launch for boats across the river to Meerzorg) and the central market. Other important thoroughfares include Henck Arron Straat, which is lined with historic buildings including Saint Peter and Paul Cathedral, the bustlingly commercial Dominee and Maagden streets, and Keizer Straat.

Less historic but no less important to tourists is the so-called Uitgaanscentrum ('Entertainment Centre'), which lies immediately east of the Palm Garden, and is separated from it by Sommelsdijck Canal. Several hotels, including the landmark Torarica, are squeezed into the compact Uitgaanscentrum, along with perhaps a dozen tourist-oriented bars and restaurants, including Sidewalk Café t'Vat, a popular all-day rendezvous. Running northeast from the Torarica Hotel, Cornelis Jongbaw Straat is lined with several restaurants, as well as the STINASU booking office and Eco Resort Inn. Further northwest, Cornelis Jongbaw Straat morphs into Anton Dragten Weg, which continues northeast to Blauwgrond (famed for its cluster of Javan-Surinamese eateries) and Leonsberg (departure point for boats to Fort Nieuw Amsterdam and sunset dolphin tours).

The most important thoroughfare heading southwest of the old city centre is Van t'Hogerhuys Straat. This extension of Zwartenhovenbrug/Saramacca Straat leads past Jules Wijdenbosch Bridge (the only road between Paramaribo and the easterly districts of Commewijne and Marowijne), and then becomes Martin Luther King Weg, the main access road to the southerly districts of Wanica, Para (for Zanderij Airport), Brokopondo and Sipaliwini.

The most important of several trunk roads leading west from the city centre, Kwatta Weg (an extension of Henck Arron Straat) runs close to Paramaribo Zoo and Weg-na-Zee before it becomes the main highway west to the districts of Saramacca, Coronie and Nickerie. Another important western trunk road is Dr J Lachmon Straat, which provides access to Zorg en Hoop Airport, the immigration office, and the adjacent TBL Cinema Complex and Hermitage Mall.

BY BIKE Fietsen In Suriname (see page 78; ⏰ *09.00–17.00 daily*) is a highly regarded operator that rents out gearless city bikes suited to pottering around town for SRD 16 per day, and four-speed bikes with handbrakes for SRD 27.50 per day. It also sells inexpensive cycling booklets covering the city and the bordering districts of Commewijne, Wanica and Saramacca.

Also recommended is **Cardy Adventures** [91 C3] (*29/31 Cornelis Jongbaw Straat;* ☎ *422518/424505;* ✉ *info@cardyadventures.com; www.cardyadventures.com;* ⏰ *08.15–17.00 Mon–Sat, 08.30–17.00 Sun*), which rents out bikes of varying types and quality for SRD 20–50 per 24 hours. It also offers very reasonable monthly specials starting at SRD 100. A refundable deposit of SRD 50 is levied on all rentals.

BY BUS Several bus lines connect central Paramaribo to suburban areas, with most vehicles leaving from within a block of the depot at Heiligen Weg. The buses are privately run, but fares are fixed at SRD 1.25–1.75 (depending on the line) and are advertised on the inside of the door, so there is no risk of you being overcharged. Drivers will usually stop anywhere *en route* to pick up or drop off passengers, and you should pay the driver directly when you board or disembark. There are no timetables as such, but buses typically run every five to 15 minutes between 05.00 and 21.30 daily, though departures tend to be less regular before 07.00 and after 18.00, and on Sundays.

In addition to the lines listed below, NVB buses leave from Heiligen Weg for Meerzorg (on the Commewijne side of the Suriname River) every 15 minutes between 05.30 and 18.30 (less frequently on Sundays), but it is quicker to get to Meerzorg by boat from Plattebrug.

The bus lines are as follows:

Line 1: Hermitage Mall; leaving from the southeast end of Dr Sophie Redmond Straat.
Line 2: Southern industrial area and Slangenhout Straat (near Parbo Brewery); leaving from Saramacca Straat near the junction with Dr Sophie Redmond Straat.

Line 3: Paramaribo North via Tourtonne and Gomper Straat; leaving from the Waterkant in front of the Central Market.

Line 4: Leonsberg via Eco Resort Inn and passing close to Blauwgrond; leaving from the Waterkant close to Plattebrug.

Line 5: Munder via Kwatta Weg; leaving from the Waterkant close to the Central Market.

Line 6: Charlesburg via Kwatta Weg; leaving from the west end of Maagden Straat.

Line 7: Latour (out past the southern industrial area); leaving from the southeast end of Dr Sophie Redmond Straat.

Line 8: Flora via Dr J Lachmon Straat, passing close to the Immigration Office, Hermitage Mall and (inbound only) Zorg en Hoop Airport; leaving from the south end of Steenbakkerij Straat.

Line 9: Flora via Dr J Lachmon Straat, passing close to Zorg en Hoop Airport (outbound only); leaving from the south end of Steenbakkerij Straat.

Line 10: Anamoe and Ruben Straat via Tourtonne Laan; leaving from Heiligen Weg.

PG Line: Geyersvlijt via Maretraite Mall and Blauwgrond; leaving from the Waterkant close to Plattebrug.

Tam-Kas Line: Kasabaholo via Verlengde Gemenelands Weg and Hermitage Mall; leaving from the northeast end of Waaldijk Straat.

BY TAXI Taxis are mostly unmetered and fares can be rather whimsical but are generally quite inexpensive. There are few taxi ranks as such, but you can usually pick one up in front of the Torarica Hotel, or at the southeast end of Heiligen Weg. Somewhat counter-intuitively, however, the fares tend to be lower if you call a taxi, or ask a hotel or restaurant to, than if you try and wave one down in the street. Recommended companies include **Tourtonne's Taxi** (*142 Tourtonne Laan;* ✆ *475734/425380;* e *info@tourtonnestaxi.com; www.tourtonnestaxi.com*), **Ulstrel Taxi** (*24 Hof Straat;* ✆ *470646;* e *info@ulstrel.com; www.ulstrel.com*), **Fany's Taxi** (*25 de Hayden Straat 25;* ✆ *450303;* m *8911600; www. fanysdiensten.com*), **Taxi Reggel** (✆ *420176*) and **Zinnia Taxi** (*49 Zinnia Straat;* ✆ *499419; www.zinniataxi.com*).

Fares within the city centre should be around SRD 10, while you're looking at SRD 17–20 to travel to Zorg en Hoop, SRD 15–20 to Leonsberg, or SRD 125–130 to Zanderij. Further afield, sample fares are approximately SRD 50–100 to various sites in Commewijn, SRD 300 to Albina, SRD 150–300 to the likes of Overbridge or Berg en Dal, and SRD 350–500 to Atjoni. Wherever you travel, it is always best to check the fare in advance and be prepared to negotiate if necessary, as some cruising taxis will ask tourists to pay up to double the going rate.

In March 2014, metered taxis were launched with a tracking system operated by Central Suriname Taxis. These taxis are easily recognisable, as they are bright yellow. They can be booked by calling ✆ 1660.

TOURIST INFORMATION

Founded in 1996 as the designated government tourism body, the **Suriname Tourism Foundation** (STF; *2 JF Nassy Laan* ✆ *424878;* e *info@surinametourism. sr; www.surinametourism.sr*) maintains tourist information centres at Johan Adolf Pengel International Airport (✆ *325194;* ⊕ *usually open to coincide with incoming flights*) and on Kleine Combe Straat in front of Fort Zeelandia [81 H7] (✆ *479200;* e *infodesk@suriname-tourism.org;* ⊕ *08.00–15.30 Mon–Fri*). Both are worth visiting, if only to pick up a good free foldout map of Paramaribo, and they also stock a good selection of brochures and leaflets.

Founded in 1969 by the biologist Johan Schulz, **STINASU** (Stichting Natuurbehoud Suriname, literally 'Foundation for Nature Preservation') is a parastatal organisation responsible for the management of several Surinamese nature reserves and for the maintenance of tourist facilities in Brownsberg, Galibi and Central Suriname (Raleigh Falls). The STINASU information and reservation office [91 C4] (*14 Cornelis Jongbaw Straat, next to Eco Resort Inn;* ☏ *421683/476597;* e *stinasu@sr.net; www.stinasu.com;* ⏰ *07.00–15.00 Mon–Fri*) remains the place to make direct accommodation bookings for Brownsberg, Galibi and Raleigh Falls nature reserves. It also stocks several useful and inexpensive bilingual (Dutch and English) booklets about the country's birdlife and primates (see pages 236–7). In theory, STINASU also offers tour packages to the reserves under its jurisdiction, but these are not as reliable as they used to be, so you'd be better off booking with a private operator. Indeed, the reputation of the foundation has been compromised in recent years by a series of corruption scandals and a general decline in efficiency, and its long-term future in its present form may be far from secure.

TOUR OPERATORS

Most visitors to Paramaribo explore the rest of the country on one or more organised day or overnight excursions put together by local tour operators. Many such tours run to fixed departure dates, and will not leave at all unless there are sufficient clients to make it financially viable (typically a minimum of two or four people). Those visitors with limited time in the country are advised to book as many excursions as they can in advance, and then make hotel bookings around those dates. Some recommended tour operators are:

All Suriname Tours Queens Hotel, 15 Kleine Water Straat; ☏ 470675; m 8644785/8204957; e info@allsurinametours.com; www.allsurinametours.com. This small new operator is a good contact for trips to relatively remote areas such as Blanche Marie, Apoera, Ananavero & Raleigh Falls, but it also offers the more usual packages to places like Galibi, Brownsberg & the Upper Suriname. Where possible, tours are led by the owner-manager Ronny Bhoelai. See ad, page 38.

Bondru Tours m 8826049/8256464; e info@bondrutourssuriname.com; www. bondrutourssuriname.com. Although it acts as an agent for tours all over the country, Bondru is the specialist operator for day tours to Warappa Creek.

Fietsen In Suriname (FIS) 13a Groote Combe Weg; ☏ 520781; m 8675757; e info@ fietseninsuriname.com; www.fietseninsuriname. nl. Catering mainly to adventurous & more budget-conscious visitors, FIS specialises in professionally guided or self-guided cycling tours ('fietsen' means bicycles) around Paramaribo, to Commewijne & to sites further afield such as the Brownsberg & Brokopondo area. Moulded in the image of its dynamic hands-on owner-manager, FIS is not only the leading exponent of cycling tours countrywide, but it also offers unique kayaking trips into the otherwise inaccessible Coesewijne Nature Reserve. The main office is in the same compound as Zus &

Zo (see below), but it also has a more central kiosk in front of Sidewalk Café t'Vat.

Jenny Tours 5c Waterkant; m 8858495; e info@suriname-tour.com; www.suriname-tour. com. Popular with students & interns, this dynamic budget operator specialises in large group tours, mostly sleeping in hammocks. Most places of interest are covered, including Galibi, Raleigh Falls, Bigi Pan, Blanche Marie & various lodges along the Upper Suriname. It is also offers a unique helicopter package to Metapica.

METS Travel & Tours 2 JF Nassy Laan; ☏ 472621/472614; e mets@sr.net; www. surinamevacations.com. Established in 1962, Suriname's most experienced operator is aimed firmly at relatively unadventurous & upmarket visitors. It offers a variety of tours countrywide, but is best known for founding & managing 2 of the interior's finest community-based jungle resorts, Palumeu & Awarradam.

Orange Travel 1 Sommelsdijck Straat; ☏ 421984; m 8773397; e info@orangesuriname. com; ⏰ 09.00–20.00 Mon–Sat. This reputable 'full-service' Dutch-based operator arranges & books professionally guided tours to pretty much everywhere in Suriname, aiming at the mid- to upper-end of the market.

Waterproof Tours ☏ 454434; m 8962927; e info@waterproofsuriname.com; www. waterproofsuriname.com. This small but highly regarded operator is best known for its regular dolphin sunset cruises (see page 117), but it also operates a number of other packages, including day trips to Moengo, a historic Commewijne 'Sugar Trail', & a great overnight package to Fort Nieuw Amsterdam & Metapica. **Zus & Zo Tours** 13a Grote Combe Weg; 520905; e info@zusenzosuriname.com; www.

zusenzosuriname.com. Though it's technically an agent as opposed to an operator, the tour office at this well-known backpackers & restaurant has its finger well on the pulse, & is a popular 1st port of call for many budget-conscious visitors trying to plan their trip. Email or ask at the office for a full list of all confirmed & scheduled departures, with prices, for the next few weeks.

SAFETY

Paramaribo is by most standards a very safe city. You have little to fear walking around by day, and even after dark you are unlikely to hit any problems if you adhere to the usual common-sense rules applicable to any large city (ie: avoid walking around alone late at night, stay clear of quiet unlit areas, don't wear expensive jewellery or other accessories, and carry only as much cash as you are likely to need for the outing). That said, people do get robbed at night, so it is probably wise to err on the side of caution and take a taxi if you stray outside the area immediately around the Torarica Hotel – they are very cheap and any bar or restaurant will call one for you. Two central areas that have a bit of a reputation by night and should definitely be avoided are the interior of the Palm Garden and the stretch of the Waterkant and Saramacca Straat west of Plattebrug.

WHERE TO STAY *Map, pages 72–3, 80–1, 87, 91 and 120–1.*

The section below includes all listed accommodation in central Paramaribo, along with a few suburban options in an area bounded by the Suriname River to the east, Leonsberg to the north, the border with Wanica District to the south and the border with Saramacca District to the west. However, with almost all of Suriname's population being concentrated within a 50km radius of the capital, it is worth emphasising that many hotels and lodgings listed under towns or regions covered in other chapters of this book could realistically be used as an alternative base for exploring the Greater Paramaribo area. Indeed, for those seeking a more rustic retreat, out-of-town options listed under the likes of the Commewijne Plantation Route, Groningen, Domburg, Lelydorp and (more remotely) in the vicinity of Zanderij might be preferable to a city hotel.

EXCLUSIVE/LUXURY ($$$$$)

Royal Torarica Hotel (105 rooms) 10 Kleine Water Straat; 473500; e reservations@torarica.com; www.royaltorarica.com. Probably the top hotel in Paramaribo, & priced accordingly, the Royal Torarica is set some distance back from the main road in large tropical mangrove-lined riverfront gardens opposite the Uitgaanscentrum. The immaculate rooms all have a balcony with a city, river or garden view, warm earthy décor, & come with a king-size bed, AC, satellite TV, minibar, free Wi-Fi & a large bathroom. There are also junior & presidential suites. Facilities include a relaxed lobby bar, terrace restaurant overlooking the large

swimming pool, tennis courts, gym, massage room & meeting rooms. The standard of service & buffet b/fast is among the highest in Suriname. From SRD 490/560 B&B sgl/dbl.

UPMARKET ($$$$)

Torarica Hotel & Casino (132 rooms) LJ Rietberg Plein, Kleine Water Straat; 471500; e reservations@torarica.com; www.torarica.com. Having celebrated its 50th anniversary in 2012 with extensive renovations, the 4-star Torarica (or 'Tor'), named after the 1st colonial settlement established along the Suriname River, remains probably the best-known landmark in

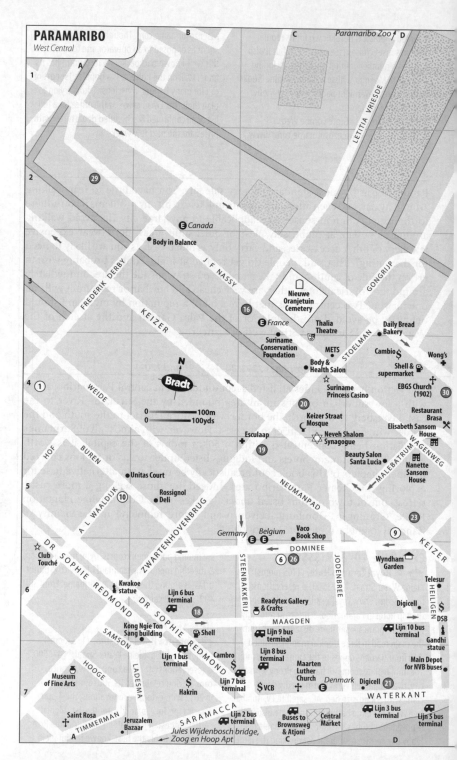

PARAMARIBO
West Central

Paramaribo Zoo

LETITIA VRIESDE

29

Ⓔ Canada

● Body in Balance

J F NASSY

FREDERIK DERBY

KEIZER

GONGRIJP

16

Nieuwe
Oranjetuin
Cemetery

Ⓔ France

Thalia
Theatre

Daily Bread
Bakery

Suriname
Conservation
Foundation

METS

STOELMAN

Cambio $

Wong's

Body &
Health Salon

Shell &
supermarket

N

Bradt

Suriname
Princess Casino

EBGS Church
(1902)

30

WEIDE

0 ___ 100m
0 ___ 100yds

20

Keizer Straat
Mosque

Restaurant
Brasa

Elisabeth Sansom
House

1

Esculaap

Neveh Shalom
Synagogue

WAGENWEG

HOF

BUREN

19

Beauty Salon
Santa Lucia

MALEBATRUM

Nanette
Sansom
House

● Unitas Court

NEUMANPAD

A L WAALDIJK

ZWARTENHOVENBRUG

10

Rossignol
● Deli

23

Germany

Belgium

Vaco
Book Shop

9

KEIZER

DR SOPHIE REDMOND

Club
Touché

Ⓔ **Ⓔ**

DOMINEE

Wyndham
Garden

Telesur

Kwakoe
statue

STEENBAKKERIJ

6 26

JODENBREE

Digicell

HEILIGEN

Lijn 6 bus
terminal

Readytex Gallery
& Crafts

DSB

18

Kong Ngie Ton
Sang building

Shell

MAAGDEN

Lijn 9 bus
terminal

Lijn 10 bus
terminal

Gandhi
statue

SAMSON

Lijn 1 bus
terminal

Cambro
$

Lijn 8 bus
terminal

Maarten
Luther
Church

Denmark

Digicell

21

Main Depot
for NVB buses

HOOGE

LADESMA

Museum
of Fine Arts

Hakrin
$

Lijn 7 bus
terminal

$ VCB

Ⓔ

WATERKANT

Saint Rosa

TIMMERMAN

Jeruzalem
Bazaar

SARAMACCA

Lijn 2 bus
terminal

Buses to
Brownsweg
& Atjoni

Central
Market

Lijn 3 bus
terminal

Lijn 5 bus
terminal

Jules Wijdenbosch bridge,
Zoog en Hoop Apt

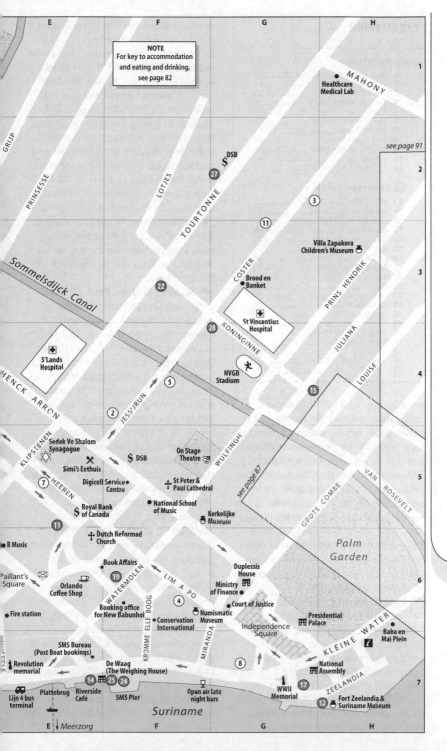

NOTE
For key to accommodation
and eating and drinking,
see page 82

see page 91

MAHONY

Healthcare
Medical Lab

$ DSB
27

3

11

TOURTONNE

LOTJES

PRINSESSE

GRIJP

Sommelsdijck Canal

22

COSTER

Brood en
Banket

Villa Zapakora
Children's Museum

PRINS HENDRIK

JULIANA

LOUISE

28

KONINGINNE

St Vincentius
Hospital

S'Lands
Hospital

NVGB
Stadium

15

5

2

JESSJRUN

HENCK ARRON

Sedek Ve Shalom
Synagogue

Simi's Eethuis

Digicell Service
Centre

KLIPSTENEN

7

HEEREN

$ DSB

On Stage
Theatre

WULFINGH

VAN ROSEVELT

see page 87

GROTE COMBE

Royal Bank
of Canada

13

St Peter &
Paul Cathedral

National School
of Music

Kerkelijke
Museum

Palm
Garden

B Music

Dutch Reformed
Church

Book Affairs

19

LIM A PO

Duplessis
House

Ministry
of Finance

Vaillant's
Square

Orlando
Coffee Shop

WATERMOLEN

KROMME ELLE BOOG

4

Conservation
International

Numismatic
Museum

Court of Justice

Presidential
Palace

Baba en
Mai Plein

Fire station

Booking office
for New Babunhol

MIRANDA

Independence
Square

KLEINE WATER

SMS Bureau
(Post Boat bookings)

Revolution
memorial

De Waag
(The Weighing House)

8

National
Assembly

WWII
Memorial

17

ZEELANDIA

Lijn 4 bus
terminal

Plattebrug

Riverside
Café

14

25

24

SMS Pier

Open air late
night bars

12

Fort Zeelandia &
Suriname Museum

Suriname

E ↓ Meerzorg

central Paramaribo & it has hosted numerous foreign presidents & celebrities over the years. The riverside garden, teeming with birds & centred on a large swimming pool is a rare enclave of tropical greenery in the city centre, & the hotel also has a lovely waterside marina clubhouse & several other bars & restaurants. The bright & spacious rooms are decorated with colourful local artworks, & have excellent facilities including AC, satellite TV, free Wi-Fi, fridge, coffeemaker, writing desk, safe & large en-suite bathroom. Other facilities include a casino, gym, aerobic centre, tennis courts, saunas, ATM in the lobby, beauty salon & massage centre. From SRD 445/480 B&B sgl/dbl.

🏠 **Courtyard Marriot Paramaribo**
(140 rooms) 52–53 Anton Dragten Weg; ☎456000/498000; www.marriott.com/hotels/travel/pbmcy-courtyard-paramaribo. Set back from the riverfront about 1km east of the city centre, this multi-storey chain hotel, though clearly aimed mainly at the business market, has a very colourful & contemporary look (it opened in 2010). The transatlantic atmosphere & fluent English-speaking staff should immediately win over

nervous 1st-time visitors to Suriname. Reached along bright corridors adorned with modern art, the huge warmly coloured rooms are arguably the best in town, with 2 dbl beds, stylish hardwood wardrobe & writing desk, AC, large flat-screen satellite TV, balcony & en-suite bathroom with tub & shower. Facilities include an onsite ATM, affordable DIY laundry, a swimming pool & patio bar currently being extended to the riverfront & a gym. The ground-floor Flavors Restaurant has a good reputation & serves an international menu of grills, burgers & pasta dishes in the SRD 45–70 range, & several cheaper eateries lie within a 500m radius. The one drawback of this otherwise top-notch business hotel is that it lies outside the historic city centre. Check the website for exact prices, which vary depending on the occupancy level, but typically start at a very reasonable SRD 420 dbl exc b/fast.

🏠 **Spanhoek Boutique Hotel** (23 rooms) 2–4 Dominee Straat; ☎477888; e reservation@spanhoekhotel.com; www.spanhoekhotel.com. Situated on the 1st floor of a small mall, 300m from the riverfront at the east end of the city's busiest shopping street, the small & stylish Spanhoek largely lives up to its claim to be downtown Paramaribo's only boutique hotel. The spacious & individually decorated rooms make liberal use of local dark wood & come with twin or queen-size beds, AC, TV, safe, Wi-Fi & en-suite hot shower. Some rooms also have a kitchenette. A drawback of this hotel is the lack of a swimming pool or of any other outdoor public area. SRD 295/330 sgl/dbl or SRD 530/600 executive sgl/dbl; all rates B&B.

🏠 **Hotel Krasnapolsky** (84 rooms) 39 Dominee Straat 39; ☎475050; e info@krasnapolsky.sr; www.krasnapolsky.sr. This modern, multi-storey business-style hotel, situated 300m from the waterfront, is a well-known landmark on Paramaribo's slickest shopping street. The well-lit rooms are very large, attractively decorated with modern artworks, & come with dark wood floor & furnishings, a king-size bed, large flat-screen satellite TV, blasting AC, free Wi-Fi, fridge, coffeemaker & small balcony. There are no gardens as such due to the downtown location, but an open-air swimming pool & b/fast area can be found on the 3rd floor, while the lobby is home to an exceptional deli/bakery & several other eateries. From SRD 405/473 standard sgl/dbl to SRD 841 dbl suite; all rates B&B.

🏠 **Best Western Suriname** (50 rooms) 99–100 Frederick Derby Straat; 📞 420007/426555; ✉ frontoffice@bestwesternsuriname.com; www.bestwesternsuriname.com. This bland but reasonably priced 4-star hotel has a rather uninspiring setting at the northeast end of the city centre, about 1km inland of the riverfront, but otherwise it should tick all the right boxes for those who place comfort before character. Facilities include 2 restaurants, 2 bars & a casino, & the comfortable rooms all come with AC, satellite TV, minibar, safe, coffeemaker & Wi-Fi. SRD 228/280 standard sgl/dbl or US$508 de luxe dbl.

MODERATE ($$$)

🏠 ✳ **Rachel's Apartments** (12 apts) 2 Sipaliwini Laan; 📞 520421; 📱 8801059; ✉ info@rachelsapartments.com; www.rachelsapartments.com. If you don't mind being tucked away on a quiet side road about 1km east of the city centre, this smart, clean & pleasant owner-managed 2-storey complex is one of the best bets in this price range. The spacious tiled 1- or 2-bedroom apts come with a well-equipped modern open-plan kitchen & a sitting room with satellite TV & Wi Fi. Common facilities include a shady 1st-floor terrace overlooking the street & free DIY laundry room. SRD 210/298 for a 1/2-bedroom apt sleeping up to 2/4.

🏠 ✳ **Greenheart Hotel** (14 rooms) 68 Coster Straat; 📞 521360; 📱 8889998; ✉ info@greenheart-hotel.com; http://greenheart hotel.com. This new hotel, situated on the opposite site of the road to, & a few doors up from, Un Pied À Terre (see page 84), was built by the same owner-managers (who live on the property) using traditional wooden construction techniques, a labour of love that took 10 years to complete. The high-quality dark wood, dedicated workmanship & quality furnishings give it an aura of classy solidity, while features include wide wooden balconies at the front & back, & a large swimming pool. Medium-sized rooms have dbl or twin beds with a good mosquito net, fan or AC & en-suite hot shower. Good value at SRD 210/300/393/438 B&B sgl/dbl/trpl/quad. See ad, page 118.

🏠 ✳ **Hotel Palacio** (22 rooms) 9 Heeren Straat; 📞 420064; 📱 8784775; ✉ info@hotelpalacio.net; www.hotelpalacio.net. Opened in 2013 & already garnering a solid reputation for offering sensibly priced & comfortable

accommodation, this family-run 3-storey hotel was custom-built in the traditional style in the heart of the old city centre. Spacious, clean & contemporarily decorated en-suite rooms all have dark wood furniture including 2, ¾ beds & a writing desk, AC, satellite TV, free Wi-Fi & fridge. Service is exceptional, as is the buffet b/fast (where for once everything tastes as good as it looks), & the bar should be supplemented by a fully operational restaurant by 2015. SRD 246/280 sgl/dbl or SRD 357 semi-suite; all rates B&B.

🏠 ✳ **Colonial Resort** (4 rooms, with more under construction) 215 Anton Dragten Weg; 📞 559400; 📱 8873659/8720306; ✉ colonialresortsur@gmail.com; www.colonialresortsuriname.net. Scheduled to open in late 2014, this potentially fabulous new resort on the Leonsberg road is centred on a 150-year-old plantation house set in pretty leafy gardens alongside a canal lined with palm trees. Accommodation will be in stylish bungalows with AC & TV, & facilities will include a swimming pool, the excellent (albeit pricey) Botralie Restaurant with terrace & indoor seating, & a colonial-style bar converted from an old garage. Rates are likely to be around SRD 150/180 sgl/dbl.

🏠 **Kekemba Resort** (10 apts) 118 Mango Laan; 📞 546904; ✉ kekemba@kekemba.info; www.kekemba.info. Set in a well-wooded area 3km north of the city centre & immediately west of Paramaribo Zoo, this comfortable lodge lies in spacious & peaceful green grounds with a swimming pool, sauna, hammocks & plenty of birdlife. The hospitable owner-managers are good cooks & reliable sources of local travel information. The 1 & 2-bedroom apts are warmly decorated & come with AC, free Wi-Fi, in-room entertainment system (DVDs & CDs can be borrowed from reception), & coffee/tea-making facilities. You can either self-cater or order meals at the small restaurant. From SRD 135/180 sgl/dbl small studio apt to SRD 400 for a bungalow sleeping up to 5.

🏠 **Hotel La Petite Maison** (12 rooms) 4 Waterkant; 📞 475466; ✉ info@hotellapetitemaison.com; www.hotellapetitemaison.com. Set in a historic 3-storey waterfront mansion built after its predecessor was destroyed by fire in 1831, this cosy owner-managed hotel is difficult to beat when it comes to the combination of a central location, hands-on service & individualistic feel. The rooms, however, are rather variable in standard – those on the ground floor are quite cramped & old-fashioned, whereas their 1st- & 2nd-floor counterparts are larger & stronger on period character – but all come with TV, AC & free Wi-Fi. Riverfront rooms have a balcony offering a wonderful view over the river & bridge, but light sleepers might be affected by the noise from the traffic & all-night waterfront bars opposite. SRD 260/315 sgl/dbl without view or SRD 315/350 sgl/dbl with river view; all rates B&B.

🏠 **Zeelandia Suites** (9 suites) 1a Kleine Water Straat; ☎ 424631; e zeelands@sr.net; www. zeelandiasuites.com. This small all-suite hotel is centred around a green courtyard tucked away behind the iconic Cafe t'Vat. The comfortable & attractively decorated suites have AC & satellite TV & are mostly spread across 2 storeys, with a ground-floor sitting room & bathroom, & 1st-floor bedroom with queen-size bed. Most have a private balcony. There is free Wi-Fi at t'Vat, right outside the entrance. An excellent choice for those seeking a comfortable mid-range accommodation option in the heart of Paramaribo's main cluster of restaurants, bars & casinos, but light sleepers & those seeking an early night find the location a bit noisy. SRD 193/245 sgl/dbl, but look out for seasonal specials.

🏠 **Guesthouse Amice** (10 rooms) 5 Gravenberch Straat; ☎ 434289; e guesthouse-amice@sr.net; www.guesthouse-amice.sr. This long-serving owner-managed guesthouse lies along a bus route on a busy suburban road about 3km west of the city centre. Facilities include a comfortable front porch, dining area with wooden tables & there's a large swimming pool at the back. Spread across 2 storeys, the comfortable & brightly decorated en-suite rooms have wooden floors, TV, AC, free Wi-Fi & a coffeemaker. SRD 184/230 sgl/dbl or SRD 210/253 with balcony; all rates B&B.

🏠 **Eco Resort Inn** (120 rooms) 16 Cornelis Jongbaw Straat; ☎ 425522; e reservations@ torarica.com; www.ecoresortinn.com. The most modest & least central of the 3 riverfront hotels in the Torarica chain, the misleadingly named Eco Resort Inn is in reality a middling to smart business-style hotel centred on an old townhouse 500m east of the city centre. Split across 4, 3-storey blocks, the rooms are modern & very comfortable, & come with a queen-size bed, AC, satellite TV, en-suite shower & private balcony. The long narrow grounds aren't especially green, but

they do lead down to a small riverside terrace bar, & the bird-feeding table next to the restaurant is usually flapping with avian activity at b/fast time. Overall, a secure, agreeable & reasonably central introduction to Paramaribo for 1st-time visitors. From SRD 315/385 B&B sgl/dbl.

🏠 **Queens Hotel** (31 rooms) 15 Kleine Water Straat; ☎ 474967/9; e info@queenshotelsuriname. com; www.queenshotelsuriname.com. This modern multi-storey hotel is in a very central location opposite the landmark Torarica & is surrounded by eateries to suit all tastes & budgets. Rooms are spacious & brightly decorated, with AC, satellite TV, free Wi-Fi, fridge, coffeemaker, safe, balcony & sizeable en-suite bathrooms. Facilities are limited but include a gym. Rates start at SRD 263/315 B&B sgl/dbl, but depend on occupancy levels.

BUDGET ($$)

🏠 ✳ **Un Pied À Terre** (11 rooms) 59 Coster Straat; ☎ 470488; m 8889998; e piedaterre.sr@gmail.com; www.guesthouse. un-pied-a-terre.com. Set in a lovely wooden 3-storey house built in the early 19th century & complete with creaky wooden floors to prove its antiquity, this owner-managed guesthouse combines the friendly, sociable atmosphere of a backpackers hostel with simple but comfortable accommodation & good facilities including free Wi-Fi, free luggage storage, a front & back balcony, a kitchen, & a cosy front room with an honesty bar & good library of English, Dutch & French novels. The dbl rooms in the main house are small but comfortable, & come with twin beds & fan, & there are also tiled family studios on the ground floor sleeping from 2 to 5. The garden is dominated by a hammock hut with its own small sitting area, toilet & shower. SRD 92/115 sgl/dbl using shared bath; SRD 138/160 sgl/dbl studio; SRD 46 additional person; SRD 81pp own hammock or SRD 101pp using a rented hammock & net; b/fast an additional SRD 14pp. See ad, page 68.

🏠 ✳ **Cardy Apartments** (5 apts) 29/31 Cornelis Jongbaw Straat; ☎ 422518/424505; e info@cardyadventures.com; www. cardyadventures.com. Spread across 2 properties opposite Eco Resort Inn about 500m east of the city centre, this small owner-managed complex offers exceptional value for money in this range, especially for long-stay visitors. The clean & spacious tiled apts come with a bedroom, a dining & sitting area, a well-equipped kitchenette with microwave, satellite TV, AC, free Wi-Fi, & attractive furniture, & the location is ideal for eating out or exploring the old city centre. SRD 138/184/230 sgl/dbl/trpl (min stay 3 nights), with discounts of 10–40% on longer stays, depending on the exact duration.

Downtown Oasis (6 rooms & apts) 9 Jessurun Straat; 521481/2; m 8578110; e info@downtownoasis.sr; www.downtownoasis. sr. Set in a tranquil green garden in a sleepy but central one-way street around the corner from the cathedral, this small owner-managed lodge, fully renovated in 2012, has a pleasant atmosphere & good facilities including a swimming pool, free Wi-Fi, coin laundry & a gazebo hung with hammocks. The large en-suite rooms, with contemporary artworks, all have a king-size bed, seating area, writing desk, flat-screen satellite TV, AC, fridge & rates include use of a common kitchen. The complex also includes several self-catering apts with their own kitchen sleeping up to 3 or 6 people. Very reasonably priced at SRD 160 dbl, SRD 210/322 for an apt sleeping up to 3/6; rates exc b/fast.

Guesthouse TwenTy4 (11 rooms) 24 Jessurun Straat; 420751; e info@ twenty4suriname.com; www.twenty4suriname. com. A conspicuous canary yellow, colonial, 2-storey wooden building on a quiet but central one-way road. This relatively new guesthouse is under the same ownership as Zus & Zo & is well suited to backpackers & others seeking affordable accommodation in a sociable atmosphere. The rooms are small but clean, with twin beds & fan, & facilities include storage lockers, Wi-Fi, a small bar & a good tour office. There's no restaurant, but it's within easy walking distance of the waterfront, & b/fast & drinks on an addictive ground-floor veranda, hung with hammocks & overlooking a lushly foliated canal teeming with birds. SRD 69/115/160/210 sgl/dbl/trpl/quad with basin only; SRD 115/160/210/253 en-suite sgl/dbl/trpl/quad.

Kampeerboerderij Suriname (2 rooms) 64 Noordpolderdam; 330410; e kittyverheul@ gmail.com; www.kampeerboerderijsuriname. nl. Situated in an agricultural area about 15km west of the city centre off the road to Saramacca, this comfortable owner-managed cottage has a well-equipped self-catering kitchen, & facilities include a swimming pool, table tennis, children's playground, free Wi-Fi & horseback trips (by prior

arrangement). It lies within easy walking distance of a bus stop, warung, supermarket & other shops. Good value at SRD 138/184 sgl/dbl, with every 7th night free.

Stardust Hotel (77 rooms) 1 Condor Straat, Leonsberg; 451544/451215; e stardust@ sr.net; www.stardust-suriname.com. The only hotel in Leonsberg is a comfortable albeit slightly rundown 2-storey block centred on a large swimming pool. The spacious en-suite rooms all come with king-size bed, TV, AC & fridge, & they seem very good value for money compared with similar hotels in the city centre, to which Leonsberg is connected by regular Line 4 buses. SRD 105/140/175 standard sgl/dbl/dbl; apts with kitchenette from SRD 263.

SHOESTRING ($)

Zus & Zo (5 rooms) 13a Grote Combe Weg; 520905; e info@zusenzosuriname.com; www.zusenzosuriname.com. Situated in a striking wooden 1930s building designed by the architect Feith Ellert Mathijsen, this small backpacker-style lodge is right opposite the Palm Garden, giving it a surprisingly rural feel despite its very central location. Facilities include a residents' lounge, free Wi-Fi & luggage storage & a laundry service. It also shares space with the excellent restaurant of the same name, a highly regarded gift shop, a tour booking agency & the bicycle-tour & rental specialist Fietsen In Suriname (see page 78). The clean rooms are small & share a bath & toilet, but come with AC & basin. Good value at SRD 69/115 sgl/dbl or SRD 184/230 for a larger room sleeping 3/4; rates exc b/fast.

Stadszending (10 rooms) 17–19 Buren Straat; 473039/473288; e stadje@parbo.net; www.moravianchurch.sr. Centrally located in the historic Moravian Stadszending (City Mission) founded in 1869, this church hostel is at the back of 2 striking 19th-century buildings with wide balconies & a small roof turret. Simple twin rooms share a bath & toilet, & should be booked in advance, since reception (in the ground-floor bookshop) is effectively only open from 08.30–14.30 Mon to Fri & 09.00–13.30 on Sat. SRD 98 twin, with every 7th night free for long-stays.

Guesthouse Albergo Alberga (19 rooms) 13 Lim A Po Straat; 520050; e reservations@ guesthousealbergoalberga.com; www. guesthousealbergoalberga.com. Boasting a very central location in a restored 3-storey wooden homestead dating to the 2nd half of the 19th century, this adequate budget lodge receives mixed reviews, depending largely on one's expectations. True, the en-suite rooms are mostly quite cramped & a little frayed at the seams, but they are clean & light, & all come with TV & fan or AC, which makes them decent value at the asking price. The historic location less than 5 mins' walk from the waterfront is a real asset, & facilities include free Wi-Fi, a very small swimming pool, & a small dining room serving b/fast for around SRD 20 from 08.00–09.00. SRD 78/111 sgl/dbl with fan or SRD 138/160 with AC.

🏠 **Bina's Inn Apartments** (26 rooms) 29 Hajary Straat; ☎473413/477535; m 8806941; e info@appartementenbina.com; www. appartementenbina.com. Under the same ownership as the adjacent Martin's House of Indian Food, this low-key apt complex wouldn't win any awards for slick architecture or tasteful décor, & rooms are very variable in standard, but it is a more than adequate budget option, particularly for students & other long-stay visitors. All rooms come with AC, satellite TV & fridge, & facilities include

free Wi-Fi, & inexpensive laundry & bike rental. Short-stay rates are SRD 92/115 sgl/dbl, dropping to SRD 50/92 per night for a week, or around SRD 35/53 per night for a month or longer.

🏠 **Guesthouse Kiwi** (16 rooms) Mahony Laan; ☎421374/471116. Split between 2 buildings a few doors apart some 10mins' walk east of the city centre, this adequate budget guesthouse has a variety of rooms sleeping from 2 to 5, all en suite & with AC & TV, but quite variable in size & quality, so ask to look at a few before you settle in. Facilities are limited but include a shared kitchen. From SRD 85 dbl to SRD 155 for a room sleeping 5.

🏠 **Zin Resort** (11 rooms) 20 Van Roosevelt Kade; ☎472224; e contact@ zinresort.sr, grandcafezin@gmail.com; www. zinguesthouseparamaribo.com. Better known for its large but rather murky swimming pool & bar than as a place to stay, this very central & budget lodge has adequate en-suite rooms with queen-size bed, AC, TV & free Wi-Fi. It is a bit of party spot, so rooms could be noisy at night, especially over w/ends. SRD 115/129 dbl with cold/hot shower or SRD 193 poolside dbl; rates exc b/fast but inc use of the pool.

✖ WHERE TO EAT AND DRINK *Map, pages 72–3, 80–1, 87, 91 and 120–1.*

The busiest cluster of tourist-oriented restaurants can be found in the small road triangle opposite the Torarica and Grand Torarica hotels. Predictably, most of the places here are on the pricey side, notable exceptions being the perennially popular Sidewalk Café t'Vat, which offers very reasonably priced daily menus, and the excellent Tangelo, a Torarica-affiliated coffee shop almost directly opposite it.

Those seeking the sort of breezy waterside ambience you'd expect from a port city such as Paramaribo should head towards the short stretch of riverfront running west from **Fort Zeelandia towards the Central Market**. Half a dozen good restaurants can be found in the area, several of them offering great views over the river, most notably the wallet-friendly Café Broki and somewhat pricier Baka Foto and Restaurant Jiji. Though it is set back from the water a little, Eetcafé de Gadri is perhaps the best traditional Javan-Surinamese eatery in the city centre.

Fast-food outlets, roti shops and sleazy-looking Chinese eateries dominate in **downtown** Paramaribo, particularly in the vicinity of the main bus station. However, two fine Asian eateries – the pricey Spice Quest and the more budget-friendly Dumpling #1 – can be found along JF Nassy Road, while Rituals Coffee House, in the lobby of the Hotel Krasnapolsky, is probably the finest such establishment in the city.

The restaurants listed **around the NVGB Stadium** all lie inland of the Palm Garden and to the northeast of Henck Arron Straat. They are all within easy walking distance of the waterfront, but are particularly convenient for those staying at Zus & Zo or at any of the quartet of budget to mid-range lodges along Jessurun and Coster roads.

Several good restaurants lie to the **east of the city centre**. Most of them are either on the Leonsberg road (aka Cornelis Jongbaw Straat/Anton Dragten Weg) or lie

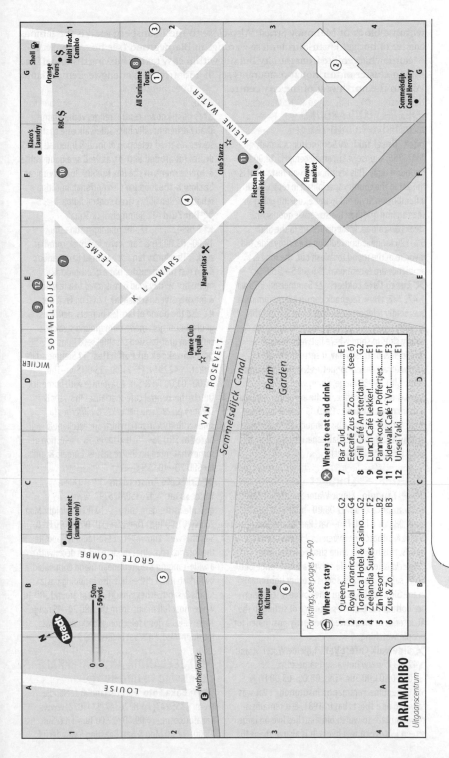

PARAMARIBO
Uitgaanscentrum

Netherlands

Palm
Garden

Sommelsdijck Canal

VAN ROSEVELT

Dance Club
Tequila ☆

Margeritas ✖

K L DWARS

Club Starzz ☆

Fietsen in
Suriname kiosk ●

Flower
market

KLEINE WATER

Sommelsdijk
Canal Heronry ●

All Suriname
Tours ●

Orange
Tours ●

Multi Track
Cambio $

Shell

RBC $

Klaco's
Laundry ●

Chinese market
(sunday only) ●

SOMMELSDIJK

WICLIER

LEEMS

GROTE COMBE

LOUISE

For listings, see pages 79–90

Where to stay

1	Queens.................................G2
2	Royal Torarica.....................G4
3	Torarica Hotel & Casino.....G2
4	Zeelandia Suites..................F2
5	Zin Resort............................B2
6	Zus & Zo..............................B3

Where to eat and drink

7	Bar Zuid..............................E1
	Eetcafé Zus & Zo..........(see 5)
8	Gril Café Amsterdam..........G2
9	Lunch Café Lekker!..............E1
10	Pannekoek en Poffertjes....F1
11	Sidewalk Café 't Vat...........F3
12	Unsei Yaki...........................E1

Bradt

N

0   50m
0   50yds

87

within a block of Mahoney Straat. Also close to the Leonsberg road is the famous cluster of budget Javan-Surinamese warungs in Blauwgrond (see box, page 93).

Somewhat remote from the city, but still within easy taxi or bussing distance (Line 1), is a cluster of top-notch restaurants set in and around Verlengde Gemenelands Weg to the **northwest of the city centre.**

TORARICA AND AROUND
Expensive to mid-range
✕ ✳ **Unsei Yaki** 20 Sommelsdijck Straat; ☎475755; e unseiyaki@gmail.com; ⊕ 18.00–midnight daily. This stylish, open-air restaurant is the 1st in the country specialised in teppanyaki, a flamboyant style of Japanese cooking using searing iron griddles. It also serves good sushi, steaks & seafood. Most dishes are in the SRD 60–120 range, admittedly on the pricey side, but if you're in the mood to splash out, the food & ambience are exceptional. $$$$$–$$$$
✕ **Lunch Café Lekker!** 22 Sommelsdijck Straat; ☎472722; www.facebook.com/lekkerparamaribo. Seemingly teleported directly from Europe, this brightly decorated contemporary continental eatery slots in somewhere between terrace café, deli & bistro. By day, it serve fresh salads, imaginatively filled baguettes & other light meals in the SRD 25–30 range, along with pastries, cakes & excellent coffee. In the evenings, the focus is more on pasta dishes (SRD 35–65) & grilled meat & fish (SRD 80-plus), though there are also usually a few cheaper daily specials. $$ (lunch); $$$$$–$$$ (dinner)

Mid-range to budget
✕ ✳ **Tangelo** Kleine Water Straat; ☎471500; www.torarica.com; ⊕ 08.00–midnight Sun–Wed, 08.00–01.00 Thu–Sat. Part of the Torarica Group & situated between its 2 more central hotels, this hybrid coffee shop, cocktail bar, *gelateria* & terrace café serves a great range of b/fasts, salads, burgers, soups & other light meals in the SRD 10–20 range. The coffee & ice cream are both good, & there's a choice of sitting in the AC interior or on a terrace perfectly positioned for people watching. $
✕ **Sidewalk Café 't Vat** 1 Kleine Water Straat; ☎424631; www.hetvatsuriname.com; ⊕ 08.00–01.00 Sun–Thu, 08.00–03.00 Fri & Sat. A genuine Paramaribo institution, 't Vat was founded as a sports bar in 1981, & it remains a popular place to watch big matches live on large-screen TVs over a few beers. It is also perhaps the

city's best-known central rendezvous, a large, shady & perennially busy sidewalk café that serves a varied selection of local & international dishes for around SRD 20, as well as a good-value 3-course menu of the day for SRD 30. Service can be slow & the food isn't exceptional, but it's a reliable & sensibly priced central fallback. $$
✕ **Bar Zuid** 17 Sommelsdijck Straat; m 8185425; ⊕ 17.00–midnight Sun–Thu, 17.00–03.00 Fri & Sat; www.facebook.com/bar.zuid.7. This funky terrace bar amid Paramaribo's main restaurant cluster has a good cocktail menu but w/day food is restricted to a few light & inexpensive snacks. After 17.00 on Fri & Sun, it's also the home of Big-Tex burgers, delicious gourmet burgers made from ground steak & served in grill-toasted sesame-seed buns. $
✕ **Pannekoek en Poffertjes** 11 Sommelsdijck Straat; ☎422914; ⊕ 11.00–23.00 Sun–Thu, 11.00–01.00 Fri & Sat. A favourite with homesick Dutch, this central café specialises in sweet & savoury pizza-style pancakes & *poffertjes* (a smaller fluffy variant), which are excellent & well priced at SRD 15–25. It also serves a selection of somewhat more mediocre salads, burgers & grills for SRD 20–40. $$$–$
✕ **Grill Café Amsterdam** 17–19 Klein Water Straat; ☎426450/426297; www. grillcafeamsterdam.com; ⊕ 10.00–midnight Mon, 10.00–01.00 Tue–Thu & Sun, 10.00–03.00 Fri & Sat. This well-known terrace restaurant opposite the Torarica combines modern urban décor with a wide-ranging Mediterranean menu dominated by Turkish meat dishes but also including pastas, salads & sandwiches. Snacks start at around SRD 10 while most full mains are in the SRD 20–45 range. There's also a good selection of cocktails & live music on Wed, Fri & Sat nights. $$$–$

FORT ZEELANDIA AND WATERKANT
Expensive to mid-range
✕ ✳ **Baka Foto** Fort Zeelandia, Zeelandia Weg; ☎355243; m 8226347/8745078; www. bakafoto.com; ⊕ 09.00–22.00 Tue–Fri & Sun, 18.00–22.00 Mon & Sat. Boasting a wonderful

riverfront setting in Fort Zeelandia, this stylish continental restaurant leads a double life as an affordable brasserie by day & a pricier fine-dining venue by night. In its 1st incarnation, it serves a decent selection of salads, sandwiches & light meals, mostly for around SRD 17–35, making it a great place to break up a day's sightseeing for lunch of coffee. By contrast, most mains on the altogether more adventurous continental-Asian fusion dinner menu are in the SRD 70–90 range, & there is also a 4-course gourmet set menu for SRD 180 (food only) or SRD 230 (including specially selected wines with each course). $$–$ (lunch); $$$$$ (dinner)

✗ **Restaurant Jiji** SMS Pier, Waterkant; ☏450899; m 8871555/8626525; e restaurantjiji@gmail.com; ☺ 09.00–14.00 Mon–Fri, 18.00–23.00 daily. Although the prime 1st-floor location overlooking the river is probably a bigger attraction than the rather variable food, this lively & breezy terrace restaurant does serve a good selection of tasty & imaginative international grills in the SRD 45–55 range, as well as burgers & other light meals, mostly for around SRD 30, on a separate 'student menu' (which anybody can order from). $$$$–$$

✗ **Ristorante Italiano De Waag** 5 Waterkant; ☏474514; e rest.dewaag@live.com. Situated in a restored *waaghuis* ('weighing house'), this stylish & well-established waterfront restaurant is known for its pleasant courtyard ambience, attentive service & quality Italian food. The lunch menu includes a good selection of filled *paninis*, burgers, salads & other light meals in the SRD 20–30 range, but dinner is a pricier affair, with pasta dishes for around SRD 50–55 & grills & seafood upwards of SRD 60. $$ (lunch); $$$$ (dinner)

Mid-range to budget
✗ ☀ **Eetcafé de Gadri** 1 Zeelandia Weg; ☏420688; m 8555173; e degradr@sr.net; ☺ 08.00–22.00 Mon–Fri, 11.00–22.00 Sat. Boasting a fabulous riverfront location opposite Fort Zeelandia, this a great place to punctuate a day of sightseeing with an affordable alfresco lunch. Choose from sandwiches in the SRD 8–13 range or a full plate of local specialities such as *bami*, *nasi*, rice or *pom* with chicken, fish, beef, pork or vegetable stew for SRD 20–32. $$

✗ **Café Broki** 5 Waterkant; m 7132538; www.facebook.com/BrokiCafe; ☺ 07.00–15.00

& 17.00–late Tue–Sun. This café-bar has one of the most attractive locations in the city, with a characterful interior leading out to a breezy wooden deck lapped by the Suriname River. It also has pool tables, plays contemporary music at a comfortable volume, & serves a varied menu of local & international dishes, all sensibly priced at around SRD 25–30. True, the food won't win any awards but it's not bad, & the riverfront setting more than compensates. $$

✗ **Grand Roopram Roti Restaurant** 37 Watermolen Straat; ☏410641; www. grandroopramroti.com; ☺ 08.00–15.00 Mon–Sat. The most central outlet of Suriname's most popular home-grown fast-food chain, open for lunch only & serves the usual tasty chicken, vegetable & other rotis for SRD 15–20. $

✗ **KFC** 74–76 Waterkant; ☏422272; ☺ 09.00–23.00 Mon–Thu, 09.00–05.30 Fri & Sat, 10.00–23.30 Sun. For those in need of a late night grease fix, this AC outlet of the international chain serves meal combos from around SRD 20 upwards. $$

DOWNTOWN
Expensive to mid-range
✗ ☀ **Spice Quest** 107 Dr JF Nassy Laan; ☏520747; m 8599920; www.facebook.com/ SpiceQuest; ☺ 11.00–15.00 & 18.00–23.00 daily. A contender for the top fine-dining restaurant in Suriname, & priced accordingly, Spice Quest boasts an eclectic fusion menu of seafood, poultry & red meat dishes, mostly with an Asian or Mediterranean influence. Starters are in the SRD 30–40 range, while mains mostly come in at SRD 75–90, & desserts at SRD 25. The high quality of the food is matched by the romantic nocturnal ambience of the garden seating, & the classy Japanese room with low tables. It occasionally hosts live music. $$$$$

✗ **Sushi Ya** 63 Henck Arron Straat; ☏475450; www.sushiyasuriname.com; ☺ 18.00–23.00 Tue–Sun. With its swish modern interior, attentive service & high-quality Japanese cuisine, this under-publicised restaurant on the edge of the old town is a must for aficionados of tempura, sushi, teriyaki & the like. Seafood dominates, as might be expected, but it also offers a few tempting meat & chicken dishes. Expect to pay around SRD 50–90 for a sushi selection or full main. $$$$$–$$$$

Mid-range to budget

✕✳ **Dumpling #1** 12 Dr JF Nassy Laan; ☎477904; m 8599920; ⏱ 11.00–15.00 Tue–Sun, 18.00–23.00 daily. Probably the best Chinese eatery in the city centre, this long-serving garden restaurant serves a limited selection of tasty meat & vegetable mains, mostly for around SRD 28, but shrimp dishes cost SRD 45. The Spanish pepper & beef is recommended for those who enjoy plenty of spice & crisp vegetables. Good value & a pleasant place to sit. $$$–$$

☕✳ **Rituals Coffee House** 39 Dominee Straat; ☎475050/420139; www.rituals.sr; ⏱ 07.30–20.00 Mon–Thu, 07.30–22.00 Fri, 08.00–22.00 Sat, 09.00–20.00 Sun. Situated in the AC lobby of the Hotel Krasnapolsky, this well-priced coffee house serves arguably the best coffee & most sumptuous range of cakes in town, along with a good selection of sweet & savoury pastries, sandwiches, snacks, soups & smoothies, mostly for under SRD 15. A great spot for a relaxed b/fast or to rest during a downtown stroll. $

✕ **Joosje Roti Shop** 9 Zwartenhovenbrug Straat; ☎472606; ⏱ 08.00–22.00 Mon–Sat. This long-serving Indian eatery has a clean AC interior, & serves delicious chicken, lamb, duck & vegetarian rotis for around SRD 15. $

✕ **Fa Tai Restaurant** 64 Maagden Straat; ☎420051/473917; m 8898888; www.fatai. sr.org; ⏱ 10.30–15.00 & 18.00–22.30 daily. This well-priced & long-serving central Chinese eatery serves a wide selection of meat & veggie dishes for around SRD 15–29, & is close to the main bus station. It's mainly a take-away, but you can also eat in the AC interior. $$–$

✕ **Grand Roopram Roti Restaurant** 23 Zwartenhovenbrug Straat; ☎410338; www. grandroopramroti.com; ⏱ 08.00–23.00 daily. The downtown outlet of Suriname's most popular home-grown fast-food chain keeps long hours & serves the usual tasty chicken, vegetable & other rotis for SRD 15–20. $

✕ **Burger King** Groot Kerk Straat; ☎470062; www.burgerking.sr; ⏱ 10.00–22.00 Mon–Thu, 10.00–23.00 Fri & Sat, 16.00–23.00 Sun. This downtown franchise has a daily deal at SRD 15, full meals in the SRD 20–30 range, blasting AC & free Wi-Fi. $$–$

✕ **McDonald's** Keizer Straat; ☎425778; ⏱ 09.00–23.30 Mon–Sat, 11.00–23.00 Sun. The downtown outlet of this global franchise serves the usual combos & meals, starting at SRD 18, & it also has free Wi-Fi & AC. There's a 2nd outlet in Heritage Mall. $$–$

AROUND NVGB STADIUM
Expensive to mid-range

✕✳ **Eetcafé Zus & Zo** 13a Grote Combe Weg; ☎520905; www.zusenzosuriname.com; ⏱ 09.00–23.00 Mon–Sat, 11.00–17.00 Sun. Among the most popular rendezvous points in Paramaribo, this funky open-air café opposite the Palm Gardens serves a varied lunch menu of sandwiches, salads, soups, burgers & other light meals in the SRD 17–40 range, while the continent-hopping dinner menu incorporates the likes of Moroccan stew, Mexican burger, Creole chicken & spicy prawn pasta, with most mains costing around SRD 40. It's a very relaxed & friendly set-up with multi-lingual waiters, contemporary music, free Wi-Fi, a well-stocked bar, & live music & other events most w/ends. $$$–$$

✕ **La Cuisine** Cnr Tourtonne Laan & Koninginne Straat; ☎425656; ⏱ noon–22.00 Mon–Thu, noon–23.00 Fri & Sat. This unpretentious eatery with spotless AC indoor seating & a shady terrace serves a few daily local specials for around SRD 25, as well as a varied selection of international dishes, from lasagne & pasta to chops or steak with a choice of mashed or sautéed potatoes, for SRD 35–70. $$$$–$$

PARAMARIBO *East Central*
For listings, see pages 82–94

⌂ **Where to stay**

1	Bini's Inn Apartments	E1
2	Cardy Apartments	C3
3	Courtyard Marriott Paramaribo	G3
4	Eco Resort Inn	C4
5	Guesthouse Kiwi	C1
6	Rachel's Apartments	C1

✕ **Where to eat and drink**

7	Bistro Don Julio	C1
8	Chi Min	E3
9	Lee's Korean	E3
	Martin's House of Indian Food	(see 1)
10	Palm Palace	D4
11	Pizza Hut	D1
12	Rita's Roti Shop	B1
13	Tangelo	B4

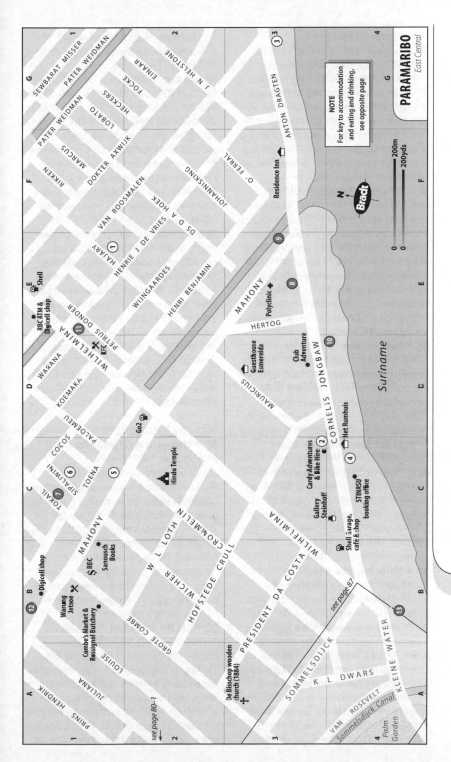

PARAMARIBO
East Central

NOTE
For key to accommodation
and eating and drinking,
see opposite page

Mid-range to budget

✗ ✳ Souposo 20a Coster Straat; ☏420351; **m** 8649893; **e** soupososuriname@gmail.com; ⊕ 10.00–23.00 Mon–Sat. This funky modern café has an attractively decorated interior as well as comfortable outdoor seating in a secluded back garden. The speciality, as the name suggests, is the soup of the day, but it also offers a tantalising menu of salads & sandwiches, all in the SRD 15–20 range, as well as full meals for SRD 40–50. Vegetarians are unusually well catered for here. **$$$–$**

✗ ✳ Sieng Jong Restaurant 21 Tourtonne Laan; ☏421049/478539; ⊕ 11.00–23.00 daily. Close to the several budget lodges along Jessurun & Coster roads, this may not look like anything special from the outside, but it serves excellent & well-priced Chinese food for around SRD 15–28 (the piquant prawns are spicily superb) & also has a very friendly owner & keeps long hours. It's mainly a take-away, but chilled beers & other drinks are served, & there are a few plastic tables if you want to eat here. **$$–$**

✗ ✳ Carili Roti Shop 6 Juliana Straat; ☏470055; ⊕ 06.30–14.30 Mon–Fri, 07.30–noon Sat. Centrally located but with a defiantly un-touristy vibe, this friendly owner-managed hole-in-the-wall must rank as the city's best-value lunch option, serving delicious chicken rotis & other Indian dishes to eat in or take-away for around SRD 10 per plate. **$**

✗ Rita's Roti Shop Verlengde Mahony Laan; ☏420625; ⊕ 08.30–17.00 Mon–Fri, 09.30–16.00 Sat. This clean & reasonably central fan-cooled local eatery serves great chicken rotis, plus regularly changing daily specials & other Surinamese dishes, mostly for under SRD 15. **$**

EAST OF THE CITY CENTRE
Expensive to mid-range

✗ ✳ Bistro Don Julio 6 Tokai Laan; **m** 7110703/8902169; www.bistrodonjulio. com; ⊕ 18.00–01.00 Tue–Sun. Tucked away on a side street off Mahony Laan about 1km east of the city centre, this characterful bar & restaurant is worth going out of your way for, especially on Wed, Fri, Sat & Sun nights, when there's live Latino or jazz music from around 20.30 onwards. A cosmopolitan tapas menu of Dutch, Asian & Mediterranean plates, mostly for under SRD 20 is complemented by an à la carte selection strong on seafood & grilled meats in the SRD 65–120 range. Vegetarians are less well catered for, but

the homemade spinach & feta ravioli (SRD 70) is something of a speciality. **$** (per tapas plate); **$$$$$–$$$$** (mains)

✗ Lee's Korean Restaurant 12–14 Mahony Laan; ☏479834; ⊕ 11.00–14.30 & 18.00–22.30 Mon–Sat. Widely regarded as one of the top Asian eateries in a city where there is no shortage, long-serving Lee's specialises in Korean cuisine but it also has a good selection of more familiar Chinese dishes for less adventurous palates. Seafood is particularly well represented, & there is plenty of choice on the meat front too, but vegetarians are more or less neglected. Mains are mostly in the SRD 40–55 range. **$$$$–$$$**

✗ Botralie Restaurant 215 Anton Dragten Weg; ☏559400; **m** 8873659/8720306; www. colonialresortsuriname.net; ⊕ noon–15.00 & 18.00–midnight Mon–Sat. Part of the soon-to-open Colonial Resort, this stylish restaurant has indoor & terrace seating in a classically decorated 19th-century plantation house looking out onto a lush green garden. The speciality is lava stone grills (you cook the meat or fish at your table on a flat volcanic stone pre-heated to 400°C in a special oven), but it also serves a variety of pasta & other dishes. Mains are mostly in the SRD 55–95 range. **$$$$$–$$$$**

Mid-range to budget

✗ ✳ Martin's House of Indian Food 29 Hajary Straat; ☏477535; www. appartementenbina.com/EN/martin.htm; ⊕ 11.00–23.00 daily. Roti shops excluded, Indian cuisine has a surprisingly low profile in Paramaribo, so this good-value genuine Hindustani eatery 1km east of the city centre is well worth the short walk or taxi ride. The extensive menu includes tandoor, curry & biryani dishes, most around SRD 20 including rice or naan bread, & unusually vegetarians have plenty of choice. There's the choice of terrace or AC indoor seating, & a good range of alcoholic drinks supplemented by lassis. **$$–$**

✗ ✳ Chi Min Restaurant 83 Cornelis Jongbaw Straat; ☏412155/427084; www. chimin-restaurant.com; ⊕ 10.00–23.00 daily. This long-serving, sprawling & perennially popular Chinese eatery, 5–10mins' walk east of the city centre, might be somewhat over the top on the oriental retro décor front, but the food is very good & the extensive menu caters to all tastes, including vegetarian. The meat & seafood sizzler plates are

CHEAP EATS IN BLAUWGROND

Regarded as the culinary heart of Javan-Surinamese cuisine, the suburb of Blauwgrond ('Blue Ground') is also the home of Paramaribo's best-known cluster of local eateries: the dozen-or-so warungs that flank Josephine Samson (JS) Green Straat, some 4km northeast of the city centre. Inexpensive, unpretentious and emphatically not aimed at tourists, these warungs are clustered within a few hundred metres along what is otherwise a mainly residential suburban road (walking here from the nearest bus route in either direction, you could be forgiven for thinking you're in the wrong place). Collectively, the warungs of Blauwgrond also form the quintessential Paramaribo culinary experience, even if the food at many of them is little different from what is served at similar local eateries countrywide. Note that many of the warungs in this predominantly Islamic area don't serve alcohol, but it is acceptable to bring your own (a couple of supermarkets selling beer are squeezed between the restaurants). Most locals have their favourite Blauwgrond warung, and while it would be pointless to list them all, here are a few (all on JS Green Straat) that stand out:

✕ ✳ **Jakarta Taste of Java** ☏ 456513; m 8873782; ⏱ 13.00–22.30 Tue–Thu, noon–22.30 Fri–Sun. Set in relative isolation a couple of hundred metres southeast of the main cluster of warungs, this exceptional terrace restaurant serves the usual Javan-Surinamese dishes as well as a great selection of genuine Javan cuisine (stir-fries, curries in coconut milk). Prices are more than reasonable (most mains SRD 18–20 with a few at SRD 30) & beer & wine are also served by the glass. Admittedly it feels less authentic than most of its neighbours, but it's a real gem nonetheless! $$–$

✕ **Warung Renah** ☏ 450987; ⏱ 18.00–midnight Wed & Thu, 18.00–01.00 Fri & Sat, 14.00–21.00 Sun. Popular family-run warung with a nice garden, varied menu & large portions, particularly well known for its fried cassava. Standard portions SRD 15–20. $

✕ **Mirosso Indonesian Restaurant** ☏ 455362; e mirosso@sr.net; ⏱ 18.00–midnight Tue–Sun. More than 20

years old, this award-winning Blauwgrond eatery is relatively upmarket & one of the few that serve alcohol. The menu is especially varied, with several dishes we've not seen elsewhere else, including *bami putih* (marinated noodles with egg, chicken & shrimp) *nasi ayam opor* (rice with coconut chicken curry) & curried duck. Most mains are SRD 28–30. $$

✕ **Warung Manis** ☏ 450942; ⏱ 11.00–midnight daily. Unlike most of the cheaper warungs, this opens for lunch as well as dinner. Typical Javan-Surinamese fare in the SRD 10–16 range, including excellent *satao* (chicken soup), is served on a brightly painted terrace with a terracotta tiled floor. $

✕ **AJ's Indo Food House** m 8482150; e ajindofoodhouse@hotmail.com; ⏱ noon–midnight daily. Set in a shady terrace with relatively modern décor, this vibrant place has a particularly varied menu, & is probably the best option in Blauwgrond for vegetarians. Mains SRD 15–20. $

To get to Blauwgrond, a taxi from the city centre shouldn't set you back more than SRD 15, and you can either ask it to collect you later, or else get the restaurant where you eat to call you another taxi when you are ready. Alternatively, PG buses from the Waterkant to Geyersvlijt run about 500m northwest of the main cluster of warungs (ask to disembark at the junction of RW Thurkow and JS Green Straat), while Line 4 buses to Leonsberg pass by to the southeast (hop off at the junction of Commissioner Roble Straat, shortly before the residence of the US Ambassador).

particularly recommended. Take-away available. Most mains are in the SRD 25–35 range. $$

✕ Palm Palace Restaurant 34–36 Cornelis Jongbaw Straat; ✆476427–9; www.palmpalace-restaurant.com; ⏱ 11.00–15.30 & 18.30–23.00 daily. Situated 500m east of the city centre next to Eco Resort Inn, this 2-storey Chinese restaurant sadly makes little effort to capitalise on its riverside position, but the food is better than adequate & the extensive menu, including the likes of ginger mussels, spicy shrimp, roast duck & stuffed veggies, is one of the few in central Suriname with a dedicated vegetarian section. Most mains are around SRD 25, but some are pricier. $$

✕ Lucky Twins Restaurant Maretraite Mall, 118 Jan Steen Straat; ✆458188; www.lucky-twins.com; ⏱ 11.30–16.00 & 17.30–22.00 daily. Located in a large mall some distance east of the city centre, Lucky Twins is probably a bit out of the way for most tourists, & you certainly shouldn't come here expecting intimacy or ambience (it proudly claims to be largest restaurant in the Caribbean, with seating for 1,200) but the food has been praised by locals & the menu certainly doesn't lack for variety. Mains start at around SRD 30. $$

✕ Pizza Hut 60 Wilhelmina Straat; ✆42444; ⏱ 11.00–23.00 Sun–Thu, 11.00–midnight Fri & Sat. Pizza lovers are usually poorly catered for in Suriname, a notable exception being this solitary outlet of the popular international franchise about 1km east of the city centre. It serves a good selection of pasta dishes, too. Pizzas start at around SRD 20. $$

✕ Subway TBL Mall, 79 Lalla Rook Weg; ✆530825; ⏱ 08.00–23.30 Mon–Sat, 11.00–23.30 Sun. Situated next to the landmark Heritage Mall, the Surinamese franchise of this popular sandwich & pizza outlet has filled subs starting from around SRD 17. $$–$

NORTHWEST OF THE CITY CENTRE
Expensive to mid-range

✕ ✳ Garden of Eden 61 Virola Straat; ✆499448; ⏱ 18.00–23.00 Mon–Sat. This Thai restaurant & lounge bar is among the highly regarded places to eat in Paramaribo. The elaborately decorated interior is adorned with an eclectic mix of vintage Asian & other artefacts, while the lovingly lit garden dining area exudes a leafy tropical ambience. Bona fide Thai chefs ensure that the delicately spiced coconut curries, stir-fries & other Thai dishes are both genuine & scrumptious. Soups & appetisers

cost around SRD 35, while mains – dominated by seafood & chicken, but with a handful of vegetarian options – are in the SRD 60–70 range. There is a good wine list too, with most bottles priced at around SRD 140. Space is limited & the restaurant is very popular & somewhat isolated, so booking is strongly recommended. $$$$$

✕ Café d'Optimist 200 Verlengde Gemenelands Weg; ✆495009; ▫ 8778939; www.cafedoptimist.com; ⏱ 18.00–24.00 Mon–Sat. Founded in 2001 & now something of a Paramaribo institution, this cosy & cheerful continental restaurant, about 7km west of the city centre, has terrace seating & a great cocktail menu. It is renowned for its excellent steaks & its baked fish, mostly in the SRD 60–75 range, but also serves pasta dishes & salads for around SRD 40–45, as well as burgers for under SRD 20. All dishes are freshly prepared, so service tends to be on the slow side. $$$$–$

Mid-range to budget

✕ ✳ Sarinah Restaurant 187 Verlengde Gemenelands Weg; ✆430661/492045; ✉ restaurantsarinah1974@hotmail.com; ⏱ 07.30–22.00 Mon–Sat. Having started life as a mom-&-pop garage-based warung in 1974, this Indonesian restaurant & take-away has since grown to become one of Paramaribo's best-known culinary landmarks. The interior, dotted with ponds, bamboo stands & breezy fans, has a rather garden-like feel, & the varied menu incorporates some 80 dishes, mostly fish- or chicken-based, & in the SRD 30–40 range. The house speciality, costing SRD 55, is *rijssttafel* (literally 'rice table'), a unique Dutch-Indonesian hybrid which (rather like Mediterranean *meze*) comprises some 15 different small dishes. $$$$–$$

✕ Gina's Restaurant 201 Verlengde Gemenelands Weg; ✆498563; ▫ 8251234; ✉ ginasrestaurant@gmail.com; ⏱ 11.00–20.00 Mon–Thu, 11.00–midnight Fri & Sat, noon–18.00 Sun. Located directly opposite the better-known Café d'Optimist, this friendly owner-managed Brazilian restaurant has pleasant terrace seating & a meat-dominated menu. It specialises in sizzling chapa hot plates, which cost SRD 55–120, depending on size, while other meat mains are in the range of SRD 30–40. The lunchtime buffet, which is charged at SRD 70 per kilo, is excellent value. $$$$$–$$$

ART GALLERIES Exhibitions featuring contemporary Surinamese artworks are held at the following galleries:

Gallery Steinhoff [91 C4] 13 Cornelis Jongbaw Straat; ☎421146; e gallerysteinhoff@sr.net
House of Art [87 G4] Royal Torarica Hotel, 10

Kleine Water Straat; ☎473821; m 8553525
Readytex Gallery [80 C6] 44–48 Maagden Straat; ☎421750/474380; www.readytexartgallery.com

CINEMA AND THEATRE TBL Cinemas [72 A5] (*79 Lalla Rookh Weg;* ☎ *463737; www.tblcinemas.com; www.facebook.com/tblcinemas;* ⊕ *box office opens from 13.00 Mon–Fri, from 11.30 Sat & Sun; SRD 19.50, with a small discount offered to pensioners & children under 12, 50% discount for everyone on Tue*) is a modern multi-screen complex based in the TBL Mall, next to Hermitage Mall and accessible on a Line 1 bus from the city centre. It usually screens around eight different films daily, including the latest Hollywood blockbusters and a slimmer selection of films from India and Europe (see the website for the latest schedule). Screenings are usually in the evenings.

The **Jeugdtheaterschool** (Youth Theatrical School) puts on regular performances at the historic Patronage Building on Wulfingh Straat, which was converted into a 200-seater On Stage Theatre in 2007. For further details, visit the office at 5 Wulfingh Straat [81 F5] (☎ *471410/471409;* ⊕ *09.00–17.00 Mon–Fri*) or visit the website www.jeugdtheaterschool-onstage.com.

Occasional theatre performances are also staged at the 500-seat auditorium of the **Thalia Theatre** [80 C4] (*4 JF Nassy Laan;* ☎*472812*), which opened in 1840 as the home of the Thalia Dramatic Society (now the oldest theatre company in the Caribbean) and was renovated in 2011 after having stood semi-derelict since the 1990s.

SWIMMING Despite its riverfront location close to the sea, there is nowhere to swim in Paramaribo except for a few hotel or public pools. If your hotel doesn't have a pool, your best bet is the central **Zin Resort** [87 B2] (*20 Van Rosevelt Kade;* ☎*472224;* ⊕ *from 09.00 daily*), which is two blocks inland of Klein Water Start and charges SRD 15 per person. Most other hotels will allow non-guests to use their pool for a fee. The closest swimming beach to Paramaribo is White Beach, on the Suriname River just past Domberg.

NIGHTLIFE

Bars Many of the restaurants listed in the preceding pages also double as bars, notably **Sidewalk Café t'Vat** [87 F3] and **Bar Zuid** [87 E1] in the Uitgaanscentrum opposite the Torarica Hotel, **Café Broki** [81 E7] with its idyllic riverside location on the Waterkant, and the more out of town **Botralie Restaurant** [off map, 73 H4]. Other popular bar-like restaurants that also put on live music some nights are the very central **Grill Café Amsterdam** [87 G2] (live music Wednesday, Friday and Saturday) and **Eetcafé Zus & Zo** [87 B3] (live music some weekends), and **Bistro Don Julio** [91 C1] (live music Wednesday, Friday, Saturday and Sunday). A popular and less touristy spot for a few cheap alfresco riverside drinks is the row of mostly anonymous local bars set along the Waterkant between Fort Zeelandia and the SMS Pier.

Nightclubs Nightclubs are not well represented in Paramaribo, and places tend to open and close with great regularity. Probably the best known is the relaxed **Havana Lounge** [72 D6] (*13 Van 't Hogerhuys Straat;* ☎*402258;* ⊕ *21.00–late Thu–Sat*), which lies 2km southwest of the city centre near the harbour. Nearby, another

Paramaribo   ENTERTAINMENT AND NIGHTLIFE   5

popular and long-serving club is the flashy **Zsa Zsa Zsu** [72 C5] (*236 JA Pengel Straat;* \ *400993; www.suitnv.com/club;* ⏰ *23.00–05.30 Fri & Sat*), which has two dance floors, one playing the latest club and reggae music aimed at the under 20s and the other a more chilled selection of oldies catering to the over 30s.

A more central stalwart is **Club Touché** [80 A6] (*Cnr Dr Sophie Redmond & Waaldijk Straat;* \ *401181; www.clubtouche.com*), which first opened its doors in 1984 and reopened in 2010 after extensive modernisation. The central Uitgaanscentrum is home to the trendy new **Dance Club Tequila** [87 D2] (*4 Van Rosevelt Kade; www.danceclubtequila.com; www.facebook.com/danceclubtequila;* ⏰ *23.00–05.00 Fri & Sat*) and the older and sleazier **Club Starzz** [87 F3] (*5–7 Kleine Water Straat;* m *7100710;* ⏰ *22.00–03.00 Wed–Sat*). Further out of town, **The Cage** (*1 Condor Straat;* m *8708680; www.facebook.com/TheCaveSuriname;* ⏰ *18.00–02.00 Thu, 22.00–04.00 Fri & Sat*) is a trendy new dance spot situated in Leonsberg's Stardust Hotel.

Casinos A striking feature of central Paramaribo is its glut of casinos. There must be half a dozen of them clustered in the small Uitgaanscentrum, and twice as many in the main downtown road grid inland of the Waterkant. The largest is the **Suriname Princess Casino** [80 C4] (*Cnr Zwartenhovenbrug & Wagenweg Straat; www.worldofprincess.com;* ⏰ *10.00–04.00 Mon–Thu, 10.00–06.00 Fri–Sun)*, which has a 1,200m² gaming area offering 12 different table games as well as a large array of slot machines. There are also plenty of others to choose from, including those attached to the Torarica, Queens and Best Western hotels.

SHOPPING

There is no shortage of shops in downtown Paramaribo, ranging from ubiquitous supermarkets to smaller shops specialising in anything from CDs, books, glasses or shoes to stationery. As a rule, the more Westernised shops that are likely to be of interest to tourists can be found in and around Dominee Straat, but there are also several relatively upmarket clothes boutiques on the ground floor of the small but central SMS Pier Mall on the Waterkant.

MALLS Outside the city centre, Paramaribo's largest suburban shopping hub is the sprawling **Hermitage Mall** [72 A5] (*229 Lalla Rookh Road;* \ *463295; www.facebook.com/HermitageMall;* ⏰ *09.00–21.00 Mon–Sat, 16.00–21.00 Sun*) that incorporates several upmarket clothes boutiques, as well as banks, a bookshop, a pharmacy and fast-food outlets such as McDonald's and Subway. Right next door to it is the **TBL Mall** [72 A5], home to the country's main cinema complex (see page 95). Line 1 buses run to the mall from Dr Sophie Redmond Straat.

Less interesting to tourists is the **Maretraite Mall** [73 G3] (sometimes spelled Ma Retraite; *118 Jan Steen Straat;* \ *459020;* ⏰ *09.00–21.00 Mon–Sat, 09.00–16.00 Sun*), which houses at least a dozen upmarket clothes shops, a Digicel service centre, several ATMs, a jewellery shop, and a first-floor food court where perhaps ten fast-food outlets specialise in everything from fried seafood and Italian coffee to Surinamese-style Indian and Javan staples. Maretraite Mall can be reached on PG Line buses from the Waterkant to Geyersvlijt.

MARKETS As much a cultural experience as a place to go shopping, the labyrinthine **Central Market** [80 C7] (⏰ *in theory 05.00–17.00 Mon–Sat, but it is generally busiest before noon*) on the Waterkant spans two storeys and is home to more than 3,000 permanent stalls. The market is divided into several different sections, with meat, fish, fruit and vegetables, Javan and Indian spices and herbs, household items and hardware dominating the ground floor, whereas the first floor is stacked high with clothes, fabrics and the like. A separate entrance to the west of the main market leads to the fascinating **Marron Market**, which specialises in traditional remedies and has a very African feel. The other central market often frequented by tourists is the **Kleine Water Straat Flower Market** [87 F3] in front of the Grand Torarica Hotel, where there are also a couple of craft stalls.

Even though the Central Market closes on a Sunday, this is an excellent day to explore a scattering of smaller (mostly suburban) specialist markets that are open in the morning only. The most central of these is the traditional **Chinese Market** [87 B1] (on the corner of Sommelsdijck Straat and Grote Combe Weg), which caters mainly to local Chinese (many stall owners speak little or no Dutch or English) and stocks a number of rather mysterious products. About 1km east of the city centre, Dutch and some English is spoken at the less traditional **Wilhelmina Straat Chinese Market** [73 G3] (on the corner with David Simons Straat), which caters mainly to other Surinamese, and sells good dim sum, other snacks, cakes, *bapao*, vegetables and plants. Also quite central, the sprawling multi-cultural **Tourtonne Flea Market** (on the corner of Tourtonne and Mahony Laan [81 H1]) is a good place to buy fruit, vegetables and other food, as well as secondhand clothes, utensils, books and such. Further northeast, out past the Maretraite Mall, **Saoena Market** (on the corner of Jozef Israel and Anamoe Straat [73 G2]) is a predominantly Javanese set-up selling Javanese food, vegetables, plants, flowers and other fresh produce. Finally, the charming **Plants and Flower Market** (off Letitia Vriesde Laan) lies below the shady trees of the Cultuurtuin's botanical garden, close to Paramaribo Zoo [73 E2].

FOOD In Paramaribo, you are never very far from a **supermarket**, which will nearly always be run by 'new' Chinese immigrants (who tend to speak very little Dutch or English). These supermarkets will generally keep very long hours (typically 07.00–22.00) and will stock a fairly predictable range of local and imported dried packaged items such as rice, cereals, pasta, tinned vegetables, biscuits, sweets, chocolate, crisps, etc. Fresh and perishable goods tend to be in shorter supply, but some supermarkets also sell frozen meat, a limited selection of fresh fruit and vegetables, and packaged cheese and cold meats. Almost all supermarkets sell cold beers and soft drinks, and many also sell a selection of wine and spirits. Recommending individual supermarkets feels like a fairly pointless task, since they are much the same.

There are often good **grocery shops** attached to filling stations and the Shell one at the junction of Cornelis Jongbaw and Wilhelmina Straats, though pricier than most Chinese supermarkets, is a good option for those staying in or around the Torarica Hotel. It sells relatively cheap take-away sandwiches and coffee, alcoholic and non-alcoholic beverages, and other imported goodies.

Self-caterers should visit the central outlet of **Rossignol Deli & Butchery** [80 B5] (*4 Weide Straat;* ℡*420984;* ⏰ *07.00–17.00 Mon–Fri, 07.00–14.00 Sat*), which stocks an exceptional selection of cold meats, cheeses, fresh produce and other quality delicacies seldom seen in normal supermarkets. There are also less central branches at the northwest end of Grote Combe Weg [91 B1] (next to Combe's Market) and on Verlengde Gemenelands Weg [72 B4].

Another worthwhile stop for self-caterers is **Soeng Ngie's Oriental Market** [73 G3] (*www.soengco.com*), which was established in 1939. It stocks a vast array of Asian spices and sauces, herbal teas, dried foods and other oriental delicacies.

The original shop is at 86 Waterkant (❨ 472031; ⏰ 07.30–16.00 Mon, Tue, Thu & Fri, 07.30–13.00 Wed & Sat) but there is a newer and larger branch in Rainville, east of the city centre (junction Wilhelmina & David Simon Straats; ❨ 550140/4; ⏰ 08.00–20.00 Mon–Thu, 08.00–21.00 Fri & Sat, 08.00–noon Sun).

HANDICRAFTS Best known as a restaurant, **Zus & Zo** (see page 90) has an excellent first-floor arts and gift shop (⏰ 08.00–19.00 daily) selling paintings, prints and decorated woodwork items made by local craftspeople, as well as items imported from parts of Asia and Africa. Otherwise, the best-known retail outlet for local handicrafts and art is the **Readytex Art Gallery** [80 C6] (44–48 Maagden Straat; ❨ 421750; www.readytexartgallery.com; ⏰ 08.00–16.30 Mon–Fri, 08.30–13.30 Sat), which represents around 20 local painters and sculptors, and also stocks crafts produced by more than 50 different artisans, as well as postcards, souvenir clothing and caps, and lots of cheaper trinkets. A good place to buy printed cloths and fabrics in African, Asian and Marron style is **Jeruzalem Bazaar** (see below).

HAMMOCKS AND OUTDOOR GEAR If you are looking to buy a hammock and mosquito net for travel outside Paramaribo, the best place to do this is **Jeruzalem Bazaar** [80 A7] (42 Saramacca Straat; ❨ 475060; ⏰ 07.30–16.15 Mon–Fri, 07.30–12.45 Sat) a few minutes' walk southwest of the Central Market. There are two types of hammock for sale: Brazilian ones with decorative edges and Surinamese ones with plain edges. Single hammocks start at around SRD 30, two-person hammocks at around SRD 45 and mosquito nets at around SRD 30. The shop also sells other gear that might be useful for people travelling in the interior, as well as hundreds of different printed cloths.

MUSIC B-Music [81 E6] (40 Keizer Straat; m 8577975; e moetjaggoe@yahoo.com; www.bmusiccddvd.webs.com; ⏰ 07.00–16.30 Mon–Fri) is a central CD and DVD shop that stocks a great selection of harder to find and current Surinamese traditional, golden oldie and contemporary music, most of it available in MP3 or CD format.

BOOKS In addition to the shops listed below, a good selection of books about Surinamese history is stocked in the **Fort Zeelandia Museum shop** (see page 104), and the **STINASU booking office** (see pages 77–8) is a good place to buy a range of titles about the primates and birds of Suriname. The gift shop at Zus & Zo (see page 90) also stocks a few worthwhile books and maps covering Paramaribo and the rest of the country.

Book Affairs [81 E6] 8 Kerk Plein; ❨ 410462; m 8969452; www.bookaffairssuriname.com; ⏰ 07.30–14.30 Mon–Fri, 09.00–13.00 Sat. This small bookshop sells predominantly secondhand books & stocks a limited selection of English-language novels. This is also a good place to look for out-of-print works about Suriname. An internet café is attached.

Faranaz Book Shop [72 A5] Hermitage Mall; ❨ 530653; ⏰ 09.00–21.00 Mon–Sat, 16.00–21.00 Sun. Though not as well-stocked as the more central Vaco, this shop has a good range of books about Suriname & also a range of mostly Dutch-language fiction.

Sanousch Books [91 B1] 67 Mahony Laan; ❨ 478697/8; ⏰ 09.00–20.00 Mon–Fri, 08.30–20.00 Sat. This large bookshop east of the town centre is stronger on stationery than on reading material but it does stock a limited selection of English-language novels.

Vaco Book Shop [80 C5] 26 Dominee Straat; ❨ 472545; www.vaco.sr; ⏰ 08.00–16.30 Mon–Fri, 08.00–13.30 Sat. This is the largest bookshop in Suriname & it stocks a comprehensive selection of books about the country, including several titles it publishes itself such as Haverschmidt and Mees's comprehensive Birds of Suriname. It also stocks a wide selection of fiction in Dutch, & a more limited selection in English.

BANKING AND FOREIGN EXCHANGE The city centre and main shopping districts are dotted with banks that operate 24-hour ATMs where local currency can be withdrawn with a foreign credit or debit card. Maestro or MasterCard are accepted at ATMs operated by most of the major banks, including the prominent **De Surinaamsche Bank** (DSB; ↘ *471100; www.dsbbank.sr*) and **Royal Bank of Canada** (RBC; ↘ *471555; www.rbtt.com/sr/personal*), as well as the smaller **Fina Bank**, **Trust Bank** and **Hakrin Bank**. Visa, Cirrus, Maestro and Plus cards are generally accepted only at RBC ATMs.

There are about 25 RBC **ATMs** scattered around town, and the most useful locations are at the bank's head office at the junction of Heeren Straat and Kerk Plein; on Sommelsdijck Straat, almost opposite the Torarica Hotel; in the Hermitage Mall; and in the lobbies of the Courtyard Marriot and Krasnapolsky hotels. There are also a number of DSB ATMs in and around Paramaribo, the most useful of these are located at the bank's head office on Henck Arron Straat, next to Saint Peter and Paul Cathedral; at the SMS Pier on the Waterkant; in the lobby of the Hotel Krasnapolsky; at the Maretraite and Hermitage Malls; in Spanhoek Passage, at the junction of Dominee and Keizer Straat; and at the SOL service station at the corner of Maagden and Dr Sophie Redmond straats. Full details of all RBC and DSB ATM branch locations are listed on the bank websites.

Many private *cambios* (bureaux de change) are dotted around central Paramaribo, offering fairly uniform rates for euros, US dollars and British pounds. One of the best is the **Multi Track Cambio** [87 G1] (↘ *477244;* m *8280920;* e *multitrackexchange@ yahoo.com;* ⊕ *08.00–21.00 daily*), which keeps unusually long hours and has branches on Sommelsdijck Straat opposite the Torarica, on Wilhelmina Straat about 500m further east, and on Steenbakkerij Straat near the junction with Maagden. Multi Track also operates two 'Multimatic' machines, where you can change euros or US dollars into SRD 24 hours a day. There is one next to the Sommelsdijck Straat branch and another in the lobby of the Hotel Krasnapolsky. Other conveniently located *cambios* include **Central Money Exchange** (*113–117 Saramacca Straat;* ↘*426841*), **Money Line** (*35c Dominee Straat or 54a Maagden Straat;* ↘*422123*), **Trade Exchange** (*78 Waterkant;* ↘*425612*) and **Surora** (*57 Henck Arron Straat;* ↘*477965*).

BEAUTY AND HAIR SALONS Conveniently located at the front of the Hotel Torarica, the long-serving **Hair Studio Dawson** [91 B4] (*1 Rietberg Plein, Kleine Water Straat;* ↘ *470602;* m *8676383/8131799;* e *hairstudiodawsonnv@hotmail. com;* ⊕ *09.00–17.30 Tue–Sat*) offers haircuts and hair treatments for women, men and children, as well as a wide range of beauty treatments. Other well-established central salons include **Body & Health** [80 C4] (*14 Zwartenhovenbrug Straat;* ↘ *425795;* m *8515892;* e *body&health4life@yahoo.com*) and **Beauty Salon Santa Lucia** [80 D5] (*Malebatrum Straat;* ↘ *426685;* e *piercingsandbeauty@hotmail.com;* ⊕ *10.00–17.00 Mon–Fri, 10.00–15.00 Sat*).

COMMUNICATIONS
Internet The easiest way to access internet and emails on a regular basis is to use a smartphone. If you are staying for a while, it might be cheaper and easier to buy a local SIM card and data bundle at any Digicell shop, rather than relying on international roaming. In addition, for those carrying phones, tablets or laptops, most hotels in Paramaribo now offer free Wi-Fi to guests, as do several restaurants including the popular and central **Sidewalk Café t'Vat** and **Rituals Coffee House**

in the lobby of the Krasnapolsky. Actual internet cafés are few and far between, but a good central option is **Book Affairs** [73 F3] (see page 98) on Kerk Plein. Also recommended, and keeping longer hours, is **Quick Copy Centre** [73 F3] (*173 Tourtonne Straat;* ✆ *420022;* m *8593030;* e *quickcopy@hotmail.com;* ⏱ *08.00–22.00 daily*), which can be reached by taking a Line 10 bus.

Telephone To use a public phone, buy a prepaid telephone card from the Telesur Head Office at 1 Heiligen Weg [80 D6] (*www.telesur.sr*). Of the main local SIM card providers, **Digicel** (*www.digicelsuriname.com*) seems to be the most efficient and well represented, with five shops and service centres dotted around the city. The central locations are 23–25 Henck Arron Straat [81 F5] (✆ *462626*), 88 Waterkant [80 D7] (✆ *411877*) and 2 Maagden Straat [80 D6] (✆ *420785*), and there are also outlets in the Hermitage (✆ *491313*) and Maretraite (✆ *554018*) malls. For those who prefer **Telesur**, SIM cards can be bought at their head office (see above), while **Uniqa** (*www.uniqa.sr*) SIM cards are sold at their service centres in JAPI airport, or the CHM Complex on Dr Sophie Redmond Straat. Whichever card you buy, it is strongly advised you do so at a formal service centre and to take your phone or tablet with you, so that the consultant can set them up.

Important phone numbers

Directory enquiries ✆108	**First Aid** ✆113 or 325177
Fire Brigade ✆110 or 473333/491111	**Police** ✆115 or 471111/477777

EMBASSIES AND CONSULATES

Barbados 386 Kwatta Weg 386; ✆432880; e rhpower@cq-link.sr

Belgium 32 Dominee Straat; ✆472545/498108; e belgconsparamaribo@interfundgroup.com

Brazil 2 Maratakka Straat; ✆400200/2; e brasemb@sr.net; www.brasil.org.sr

Canada 50 JF Nassy Laan; ✆424527; e: cantim@sr.net

China 154 Anton Dragten Weg; ✆451570; e chinaemb_sr@mfa.gov.cn; http://sr.chineseembassy.org

Denmark 92–94 Waterkant; ✆471222

France 23 JF Nassy Laan; ✆475222; e ambafrance.paramribo@diplomatie.gouv.fr; www.ambafrance-sr.org

Germany 36–38 Dominee Straat; ✆471150

Guyana 82 Henck Arron Straat; ✆477895; e guyembassy@sr.net

India 239 Dr Sophie Redmond Straat; ✆498344/531448/531449; e india@sr.net; www.indembassysuriname.com

Netherlands 5 Van Rosevelt Kade; ✆477211; e prm@minbuza.nl; www.nederlandseambassade.sr

UK Contact the British Honorary Consul; ✆402558/402870; e britishconsulate@vshunited.com; or the British High Commission in Guyana; 44 Main Street, Georgetown; ✆+592 226 5881/2; e bhcguyana@networksgy.com

USA 129 Dr Sophie Redmond Straat; ✆472900; http://suriname.usembassy.gov

IMMIGRATION All visitors planning on staying in Suriname for longer than the 30 days initially stamped in their passport will need to obtain an extension at the **Immigration Department** [72 A5] (✆ *532109/532123;* ⏱ *07.00–14.00 Mon–Fri*), which lies a few kilometres out of town on the south side of J Lachmon Straat opposite the junction with Lalla Rookh Weg. To obtain an extension, you need to bring your passport and a hard copy of your air ticket. It would also be wise to dress quite formally and conservatively, as we have heard of women in particular being refused assistance for wearing skimpy attire. Assuming your papers are in order, your dress is deemed appropriate, and there is no queue, the extension can be issued on the spot and there is no charge.

LAUNDRY Most hotels provide a laundry service, typically charging SRD 30–50 per machine load for a same-day or overnight service. Elsewhere, **Klaco's Laundry** [87 F1] (*Sommelsdijck Straat;* m *8548904;* ⊕ *09.00–16.00 Mon–Fri*) charges SRD 10/kg and usually has clothes ready within 48 hours.

MEDICAL FACILITIES
Hospitals Founded in 1916, **Sint Vincentius Ziekenhuis** [81 G3] (*4 Koninginne Straat;* \ *471212; www.svzsuriname.org*) is a well-regarded central hospital with emergency rooms, an intensive care unit, a pharmacy and several resident specialists. Slightly less central but equally reputable is the **Academisch Ziekenhuis Paramaribo** [72 C3] (*Flu Straat;* \ *442222; www.azp.sr*), which has similar facilities, a wider range of specialists and a good laboratory.

Pharmacies Central standalone pharmacies include **Esculaap** (*34 Zwartenhovenbrug Straat;* \ *473102;* ⊕ *07.00–13.00 Mon–Sat &* 16.00–19.00 Mon–Fri) and **Wong's** (*88 Henck Arron Straat;* \ *424261;* ⊕ *07.00–19.00 Mon–Fri, 07.00–13.00 Sat*). Pharmacies stay open 24 hours on a roster system, which is announced in the local newspapers every Friday.

POST The best place to post mail and parcels is the **Surpost** head office at the corner of Kerk Plein and Keizer Straat [81 E6] (\ *425424/477524;* e *mail@surpost.com; www.surpost.com;* ⊕ *07.30–14.00 Mon–Thu, 07.30–13.30 Fri*). The post office also contains a cambio and a philately counter selling first-day covers.

WHAT TO SEE AND DO

Paramaribo's main attraction is the old inner city, which is liberally scattered with pre-20th-century architectural gems, including Fort Zeelandia, the magnificent wooden Saint Peter and Paul Cathedral, and dozens of old colonial homesteads. For those with limited time, it is worth dedicating at least half a day to Fort Zeelandia (which now houses the Suriname Museum) and its immediate environs. A full day is required to explore the old city centre more thoroughly. Further afield, popular goals for day excursions, all easily visited using public transport or on foot or by bicycle, include Paramaribo Zoo, Wegna Zee and the Neotropical Butterfly Park at Lelydorp, as well as several east bank sites described in the Commewijne chapter, notably Fort Nieuw Amsterdam and Peperpot Nature Park. Also worth highlighting are the popular dolphin sunset cruises that explore the waters around the confluence of the Suriname and Commewijne rivers. The section below also includes brief coverage of day and overnight tours to sites covered in greater details elsewhere in the book, such as Brownsberg Nature Park, the turtle-nesting beaches at Matapica and Galibi, Joden Savannah and the upmarket Berg en Dal Resort.

HISTORIC INNER CITY The Historic Inner City of Paramaribo was inscribed as a World Heritage Site (WHS) in 2002 by UNESCO, which considers it to represent an 'exceptional example of the gradual fusion of European architecture and construction techniques with indigenous South American materials and crafts to create a new architectural idiom'. The street plan of the inner city has changed little since the 1760s, although around 400 of the original buildings were lost to the fires of 1823 and 1831, and have subsequently been rebuilt. The WHS comprises a 30ha core conservation area incorporating Fort Zeelandia and bounded by the Suriname River to the south, Sommelsdijck Canal to the northeast and Heiligen Weg, Klipstenen Straat and Tourtonne Straat to the west. An additional area of 60ha

5

east and northwest of the WHS is UNESCO-listed as a buffer zone. There are also several important historical buildings that lie just outside both zones.

Getting around The WHS and its immediate environs are most easily explored **on foot**, and the main cluster of historic sites is sufficiently compact – less than 1km² – so that there's no overwhelming reason to follow a prescribed route. Nevertheless, for those who prefer to plot out their sightseeing in advance, a useful 5km circuit, leading past most of the more important buildings, would start at Fort Zeelandia, crossing to the adjacent Independence Square, then run east along Klein Combe Weg, northwest through the Palm Garden, Grote Combe Weg and Henck Arron Straat, then weave in a broadly westerly direction to Dr Sophie Redmond Straat via Klipstenen, Heeren, Malebatrum, Keizer, Jodenbree, Dominee, Steenbakkerij and Maagden straats, then follow the Waterkant east, possibly diverting back inland to Kerk Plein, before returning to Fort Zeelandia. The sites described below are listed sequentially more or less following the above route.

Two worthwhile **printed companions** to a walk through the old city centre can be bought at Zus & Zo (see page 90) or Vaco Book Shop (see page 98). The *Paramaribo Monumentkaart* (Aimée de Back, ME Productions, 2008; SRD 25) is a compact foldout map annotated with photographs of more than 100 key buildings and monuments in and around the old city, as well as informative Dutch and English text. *Paramaribo Monument Walking Guide* (Philip Dikland, Vaco Publications, 2013; SRD 45) is a more substantial booklet with detailed Dutch and English background to around 40 key buildings, as well as plenty of photos.

Guided city tours are offered by the acclaimed historical novelist Cynthia McLeod for SRD 30 per person – contact her directly (◑ 451620/479502; m 8838186) or book through Waterproof Tours (see pages 78–9). Also worth considering are the three-hour guided **Paramaribo Bus Tours**, which start at 09.30 every Monday, Wednesday and Friday, are run by Orange Travel and cost SRD 135 per person (see page 78).

Fort Zeelandia and the Suriname Museum [81 H7] (*1 Abraham Crijnssen Weg*; ◐ 425871; e *museum@cq-link.sr*; *www.surinaamsmuseum.net*; ⊕ 09.00– 14.00 Tue–Fri, 10.00–14.00 Sun; *free guided tours every Sun at 10.30; entrance SRD 15*) The oldest building in Paramaribo, Fort Zeelandia stands sentinel on the west bank of the Suriname River in the heart of the old city centre opposite Independence Square and the Palm Garden. Set on a shingle reef that stands 5m above the river at low tide, the fort started life in 1640 as a simple stockade built to protect a small French trading centre, and it was greatly expanded in the 1650s after the site was captured by Baron Willoughby. In 1667, Fort Willoughby was itself captured by the Dutch commander Abraham Crijnssen, who renamed the fort after his home country of Zeeland. The fort took its modern shape under the direction of Crijnssen, who built the outer walls and five bastions using red bricks and tiles imported as ballast by mercantile ships from Europe. Fort Zeelandia changed hands several times over subsequent decades, but its military importance diminished after 1747, following the completion of Fort Nieuw Amsterdam further downstream, and the two landward bastions were demolished. A second storey was added in 1784, and the fort still served as a garrison for most of the 19th century. Between 1872 and 1967, the inner fort was used as a prison. Following extensive restoration work, it opened as the Suriname Museum in 1972. However, in the wake of the 1980 Sergeants' Coup, the fort was seconded to the military and was used as Dési Bouterse's headquarters, under whose tenancy it witnessed the notorious 'Decembermoorden' (December Murders) of 1982 (see box, opposite page). The

Fort Zeelandia was the setting for one of the most brutal excesses committed under the de facto leadership of Dési Bouterse and his Nationale Militaire Raad (NMR) in the 1980s. On 7 December 1982, 16 prominent journalists, lawyers, university lecturers and other critics of the Bouterse regime were abducted from their homes during the early hours of morning and taken to Fort Zeelandia. One of the detainees, the prominent unionist Frederik Derby, was released the next day, possibly because the NMR believed his influence over the unions was too important. The other 15 captives, according to a national television broadcast made by Bouterse on 10 December, were shot dead in an aborted attempt to escape from military custody. Few believed this improbable version of events at the time, and it later emerged that the victims had been tried for unspecified crimes by a self-styled court composed of NMR leaders, tortured for up to two days, and then shot dead on Bastion Veere.

In the wake of the December Murders, the Netherlands immediately suspended all aid to Suriname, and the Bouterse regime was roundly condemned by several other Western governments. In addition, many opponents of the NMR, particularly those of Hindustani descent, went into exile in the Netherlands or elsewhere. Frederik Derby, the only survivor, went on to become a prominent opponent of Bouterse, co-founding the Surinaamse Partij van de Arbeid (SPA), which (unsuccessfully) contested the 1987 election. He only went public with his account of the events of December 1982 on the 18th anniversary of his release, in the hope that it would instigate a long-overdue official investigation. Derby died in May 2001.

In December 2002, a preliminary inquiry headed by Magistrate Ramnewash asked the Nederlands Forensisch Instituut (NFI) to conduct an autopsy on the victims' remains. Based on the NFI's findings and other evidence, a notice of prosecution was served on Dési Bouterse and 33 other suspects in December 2004. This list had been reduced to 25 by November 2007, when criminal proceedings started in Domberg, but Bouterse was still the prime suspect. Despite this, however, Bouterse, still active in politics, never once attended the trial, and went on to become the president of Suriname when his Nationale Democratische Partij (NDP) won the 2010 election. On 19 March 2012, the National Assembly, led by President Bouterse, voted in a controversial amnesty bill protecting all suspects in the December Murders from criminal prosecution. In theory, this bill still requires ratification by the constitutional court, but since no such entity exists in Suriname, the trial is effectively on hold indefinitely.

fort was vacated by Bouterse and his soldiers in the late 1980s, and reopened as the country's pre-eminent museum in 1995.

Allow at least one hour, or better two, to explore the museum thoroughly. Ground-floor displays include a replica of a 19th-century apothecary, a section on the early days of the fort, and a collection of Marron artefacts demonstrating the pervasive influence of their African origins. The undoubted highlights, however, are the superb first-floor collections of pre-Columbian and Amerindian artefacts accessed from Bastion Middelburg. These displays include a unique pre-Columbian ceremonial stone mask unearthed near Albina in 2000, a collection of four intact pre-Columbian stone axes dredged from various sites along the

Suriname and Marowijner, several rainbow-coloured feather headdresses, as well as ceremonial drums, neatly sculpted jars, clay figurines, and stone arrowheads and other tools. Also on the upper floor, the Bastion Veere National Monument, unveiled in 2009, incorporates a plaque commemorating the 15 victims of the 1982 'Decembermoorden' and there are several bullet holes dating back to the day of the executions. A ground-floor shop stocks several interesting books covering various aspects of Surinamese culture and history, as well as a series of historic monochrome postcards. Refreshments are available on the terrace of Baka Foto (see pages 88–9). A red, 18th-century letter box stands outside the fort entrance.

Around Fort Zeelandia The tranquil and rather park-like area immediately around Fort Zeelandia is studded with several buildings of antiquity. These include six similar wooden buildings, all double-storied and wide-balconied, that were originally built between 1750 and 1839 as officers' houses, though most have been greatly expanded since then. These houses were used by the military following the 1980 coup but were evacuated in 1987 and left empty until the mid-1990s. They have since been restored one by one by the Suriname Museum, with the assistance of the Netherlands Embassy. The old houses now mostly serve as offices for the likes of the Surinamese museum, the Stichting Gebouwd Erfgoed Suriname (Foundation for the Built Heritage), the Nola Hatterman Art Institute and the Staatsraad (State Council).

Other buildings of note in the fort gardens include the former prison guardhouse, which now houses the tourist information centre, and a derelict shell of the largest-ever brick structure in Suriname, a riverfront warehouse originally built in 1790 and later used as military barracks and by the Ministry of Education prior to it being partially destroyed by fire in 1990. Overlooking the river west of Fort Zeelandia is a statue of Queen Wilhelmina unveiled in 1923 to commemorate her silver jubilee. This originally stood on Government (now Independence) Square, but was relocated during independence celebrations in 1975 to make way for a flagpole adorned with the new Surinamese flag.

Independence Square [81 G6] Known as Government or Orange Square prior to 1975, Onafhankelijkheids Plein is a large grassy rectangle formerly used as a parade ground but now best known as the site of the city's regular Sunday morning songbird competitions (see box, opposite page). Landmarks on the open square include the forest of flagpoles at its eastern end, the so-called Wilhelmina Boom ('tree') planted in 1898 when its namesake ascended to the Dutch throne, and statues of two late politicians: Prime Minister Johan Pengel and the Hindu leader Jagernath Lachmon (the latter officially recognised as the world's longest-serving parliamentarian when he died in 2001, having first been elected in 1949).

Several important buildings flank Independence Square. On the northeast side, backing onto the Palm Garden, the **Presidential Palace** (formerly the Governor's Palace) is a massive three-storey building with a tiled slate roof, whitewashed exterior and wide ground-floor veranda hemmed in by more than a dozen Corinthian arches. The oldest part of the mansion was constructed in 1685 as the residence of Governor van Sommelsdijck, but it was greatly expanded under Governor-General Karel Cheusses in 1730, and has since undergone several further renovations. Although the palace is closed to visitors, its imposing façade – adorned with the coat of arms of the 18th-century Geoctrooieerde Societeit van Suriname – can be seen clearly from Independence Square.

The most distinguished building at the northwest end of the square is the **Ministry of Finance**, a double-storey redbrick construction with four tall Doric pillars in front,

SONGBIRD COMPETITIONS

The most popular leisure activity among Surinamese men is, rather unexpectedly, bird-keeping. And we're not talking about chickens or other edible fowl, nor even colourful parrots or toucans, but three select species of relatively drab sparrow-sized seedeaters renowned primarily for the singing ability of the pugnacious males. Indeed, bird-keeping is not so much a hobby among Surinamese males as it is a national obsession: wherever you travel in the country, you'll see men walking down the street birdcage in hand, chilling on their balcony with their feathered friend perched by their side, or fishing in a canal while their avian companion sits in a cage hung from the nearest branch or the door of their parked car.

Surinamese songbird enthusiasts are also highly competitive, with the most popular competition taking place on Paramaribo's Independence Square early on Sunday mornings, weather permitting. Here, dozens of pedigree bird-owners come together to pit their finches against each other in a musical duel, for prizes such as cups, new cages and bags of birdseed, but above all to determine who owns the finest songster. Three categories of indigenous bird compete, known locally as *twatwa* (great-billed seed-finch *Oryzoborus crassirostris*), *picolet* (chestnut-bellied seed-finch *Oryzoborus angolensis*) and *rowtie* (various *Sporophila* finches). The system is that two caged males of the same species are hung from posts set 50cm apart to trigger their competitive instinct, and the winner is the bird that whistles the most often or fastest during a specified period (usually ten to 15 minutes). Competitive though it might be, the atmosphere is genial and welcoming, and most bird-owners will be delighted to let you photograph them and/or their favourite finch.

and a prominent octagonal white clock tower rising 34.5m above the square. Designed by Johan August Voigt in the then popular Greek revival style, it originally served as the town hall before becoming a ministry, but it is otherwise almost unaltered since its original 1836–41 construction, though the bronze medallion depicting King Willem III was added to the triangular pediment in 1913. To its left, the **Court of Justice** was constructed for that purpose in 1793 reusing the foundations and other materials from an older house built on the same site in 1755. To its right, the so called **Duplessis House** is one of the oldest extant residences in the city, built in the mid 18th century and rented by the notorious slave owner Maria Susanna Duplessis (see box, page 160) for several years prior to her death in 1795. A handsome double-storey building with a wide-arched veranda opening out to the street, it later served as the Home Office and now houses the National Institute for Environmental Research.

Numismatic Museum [81 F6] (*7 Lim A Po Straat*; ☏ *520016*; e *numismatischemuseum@cbvs.sr*; ⊕ *08.00–14.00 Mon–Fri*; *free entrance*; *photography forbidden*) Situated diagonally opposite Independence Square along a road lined with historic buildings, the surprisingly diverting Numismatic Museum is operated by the Central Bank of Suriname, which was founded in 1957 to replace the private DSB as the national governing body in monetary and economic affairs. Its air-conditioned interior incorporates a collection of Surinamese banknotes and coins dating back to 1679, when the first *papegaaienmunt* ('parrot coin') was issued, depicting a parrot on a branch, and valued at one pound of sugar (which then cost

PARAMARIBO'S WOODEN ARCHITECTURE

The distinctive wooden architecture associated with Paramaribo is largely a product of the city's location. Paramaribo has been prone to rapid expansion since its foundation in the mid 17th century, and while stone has always been in short supply, and the waterlogged soil is less than ideal for rapid brick production, Suriname possesses an almost unparalleled natural supply of timber. Therefore in the early days of the small settlement most construction was undertaken in wood, using techniques learned from ships' carpenters and Moravian migrants. As is also the case in some parts of Asia as well, the finest traditional builders did not use nails or glue to hold the wood together but cut the pieces so perfectly that none was necessary.

Most of the city's wooden houses are built along similar lines. They have a rectangular base, with the street façade usually being the longer side, though on narrow lots they may be orientated with a street-facing gable. The foundations are almost invariably made of bricks, which support the floor beams, aided by at least one brick or stone base block in the centre, and the outside steps are also usually made of bricks. Perimeter beams are then set in place to support a timber skeleton on which 30cm-wide boards, usually painted white, are fixed to create a symmetrical façade of horizontal boards. Windows, doors, shutters, frames and louvres are usually painted dark green or black. Most houses feature detailed embellishments on the meticulously hand-carved balconies, balustrades, joints and banisters.

A typical feature of Paramaribo's wooden houses is the high sloping roofs inset with one or more gabled dormers. These dormers usually have two rectangular windows each, sometimes set below a third semicircular window. The reason for the use of dormers to create additional headroom and let in more light was because early roofing materials – mostly pina leaves, wooden shingles, slates and flat tiles – enforced the use of steep slopes to combat Suriname's rainy climate. That changed with the introduction of galvanised zinc roofing in the 1870s, but by then the steep sloping style was well established. Houses constructed prior to 1850 usually had small balconies or none at all. By contrast, many buildings constructed or extended in the latter half of the 19th century possess wide balconies supported by arches or pillars, and some also have grandiose colonnaded porticos, the latter influenced by the southeast USA. These large balconies and porticos were probably built as a sign of prosperity.

five cents). It also includes the colony's earliest paper money, issued in 1779, and a display documenting traditional currencies used by older societies, such as cowry shells and manila armbands.

The Palm Garden [87 D4] The only park in central Paramaribo, the 4ha Palmentuin is also, according to local tradition, the site of the original Amerindian village bordering Paremuru Creek (now Sommelsdijck Canal). In the 1680s, Governor van Sommelsdijck developed the site as a fruit and vegetable garden to help feed the troops stationed at the facing Fort Zeelandia. It is thought that the first of the tall *Roystonea oleracea* palms that now dominate the garden were planted by him. During the 18th century, the garden was developed as a general service area for the nearby Governor's Palace, and it incorporated several warehouses, two long rows of cramped slaves' quarters, as well as a small working garden. Following the abolition of slavery, it was transformed into a primarily recreational area in the late 19th century, with the southwest section remaining a private extension of the governor's garden, and the northeast section being set aside as a public park.

There are now estimated to be 1,000 palms in the garden, which was opened to the public in its entirety in the early 20th century and declared a national monument in 1999. Today, it is a pleasant enough spot to enjoy a shady break, and there are plenty of birds about, though no longer, as far as we can ascertain, a resident troop of capuchin monkeys. Of the several statues in the park, the most macabre – depicting a little boy who died after being trapped in a refrigerator – was sculpted by the child's father to warn other parents against similar acts of carelessness. On Klein Combe Weg, immediately opposite the Palm Garden, the Baba en Mai Plein (Father and Mother Square) Statue was erected in 1994 to commemorate the arrival of the first Hindustani workers in the wake of the abolition of slavery on 5 June 1873.

Henck Arron Straat [81 E4] Exiting Palm Garden to the north, a left turn into Grote Combe Weg (with the Ministry of Finance clock tower standing prominently ahead) brings you to Henck Arron (formerly Graven) Straat, the most important thoroughfare leading northwest out of the city centre. Several very old houses line this road, which was evidently largely untouched by the fires of 1823 and 1831.

The redbrick **Bisschopshuis** (Bishop's Residence) at 12 Henck Arron Straat is one of the city's oldest buildings, which was owned by a Sara Lemmers in 1750 but was probably built 20 years before that. It was bought by the Roman Catholic Church in 1917 and became the bishop's residence four years later. The interior houses a small neo-Gothic chapel and the striking rear incorporates a first-floor wooden extension that creates an external arched gallery on the ground floor.

Next door, **14 Henck Arron Straat** is another very old house, built in 1740 by the French plantation owner Jean David Cellier, whose initials are embossed in wrought iron on the skylight above the front door. Like its neighbour, it has a particularly attractive rear façade, with wide balconies on both floors and a flight of redbrick steps fanning out into a courtyard that is shared with a school that was founded by the Sisters of Charity of Roosendaal in 1863. Restored in 2002, the building is now the headquarters of the **Catholic Diocese of Paramaribo**, so you should be allowed to take a look at the impressive interior during working hours, and can certainly walk around to the back to visit the small **Kerkelijk (Ecclesiastical) Museum** (✎ 426092; ⊕ 08.30–13.30 Mon–Fri).

On the other side of the road, at 21 Henck Arron Straat, the former **Pastorie** (Friar House) is a massive wooden structure amalgamated from three older houses between 1863 and 1873 to be used as living quarters for monks belonging to the Congregation of the Redemptorists. A third storey was added in 1916. Abandoned in 1990, this handsome wide-balconied building reopened in 2006 after extensive restoration, and the first two floors now house the **National School of Music**, while the third floor is used for student accommodation.

Saint Peter and Paul Cathedral [81 F5] (*22 Henck Arron Straat;* ✎ *472521;* e *secretariaatpetrusenpaulus@gmail.com; www.bisdomparamaribo.org;* ⊕ *the cathedral usually keeps its doors open throughout the morning & for part of the afternoon; Mass 06.30 & noon Mon–Fri, 19.00 Sat, 10.00 Sun, & the church also often hosts weddings & other ceremonies, particularly at w/ends; no entrance fee but donations welcome*) Paramaribo's most distinctive architectural landmark – and the

HISTORY OF A BASILICA

The first recorded Roman Catholic church in Paramaribo was converted from a private residence on Wagenweg Straat in the 1780s and it burned down in 1821. Initially, the church relocated to a building on the corner of Zwartenhovenbrug and Wagenweg Straat, but this proved to be too small. So, in 1824 the church bought an abandoned Dutch Jewish theatre called De Verrezene ('Risen') Phoenix on the site of the present-day cathedral, adapted it for use as a church, and consecrated it in 1826, dedicating it to saints Peter and Paul. By 1882, however, it was clear that the former theatre was in imminent danger of collapse, so construction work began on a much larger wooden building under the supervision of Friar Frans Harmes, a professional carpenter and member of the Congregation of the Redemptorists. Re-consecrated in 1885, the new church was completed in 1887, and the twin spires were added a few years later.

The church of Saint Peter and Paul was upgraded to a cathedral in 1958, when Paramaribo was made a diocese. Unfortunately, however, the combination of a roof design prone to leaks and perishable building materials meant that it was already starting to show signs of deterioration. Extensive renovations were undertaken between 1977 and 1979, but even so, by 1989, the cathedral had deteriorated to such an extent that it was no longer considered safe to hold services or other events there. In 1995, the dilapidated church was subjected to a more extensive programme of structural restoration under the guidance of a Dutch architect and the engineer WBJ Polman. Following further EU-funded renovation, Saint Peter and Paul finally came back into active service in 2010. On 6 April 2014, Pope Francis elevated the status of this, the most impressive of Paramaribo's old wooden buildings, to basilica, a papal endowment that, among other things, acknowledges it as a substitute for people unable to make the pilgrimage to the seven basilica churches in Rome.

city's one genuine architectural 'must see' – is the Kathedraal Basiliek van Sint Petrus en Paulus (Cathedral Basilica of Saint Peter and Paul), which has stood opposite the old Pastorie since the 1880s (see box above). Reputedly the largest wooden building in the western hemisphere, the cruciform cathedral has a capacity of $15,500m^3$ and can hold around 900 people, while its neo-Gothic twin spires, standing 44m high, are visible from several vantage points on surrounding streets. The outside of the building is painted pastel yellow and grey, but the unpainted cedar interior exploits the natural grains and patterns of the wood to impressive effect, and is also embellished with carved capitals, gates and doors. The west tower contains three 19th-century bells called Alphonsus, Rosa and Johannes, the largest of which weighs 375kg, and all three of which toll on Sundays and church holidays. Also dating to the late 19th century, the German-made pipe organ originally comprised 1,550 pipes, many of which have been stolen over the years.

Visitors are welcome to attend Mass (see above for times) and other services, but may not take photographs of the interior when the church is in use. On the third Sunday of the month, the cathedral hosts a free classical music concert, starting at 18.00. **Guided tours**, in Dutch, cost SRD 20 per person, and are held at 10.00 every Saturday (register at the souvenir kiosk next to the main entrance 30 minutes in advance) and at other times by prior arrangement for groups of five or more.

West towards Dr Sophie Redmond Straat Starting from Saint Peter and Paul Cathedral, a westward meander of around 1.5km takes you across the inner city to Dr Sophie Redmond Straat, passing several notable buildings *en route*.

S' Lands Hospital [81 E4] Continue northwest along Henck Arron Straat – passing the late 19th-century Hendrik School on your right – until you reach the junction with Klipstenen Straat and immediately after this junction, also on the right side of Henck Arron Straat, is the oddly named S' Lands Hospital. Formerly the military hospital, it is the city's largest national monument, comprising six historic buildings, most of which date to the late 19th or early 20 century. The hospital's oldest building, 64 Henck Arron Straat, constructed in the 1760s and completely remodelled in 1925, is now home to the Ministerie Van Volksgezondheid (Ministry of Health).

Sedek ve Shalom Synagogue [81 E5] Turning left into Klipstenen Straat, the isolated white building at the centre of a large and rather bare plot to your left is the Sedek ve Shalom ('Justice and Peace') Synagogue, built in 1736 by Sephardic Jews from Portugal after they split with the Ashkenazic (German Jewish) community associated with the older synagogue on Keizer Straat. Remodelled and extended several times since then, the seven-bay synagogue was decommissioned in the 1990s when the city's few remaining Sephardic Jews decided to relocate their services to Keizer Straat. It is now used as an office.

The Samson houses [80 D5] At the next intersection turn right into Heeren Straat and follow it as it curves left to become Malebatrum Straat. Flanking the junction with Wagenweg Straat, you'll see two large houses that were lived in during the mid 18th century by the Samson sisters Elisabeth and Nanette, so-called 'free negresses' whose mother Nanoé had been a slave and planter's concubine. The sisters were successful businesswomen who ended up owning several coffee plantations and a ship that used to transport their produce to Amsterdam. However, they are probably best remembered today after Elisabeth (the subject of Cynthia McLeod's semi-biographical novel *The Free Negress Elisabeth*) won a protracted and controversial court case that allowed her to become the first black woman in Suriname to marry a white man, in 1767. Elisabeth Samson resided in the impressive wooden homestead at 22 Wagenweg Straat from 1750 until her death in 1771, though it seems likely this building was significantly extended circa 1800 by its then owner Pieter Heydoorn, whose initials are embossed above the front door. Nanette lived at 47 Wagenweg Straat from 1750 until her death in 1790, by which time she owned half the properties on the street. Though the original house was partially razed in the fire of 1821, the foundations and entrance stairs of the current house clearly show its 18th-century origins.

Nieuwe Oranjetuin [80 C3] From the Samson houses it is possible to follow Wagenweg Straat north across Swalmberg Straat, passing the Thalia Theatre on your right, until you reach JF Nassy Laan, which is flanked by the Nieuwe Oranjetuin (New Orange Garden) Cemetery. Founded in 1758, this large cemetery, surrounded by tall brick walls, is where many of the city's more influential Christian citizens (among them Elisabeth Samson) were buried prior to its closure in 1961. It contains more than 1,500 engraved gravestones, many of which were imported from Holland. Unfortunately, it is also very overgrown and appeared to be closed when we visited in April 2014.

Neveh Shalom Synagogue [80 C5] Continue along Malebatrum Straat to the T-junction with Keizer Straat, and a right turn will bring you to the Neveh Shalom ('Oasis of Peace') Synagogue at 82 Keizer Straat. This large plot was bought by Sephardic Jews of Portuguese origin in 1716, and the first synagogue was built here in 1717–23 to replace its predecessor further upriver at Jodensavanne. In 1735, the plot was sold to the Ashkenazic (German) community, who built the current synagogue – a magnificent wooden construction along clean neoclassical lines – in the 1830s. Since 1999, the small Sephardic and Ashkenazic communities, numbering around 500 people in total, have both used Neveh Shalom as their primary place of worship. The synagogue contains several centuries-old Torahs, and the Holy Ark, dais and benches are all beautifully crafted from wood. A unique feature of the building is its sandy floor, which commemorates not only the Hebrews' 40-year desert sojourn after their exodus from Egypt, but also the grim days of the Spanish Inquisition, when many Sephardic Jews who were forced to convert to Christianity continued to hold Judaic services in cellars where the floors were covered in sand to muffle the prayers. The large neat grounds of Neveh Shalom house a ritual bath dating to 1830, as well as a collection of several hundred 18th-century gravestones relocated from a disused Sephardic cemetery on Kwatta Weg. Services are held at 19.00 on the first and third Friday of the month and at 08.30 on the second and fourth Saturday. Entrance during services is at the back of the building on Wagenweg Straat.

Keizer Straat Mosque [80 C4] An oft-vaunted example of Suriname's dedication to religious tolerance is the fact that the capital's only extant synagogue and its largest mosque stand adjacent to each other on Keizer Straat. The headquarters of the Surinaamse Islamitische Vereeniging (Surinamese Islamic Society), the current Keizer Straat Mosque, was inaugurated on 27 July 1984, and is a modern, rectangular, two-storey building with numerous arches along the sides and an additional four-storey minaret on each of its four corners. Reputedly the largest mosque in the Caribbean, its construction necessitated the demolition of a more modest but characterful wooden mosque, with two domed minarets, built in 1932.

Dominee and Steenbakkerij Straats [80 C6] Opposite the Neveh Shalom Synagogue, follow Jodenbree Straat south for a block and then turn right into Dominee Straat, which is arguably the most popular downtown shopping road. The best-known landmark here is the ultra-modern Hotel Krasnapolsky, home to Rituals Coffee House, which is a great place to stop for liquid or more substantial refreshment in air-conditioned surroundings. Several other two-storey buildings on this road (and parallel Maagden Straat) were constructed in the late 19th century by Moravian traders, who lived upstairs and operated their business on the ground floor. A good example of this is the recently restored **Kersten Building** at 38 Dominee Straat. The Moravian community was focused on this part of Paramaribo largely because of the long-standing presence of the Evangelische Broedergemeente van Suriname (EBGS) church a block south of Dominee Straat on the corner of Steenbakkerij and Maagden Straat. The first Moravian church was built here in 1739, but it was replaced by the current building in the late 1820s, and enlarged in 1947. Three storeys high, 30m wide and constructed almost entirely from wood, it has a truly impressive white-painted interior, comprising a large central hall of worship surrounded by internal balconies.

Kong Ngie Tong Sang (KNTS) Building [80 B6] From the intersection with Steenbakkerij Straat, follow Maagden Straat west to the T-junction with Dr Sophie

The first 18 Chinese immigrants arrived in Suriname in 1853 to work on the government sugar plantation Catharina Sophia. By 1869, around 2,500 Chinese indentured labourers worked on the colony's various plantations, and while many returned home after their contracts expired, others stayed behind to form a tight-knit community of long-term settlers. Mostly retail traders, these Chinese settlers also formed several cultural associations, the most influential of which, Kong Ngie Tong, was founded in April 1880. Kong Ngie Tong used a small building on Virgin Street as its clubhouse, before moving to its present location in 1888. Funded by annual dues as well as donations from wealthier Chinese, Kong Ngie Tong provided sanctuary and a meeting place for members of a young immigrant community often subjected to suspicion and prejudice by more established settlers. The *huiguan* also played an important role in education, integration and the development of social activities, for instance by offering Dutch lessons to new arrivals, by supporting music and dance events, by housing an important traditional temple shrine, and by introducing sports such as boxing and basketball to the city.

In the 1920s, the Kong Ngie Tong huiguan became strongly associated with *piauw*, a Chinese-style lottery that flourished between the wars as a result of the strict laws regulating other forms of gambling in Paramaribo. Tolerated by the authorities as long as it was restricted to the Chinese community, the piauw lottery was bankrolled by wealthy Chinese traders affiliated with Kong Ngie Tong, and it helped provide a livelihood to the new immigrants who generally acted as ticket sellers. By the mid-1920s, however, the majority of tickets were being bought by Creole and other non-Chinese urban workers, many of whom became addicted to the game. In 1926, the colonial government made piauw illegal, and the police set up a special 'Piauw Brigade' charged with enforcing the ban. However, this ban merely drove the game underground, or more specifically to the upper floor of the Kong Ngie Tong huiguan, which reputedly also doubled as an illicit opium den. Following several police raids on the building, the government finally stripped Kong Ngie Tong of its corporate capacity in June 1930, closed the huiguan, removed the temple, and auctioned off all its assets. Critics claimed that this rather heavy-handed assault on Kong Ngie Tong was motivated largely by racism, and certainly it seemed to precipitate an increase in poverty and destitution among the Chinese community. The huiguan, by contrast, was soon bought by a wealthy Chinese businessman and the cultural society was revived as Kong Ngie Tong Sang (*sang* means 'reborn'), though the temple removed by the authorities was never replaced.

Redmond Straat, which is overlooked by the colourful and rather architecturally anomalous *huiguan* (assembly hall or clubhouse) of the KNTS (see box, above). Constructed in 1888, this was originally one of the most beautiful architectural landmarks in Paramaribo, a double-storeyed construction with wide open-sided balconies that combined the elaborate woodwork typical of Suriname with distinctive Chinese flourishes. The original huiguan burned down in April 1995, probably due to faulty wiring, and the rather gaudy and more overtly Chinese replacement, completed in 2005, arguably lacks its peculiar charm. Nevertheless, it is still one of the city's most strikingly incongruous buildings, and it remains an important cultural centre, its exterior and interior adorned with many Chinese artefacts and artworks. Open to the general public, the KNTS building is entered via a traditional *pailou* commemorative arch, flanked by statues of lions and a bust of Dr Sun Yat Sen, the revolutionary who founded the Republic of China in 1912 following the overthrow of the Qing Dynasty, and who served as its first president. The building also houses the press that produces the *Ngie Kong Tong Sang Dagblad*, Suriname's main Chinese-language newspaper. A small balcony on the eastern side reflects an ancient belief that Chinese people living in another country need only look east for part of their soul to return to China. The huiguan is a focal point of Suriname's Chinese New Year celebrations, a moveable feast that falls between 21 January and 20 February depending on the lunar calendar.

Kwakoe statue [80 A6] A block north of the KNTS building, at the busy junction of Dr Sophie Redmond and Zwartenhovenbrug Straats, stands the most beloved of the many statues scattered around central Paramaribo. Unveiled by Prime Minister JA Pengel in 1963 to mark the centenary of the abolition of slavery (on Wednesday, 1 July 1863), the Kwakoe statue is a life-size sculpture of a bare-chested former slave who has just broken his chains. Cast by Jozef Klas, a pupil of the well-known Dutch-born, Suriname-based artist Nola Hatterman, the statue is sometimes said to represent an individual escaped slave called Kwakoe, but more likely it is a symbolic reference to the Krimanto Marron name for boys born on a Wednesday (itself derived from Kwaku, the Wednesday birth-name used by the Akan-speaking people of Ghana).

Saint Rosa Church [80 A7] A short diversion southwest of Dr Sophie Redmond Straat leads you to the Saint Rosa Church at the junction of Prinsen and Timmerman Straat. This is the city's second-largest Roman Catholic church, a wooden construction with twin spires and a yellow-and-grey exterior that strongly resembles a scaled-down version of the Saint Peter and Paul Cathedral. It was built in 1911 on the site of an older single-spired church dating from 1860. If you decide to visit this church, cut directly south from Timmerman Straat to Saramacca Straat, then follow the road east back to where Dr Sophie Redmond Straat intersects with the Waterkant.

East along the Waterkant The southeast end of Dr Sophie Redmond Straat brings you out on the Waterkant, the main road along the waterfront. If you're feeling leg weary, it's only 800m east from here to Fort Zeelandia and Independence Square, passing several landmarks *en route*, but otherwise you can follow the road east for about 400m, then take a short diversion inland along Heiligen Weg to Kerk Plein before returning to the Waterkant via the brilliantly named Kromme Elleboog ('crooked elbow') Straat.

Maarten Luther Church [80 C7] Situated roughly opposite the Central Market (see pages 96–7), the Maarten Luther Kerk is the oldest Lutheran church in Paramaribo. Inaugurated in 1834, it was designed by the architect Charles Antoine Roman to replace an older wooden building constructed on the same spot in 1747 and razed by the fire of 1831. It is made almost entirely from brick and stone, and the white-plastered façade with arched black window frames is slightly reminiscent of the Cape Dutch style associated with South Africa. The beautiful interior comprises three aisles separated by six Doric pillars, as well as a pulpit, organ and internal balcony made from rich dark mahogany. Most features have remained unchanged since its construction.

Revolution memorial [81 E7] This memorial commemorating the 1980 military coup is the central feature of a park-like square on the east side of the intersection of the Waterkant and Heiligen Weg. It is the work of Jules Chin a Foeng, a well-known political artist who founded Suriname's first Academy of Fine Arts in 1966 and who created the memorial after winning a design competition staged by the military government in 1981. The monument stands on the ashes of the former police station, a stark three-storey wooden monolith that was built in 1925 and burned to the ground during the 1980 coup. All that remain of the police station today are five thick round pillars that have been incorporated into the memorial.

Vaillant's Square [80 D6] More triangle than square, Vaillantsplein was created in 1821, when it was decided not to rebuild a block of houses destroyed by fire at the north end of Heiligen Weg. Originally a park, it was made the city terminus of the Lawa Railway (which ran inland to near present-day Brownsberg) in 1902. The station was relocated from Vaillantsplein to Beekhuizen, a few kilometres further south, in 1958. There was also a market here until the early 1960s, but in 1966 this was replaced by a large fountain, at the centre of which stands the impressive State Monument designed by Stuart Robles de Medina to commemorate the centenary of the Surinamese parliament. In 1975, the monument was joined by a 25-bell carillon donated by the Dutch government to celebrate Suriname's independence.

Dutch Reformed Church [81 E6] In the early 18th century, Kerkplein (Church Square), a block east of Vaillantsplein, was known as Oranjetuin (Orange Garden) and it housed a large multi-functional building that served as the town hall and police court as well as the church for Nederlandse Hervormde (Dutch Reformed) and Lutheran settlers. By 1750, however, the Lutherans had built their own church on the present-day Waterkant, and the state services had also relocated elsewhere. A larger-domed Dutch Reformed Church with an eight-sided base built on the site in 1810 was lost to the fire of 1821, but it clearly served as a model for the replacement, which was constructed between 1833 and 1837. Little has changed since then, the palm-shaded church still has its unusual octagonal shape, the large tilting windows that give it a very light airy feel during services, and the two rows of four Ionic pillars still separate the aisles. The handsome mahogany organ and pulpit both date to the 1840s. Several gravestones outside the church are relics of the days prior to the establishment of the Nieuw Oranjetuin Cemetery (see page 109), when its older namesake also served as a cemetery for wealthy Christian settlers.

The Weighing House [81 E7] Returning to the Waterkant via Kromme Elleboog Straat, you come out opposite De Waaghuis, a handsome two-storey building where the open ground floor contains four massive pillars that support the upper floor. One of the first buildings to be constructed after the fire of 1821 (there is an engraved foundation stone dating back to July 1822 in the outer wall), the weighing house stood at the heart of Paramaribo's harbour from 1824 until 1965. In its prime, the building was flanked by two long wooden piers where boats from the many plantations along the Commewijne and Suriname rivers would unload their cargoes of sugar and coffee ready to be weighed. The weighing house fell into disuse after 1965, when the harbour was relocated to its present more southerly site, and had deteriorated to a state of near dereliction by the late 1980s. Extensive restoration took place between 1995 and 2000/2002, and since 2007 'De Waag' has housed an eponymous courtyard restaurant (see page 89).

5

Eastern Waterkant and around [81 F7] East of De Waag, the landward side of the Waterkant is lined with the impressive façades of two- and three-storey mansions built in the aftermath of the 1821 fire. Coming from the west, these include the former Ministry of Social Affairs at 30 Waterkant, the Central Bank of Suriname at 26 Waterkant, the beautifully restored Vervuurt at 12 Waterkant, the brick-faced three-storey mansion at 10 Waterkant, and the Corner House at 2 Waterkant. There are also several gracious old buildings immediately inland, especially along JC De Miranda and Dr Lim A Po Straat.

OTHER PLACES OF INTEREST

Sommelsdijck Canal Heronry [87 G4] (*Closed to the public*) Since the late 1980s, the mangrove at the mouth of Sommelsdijck Canal has supported impressive numbers of heron and egret during the main breeding season (April to September). The most prolific species here is the ubiquitous cattle egret – several hundred pairs descend on the site annually – but small numbers of snowy egret, little blue heron and tricoloured heron have also been regular visitors for the past 20 years. More recent arrivals are the rather elusive black-crowned night-heron, which first made an appearance circa 2000, and the secretive and eagerly sought after boat-billed heron, which has bred here regularly since 2011. Among the most singular of South American waterbirds, the handsome boat-billed heron is placed in a monotypic genus *Cochlearius*, and is named for its massive flattened black bill, which it uses to scoop prey from the mangrove beds it typically inhabits. More than 100 pairs of boat-billed heron have been present at times, which is all the more remarkable given that these nocturnal birds usually choose highly inaccessible nesting sites in the heart of seasonal or perennial black mangrove swamps along the coast.

Situated on the east bank of the Suriname River between the Royal Torarica Hotel and Cabinet of the President, the site is closed to the public (probably no bad thing conservation-wise) but it is usually quite easy to see the herons from the gardens of the Royal Torarica. Failing that, you could charter a boat at Platte Brug, which is only 500m further west, so it shouldn't be prohibitively expensive.

Museum of Fine Arts [80 A7] (MoFA; *107–109 Zwartenhovenbrug Straat;* m *8130521;* e *info@mofa-p.com; www.mofa-p.com;* ☉ *11.00–16.00 Wed–Fri; entrance fee depends on the current exhibition*) This central museum was established by the Dutch-born creative designer Tejuna Nandoe Tewarie-Veldhuizen in 2011. Housed in a two storey-building, the ground floor currently houses temporary exhibitions by upcoming young Surinamese artists and other painters and fine-art photographers, but there are plans to install a permanent collection of fine art on the upper floor.

Villa Zapakara Children's Museum [81 H3] (*17b Prins Hendrik Straat;* ☎ *422212;* e *info@villazapakara.com; www.villazapakara.com;* ☉ *09.00–16.00 Sat*) Aimed mainly at local schoolchildren, Villa Zapakara isn't so much a museum as an interactive installation dedicated to exposing youngsters to exotic cultures and to promoting cultural tolerance. The themes change every two years: the original 2009 incarnation replicated the Ashanti Palace in Kumasi (Ghana), and was replaced by a Mumbai-themed installation in 2011 and the current Qi of China exhibition in 2013. It is open to school groups only during the week, but the public can visit on Saturdays, when there is a Qi of China tour at 11.30, and workshops at 09.15, 10.30 and 13.15.

Het Surinaamsch Rumhuis [91 C4] (*18 Cornelis Jongbaw Straat;* ☎ *473344; www.rumhuis.sr;* ☉ *10.00–14.30 Tue–Fri; no entrance fee*) This small museum next to the Eco Resort Inn is operated by Suriname Alcoholic Beverages (SAB), the national rum producer founded in 1966 and responsible for the ubiquitous Black Cat and Borgoe brands, both of which have won several international awards. The museum has several interesting displays about the history of rum production in Suriname, as well as a collection of old labels, and a tasting room and gift shop selling various SAB products. Guided tours of the museum and factory, including a tasting session, run every Tuesday at 09.30, or upon demand for groups of eight or more, and cost SRD 65 per person.

Arya Dewaker Temple [72 C5] Situated on JA Pengel Straat about 1km west of the city centre, the Arya Dewaker Temple is the largest Hindu edifice in Suriname. It is a rather fantastic four-storey construction, and the balconied octagonal main building is set below a large red dome, and flanked by two smaller parapets each topped with what looks like a strawberry ice-cream whirl. Constructed over 25 years, the present-day temple was inaugurated on 11 February 2001 on the site of an older and smaller predecessor built in 1936 and demolished in 1975. It is managed by, and named after, the Arya Dewaker (literally 'Aryan Sun'), a Hindu association founded in 1929 by Mehta Jaimini, a follower of the Arya Samaj reform movement founded by the ascetic Swami Dayananda Sarasvati in 1875. It is the main spiritual home of 30,000 Surinamese who adhere to this school. A striking feature of this and other Arya Samaj temples is that they contain no images or statues of divinities, reflecting the movement's rejection of what it regards as the idolatrous nature of other religions and other Hindu sects.

Paramaribo Zoo [72 E2] (*Kananga Straat;* 545275; e *paramaribozoo@yahoo.com;* ⊕ 09.00–18.00 *daily; entrance SRD 5/10 child/adult*) Around 3km north of the city centre, Paramaribo Zoo lies at the heart of a forested enclave known somewhat obtusely as the Cultuurtuin (Cultural Garden). Initiated by Prime Minister Johan Pengel in 1966 and formally opened in 1972, the zoo lost many of its original animal inhabitants during the civil war years, but has undergone major renovations since being offered official support by Rotterdam Zoo in 2004. As with most zoos, it provokes mixed reactions: on the one hand it offers visitors and locals an opportunity to observe several indigenous animals seldom encountered in the wild, but on the other it can be quite depressing to see some of these creatures (the large cats in particular) held captive in small cages.

Among the more interesting species represented are lowland tapir, giant river otter, giant anteater, jaguar and various smaller cats and other predators. Most primate species present in Suriname are represented, with pride of place going to two well-constructed island retreats inhabited by troops of the remarkably supple black spider monkey. There are also plenty of striking birds, including king vulture, harpy eagle, scarlet ibis, and various toucans, macaws and parrots, while reptiles include yellow-footed tortoises, caimans, anacondas and various other snakes. Perhaps the best feature of the zoo, however, is the remarkable volume of wildlife that crosses between the zoo and adjoining Cultuurtuin of its own accord. Spider monkeys and black capuchins are often seen and heard in the surrounding trees, brightly coloured toucans and various raptors are often spotted in the vicinity of their caged kin, while a quiet vigil at the canal running behind the spider monkey islands will sometimes reward you with a caiman, peccary or agouti sighting.

The zoo is about a 45-minute walk from the city centre. To get there, follow Henck Arron Straat inland from Independence Square for about 1km, then turn right into Swalmberg Straat, which shortly thereafter becomes Letitia Vriesde Laan, passing the Andre Kamperveen Stadium and the flower market on your left. After about 1km, you come to a T-junction where you need to turn left into Kananga Straat and then follow it as it curves 90° before passing through a patch of forest and emerges (to the left) at the zoo entrance after another 1km. The zoo is best visited on normal weekdays, as it is also home to a playground and a petting zoo and these attract lots of families at weekends and public holidays.

Chocopot [off map, 72 A3] This isolated 1km patch of swamp forest is around 8km from the city centre. Though not formally protected as a nature reserve, it is one of Paramaribo's most rewarding and accessible sites for birdwatching and monkey spotting. More than 140 bird species have been recorded here, with some of the more common and conspicuous residents being limpkin, American pygmy kingfisher, black-crested ant-shrike, black-chinned ant-bird, cinnamon attila, chestnut-vented cone-bill and cocoa thrush (the latter giving the site its informal name of Chocopot, a pun on Peperpot). More than 15 raptor species have been noted here, along with seven types of parrot (including chestnut-fronted and scarlet macaw, though neither is common), and there is also a fair chance of seeing howler monkeys, squirrel monkeys and brown capuchins. The wildlife is most active in the first few hours of the morning.

To get to Chocopot, follow Kwatta Weg out of town for 6km, then turn right into Noordwijk Weg and continue along it for about 1.5km. Buses from Heiligen Weg to Weg-na-Zee (see below) can drop passengers at the junction of Kwatta and Noordwijk Weg, from where it is a 15- to 20-minute walk to the forest edge.

Weg-na-Zee [off map, 80 A3] As indicated by its fabulously prosaic name, Weg-na-Zee ('Road-to-Sea') offers the closest direct access to the open ocean from central Paramaribo, though it should be said that its Atlantic shoreline of stark tidal mudflats lapped by murky shallow water is unlikely to attract too many sun-worshippers or bathers. The main attraction of this small suburb, which lies about 15km northwest of the city centre, is the **Tirat Sthaan Rameswarem Temple**, one of the country's largest Hindu shrines, built in 1968 and set in green gardens adorned with dozens of colourful statues of deities, some of which stand more than 10m tall. Visitors are also welcome to visit the country's largest Hindu crematorium, which lies about 2km from the temple. Cremations are usually held at 14.00 on weekdays, and ashes are collected by the relatives and scattered over the ocean the next morning.

Weg-na-Zee is also an excellent place to see marine and aquatic birds. Excluding Warappa Creek, which is accessible only by boat, this is probably the best place in the world to look for the very localised rufous crab-hawk. Other marine birds often recorded here include the magnificent frigate-bird, scarlet ibis, wood stork, osprey, black skimmer, and a wide diversity of herons and egrets, plovers and sandpipers, and gulls and terns. Others associated with the mangroves here include the toco toucan, bicoloured conebill and red-breasted blackbird.

To get here, take Kwatta Weg out of town for about 9km, then turn right into Henry Fernandes Weg and follow it north until it ends in front of the temple and beach. The NVB operates ten buses in either direction daily except Sunday between Heiligen Weg and Weg-na-Zee, leaving at 05.30, 06.00, every hour on the half-hour between 07.30 and 15.30, and 17.00. The trip take about 40 minutes and the fare is SRD 1.10. There is no bus on public holidays.

Dolphin and sunset cruises This popular excursion in a traditional Surinamese tent-boat runs downstream from Leonsberg, past the confluence with the Commewijne River, towards the mouth of the Suriname River, one of the most reliable sites in the country for sighting the Guinean dolphin, a smallish long-beaked species that usually swims in schools of up to ten. Dolphins are present here throughout the year, at almost all times of the day, and while sightings are not guaranteed, the success rate stands at around 95%, though this might vary from a few quick glimpses of one or two surfacing individuals to an extended encounter with a school playing in the boat's wake. The trip is also rewarding for marine bird sightings, with the striking greater frigate-bird (look out for its heavy bill and long streamlined tail) likely to be seen circling overhead amongst the gulls and terns, and the mangrove-lined eastern riverbank often supporting the likes of scarlet ibis, little blue heron, and various gulls and waders.

The tours are run by a few different operators, but we can recommend Waterproof Tours (see pages 78–9), a very ethical organisation that charges SRD 125 per person for adults or SRD 100 for children under 12. Drinks are included in the tour, which leaves from Leonsberg Jetty at 16.00 on Wednesday, Friday and Sunday, continues up the Commewijne for a free sunset snack platter at the village of Margaretha, and then returns at around 17.00. The tour can optionally be extended past sunset to go caiman spotting by canoe in the swamps north of Margaretha.

Coming from Paramaribo, you can catch a Line 4 bus to Leonsberg (at most 15 minutes) but you will need to get a taxi back, which the guide can arrange.

Post boat [81 F7] (*SMS Hse, 44 Waterkant;* \ *410281/479061;* m *8540558;* ⏱ *office 08.00–17.00 Mon–Fri*) Based at the SMS Pier on the Waterkant, the post boat runs several relatively affordable trips that may be of interest to tourists. The best known of these is the seven- to eight-hour **Commewijne Post Boat**, which follows the Commewijne River upstream to the Bakkie and Alliance plantations (see page 133), leaving at 07.00 every Friday and Sunday, and returning the same afternoon. This costs SRD 75 per person for foreigners or SRD 38 for locals, including a guide, but excluding drinks and lunch (these can be bought at the Alliance plantation, though meals should be arranged in advance when you book).

During the busiest tourist months of April, August and September, the post boat also runs a twice-weekly excursion to Jodensavanne (see page 180), which leaves in theory at 07.00 on Thursday and Saturday. The trip costs SRD 175 per person for foreigners or SRD 145 for locals, including a guided tour of Jodensavanne, entrance fees and lunch. This trip was not running in April 2014 due to the dangerous state of the jetty at Jodensavanne, and while it should resume in 2015 it's best to check in advance.

The monthly post boat to Donderskamp, Batavia and Kalebaskreek on the Lower Coppename River (see page 155) had been suspended in early 2014 due to the silting up of the Saramacca Canal, but it should resume once dredging is complete.

Enquiries can be made by calling the numbers given above, or by contacting the tourist office on the ground floor of SMS House at the junction of Waterkant and Watermolen Straat. Details of planned departures are also usually posted on a whiteboard at the SMS Pier.

FURTHER AFIELD Given that most of Suriname's population lives within an hour's drive of the capital, it should come as no surprise that many attractions covered in other chapters in this book are normally visited on day or overnight trips from Paramaribo. This includes almost all sites of interest in Commewijne, Wanica and Parad, most of which can either be visited as part of an organised tour, or independently using public transport or a hired bicycle, depending on your preference and budget. Further details are included under the specific destination, but the following overview of highlights within day-tripping and overnight distance, including the more remote sites, might also be useful.

Top destinations for easy day trips out of Paramaribo include Fort Nieuw Amsterdam, Peperpot Nature Park, the Neotropical Butterfly Park in Lelydorp, Para Flor Botanical Resort in Onverwacht, Domberg and White Beach. More remote destinations include Jodensavanne, Warappa Creek and Brownsberg Nature Park (the latter two can be visited on an organised tour only).

Among the popular overnight destinations are the turtle-nesting beach at Matapica, Brownsberg (often combined with Stoneiland), the upmarket Berg en Dal Resort, the Marron village of Santigron, and the various riverside camps around Zanderij. Some operators also offer overnight tours to Nieuw Nickerie and Bigi Pan, and to Galibi Nature Reserve via Albina.

Most visitors to Suriname also undertake at least one longer trip further afield from the capital. For independent travellers, the easiest area to visit on a longer trip is the Upper Suriname River, which is serviced by several affordable camps and can be accessed and explored using public transport. More remote areas are realistically accessible only by air or on an organised tour, and these include Kabalebo Nature Reserve, Palumeu, Raleigh Falls, Blanch Marie Falls and Ananavero.

6

Commewijne

Running east from the Suriname River directly opposite Paramaribo, the historic district of Commewijne is named after a wide waterway that has served as an important trade conduit since the 17th century, when the first of many plantations was established along its banks. Commewijn is a bastardisation of the local Arawak phrase *kama wini*, meaning 'river of tapirs', and while you would be very lucky to see any terrestrial wildlife quite that large along the river's banks today, the area does still support plenty of monkeys, birds and caimans, while Matapica Beach is arguably the top site in Suriname for turtle viewing.

Due to Commewijne's proximity to Paramaribo, many of its top tourist sites are most regularly visited on a day trip from the capital. These include the pedestrian-friendly Peperpot Nature Park, the historic Fort Nieuw Amsterdam and centuries-old plantations such as Mariënburg, the site of an abandoned sugar factory, and Katwijk, the country's only surviving coffee producer. Most of these sites are regularly included in organised tours, but can also be visited independently without too much effort, or explored whimsically by bicycle. Further afield, the turtle-nesting beach at Matapica and more remote plantations along the bird-rich Warappa Creek are most easily visited on organised tours, or in the case of the latter, the affordable Commewijne Post Boat that leaves Paramaribo's SMS Jetty twice a week (see page 117)

COMMEWIJNE PLANTATION LOOP

This section covers a 60km road loop that runs past several of the more popular and worthwhile sites in Commewijne District, notably Peperpot Nature Park and Fort Nieuw Amsterdam. Although the sites included here are thematically diverse, and any one of them could be visited without the others, it seems practical to group them together for logistical reasons. The main transport hub along the plantation loop is Meerzorg, a small town on the east bank of the Suriname River directly opposite Paramaribo, and linked to it by the Wijdenbosch Bridge and regular taxi-boats. From Wijdenbosch Bridge, the road loop runs west for about 4km through Meerzorg to a major intersection close to the entrance of Peperpot, then north for 15km to the district capital Nieuw Amsterdam, site of the eponymous fort. From here, it follows the Commewijne River east for around 15km to Alkmaar, offering access to the Mariënburg and Katwijk plantations (as well as a jetty from where you can cross to the north bank), then runs south to rejoin the main road between Meerzorg and Albina at Tamanredjo Junction.

GETTING THERE AND AROUND Although Commewijn District lies on the east bank of the Suriname River, most sites along the plantation loop are readily accessible from Paramaribo, by boat, bus, car, bicycle, organised tour, on foot,

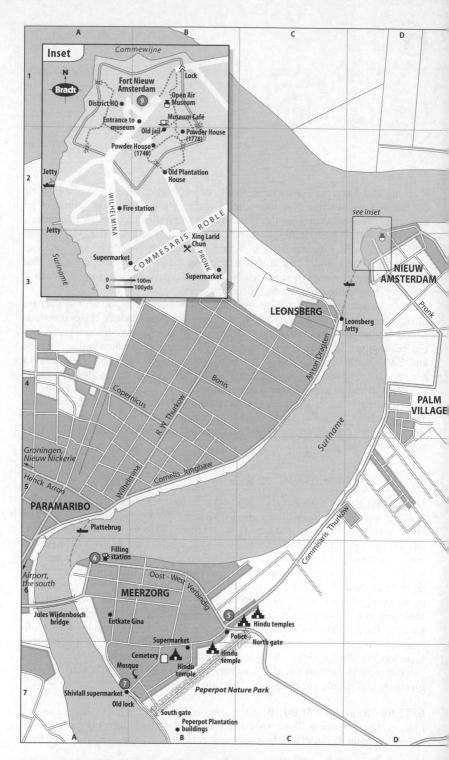

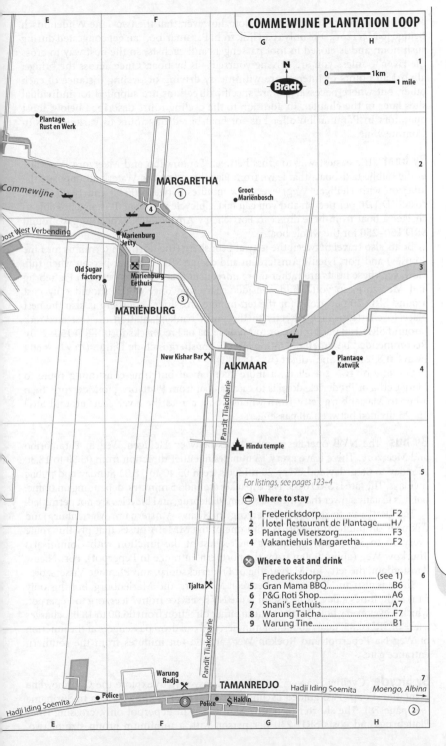

Bradt

0 |———————| 1km
0 |———————| 1 mile

N

E

F

G

H

1

2

Plantage
Rust en Werk

Commewijne

MARGARETHA
①

Groot
Mariënbosch

4

Oost West Verbending

Marienburg
Jetty

3

Old Sugar
factory

Marienburg
Eethuis

MARIËNBURG

③

New Kishar Bar ✕

ALKMAAR

Plantage
Katwijk

4

Pandit Tilakdharie

Hindu temple

5

For listings, see pages 123–4

🛏 **Where to stay**

1	Fredericksdorp..............................	F2
2	Hotel Restaurant de Plantage.......	H7
3	Plantage Viserszorg.......................	F3
4	Vakantiehuis Margaretha..............	F2

✕ **Where to eat and drink**

	Fredericksdorp............................	(see 1)
5	Gran Mama BBQ............................	B6
6	P&G Roti Shop................................	A6
7	Shani's Eethuis...............................	A7
8	Warung Taicha...............................	F7
9	Warung Tine...................................	B1

Tjalta ✕

Pandit Tilakdharie

Warung
Radja ✕

Police

TAMANREDJO   Hadji Iding Soemita   *Moengo, Albina →*

Police $ Haklin

Hadji Iding Soemita

6

7

②

E

F

G

H

or by a combination of the above. Note, however, that the two-lane Wijdenbosch Bridge to Meerzorg, the only road link from Paramaribo, can get congested during rush hour, and is closed to foot passengers and cyclists, so the best way to cross the river – unless you are driving yourself – is by boat. Once across the bridge, almost all points of interest are within easy driving or cycling distance of each other, but where necessary, more specific directions are supplied for individual sites later in the chapter. In addition to the cycling tours described below, most operators in Paramaribo offer bus- or boat-based day tours to various sites in Commewijne.

By boat The easiest way to cross between Paramaribo and Meerzorg is on one of the public taxi-boats that leave from Plattebrug (on the Waterkant opposite the junction with Heiligen Weg) every few minutes between 06.00 and 18.00. These cost SRD 1.20 per person and you can take a bicycle with you. It is also possible to charter a boat from here direct to Fort Nieuw Amsterdam; expect to pay around SRD 150–250 for the whole boat.

Boats also travel between the jetty at Leonsberg (the northern terminus for Line 4 buses) and Fort Nieuw Amsterdam and charge SRD 1.25 per person when full. However, these boats are rather more infrequent that the ones between Plattebrug and Meerzorg, so you could consider chartering one, which should only cost around SRD 20 per group for the ten-minute crossing. Leonsberg is also the best place to charter a boat directly to the north bank plantation of Rust en Werk (around SRD 100 per group), or to Margaretha or Fredericksdorp (SRD 150–200). Recommended boatmen operating out of Leonsberg include Djiran (**m** 7149660), Iwan (**m** 8524677) and Albert (**m** 7154375).

For one or two travellers, a more economical but time-consuming route to Margaretha or Fredericksdorp is to catch a boat from Plattebrug to Meerzorg, then a bus to Mariënburg Jetty, from where a boat across the river costs around SRD 15–25 divided between all passengers.

By bus The NVB operates regular buses between Heiligen Weg in Paramaribo and Meerzorg. These leave every 15 minutes in either direction from 05.30 to 18.30 Monday to Saturday and every 20 minutes from 05.40 to 18.00 Sunday and public holidays. The fare is SRD 0.85. The trip takes around 15 minutes, depending on traffic, but it is usually slower than the boats from Plattebrug, and bicycles are not permitted.

The best way to get from Meerzorg to Nieuw Amsterdam, Mariënburg and Alkmaar on public transport is with one of the MMHA buses that ply this route every 15 to 30 minutes, stopping on request at the junction with Commisaris Thurkow Weg (about 500m from the northern entrance to Peperpot), Fort Nieuw Amsterdam, the jetty for Margaretha or Fredericksdorp, and Plantage Visserszorg.

There is also an NVB service between Meerzorg and Mariënburg, but this only runs eight times a day. More useful is the NVB service from Meerzorg to Peperpot, which leaves every hour on the hour in either direction from 06.00 to 18.00, charges a fare of SRD 0.85, takes about ten minutes, and can drop passengers at the junction of Weg Na Peperpot and Roekon Weg, around ten minutes from the southern entrance gate.

By bicycle Cycling is a very popular and easy way to explore the Commewijne Plantation Loop. Two guided cycling day trips are offered by Fietsen In Suriname (see page 78). The shorter (around 18km) takes in Peperpot only, crossing from Plattebrug, and costs SRD 230 per person with a minimum group size of two, while the longer (about 60km) crosses by boat from Leonsberg to Rust en Werk Plantation, then continues east along the north bank to Margherita, crossing by boat to Katwyk, and costs SRD 340 per person, with a minimum group size of four.

It is also easy enough to explore the area independently using a bicycle hired from Fietsen In Suriname or Cardy Adventures (see page 76). An advantage of going with the former is that they can supply you with a useful descriptive booklet covering cycle routes in Commewijn. Note that it's forbidden to cycle or walk across Wijdenbosch Bridge, and most buses don't allow bicycles on board, so the only way for cyclists to cross between Paramaribo and Commewijne is by boat.

WHERE TO STAY *Map, pages 120–1*
Upmarket ($$$$)
⌂ ✳ **Hotel Fredericksdorp** (6 houses) ☏453083; m 6804403/8984747; e m.hagemeijer@hotmail.com; www.frederiksdorp.com. This absolutely lovely hotel lies on the eponymous former coffee & cocoa plantation, which was founded in 1747, bought by its present owner in 1976, & opened in its present incarnation in 2004. Several buildings, including the old plantation house, date to the late 18th century, & newer buildings have been restored or built in traditional style. Accommodation is in characterful & attractively furnished dbl-storey wooden houses each of which has 2 bedrooms (sleeping a total of 4), a living room with TV, shared bathroom, kitchenette with fridge, & balcony. A good-value restaurant is attached, & the lovely gardens support a wide variety of birds (up to 60 species have been recorded in 1 day). The management also offer a variety of day trips to overnight guests, & special all-inclusive packages out of Paramaribo (see website for details). Access is by boat only. Good value at SRD 210/325/350/550 B&B for 1/2/3/4 people.

⌂ **Hotel-Restaurant de Plantage** (8 cabins) ☏356567; e info@deplantagecommewijne.com; www.deplantagecommewijne.com. Signposted on the south side of the Albina road about 4km east of Tamanredjo Junction, this smart owner-managed lodge is situated on the old Montpelier Plantation, which still support substantial tracts of forest & plenty of wildlife, most conspicuously birds, monkeys & sloths. Accommodation is in colourfully decorated cottages with tiled floors, banana leaf roofs, cane furniture, queen-size beds, large en-suite bathrooms, private balconies with hammock & seating, & facilities include a swimming pool, guided forest & bird walks, & an excellent restaurant serving fusion cuisine in an octagonal dbl-storey building with a palm-leaf roof. Lunch

& light snacks are in the SRD 25–35 range, & a 3-course dinner costs around SRD 100. Stays are for a min 2 nights & include b/fast. It works out at SRD 265/380 per night sgl/dbl occupancy of a dbl chalet, or SRD 530/665 per night for 3/4 people occupying a 4-person chalet, & feels a little overpriced compared with the option below.

Moderate ($$$)
⌂ **Plantage Visserszorg** (4 cabins) Zuster Jensen Weg; ☏322725; m 8754181; e info@surinamevakantiehuisje.nl; www. surinamevakantiehuisje.nl. Situated in a row of large suburban properties separating the villages of Mariënburg & Alkmaar, this rustic & friendly owner-managed lodge is named after the defunct plantation on which it lies. The lush tropical gardens are alive with birds (parrots fly over at dusk & dawn), & the small palm-lined canal running through it also attracts the occasional caiman. Accommodation is in cosy screened dbl or 5-bed wooden cabins with self-catering facilities, mosquito nets, en-suite shower & a private balcony, & facilities include a swimming pool, Wi-Fi & honesty bar. All in all, it's an excellent base for exploring Commewijne by car or bicycle. From SRD 160/230 B&B sgl/dbl, with discounted weekly rates. Lunch or dinner can be prepared on request for SRD 46 a meal.

Budget ($$)
⌂ **Vakantiehuis Margaretha** (4 rooms) m 6804054. This 3-storey riverfront wooden house in the north bank village of Margaretha is run by a family who also regularly arrange trips to nearby Matapica (see pages 130–3). It has twin & dbl rooms, some with AC, shared bath & toilet, & a neat little lounge & balcony overlooking the jetty & river. Decent value at SRD 75 per room.

✕ WHERE TO EAT Map, pages 120–1

There are plenty of decent *eethuises*, warungs and roti shops dotted along the Commewijne Plantation route, with the main concentrations being in central Meerzorg and along the main road immediately west of Tamanredjo Junction. There is also at least one adequate eatery in Nieuw Amsterdam, Mariënburg and Margaretha (the main village on the north bank). Standouts are as follows:

✕ Restaurant Fredericksdorp ☎453083; ⊕ daily. The pick of the Commewijne eateries, this stylish terrace restaurant offers shady seating overlooking the attractive north bank gardens of Fredericksdorp, & a selection of typical Javanese & Surinamese dishes in the SRD 15–20 range. It's well worth catching a boat across the river just to eat here. $

✕ Gran Mama BBQ, Restaurant & Grill Commisaris Thurkow Weg, Meerzorg; m 6804502; ⊕ 10.00–20.00 Wed–Sun. About 200m north of the main junction with Hadji Iding Soemita Weg, within walking distance of the northern entrance to Peperpot, this clean owner-managed eatery serves an unusually wide range of Javanese dishes in the SRD 15–20 range. The food is very tasty, & there's comfortable seating on the wood & tile terrace. $

✕ P&G Roti Shop Zaagmolen Weg, Meerzorg; ⊕ daily. Offering a change from the Javanese fare on offer at most of the restaurants in the area, this small Hindu eatery a few hundred metres from Wijdenbosch Bridge serves excellent chicken & other rotis for around SRD 15–20. $

✕ Shani's Eethuis Weg Na Peperpot, Meerzorg; ⊕ daily. This decent local 'eat house' is distinguished by its bright pink exterior & convenient proximity to the southern entrance of Peperpot. $

✕ Warung Tine Nieuw Amsterdam; ⊕ 10.00–17.00 Tue–Sun. Situated next to the entrance to the fort, this serves the usual Javanese dishes for SRD 10–15 per portion. $

✕ Warung Taicha Hadji Iding Soemita Weg; ☎356222; m 8713809. The pick of half a dozen warungs on the Albina road immediately west of Tamanredjo Junction, this Chinese-run place serves mostly Javanese dishes for around SRD 12–15. $

WHAT TO SEE AND DO

Peperpot Nature Park (*Hadji Iding Soemita Weg, Meerzorg;* m *7230070/7125953;* e *info@peperpotnaturepark.org; www.peperpotnaturepark.org;* ⊕ *08.30–15.00 Tue–Sun, 08.30–noon public holidays; entrance SRD 18 (foreigners), SRD 6 (local adults) SRD 3 (children under 12)*) Centred on the disused Mopentibe Plantation only 5km southeast of central Paramaribo, the 26ha Peperpot Nature Park protects a small but astonishingly biodiverse enclave of lush swamp forest in the heart of an otherwise rapidly urbanising area. The park is renowned for its varied fauna, which includes several mammal and more than 250 bird species, and is bisected by a short cycling and walking trail that ranks as perhaps the best birdwatching site in the immediate vicinity of the capital. This park is particularly rewarding for visitors who don't have the time or means to travel deeper into the Surinamese jungle. It is earmarked to play an important role in generating greater local ecological awareness, and there are plans to construct an educational facility over the next few years.

History and future developments The nature park is named after the adjacent Peperpot (Pepper Pot) Plantation, which is one of Suriname's oldest, established in the 1680s, initially to farm tobacco, but later given over to coffee and cocoa production. Peperpot changed hands several times prior to its closure in 1998. Today, the nature park is managed in conjunction with the Guianas branch of WWF, which was also involved in the establishment in 2009 of the adjacent Peperpot Nature Corridor, an 800ha stand of swamp forest running south to Paulus Creek via the disused plantations of Peperpot, La Liberté, Puttenzorg and t'Yland. This corridor is earmarked for several exciting developments, notably the construction of a world-class Discovery Centre (incorporating a research centre, additional nature trails and a digital education platform for schoolchildren) funded by a grant from the Dutch Embassy and a donation by the Dutch Postcode Lottery, and scheduled for completion by 2017. It is also hoped that restoration of the original plantation compound (about 1km southeast of the park's southwest gate) will follow, as it includes several rundown houses and sheds dating to the 18th or 19th century.

Getting there and away There are two entrances to Peperpot, one at the northeast end of the Mopentibe Trail, on Hadji Iding Soemita Weg (the main road towards Albina) about 500 east of the junction with Commisaris Thurkow Weg, and the other tucked away on Weg Na Peperpot at the southwest end of the trail, about 3km from the main road. Arriving by bicycle or car, the northeast gate is the better signposted, easier to find and more accessible of the two, and it also lies within easy walking distance of the MMHA bus route from Meerzorg to Alkmaar. Self-drivers will need to return to whichever gate they entered, and walkers will probably also find this to be more convenient than using the longer and more circuitous road route to/from the southwest gate. However, cyclists and walkers could also take a shortcut one-way between the southwest gate and Meerzorg via Weg Na Peperpot and Pandit Murli Weg, or use the hourly NVB bus service from Weg Na Peperpot (near the southern gate) to Meerzorg.

What to see and do The only activity currently offered at Peperpot Nature Park is the 3.2km **Mopentibe Trail** (which many visitors extend to 6.4km by walking or cycling in both directions). The trail runs parallel to a canal through an area of dense forest, which is dominated by the moco-moco shrub (*Montrichardia arborescens*), a bushy swamp-associated perennial flowers and fruit that attract large numbers of birds and monkeys. The forest also contains various larger trees, as well as shade-loving cocoa and coffee plants. Brown capuchin and squirrel monkeys are the most frequently observed mammals, giant iguanas can often be seen crashing through the undergrowth, and a varied cast of invertebrates includes several spectacular species of butterfly.

The main attraction of the trail is its rich birdlife, which includes several forest species normally associated with more remote sites. This is the best place in the vicinity of Paramaribo to see three very localised species: the blood-coloured woodpecker, arrowhead piculet and ashy headed greenlet. Other regularly observed forest birds of interest include the cinereous tinamou, black hawk-eagle, slender-billed kite, green-rumped parakeet, green parrot, little cuckoo, white-tailed trogon, black-necked aracari, great potoo, Guianan piculet, green-tailed jacamar, spotted puffbird, black-crested ant-shrike, blackish ant-bird, cinnamon attila and crested oropendola, while the canals are the favoured habitat of green ibis, limpkin, rufescent tiger-heron and five species of kingfisher.

Serious birders and wildlife enthusiasts are advised to allow at least three hours, preferably longer, to explore the Mopentibe Trail, and to bring binoculars. Also, bearing in mind that birds and monkeys tend to be most active and conspicuous in the early morning and late afternoon, you could consider forking out an extra SRD 18 for a special pass (available on the spot) that allows access through the northeast gate as early as 06.30 or until 18.15. In addition to wildlife being more active in the early morning, there are usually no other visitors around to create a disturbance. Finally, it is worth buying a copy of the WWF booklet *Birds of Peperpot*, which includes a full bird checklist, plus photographs and descriptions of 30 of the more common species with English and Dutch text, and is stocked at the entrance gates (where it effectively costs SRD 19.50, as the cover price includes one person's entrance fee).

Nieuw Amsterdam One of the most popular day trips from Paramaribo is to the modest hamlet of Nieuw Amsterdam (population 1,200), which stands on the east bank of the Suriname River at its confluence with the Commewijne, directly opposite Leonsberg and about 10km northeast of the city centre. The administrative capital of Commewijne District since 1907, this small settlement is dominated by Fort Nieuw Amsterdam, which was built in the mid 18th century as a first line of defence against naval attacks on Paramaribo and the plantations of Commewijne. The strategically located fort was the most important military installation in Suriname for at least a century thereafter, and it would go on to serve as the country's main prison for long-term offenders from the late 19th century until the 1960s. Extending over some 15ha of green swampy land drained by several canals, the fort today operates a rewarding open-air museum.

History The earliest plantations on the Commewijne River were established in the mid 17th century and lay some distance upriver of its mouth, closer to the confluence with the Cottica, which was chosen as the site of the district's first fortified building. This was Fort Sommelsdijck, founded in 1686 and named after Governor Cornelis Sommelsdijck, and strengthened in 1715. However, in 1734, Governor-General de Cheusses decided to build a larger fort closer to Paramaribo, at the confluence of the Commewijne and Suriname rivers, a site known to the earliest settlers as Tijgershol (Jaguar's Den). Construction, which started in 1735, went less than smoothly. It turned out that the local clay was too moist and saline to bake bricks on site as initially planned, and also that the ground was too soft and marshy to support a structure made entirely from bricks. By 1747, however, Fort Nieuw Amsterdam was more-or-less fully operational. Fort Sommelsdijck was decommissioned a year later, and though it continued to serve in a non-military capacity after that, it was abandoned completely in 1870 and few traces of it remain today.

Strategically positioned to protect both Paramaribo and the upriver plantations from naval attacks, Fort Nieuw Amsterdam was originally supported by armed batteries on the west bank of the Suriname River and north bank of the Commewijne. It was built in the shape of a regular pentagon, with five bastions named after various Dutch provinces, and a surrounding trench (crossed by a drawbridge) that could be transformed into a moat simply by opening a sluice gate. Within the ramparts were several barracks and officers' housing, a blacksmith and a wind-powered flour mill, two powder houses and several reservoirs. Despite this, it met with limited success in its primary role as a military installation, falling to the British in 1799 and again in 1804, reputedly without a shot being fired.

As the importance of the fort waned towards the end of the 19th century, the high maintenance costs became increasingly hard to justify. In 1872, the Dutch administration transformed one of the former barracks into a prison. In 1907, Nieuw Amsterdam replaced Fredericksdorp as the administrative centre of Commewijne, and the fort was totally abandoned by the military. The fort enjoyed a short military revival during World War II, when the USA installed large guns on the bastions to protect its bauxite mining interests at Moengo and Paranam. It also served as a concentration camp, as several German sailors from the sunken *Goslar* were interned in the cells, along with 146 Dutch East Indian prisoners with suspected affiliations to the Nazi-sympathising Nationaal-Socialistische Beweging

(NSB). The prison was finally shut down in the 1960s. It 1965, funded largely with money donated by Parbo Brewery, the rundown fort underwent major renovations before reopening as an open-air museum in 1968. It was accorded national monument status in 2005.

Getting there and away Nieuw Amsterdam lies on the east bank of the Suriname River, a 15km drive south of Meerzorg and the Wijdenbosch Bridge, following Commisaris Thurkow Weg then Pronk Weg. Most organised tours to Commewijne stop at the fort. Travelling from Paramaribo on public transport, you can either take a bus to Leonsberg and then a boat across the river to the jetty in front of the fort, or a taxi-boat from Plattebrug to Meerzorg, then the MMHA bus towards Alkmaar, asking to be dropped at Nieuw Amsterdam.

What to see and do The focal point of the small town is the **Fort Nieuw Amsterdam Openlucht (Open Air) Museum** [120 B1] (*Wilhelmina Straat, Nieuw Amsterdam;* \322225/7; e *info@fortnieuwamsterdam.sr; www.fortnieuwamsterdam. sr, www.fortnieuwamsterdam.com;* ⊕ *09.00–17.00 Mon–Fri, 10.00–18.00 Sat, Sun & public holidays; entrance SRD 10 (foreigners), SRD 5 (locals); optional guide fee SRD 35 per party),* which incorporates the half of the fort north of Wilhelmina Straat. The core of the museum is the 'House of Correction', or prison, built under Governor Willem van Idsinga in 1872. Here, several of the old solitary confinement cells are preserved in their original almost lightless state, while larger cells house displays on the history of the fort, the Commewijne plantations, the transatlantic slave trade, and the Ashanti Kingdom and coastal forts of Ghana (a major source of the slaves shipped to Suriname). There is also an interesting display comparing photographs of various streets in central Paramaribo in the early 20th century with ones taken at the same site in more recent times – some, like the trio of early 19th-century buildings at the junction of Waterkant and Watermolen Straat, are practically unchanged, while others, such as Vaillantsplein, are barely recognisable. Opposite the old prison buildings, the museum café sells a limited selection of drinks and snacks.

From the old prison, you can continue to the open-air part of the museum, which incorporates the original whitewashed *kruithuis* ('gunpowder house') built in 1740, and its more water-resistant redbrick 1778 replacement, ironically enclosed by a pretty lily-covered moat. There's also a 19th-century *koetshuis* ('coach house') complete with several old carriages, the original 18th-century brick sluice, a lighthouse dating to 1905, two large sealed water reservoirs built in 1740, and a barrage of cannons dating from 1722 onwards. Look out too for one of the massive *kappas* (metal pots) that were used to boil sugarcane, which was grown on several of the surrounding plantations, to transform it into sugar, a process that required continuous stirring to prevent it from caramelising. The impressive plantation house north of the main cluster of buildings is not the original, but an accurate replica constructed in 1986.

Outside the fenced open-air museum, the southern half of the fort incorporates a few time-worn administrative buildings, and a monument, erected in 2008, commemorating the arrival of the first Chinese workers in 1853. Overlooking the Suriname River, immediately outside the southeastern buttress, is the American battery installed during World War II. It is said that the range of these cannons extended all the way to the mouth of the Suriname River, and that the whole of Nieuw Amsterdam shook when the guns were fired. The waterways and marshes around the fort also harbour caimans, monkeys and varied birdlife (look out in particular for the localised white-headed marsh tyrant). Looking out from the bastion over the river confluence, you can sometimes see dolphins.

Mariënburg Situated around 6km east of Nieuw Amsterdam, Mariënburg is probably the largest town in Commewijne, with a population estimated at around 4,500. It lies close to the south bank of the Commewijne River, stretching inland for about 1km from the taxi-boat jetty facing the north bank estate of Margaretha. The town itself is of limited interest to tourists, but it does boast a few cheap eateries and bars, and is also accessible by MMHA bus as they run regularly between Meerzorg and Alkmaar.

Of greater interest is the disused and rather dilapidated **Mariënburg Sugar Factory** [121 F3] (see box, below), which can be reached by following the main road through town south for 1.3km past the junction with the Nieuw Amsterdam road, then turning right onto a well-marked 200m dirt road that leads to the parking area. The best guide is the enthusiastic Mr Soekhardi (m 8519239), a former factory worker who can almost always be found at the site. If he is not there, however, other guides are usually ready to show visitors around. The old director's house, next to the parking area, has been restored as a mini-museum dedicated to the history of Mariënburg and its sugar factory. In theory, the museum is open from 10.00 to 17.00 daily, but in practice it is often closed, so best to call Mr Soekhardi ahead if you want him to try and make sure the people responsible for the museum are there. There are also two large monuments in the old factory grounds. The one in front of the mini-museum commemorates the first Javanese workers to arrive at Mariënburg in August 1890, while the other, about 100m to its

MARIËNBURG SUGAR FACTORY

Founded in 1745 by the widow Maria de la Jaille, the Mariënburg Sugar Plantation underwent several changes of ownership and fortune prior to being bought by the royally decreed Nederlandsche Handel-Maatschappij (NHM) in 1882. It was subsequently transformed into one of the largest enterprises in Suriname: a massive mechanised sugar factory was constructed by the NHM, which then laid a 12km railway track to carry cut cane there for processing, and shipped across large numbers of Javanese and Indian contract workers from August 1890 onwards.

On 29 July 1902, the (mostly Hindu) workers at the sugar factory went on strike to demand better wages and working conditions, a tense and violent uprising that led to the infamous Mariënburg Massacre wherein 24 workers were shot dead by the colonial military forces. Another 32 workers were injured, and eight of the strike leaders were sentenced to 12 years hard labour. The bodies of the slaughtered workers were deposited in a mass grave and its undocumented location is currently being investigated by archaeologists.

After World War II, Mariënburg became an important supplier of molasses to Suriname Alcoholic Beverages (SAB), the producers of several brands of rum including the very strong (80–90% alcohol) Mariënburg brand. In 1957, a refinery was added to produce granulated sugar. In 1964, the factory was sold to Rubber Cultuurmaatschappij Amsterdam, which ceased to invest in it, leading to its eventual closure in 1986. On 30 July 2006, more than a century after the Mariënburg Massacre, a monument to its victims was unveiled *in situ* by Vice President Ramdien Sardjoe.

southeast, is dedicated to the 24 labourers killed during a strike action in 1902 (see box, opposite). A visit to the factory is incorporated into the 'Sugar Trail' day tour offered by Waterproof Tours (see pages 78–9).

Alkmaar and Plantage Katwijk The most easterly town on the south bank of the Commewijne River is Alkmaar [121 G4], which lies about 12km upriver of Nieuw Amsterdam at the junction of the surfaced road leading south to Tamanredjo Junction on the main Albina Road. Sometimes referred to locally as Goedoefrow (a corruption of the name of a former plantation owner that literally means 'rich woman'), Alkmaar supports a slightly smaller population than Mariënburg, but is rather more sprawling in nature, and sites of interest are limited to a Moravian church built in 1923, and a few local bars and eateries.

Alkmaar's main touristic claim to fame is that it's the gateway town to **Plantage Katwijk** [121 H4] (✆ 421750; m 8513377/8803342; e plantagekatwijk@gmail.com; www.facebook.com/Plantage.Katwijk.Suriname; ⊕ Mon–Sat), which lies about 3km further east along the dirt Tjetje Weg (signposted to Bar Jurgen). Katwijk is currently the sole remaining coffee plantation in Suriname, growing a combination of arabica and robusta varietals, which it then processes and packs onsite for its own KW brand. It is also one of the oldest Commewijn plantations, established in 1746 when the governor of Paramaribo issued some 200ha (530 acres) of land to the 13-year-old Alida Wossink, who developed it as a coffee estate with three successive husbands prior to her death in 1885, and gained a reputation for being a particularly harsh task mistress 'who, for the slightest mistake, had her slaves whipped'. Katwijk underwent several changes of ownership prior to being bought by its present owners in 1974, but coffee has evidently remained its primary crop throughout its long history. Informative three-hour guided tours explaining coffee production, and ending with a cup of home-grown KW coffee and a dip in the swimming pool at the plantation house, cost SRD 50 per person.

North bank plantations Accessible by boat only, a string of historic plantations runs along the north bank of the Commewijne River east of its confluence with the Suriname. The most westerly of these, **Plantage Rust en Werk** [121 E2] ('Rest and Work'; m 6804141; e vcm.rustenwerk@sr.net; www.vcm.sr) is now the centrepiece of a 5,600ha livestock and shrimp farm amalgamated from a dozen old plantations by the private Verenigde Cultuur Maatschappijen (VCM) since 1947. One of the oldest north bank plantations, Rust en Werk was established in 1750 by Lieutenant Colonel Wigbold Crommelin, a Dutch military leader who had arrived in Suriname two years earlier and would later serve as governor-general (the 18th-century cemetery where several members of the Crommelin family are buried can still be seen on the estate). In the mid 19th century, Rust en Werk was home to the largest sugarcane factory in South America, but this was later relocated south of the river in Mariënburg. Today, the large estate is popular with cyclists, but it also operates motorised tours (in a double-decker bus) and offers excellent walking, birdwatching and fishing opportunities.

About 4km east of Rust en Werk, **Margaretha** (or Margrita), set on the defunct plantation of Johan en Margaretha, is a riverside village of a few hundred inhabitants. The village sees quite a bit of tourist traffic, as it is the launching point for boats to Matapica Beach (see pages 130–3) and also where dolphin and sunset cruises stop for a sundowner snack and drink. There are a couple of good warungs in town, and several supermarkets, while the waterfront Vakantiehuis Margaretha (see page 123) is a good budget place to stay for those keen to explore the north bank at a more leisurely pace.

Less than 1km further east, **Plantage Fredericksdorp**, now an attractive and well-priced hotel and restaurant (see page 123), is named after Johan Friedrich Knoffel, who founded it as a coffee plantation in 1747. It incorporates several historical buildings, most notably a director's house dating from the 1760s and prison cells from the plantation's lengthy stint as the capital of Commewijne prior to the administration being relocated to Nieuw Amsterdam in 1907. The well-wooded grounds, running down to the river, are alive with birds, and day visitors are welcome to look around, making it a great place to stop for a relaxing lunch. If you are feeling energetic, you could head another 2km east to **Groot Mariënbosch** [121 G2] (✆ +31 65 1230070; www.landgoedgrootmarienbosch.com), a little-visited but still operational plantation noted for its historic buildings. These include the original plantation house, whose ground floor was built in 1774 (the date is inscribed in bricks on the veranda) and an impressive 19th-century sluice gate.

Getting there and around If you are already in Commewijne, the best way to get to the north bank plantations is by taking one of the inexpensive taxi-boats that run regularly from Mariënburg Jetty (✆ N5 53.132 W55 02.755) to Margaretha and Fredericksdorp. Coming from Paramaribo, as most people do, the cheapest option is to take a bus from the city centre to Leonsberg, and charter a boat from there (see page 122). A costlier but perhaps more convenient way is to charter a boat directly from Plattebrug in the city centre. Finally, the longer guided bike tours offered by Fietsen In Suriname (see page 78) incorporate visits to the main north bank plantations. Once on the north bank, a flat cycling and walking track connects Rust en Werk to Mariënbosch via Margaretha and Fredericksdorp, a total distance of around 7km.

MATAPICA BEACH

One of the region's most important marine turtle-nesting sites, Matapica Beach is the name loosely applied to the 20km of wild uninhabited Atlantic coastline that stretches east from Braamspunt (on the combined estuary of the Suriname and Commewijne rivers) to the mouth of the smaller Matapica Creek. Unusually for Suriname, the coastline here is predominantly sandy, and while the water might be a little too rough and murky for it to qualify as a conventional beach resort, it does provide ideal conditions both for the turtles to lay their massive clutches of eggs, and also for visitors to witness this thrilling phenomenon. In terms of turtle encounters, we regard Matapica as the best site in Suriname, since you are based right on the beach, and thus have a better chance of daylight sightings than you would at better-known rival Galibi. The most common species here, as in Galibi, is green turtle, but leatherbacks are also quite frequent. Olive ridley and hawksbill turtles also nest here, but very occasionally and sightings are rare. The main nesting season for green turtles runs from February to May, and for leatherbacks from April to July. Turtles are highly unlikely to be seen at other times.

GETTING THERE AND AWAY Though it lies only 20km northeast of Paramaribo as the crow flies, Matapica has a very remote feel and is accessible only by boat or by helicopter. The normal point of departure is the north bank village of Margaretha, from where small motorboats follow the artificial Matapica Canal north for about 10km, crossing a slipway en route and then heading west for about 7km to Diani Beach, which is currently the best site for turtle viewing and is lined with perhaps five hammock shelters. The ride out, mostly through mangrove-lined canals and patches of still open water, is usually very smooth and dry, unless it rains. The journey takes up to two hours from Margaretha, but might require a bit longer if you stop to admire any birds or monkeys *en route*.

Most operators in Paramaribo can offer all-inclusive overnight tours to Matapica. These usually range in price from around SRD 400–700 per person, with some added negotiability for large groups. In addition, Fietsen in Suriname (see page 78) runs a one-day bike and boat tour for SRD 640 per person, as well as a more adventurous two-day kayak trip for SRD 790 per person. Jenny Tours (see page 78) offers a boat-in, helicopter-out package for SRD 900 per person. All tours include transport to/from Paramaribo, meals, soft drinks and sleeping gear (tent or hammock) if staying overnight.

Although the overwhelming majority of tourists follow the path of least resistance and visit Matapica with a Paramaribo-based operator, the on-the-ground arrangements (boats, food, etc) for these tours are generally handled by experienced locals based in Margaretha, and it is possible to make your arrangements with them directly. Typically, you'd be looking at a straight boat hire of around SRD 350 for a group of up to four, which would literally just include transport between Margaretha and Matapica, but would require you to bring all your own food, drinks and sleeping gear. Alternatively, an all-inclusive trip with a pickup in Margaretha or Leonsberg should coat around SRD 350–420 per person (minimum group size four, with discounts for larger groups). Contact Winkel Robby (m *6804054*) or Albert (m *8621859*).

WHERE TO STAY AND EAT Matapica Beach is more or less uninhabited and there is no formal accommodation here. Most tours stay in one of the four or five hammock huts that have been constructed along the Diana Beach by various local operators. Usually the operator will provide either a hammock with a mosquito net, or a tent with mattress and sheet, but you may want to confirm this when you book. The operator will also supply all meals, snacks and soft drinks. There is no shop at the beach, so bring all alcoholic beverages with you (local beers and brandy are sold at a few shops in Margaretha) and anything else you might need.

WHAT TO SEE AND DO The main activity, with luck, will be **turtle watching**. This is usually undertaken at night, but it is well worth strolling along the beach every hour or so in daylight. Leatherbacks often nest by day, and when tides are suitable, green turtles might also be out of the water towards dusk or in the early morning. The tell-tale sign of a nesting turtle is a fresh trail (like a giant one-wheeled truck), close to the water that has yet to be washed away. If you do locate a turtle while she is laying eggs, maintain a comfortable distance and try to stay out of her line of vision, so you don't spook her before she has completed her task. Once the eggs have been laid, she will usually spend at least 30 minutes burying them before she returns to the sea, and this is when, with some sensitivity, it is possible to approach more closely, quietly and in small groups (see box, page 132).

For **birders**, a highlight of a trip to Matapica will be the boat journey through the mangroves, assuming you can persuade the skipper to cut back on the speed a little. Expect to see a good range of herons and egrets, along with wattled jacana, purple gallinule, various kingfishers and a fair number of raptors, and marsh-associated passerines such as carib grackle, yellow oriole and yellow-headed blackbird. Once at Matapica, the beach is well suited to long seaside rambles and runs, with a chance of spotting a few waders along the way, but swimming should be undertaken with caution, as there is no lifeguard, the water is often rough and the undertow can be quite strong.

The four species of marine turtle that nest on the beaches of Suriname are all listed as endangered due to global threats such as habitat destruction, direct harvesting for food, incidental capture by fishermen, and eggs being preyed upon by domestic animals. People seldom have an opportunity to observe turtles in the wild because they are so rare and difficult to find. However, tourists who visit the Surinamese beaches of Galibi and Matapica during the nesting season of February to July (sometimes running into August) are provided with an excellent chance of watching a sea turtle come ashore to nest. Unfortunately, however, keep in mind that guiding standards in Suriname are not always what might be hoped for, which places some responsibility on the individual tourists to ensure that any sighting is handled in a manner that minimises the disturbance of these sensitive creatures whilst maximising the chances of having a great experience:

- Sea turtles are very sensitive to light and a photographic flash can damage their eyes. For this reason, flash photography is prohibited in most turtle-breeding sites globally, and you are urged not to use a flash even if your guide permits or encourages it.
- Use a torch (flashlight) or headlamp with a red filter. Sea turtles are less sensitive to red light. But avoid shining any light in the turtle's eyes or near her head.
- Wear dark clothing to reduce the chances that a turtle will see you approaching.
- Wear closed-toed shoes with socks. Although sandals are fun to wear on the beach, they can cause blisters when walking for a long time.
- While walking, always stay with your guide and feel free to ask lots of questions about turtles and their conservation needs.
- It is best to walk on the wet sand close the waterline, but do watch out for waves.
- Speak softly and move slowly when you are around the turtle to avoid disturbing her. Too much disturbance will cause her to return to the sea without nesting.
- Always stay behind the turtle's front flippers. Stay about 3m behind the turtle when she is covering her nest, or the powerful flippers will cover you with sand.
- When she begins returning to the ocean, shift your position so that you stay behind her and on the landward side, giving her a clear path and view of the ocean. When she is crawling back to sea, do not get between her and the ocean.
- Remember that sea turtles are endangered so you should feel very lucky if you are able to observe one in the wild. No-one can predict when or where a sea turtle will come ashore, so do not become frustrated if your guide is unable to find one. Not finding a turtle only illustrates the need to provide better protection for these amazing but endangered animals. Whether you see a turtle or not, consider tipping your guide if they were knowledgeable and sincere.

Caimans are abundant in the swamps between Margaretha and Matapica, but are most easily seen at night when you can ask your guide or boatman to take you out looking for them – even if you don't get lucky, paddling through the swamp by night, with the lights of Paramaribo glowing on the western horizon, is a rather spooky and wonderful experience.

WARAPPA CREEK

Running north from the Commewijne River, 3km west of its confluence with the Cottica, Warappa Creek was an important travel route in the 18th century, when its banks were lined with sugar, cotton and coffee plantations, and a northerly extension leading to the Atlantic was dug by slaves. Following the abolition of slavery in 1863, most of the Warappa plantations were abandoned as unprofitable, and a long stretch of the creek silted up, rendering it unnavigable for more than a century. Its revival dates to 2007, when Dutch-born Marcha Mormon traced her roots to the former Reynsdorp Plantation, and together with her husband Bas van der Spek decided to develop it as a tourist facility. The silted up waterway was reopened all the way to the Atlantic in 2008, and Reynsdorp, often referred to as Bakkie (the name of the administrative resort in which it lies) is now the headquarters of the Warappa Foundation (*www.warappakreek.com*), which is concerned with the deployment of sustainable tourism and educational facilities in the area.

The creek is a particularly worthwhile place for **birdwatchers** to visit. Running through dense stands of mangroves, it protects a similar variety of coastal species as the Matapica Canal, before opening out onto a stretch of Atlantic coastline where a bird observatory overlooks a series of mudflats. Here, depending to some extent on the season, you can expect to see large flocks of wading shorebirds, along with such eagerly sought larger aquatic species as black skimmer, scarlet ibis, roseate spoonbill and wood stork. This is also regarded as the top site in the world for the localised rufous crab-hawk, while interesting species often seen in the mangroves include pygmy kingfisher, blood-coloured woodpecker, arrowhead piculet and the elusive ashy-headed greenlet. The area is also rich in **historic attractions** such as a 1830s sugar factory with steam engines, old locks and gates, and an excellent private museum at Reynsdorp that houses a large collection of historic books, prints, maps, paintings, and old household utensils and artefacts such as slave shackles. A lodge comprising a dozen houses is also under construction at Reynsdorp.

GETTING THERE AND AWAY Several operators offer full-day tours to Warappa Creek, but as far as we can ascertain they are all ultimately organised and guided by **Bondru Tours** (m *8826049/8256464*; e *info@bondrutourssuriname.com; www. bondrutourssuriname.com*), cost around SRD 350 per person and the minimum group size is four. The tour involves taking the bus to Alkmaar, travelling by boat to the creek and the Atlantic bird observatory, stopping *en route* at Reynsdorp and its museum, and having lunch at Alliance, a citrus plantation situated at the confluence of the creek and the Commewijne River. Dedicated bird tours led by an ornithologist can be arranged on request.

A more affordable option is the Commewijn Post Boat (` *410281/479061*), which runs from the SMS Jetty in Paramaribo to Alliance and Reynsdorp/Bakkie every Friday and Sunday. This costs SRD 75 for tourists or SRD 38 for locals, inclusive of a guide, and lunch can be served by prior arrangement at Alliance. The boat leaves at 07.00, spends about six hours on the water, and around one hour at each plantation, getting back to Paramaribo at around 16.00. Be aware, however, that it doesn't travel up the creek beyond Reynsdorp, so you won't catch sight of the ocean.

The most easterly settlement in Commewijne, the tiny hamlet of Stolkertsijver (literally 'Stolkert's Diligence') lies alongside the Commewijne River on the main road to Albina, perhaps 5km before it crosses into Marowijne District. The site of an impressive metal bridge constructed in 1980, the village is also home to a comfortable eating shelter, a supermarket and a well-known vegetable stall. Most eastbound organised tours from Paramaribo make a stop there. The town is named after the disused plantation Stolkertsijver, which was one of the earliest in the country, founded in the 1660s under the name Courcabo. It was also the site of one of the country's earliest churches, but this had been abandoned by 1702 and no trace of it remains today. Stolkertsijver plantation was later associated with two of Suriname's most notoriously cruel female slave owners: Anna Magdalena Bleij (1724–81) and Maria Susanna Duplessis (see box, page 160). The plantation is named after Duplessis's second husband, Frederik Cornelis Stolkert, who inherited it in 1775 and farmed sugar there until his death in 1804.

About 20 minutes boat trip upriver of Stolkertsijver, another abandoned plantation called Concordia is the site of an old steam train and an overgrown cast-iron mill of a type unknown elsewhere in Suriname. The only operator to explore this area much beyond the supermarket and eating shelter at Stolkertsijver is Waterproof Tours (see pages 78–9), and their 'Sugar Trail' itinerary includes a boat trip to Concordia, by exclusive arrangement with the board of the plantation's descendants. For independent travellers, though any public transport headed between Paramaribo and Albina could drop you at Stolkertsijver, it would be difficult (and possibly illegal) to visit the old plantations outside the context of the aforementioned tour.

7

Marowijne

This 4,627km² administrative district is named after the Marowijne (or Maroni) River, which runs along the eastern border with French Guiana, and whose name derives from the local Karina phrase *mara-uni*, meaning 'endless river'. The district supports a population of around 20,000, most of which is concentrated in two port towns: the administrative capital Albina, on the Marowijne River, and the former bauxite mining centre of Moengo on the Cottica. Prior to the construction of the Moengo to Albina road in 1964, the district was somewhat isolated from the rest of the country, and its two main towns were accessible only by river. It was again largely cut off from the rest of the country in the late 1980s, when it became the focal point of a long civil war that resulted in the partial abandonment of Albina and Moengo and the destruction of several bridges. Today, however, a good surfaced road and bridge serviced by regular buses connect Paramaribo to Albina and Moengo. The district's main attraction is the Galibi Nature Reserve, an important turtle-nesting site situated at the mouth of the Marowijne about a two-hour boat ride north of Albina. Other sites of interest include the French Guianan city of Saint-Laurent-du-Maroni (easily visited on a day trip from Albina) and the Tembe Art Studio in Moengo, and visitors can also explore the Cottica and Marowijne rivers by boat.

MOENGO

The largest urban centre in Marowijne and the fourth largest in the country, Moengo is an attractive river port set on the east bank of the Cottica, a navigable tributary of the Commewijne. A company-built town founded in the early 20th century and the birthplace of Suriname's bauxite mining industry, Moengo has suffered a prolonged economic slump since the 1980s. Today, the town's spacious neat layout and scattering of grandiose old company buildings seem to emphasise rather than disguise its subdued and rather rundown aura. Still, Moengo is an intriguing place, not least due to the proximity of the forest-fringed Cottica River, and it is also emerging as a latent cultural hub, largely thanks to the efforts of Marcel Pinas, the founder of the Tembe Art Studio (which has invited a number of international artists to adorn the town with their work) and the new Moengo Festival of Theatre and Dance. Rather more lively than the old town centre is Wonoredjo, a less ostentatiously conceived residential area that lies immediately to the east.

HISTORY Formerly the site of a remote Marron village, Moengo (a local Amerindian word meaning 'hill', and sometimes spelled Mungo) was founded in 1916 by the Suriname Bauxite Company, a subsidiary of the US-owned Aluminium Company of America (Alcoa), to exploit the region's rich deposits of extractable bauxite. Bauxite was first mined in Moengo in 1920, and it reached the USA two years later, exported via the Cottica River and then Trinidad. A customised mining town, designed to accommodate 1,000 families, Moengo was built on residentially segregated lines (with easterly Wonoredjo being the 'lower class' suburb), and the company management enforced a rigid social hierarchy, one initially based largely on ethnicity, and later on income and occupation. That said, most sources concur that the across-the-board standard of living at Moengo was far higher than the national average, as were wages.

Despite its growing economic importance to the national economy, Moengo suffered a temporary slump linked to the Great Depression in the early 1930s. This led to the retrenchment of many workers. Even so, Moengo replaced Albina as the administrative centre of Marowijne in 1932, and four years later a bi-weekly passenger boat service to Paramaribo was introduced. Bauxite production and export increased greatly during World War II, when Suriname emerged as one of the world's largest producers of the aluminium-bearing ore, and the port at Moengo was protected by a significant US military presence. Moengo relinquished its short-lived status as district capital to Albina in 1945.

In the early days, the town's inherent isolation was enhanced by several company policies. These included the decision to increase productivity by putting back the clock one hour, which placed it in a different time zone to the rest of Suriname, and a ban on unauthorised outsider visits. Moengo remained accessible only by river until 1955, when an airstrip was cleared about 1km to the south. The main road connecting Paramaribo to Albina followed in 1964.

Bauxite production at Moengo fell into slight decline during the 1970s, primarily due to the depletion of readily extractable reserves. The closure of mining operations was hastened by the civil war in the 1980s and subsequent tensions between striking workers, the US management and the military government. Alcoa suspended all mining operations in Suriname over the course of 1986/87, when the area around Moengo emerged as the main centre of fighting between government forces and Ronnie Brunswijk's 'Jungle Commando'. Indeed, the town was more or less evacuated in the late 1980s, as former company employees either returned home or took refuge in French Guiana. Those who returned following the 1992 ceasefire found that civil amenities had ground to a virtual standstill. The mine at Moengo remained non-operational even after an agreement between Alcoa and the government was reached in 1993 (leading to the reopening of mines elsewhere in the country), and it still is today. Nevertheless, the population has grown steadily from around 7,000 in 1997 to an estimated 10,000 today. Even so, Moengo feels strikingly less prosperous than most other urban areas in Suriname.

GETTING THERE AND AROUND
By road Moengo lies about 100km east of Paramaribo and some 2km north of the main road to Albina. The junction is clearly signposted. The only tour operator offering day and overnight trips to Moengo is Waterproof Tours (see pages 78–9), which works closely with the Tembe Art Studio and associated artists. Its itineraries also include a short boat trip up the Cottica.

Three buses daily travel between Paramaribo's Heiligen Straat station and Moengo on Mondays to Saturdays. They leave at 07.00, 08.30 and 12.30 in either direction. There is just one bus on Sunday, leaving at 08.30. The fare is SRD 6.50 and the trip takes up to three hours. In addition, three buses daily connect Moengo to Albina (Monday to Saturday). These also leave at 07.00, 08.30 and 12.30 in either direction. The only bus on Sunday leaves at noon in either direction. The fare is SRD 6 and the trip takes about one hour.

For listings, see pages 137–8

⊝ **Where to stay and eat**

1   Masanga Guesthouse

Off map

Afaka Guesthouse

By boat The NVB (*www.nvbnvsuriname.com*) operates three local boat services out of Moengo. Up-to-date details of timetables can be obtained from their Moengo depot in the Commissariat Building on Juliana Straat (\341414).

The most interesting of these is a daily weekday service that follows the Cottica about 60km downriver to Wanhatti via the smaller riverside villages of Manja-Bon, Malokko Kondre, Langa Hoekoe, Tamarin, Pikinsanti, Pinatjami and Latour Weg. Boats leave Moengo at 13.00 and Wanhatti at 06.30 (Monday to Friday only), take around three hours to complete the full one-way trip in either direction, and tickets cost SRD 12.50 one-way.

There is also a ferry service between Moengo and Ricanaumoffo, 15km further downriver, leaving Ricanaumoffo at 06.30 and Moengo 13.00 daily except Tuesday. The journey costs SRD 2.75, and takes about one hour to 90 minutes in either direction. The only boat upriver is a daily service leaving Dang-Tahoe at 06.30, returning from Moengo at 13.00; the journey takes one hour and it costs SRD 5.50 per person.

⌂ WHERE TO STAY *Map, above*

⌂ **Masanga Guesthouse** (11 rooms) Sumatra Laan; see contact details for Tembe Art Studio, pages 138–9. This newly opened guesthouse, also part of the Tembe Art Studio

project, has a row of clean en-suite dbl rooms with fan. SRD 80 dbl bed only or SRD 100 B&B. **$**

⌂ **Afaka Guesthouse** (3 rooms) Achmed Khalil Straat; \341251; m 8719729; e info@

tembestudioart.com; www.tembeartstudio.com. This older guesthouse, part of the Tembe Art Studio project, comprises 2 apts with 3 bedrooms, cooking facilities, bath & toilet & a living space. SRD 175 for the whole guesthouse. **$**

✕ WHERE TO EAT AND DRINK *Map, page 137*

The only place to eat in central Moengo is the **Cafe-Restaurant Masanga**, on the ground floor of the eponymous guesthouse (see above). It serves local dishes such as *nasi*, *bami*, *her'heri*, *moksi alesi*, or rice with chicken, fish, pork or beef, as well as various traditional soups, all in the SRD 15–20 range. It also offers fresh juices, beer, tea and coffee. In addition, the main road through Wonoredjo is lined with local and Chinese eateries, including the **Jinrong Restaurant & Bakery** and the **King Long Bar & Restaurant**, serving the usual inexpensive local fare. A resident has also recommended the **Letje Sranan Oso Njan**, a local eatery at 26 Achter Straat (m *08848112/08632056*).

OTHER PRACTICALITIES

Banking The DSB on the main road out of town, a block south of the bus station, has an ATM outside. It accepts MasterCard but probably not Visa.

Shopping Loosely affiliated with the Tembe Art Studio, **Koni Marwina Pikin Craft Shop** (m *8775940; http://craftshopmoengo.wordpress.com*), on Abraham Crijnssen Laan opposite St Theresa Church sells an interesting selection of beaded jewellery, clothing, herbal toiletries, woodcarvings, bags and other artefacts made by around a dozen local craftspeople. There are plenty of **supermarkets** scattered around town, including a very good one right next to the bus station.

WHAT TO SEE Moengo is an agreeable town to stroll around. It is worth heading south and uphill from the old town centre, along Abraham Crijnssen Laan, through the old and now mostly disused managerial recreational area, with its swimming pool, tennis courts and gardens, to the so-called Casa Blanca. This three-storey hilltop colonial mansion, the former residence of the director of Suralco, offers great views over the river and positively begs to be restored as a hotel.

In the opposite direction, Juliana Straat curves northward and downhill to the riverfront, site of the now rather soporific port, a sporadically lively waterfront market, and one of the more intriguing of the town's artworks, an installation by the locally born artist Remy Jungerman featuring 21 cast-cement frogs. A metal bridge leads across the river to a long dirt road that offers plenty of potential for birdwatching and possibly monkey spotting. Also worth a look is Wonoredjo, which is most easily reached by heading east along Juliana Straat for a few minutes. It has a far more vibrant feel than the main town centre.

Tembe Art Studio (TAS; *Juliana Straat;* \ *341041;* e *info@tembestudioart.com; www.tembeartstudio.com;* ⊕ *16.00–20.00 Mon–Fri*) The centre of most artistic and touristic things in Moengo is the Tembe Art Studio, which stands in the old town centre a block west of the bus station. The brainchild of local artist Marcel Pinas, it is a multi-faceted set-up that offers free tuition in traditional Marron woodcarving and other artistic disciplines to local children. It also operates the new **Contemporary Art Museum of Moengo** at 40 Abraham Crijnssen Laan and **Marowijne Art Park** located on the road to the harbour.

The artist-in-residence scheme has thus far resulted in around a dozen large outdoor installations by Surinamese, Dutch and other sculptors adorning Moengo and its environs – including an unmissable wooden statue of Mickey Mouse on the feeder road into town, and a traditional Marron Faaka Tiki decorated with traditional artefacts, drawings and Afaka signs. Another initiative of TAS is the three-day **Moengo Festival of Theatre and Dance**, first held in September 2013 and likely to be held in the same month in subsequent years, and a new **Festival of the Arts** planned for 2015. Check out the website or ask at Masanga Guesthouse (see page 137) for details.

Ronnie Brunswijk Stadium Football enthusiasts might be surprised to learn that sleepy Moengo is home to not one but two of the country's top-flight football teams. The more successful is Inter Moengotapoe, which has won six out of eight premier domestic 'Hoofdklasse' league cups, up to and including the 2013/14 season. If you are in town during football season (October to May), see whether you can catch Inter Moengotapoe playing at home in Ronnie Brunswijk Stadium (owned and operated by the eponymous Surinamese politician), which lies on the Ricanaumoffo Road a few hundred metres north of the bus station.

Cottica River One of the most beautiful rivers in Suriname, the sedate and forest-lined Cottica is navigable all the way to its confluence with the Commewijne, and then on to the open sea – indeed, until the mid-1950s, all passenger and cargo traffic in and out of Moengo travelled by river. Three passenger ferry services still operate on the Cottica (see page 137), and while none is aimed specifically at tourists, or used by them much, they could offer adventurous travellers a great opportunity for inexpensive riverine exploration. The service 60km downriver to Wanhatti, a remote Saamaka village of around 400 inhabitants, is the most interesting to travellers, as there is a small guesthouse in Wanhatti where you can spend the night (details obtainable from TAS or its guesthouses in Moengo). The timing of the other two services, to Ricanaumoffo and Dang-Tahoe, would also necessitate an overnight village stay, which could prove problematic without local contacts.

ALBINA

Situated on the Marowijne River, 140km east of Paramaribo, the compact border town of Albina has a bustling feel unusual for Suriname, and one that belies its official population estimate of around 4,000. This is probably because, as an important trade centre and base for gold prospecting further upriver, it provides unofficial sanctuary to many illegal immigrants from Brazil, French Guiana, China and elsewhere. The administrative capital of Marowijne District, it is located directly opposite the much larger city of Saint-Laurent-du-Maroni in French Guiana, and the two are linked by a regular vehicular ferry as well as by plenty of informal taxi-boats. Though it is quite a well-equipped town, Albina is of interest to tourists mainly as a springboard for boat trips to the Galibi Nature Reserve, which lies at the mouth of the Marowijne River and is one of the most important turtle-nesting sites in Suriname.

HISTORY Little is known about Albina's early history, but it is thought that it was formerly the site of a small Amerindian village under a chief called Kwaku. The present-day town was founded by a German military officer, August Kappler, who had served as the commander of a small fort at Galibi, close to the mouth of the Marowijne River, from 1836–42. After retiring from the military in 1846, aged only 31, Kappler was granted a concession upriver from Galibi, which he named after his fiancée (and later wife) Albina Liezen Maier. A keen amateur naturalist, Kappler established a small

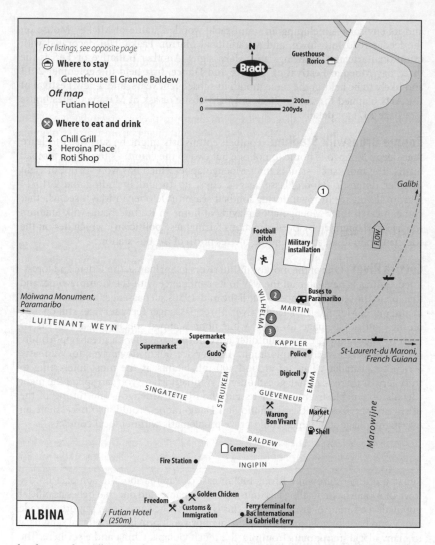

For listings, see opposite page

Where to stay
1 Guesthouse El Grande Baldew

Off map
Futian Hotel

Where to eat and drink
2 Chill Grill
3 Heroina Place
4 Roti Shop

ALBINA

lumber yard at Albina, and was allowed to purchase the land in 1861, three years after the French established Saint-Laurent-du-Maroni on the opposite bank.

In the early 1870s, the discovery of gold at Lawa, a remote southern tributary of the Marowijne, prompted the Surinamese government to take advantage of a clause in the original sale deed obliging Kappler to sell the land back on demand. In 1876, Albina was made the seat of Marowijne District, and it grew rapidly after that, largely as a result of the gold boom. Even after the boom ended, it prospered as a centre of trade with French Guiana, and as a stylish riverside resort whose waterfront, along present-day Emma Street, was lined with handsome whitewashed wooden houses similar to those still found in Coronie or central Paramaribo.

Albina's recent history has been more troubled. The surrounding area was the site of several of the bloodiest battles during the 1986 civil war. As a result much of Albina was razed by fire, while homes and businesses were plundered by the military, and many of the town's residents were forced to flee across the river to

French Guiana. In addition, the district's infrastructure was undermined by the destruction of several important bridges along the road to Paramaribo. Since then, the town has been restored with Dutch development aid, as has the road to Paramaribo and the ferry service to Saint-Laurent-du-Maroni.

Ethnic tensions associated with the high number of foreign prospectors and illegal immigrants in the town came to a head in December 2009, when the fatal stabbing of a local man, allegedly by a Brazilian prospector, precipitated a riot in which several hundred local Marrons attacked gold diggers from Brazil, Colombia and Peru. Depending on which reports you believe, between one and seven people died in the riots, up to 24 were seriously wounded and at least 20 women were raped. Many foreign prospectors were relocated by the government in the wake of the violence and 35 people were arrested, but Albina still retains a slight air of instability and lawlessness.

GETTING THERE AND AWAY Three buses travel between Paramaribo's Heiligen Straat station and Albina daily from Monday to Saturday, leaving at 07.00, 08.30 and 12.30 in either direction. There is just one bus on Sunday, leaving at 08.30. The fare is SRD 8.50 and the trip takes up to four hours. A few shared taxis usually cover the same route daily, leaving when full, but these are a costlier SRD 70 divided between up to five passengers.

Three buses connect Albina and Moengo from Monday to Saturday. These also leave at 07.00, 08.30 and 12.30 daily in either direction. The only bus on Sunday leaves at 12.00 in either direction. The fare is SRD 6 and the trip takes about one hour. All road transport leaves from Martin Straat next to The Chill Grill.

For details of boat travel to Galibi, see page 144. For the boat and ferry to Saint-Laurent-du-Maroni in French Guiana, see page 143.

WHERE TO STAY *Map, opposite*

Guesthouse Rorico (9 rooms) 342031. This neat little guesthouse a few hundred metres north of the town centre is in an L-shaped building & the clean en-suite dbl rooms all have a balcony. It's best to call in advance so they know to expect you. SRD 65/85 dbl with fan/AC. **$**

Futian Hotel (20 rooms) m 7191363. Set on the 1st floor of a converted warehouse south of the town centre, this rather peculiar hotel has large tiled en-suite rooms with king-size bed, wooden furniture, AC & TV. There's an affordable Chinese restaurant downstairs. It's OK, but seems wildly overpriced compared with the more agreeable Rorica. SRD 150 dbl. **$$**

WHERE TO EAT AND DRINK *Map, opposite*

Heroina Place Restaurant Kappler Straat; m 8837406/9272727; ⊕ daily. Owned by a French-speaking chef from across the border, this cosy terrace restaurant serves a varied selection of French & Surinamese dishes for around SRD 35–40 per plate. **$$$**

The Chill Grill Martin Straat; m 8551234/8667653/8857599; e ralph_aj@hotmail.

com; www.facebook.com/thechillgrillalbina; ⊕ 10.00–16.00 Mon–Sat. This pleasant modern eatery has terrace seating & a daily changing menu of local, Asian & Western dishes, mostly in the SRD 15–25 range. **$–$$**

Roti Shop Wilhelmina Straat; ⊕ 10.00– 17.00 Mon–Sat. Tasty chicken rotis & other local dishes in the SRD 10–15 range. **$**

OTHER PRACTICALITIES

Banks and foreign exchange There is a Gudo Bank in Albina, but there doesn't appear to be any ATM or foreign exchange facility. However, euros, as the official currency of neighbouring French Guiana, are widely accepted and it shouldn't be too difficult to find somebody to change enough money to see you through to Paramaribo.

Shopping Plenty of **supermarkets** are dotted around town, and there is a busy little waterfront **market** on Emma Straat. If you are heading to Galibi and don't have waterproof clothing, ponchos are sold in a couple of the supermarkets on Emma Straat opposite the main beach.

Telephone Visitors newly arrived from French Guiana can buy a local SIM card and airtime or a data bundle from the Digicell shop on Emma Straat.

WHAT TO SEE AND DO

Moiwana Monument Standing prominently on the north side of the Paramaribo road about 5km west of Albina, the Moiwana Monument was erected in 2007 to mark the 21st anniversary of the Moiwana Massacre of 1986. The Ndyuka Marron village of Moiwana was the home of Ronnie Brunswijk, the leader of the Surinamese Liberation Army, the rebel 'Jungle Commando' that took on the Surinamese government in the 1986 civil war. The village was attacked by the Surinamese military on 29 November 1986, under the pretext of trying to locate Brunswijk, and when the attackers couldn't locate their target, they burned down his house and took out their frustrations on the villagers, killing at least 38 inhabitants, mostly women and children. It was in the wake of this punitive attack on a civilian village that many residents of the Marowijne interior decided to flee across the river to French Guinea. A theoretically ongoing police investigation into the unprovoked massacre has not yet lead to any arrests or prosecutions, and the cold-blooded assassination of the lead investigating officer, Chief Inspector Herman Gooding, outside Fort Zeelandia in August 1990, remains unsolved. However, the victims' relatives and other survivors of the Moiwana Massacre won a landmark victory in August 2005, when the Inter-American Court of Human Rights ordered the government of Suriname to pay them three million US dollars in compensation. The Moiwana Monument, erected on the site of the massacre, is the work of the Moengo-based artist Marcel Pinas and pays simple but moving testament to the brutal killings. It incorporates a tall spire-like structure adorned with characters in Afaka (a unique syllabary, rich in West African symbols, devised in 1910 to transcribe the Ndyuka language) that read Kibii wi ('Protect us'). Around it are several smaller headstone-like structures inscribed with the names of the known victims.

SAINT-LAURENT-DU-MARONI

Located on the east bank of the Marowijne River, only ten minutes from Albina by taxi-boat or ferry, Saint-Laurent-du-Maroni is the second most populous city in French Guiana. It has around 45,000 inhabitants, making it significantly larger than any Surinamese town outside Paramaribo. The city was founded in 1858, in the wake of the Napoleonic wars and the French abolition of slavery, initially as a Camp de la Transportation for political deportees and convicts condemned to hard labour in the infamous Salvation Islands offshore of the Guianan capital Cayenne. In 1880, however, Saint-Laurent-du-Maroni was officially declared a French penal colony, a role it technically retained until 1938, though the intervention of World War II meant that the prison remained open until 1946. An estimated 70,000 convicts were detained in the prison during its 60-plus years of service, most famously Henri 'Papillon' Charrière, a convicted murderer who was incarcerated there for 11 years prior to escaping to Venezuela, reputedly using a bag of coconuts as a makeshift raft. Published in 1970, Charrière's autobiographical book *Papillon*, describing his imprisonment and escape, became a worldwide bestseller, and was later made into an Oscar-nominated movie starring Steve McQueen and Dustin Hoffman.

GETTING THERE AND AWAY Unless you have a vehicle, the easiest way to travel to or from Saint-Laurent-du-Maroni is by taking a taxi-boat from the main beach on Emma Straat in Albina. This will cost around SRD 20 divided by the number of passengers. Alternatively, a motor ferry called the *Bac International La Gabrielle* (e *bac.gabrielle@orange.fr*) travels in either direction at least twice in the morning from Monday to Saturday and at least twice in the afternoon daily. The fare is SRD 156 for an ordinary car (including the driver), more for a heavy vehicle, while additional or foot passengers pay SRD 14 per person.

At the time of writing, no paperwork was involved in making a day trip to Saint-Laurent-du-Maroni. This is partly because the international border is in the Marowijne River, which makes it difficult for Surinamese officials to distinguish between boats crossing from one side to the other and those bound for domestic destinations. Furthermore, since French Guiana is officially part of France, with entry regulations similar to any other part of the EU, most EU-passport holders can enter freely (and in any case, the first immigration post where passports are checked is 30km out of town along the road to Cayenne).

The only possible complication is that the tourist pass issued upon arrival at Zanderij Airport is valid for one entry to Suriname only, so if your passport were to be stamped upon exiting Suriname, you would need to buy a second tourist pass (which cannot be obtained in Albina) in order to re-enter. In practice, however, the officials at Albina seem to take the attitude that cross-border tourism and trade are more important than visas and passport stamps. Which means that locals move freely between the two riverside towns, most tours to Galibi include a short visit to Saint-Laurent-du-Maroni (asking only that their clients bring along a passport, which as often as not won't be checked), and there is little to prevent independent travellers from popping over to Saint-Laurent-du-Maroni for the day, provided they carry a passport. Having said that, it would be remiss of us not to point out that that it's all a bit of a legal grey area, and that official attitudes may change, so best to ask around before you make the crossing.

WHAT TO SEE Saint-Laurent-du-Maroni is well equipped to receive day trippers from Albina. There is a helpful **tourist office** (*Esplanade Laurent Baudin;* \ *0594 342398;* e *infoslm@wanadoo.fr; www.ot saintlaurentdumaroni.fr;* ⊕ *08.00–12.30 Tue–Sun & 14.30–18.00 Mon–Sat*) at the main boat jetty, as well as an open square adorned with various monuments. The main tourist attraction, about 100m inland of the tourist office, is the old **Camp de la Transportation** (\ *0594 2789596;* ⊕ *09.30–18.00 daily; entrance €5pp*), which can be explored on your own or with one of the hour-long guided tours that leave from the tourist office at 09.30 and 11.00 Tuesday to Sunday, and 15.00 and 16.30 Monday to Saturday. Effectively a high security prison, the old camp is now a well-maintained museum, and the cell where Henri Charrière was held is still intact.

Also of interest in Saint-Laurent-du-Maroni is the colourful Central Market (*Av General de Gaulle;* ⊕ *07.00–14.00 Wed & Sun*), where you can sample inexpensive Chinese and Guianan street food. Alternatively, the tourist office website lists a good selection of restaurants, as well as hotels and lodges in and around town.

GALIBI NATURE RESERVE

Situated at the mouth of the Marowijne River about 20km northeast of Albina, the 40km² Galibi Nature Reserve was created in 1969 to protect an area of sandy river frontage and coastline used as a nesting site by more than 1,000 marine turtles annually. The reserve is named after the quiet riverfront village of Galibi, which lies at its southern border, about two hours boat ride north of Albina. Serviced by four lodges, a shop, a visitor centre and various other tourist facilities, Galibi village is the most normal base for overnight tours to the nature reserve, and it is also a very agreeable settlement in its own right, thanks to its peaceful, welcoming atmosphere and attractive riverfront location, which usually offers safe swimming.

Until as recently as the early 1970s, Galibi was renowned as one of the few sites in the western hemisphere to host regular *arribadas*: hundred-strong aggregations of female olive ridley turtles that amassed on the beach to lay their eggs simultaneously. Today, sadly, the olive ridley is a rare sight, but the beaches at Galibi – being more stable than their regularly shifting counterparts at Matapica – remain the most important nesting site in Suriname for green and leatherback turtles, and are also occasionally visited by hawksbill turtles. It should be noted, however, that Galibi is generally less rewarding than Metapica in turtle-viewing terms, since most tourists only visit the nesting beaches in the dark. The one exception to this is if you arrange to stay at Warana Lodge, which actually lies within the reserve rather than in Galibi village. Galibi also has the edge for budget-conscious independent travellers, who could try their luck turtle spotting in the village for a few days. The main nesting season for green turtles runs from February to May, and for leatherbacks from April to July. Turtles are highly unlikely to be seen at other times.

GETTING THERE AND AWAY Galibi can only be accessed by boat along the Marowijne River. Boats usually leave from Albina and the trip takes up to two hours in either direction. The water can be quite choppy and is sometimes very rough, so bring a poncho and make sure that cameras and any other electronic equipment are well protected.

Most people visit Galibi as part of an organised overnight tour from Paramaribo. These are offered by several operators and prices range from SRD 550–920 per person, depending on the quality of operator, group size and accommodation. If you are serious about turtle viewing and are not too strapped for cash, we would strongly recommend you consider joining a tour staying at Warana Lodge, since it is far better situated for daylight or dusk and dawn sightings than the lodges in Galibi village.

There is no formal pubic transport to Galibi, but enterprising travellers should be able to make their way there independently. For larger groups, a realistic option is a return charter from Albina, costing around SRD 1,350 (for up to 15 people), inclusive of a trip out to the reserve's turtle-nesting beaches. For budget-conscious solo travellers, couples and small groups, a couple of private fishing boats ply back and forth to/from Albina most days. The best days to travel are Wednesday and Saturday, when the central market in Saint-Laurent-du-Maroni is in full swing, and there is plenty of traffic to Galibi between 14.00 and 16.00. Another possibility, assuming it has space, is the boat that takes secondary school pupils from Galibi to Albina on school days, leaving Galibi at 06.00 and starting the return trip at about 14.00. Expect to pay around SRD 75 per person each way. Note, however, that these boats only travel as far as Galibi village, and while you might well see turtles there if you take the odd stroll around at night, you would need to charter a boat from the village (around SRD 600 for a group of up to 15) to get out to the beaches in the nature reserve. You could also ask around about lifts or charters in Albina, at the supermarkets opposite the beach, but a better idea would be to call George at Wajoe Lodge (see opposite) a day or two ahead – he usually knows about all boats heading back and forth – and he can put you in touch with a reliable captain.

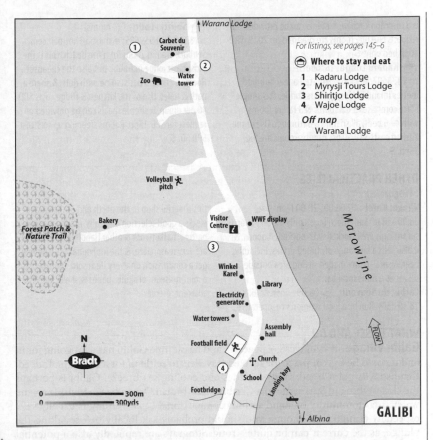

For listings, see pages 145–6

Where to stay and eat

1 Kadaru Lodge
2 Myrysji Tours Lodge
3 Shiritjo Lodge
4 Wajoe Lodge

Off map
Warana Lodge

Warana Lodge

Carbet du Souvenir

Water tower

Zoo

Volleyball pitch

Forest Patch & Nature Trail

Bakery

Visitor Centre

WWF display

Winkel Karel

Library

Electricity generator

Water towers

Assembly hall

Football field

Church

School

Footbridge

Landing bay

Albina

Marowijne

FLOW

N

Bradt

0   300m
0   300yds

GALIBI

WHERE TO STAY AND EAT *Map, above*

Warana Lodge (5 rooms)
421683/476597; e stinasu@sr.net; www.
stinasu.com. Situated on the northern border
of the nature reserve along the otherwise
uninhabited Babunsanti Beach, this remote
STINASU lodge offers the most reliable turtle
viewing due to its isolated location, 8km north
of the village, in prime nesting territory. The
accommodation, though a little overpriced, is
also marginally the best in the area, comprising a
large house with 5, 4-berth en-suite bedrooms, a
kitchen & a dining/sitting area. Named after the
troops of *babun* (howler monkey) that frequent
the area, Babunsanti Beach is lined with palms &
forest, & supports a good range of birds too. SRD
280 for a room sleeping up to 4. **$$$**

Myrysji Tours Lodge (15 rooms) 453151;
m 8835036; e info@galibi-tours.com, myrysji@
yahoo.com; www.galibi-tours.com. Situated on a
good swimming beach at the north end of Galibi

village, this is the most resort-like lodge in the
area, with accommodation mainly in en-suite
rooms sleeping from 2 to 7 people. It also has a
restaurant & bar, & activities (other than turtle
viewing) include kayak trips up a nearby creek &
sunset cruises, both of which should be booked in
advance. The lodge caters mainly to people who
book an all-inclusive Galibi trip with Myrysji Tours
(which start at SRD 800pp), but walk-in guests are
also accepted subject to availability. SRD 100/150
sgl/dbl B&B. **$$**

Wajoe Lodge (16 rooms)
m 8712385/8228096. This long-serving owner-
managed lodge lies at the heart of the village,
next to the primary school, & 100m from a nice
swimming beach. The clean rooms come with 2
or more beds & nets, & are in blocks of 5 with a
private balcony. The helpful owner George speaks
good English & is a useful contact when it comes
to arranging cheap transport from Albina. There

is a common kitchen, & meals can be provided on request. En-suite rooms are planned for 2015. SRD 40pp bed only. **$**

🏠 **Kadaru Lodge** (8 rooms)
m 7175687/8595863. Situated a few hundred metres inland of Myrysji Tours Lodge, this simple place comprises 5 dbl rooms & 3 larger rooms with 4–6 beds, all sharing a bathroom. Use of the kitchen costs SRD 50 per group. Rooms are SRD 35pp. **$**

🏠 **Shiritjo Lodge** (4 rooms)
m 8244024/8959685; e shiritjo@hotmail.com. Set back around 200m from the beach, this is the most basic lodge in Galibi, but also the cheapest. Rooms all have 3 beds, some with nets, & share a bath & toilet. Use of the kitchen & fridge costs SRD 40 per group, & simple meals can be provided on request for SRD 15pp. Rooms sleeping up to 3 cost SRD 50. **$**

OTHER PRACTICALITIES
Shopping
Winkel Karel ⊕ 08.00–20.00 Mon–Sat, 08.00–18.00 Sun. The village's only grocery shop is surprisingly well stocked with packaged goods, & it also sells a fair range of chilled drinks, including beer. A small palm-shaded sitting area outside serves as Galibi's local bar.
Carbet du Souvenir ⊕ 08.00–noon & 16.00– 18.30 daily. Run by a local women's co-operative, this cheerful shop at the north end of the village stocks a good selection of locally-made jewellery, pottery, basketwork & other handicrafts. Prices are very reasonable, & the individual craftspeople get a commission on every item sold. It also hosts a mini-museum of skulls, bones & shells from the adjacent reserve.

WHAT TO SEE AND DO
Galibi village As villages go, peaceful and hassle-free Galibi has a lot going for it, and it could be a great place for relaxed travellers to settle in for a few days. Indeed, thanks to its palm-lined sandy beaches and cooling sea breeze, Galibi is perhaps the closest thing in Suriname to a Caribbean or Indian Ocean beach idyll. True, the water is far too murky to stand serious comparison, but swimming is usually safe, especially at high tide, though you should probably ask locally before taking the plunge, as the current can be quite strong. Stingrays are reputedly also a potential nuisance at low tide.

Running for almost 2km along the beach, Galibi was established in the 1860s by two Amerindian brothers and former slaves called Christiaan and Langaman (with the former's name presumably indicating he was an early Catholic convert), at what was then a recently abandoned colonial military post. Today, the village supports around 800 people and is divided into two parts named after the two brothers: the smaller traditionalist Langaman Kondre runs south from the Saint Antonius Church and primary school, while the Catholic-dominated Christiaan Kondre lies to the north. Agriculture and fishing remain the main source of income locally, but tourism has also brought a fresh source of income in recent years, as well as providing an outlet for the local handicrafts sold at the Carbet du Souvenir (see above). Despite this, Galibi doesn't market itself as a voyeuristic 'cultural experience' in the way of so many other Amerindian and Marron villages in Suriname, meaning that you can just hang out and interact with locals in an uncontrived way.

In season, you'll see plenty of evidence of turtle activity within the village, mostly in the form of recent trails along the beach, and might well catch a turtle nesting if you keep an eye open at night. There is also an excellent WWF-funded **open-air display** about marine turtles on the beach. Behind this is a visitor centre, the purpose of which is unclear but which claims to be open 08.30–13.30 and 16.30–19.00 Monday to Saturday and 10.00–13.00 Sunday, but was resolutely closed throughout our visit.

Further north, next to the Carbet du Souvenir, **Galibi Zoo** is a rather undercooked affair that protects a few parrots, monkeys and small carnivores, most of which are free-ranging rather than caged, and presumably hang around because they are fed by the zookeeper. If you do visit the zoo, please don't feed the animals sweets or other junk food, and try to dissuade the zookeeper from doing the same – cute as it might seem to see a monkey sucking on a lollipop, if it happens on a regular basis it will mess up the animal's metabolism.

The WWF cut a 2km walking trail through a patch of forest behind the village in 2006. It has never been used much, and most of it is now overgrown, but the forest is still there and is home to agouti, monkeys and a wide variety of birds.

The nature reserve For most visitors, access to the reserve will amount to a three- to four-hour nocturnal excursion, the exact timing of which is dictated by the tides. The trip out can be rough, so bring waterproof clothing and something to protect your camera gear. The odds of encountering a nesting turtle are very high in season, but you might well end up sharing the sighting with many other parties that have boated in from the village, which can be rather unsatisfying for you and disturbing for the turtle. By contrast, if you stay at Warana Lodge, which is right on Babunsanti Beach, the experience is more like that at Matapica, with a good chance of daylight sightings or night-time encounters exclusive to your party.

Galibi is also highly rated for marine birds. The best site is probably Samsambo Beach, which lies outside the reserve about 10km northwest of Babunsanti, and is accessible by boat only. Formerly the site of a research centre, Samsambo is surrounded by mudflats and lagoons that regularly attract scarlet ibis, along with a wide variety of waders and small herons.

8

Saramacca, Coronie and Nickerie

The long coastal belt west of Paramaribo, though relatively accessible, is among the least touristy parts of Suriname, lacking as it does the well-maintained plantations and excellent turtle-viewing opportunities associated with Commewijne and Marowijne. But while it is short on big-name attractions, the northwest has much to offer independently minded travellers on a self-drive holiday or using public transport. True, the administrative districts of Saramacca, Coronie and Nickerie might not be as wild as the deep interior, but they are surprisingly sparsely populated, incised with a succession of wide forest-fringed rivers and estuaries, and dotted with characterful and reasonably well-equipped small towns that struggle and just about succeed in keeping the jungle at bay. The region's largest settlement, Nieuw Nickerie, is also the most remote from the capital, practically within walking distance of the Guyanese border, and it offers easy access to Bigi Pan, the northwest's biggest single tourist attraction and a genuine 'must-do' for serious birdwatchers. Also of interest are Groningen, perched on the south bank of the wildlife-rich Saramacca River, and tiny Totness, the sedate capital of Coronie District. Accessible only by boat, the former leper colony at Batavia and remote Amerindian village of Kalebaskreek both lie on the east bank of the Coppename, the region's largest river.

GRONINGEN

Situated 35km west of Paramaribo, the rustic capital of Saramacca District is a sprawling but lightly populated settlement nestled on the west bank of the Saramacca River. Like many small towns in Suriname, Groningen feels like it has been carved out of the jungle, with the dominant presence being the wide forest-fringed river that meanders past the small main square. And while the town itself isn't much to write home about, it is a very peaceful place, offering some accessible and affordable wildlife-viewing opportunities. The stretch of river immediately around town is regarded as one of the best places in Suriname to look for manatee and giant otter, and it also supports a dazzling variety of birds, plenty of sloths and several species of monkey – indeed, it is not unusual to hear the distinctive communal growling call of howler monkeys from the main square and jetty. There are a couple of adequate budget hotels in town, as well as a few decent local eateries, but the most attractive overnight options are to be found a short way south of town along the Saramacca Weg.

HISTORY The first known settlement at Groningen was a four-bastioned fort built on a riverfront site encompassing the present-day main square, police station and District Commissioner's Residence. The fort was named after the Dutch town of Groningen, birthplace of Governor Jan Gerhard Wichers, who oversaw its construction in 1790. Wichers intended the fort to form the centrepiece of a colonial settlement that never materialised within its short lifespan. Indeed, when the soldier August Kappler visited Groningen in the late 1830s, he noted that while it did incorporate a Moravian church and cemetery, there were no residential houses to be seen.

In late 1845, Groningen was settled by the so-called Boeroes, a pioneering group of around 400 farmers, led by the Pastor Arend van den Brandhof, who immigrated to Suriname from the Groningen and Gelderland regions of the Netherlands. Within six months of their arrival, however, around half of the settlers had succumbed to a typhoid epidemic, among them van den Brandhof's wife Anna Pannekoek, who is buried in the old cemetery. By 1854, only 45 settlers remained, the rest having either died of a tropical disease or fled to the relative safety afforded by Paramaribo, and the ill-fated settlement was formally abandoned. Van den Brandhof's old house was resurrected as the official District Commissioner's Residence when Groningen was chosen as the capital of Saramacca District in 1863.

From the late 19th century until 1910, Groningen housed an asylum and hospital for victims of yaws, an infectious skin disease now largely eradicated by antibiotics. Back then, access from Paramaribo was by boat only, following the artificial Saramacca Canal to the sluice at Uitkyk, then the Saramacca River to Groningen. In 1936, the first road to Groningen was laid, connecting it to Hamburg (on the west bank opposite Uitkyk). However, it was only after the construction of the main road from Paramaribo towards Nickerie in 1960 that Groningen experienced any significant urban development. Today, it is the tenth-largest town in Suriname, with a population estimated at around 3,200.

TOURIST INFORMATION The website www.saramaccainsuriname.com includes several useful links for tourist facilities in Groningen and elsewhere in Saramacca.

GETTING THERE AND AWAY
By car Depending on traffic, Groningen is up to an hour's drive west of Paramaribo. For self-drivers, the most direct route is to follow Kwatta Weg west out of the city centre in the direction of Nickerie. After leaving the city, as the road name changes to Garnizoen Weg and then Wayambo Weg, keep going straight until you cross the impressive Saramacca Bridge after about 30km. Shortly after the bridge, you reach a large traffic circle where you need to branch left onto the Sidodadi road. It is another 5km from here to the town centre, passing several supermarkets, warungs and filling stations on the way.

A slightly longer alternative route from Paramaribo entails turning left onto 5de Rij Weg about 10km out of Paramaribo, and then crossing the Saramacca River further upstream at Uitkyk Bridge. This is probably the preferable route if you are heading to the accommodation options south of the town centre.

New arrivals could drive directly to Groningen from Zanderij International Airport, a 70km trip that shouldn't take longer than 90 minutes. Follow JFK Highway north in the direction of Paramaribo through to Lelydorp, then about 3km further on turn left onto Welgedacht A Weg, and follow it for about 10km until you reach the Uitkyk Bridge across the Saramacca River.

By bus Two or three buses run in either direction between Paramaribo and Maho via Groningen. From Monday to Saturday, they leave from Heiligen Weg in Paramaribo at 05.30, 09.00 and 16.00, and on Sunday (and public holidays) they leave at 08.00 and 13.00. These buses pass Appartments Bloemendaal and Hotel SJV Groningen *en route* between Groningen and Maho, and will drop passengers at

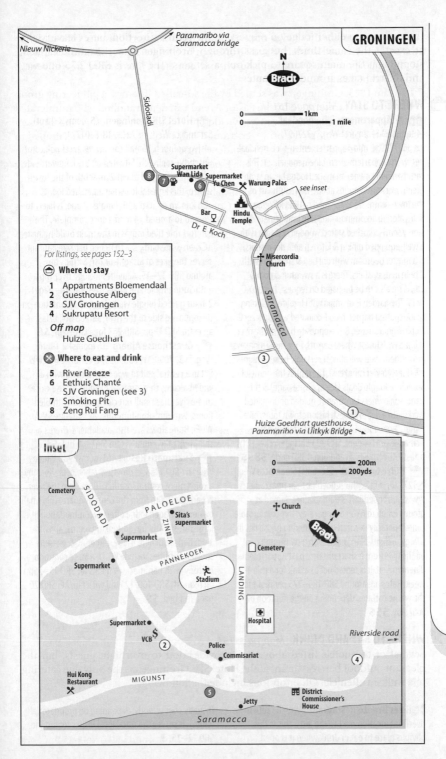

Paramaribo via
Saramacca bridge

Nieuw Nickerie

N

Bradt

0 — 1km
0 — 1 mile

Sidodadi

Supermarket
Wan Lida   Supermarket
8 7   6 Yu Chen Warung Palas
                                      see inset

Bar
Hindu
Temple
Dr E Koch

Misercordia
Church

Saramacca

3

1

For listings, see pages 152–3

⌂ **Where to stay**

1 Appartments Bloemendaal
2 Guesthouse Alberg
3 SJV Groningen
4 Sukrupatu Resort

Off map
   Huize Goedhart

✕ **Where to eat and drink**

5 River Breeze
6 Eethuis Chanté
   SJV Groningen (see 3)
7 Smoking Pit
8 Zeng Rui Fang

Huize Goedhart guesthouse,
Paramaribo via Uitkyk Bridge

Inset

0 — 200m
0 — 200yds

Cemetery

SIDODADI

PALOELOE

Sita's
supermarket
ZINHA

Supermarket

PANNEKOEK

Supermarket

✝ Church

Cemetery

N
Bradt

Stadium

LANDING

✚
Hospital

Supermarket
VCB $
2

Riverside road

Police
Commisariat

4

Hui Kong
Restaurant
✕

MIGUNST

5

Jetty

District
Commissioner's
House

Saramacca

the entrance to either lodge on request. In the return direction, buses leave Maho at exactly the same times, but pass through Groningen about 20 minutes later, stopping at the main square to pick up passengers. The fare is SRD 2.75 one-way and the trip takes around 90 minutes.

🏠 WHERE TO STAY *Map page 151*

🏠 ✳ **Appartments Bloemendaal**
(4 cottages) Saramacca Weg; ☎ 327097; m 8607720; e info@appartementen-bloemendaal. net; www.appartementen-bloemendaal.net. This commendable owner-managed lodge lies in large green riverfront grounds about 4km southeast of the town centre along the road to Uitkyk Bridge. Self-catering accommodation is in immaculate dbl-storey semi-detached stilted wooden cottages with a well-equipped dining & kitchen area downstairs, & a master bedroom with dbl bed & small loft with 2 twin beds upstairs. There is a swimming pool & bar, & meals can be prepared on request, but no AC or TV. The garden is teeming with birdlife, including black-spotted barbet, blood-coloured woodpecker & tropical gnatcatcher, & the opposite bank of the river is lined with forest where parrots, toucans & monkeys are resident (you will almost certainly hear & might even see howler monkeys). The jetty is the home of Suriname Jungle Boats (see opposite page) & the hands-on owners can arrange guided or unguided walks into a nearby forest, historic town tours, bike rental, & possibly visits to a nearby creek where manatees are resident. SRD 393 dbl inc excellent DIY b/fast; other meals an additional SRD 46pp. **$$$$**

🏠 **Huize Goedhart**   (3 rooms) Saramacca Weg; ☎ 327320; e info@huizegoedhart-saramacca.net; www.huizegoedhart-saramacca.net. Aimed at groups (of up to 6) on a longer stay, this comfortable contemporarily decorated self-catering house lies in a large orchard-like garden with a swimming pool on the riverfront a short distance past Appartments Bloemendaal. It is rented out as a unit for a min 1 week. Rates are around SRD 185–275 per night for the whole cottage, depending on the duration of your stay. **$$$**

🏠 **Hotel SJV Groningen**   (5 rooms & 1 apt) Saramacca Weg; m 7269218/8801771; e sjvgroningen@gmail.com; www.facebook.com/ HotelSJVGroningen. Situated on the landward side of Saramacca Road about 2km south of the town centre, this agreeable owner-managed lodge, also known as Suriname Jungle Village, is likely to expand to around 14 rooms once complete. The comfortable tiled rooms in the main building have AC & en-suite bath, & a thatched bar & restaurant serves the likes of lasagne or fish & chips for around SRD 12–15. Activities include river trips with Suriname Jungle Boats (see opposite page) & 2-hour guided jungle walks in an old plantation on the opposite side of the river. SRD 88 dbl, b/fast is an extra SRD 18pp; SRD 263 for a large apt. **$$**

🏠 **Guesthouse Alberg**   (6 rooms) 2 Tibitie Weg; ☎ 327090; m 8539633; e caribrice@sr.net. Set in a central stilted wooden building with a wide balcony, this comfortable guesthouse close to the river has small but clean rooms with tiled floors, wrought-iron furniture, AC, satellite TV & Wi-Fi. Bungalows are also available, & there's a children's playground. From SRD 100 dbl. **$$**

🏠 **Sukrupatu Resort**   (4 rooms) 9 JB Panday Weg; m 8613788; e droytje@yahoo.com. Boasting a convenient central location 100m from the river & perhaps 200m from the central square, this small owner-managed lodge offers accommodation in large but slightly frayed-looking rooms, all with 1 dbl bed, 1 sgl bed, fridge, fan or AC & en-suite shower. Facilities include Wi-Fi, a large common balcony with hammocks & meals for SRD 15–25pp on request. SRD 100/125 dbl with fan/AC; SRD 20 per extra bed. **$$**

🍴 WHERE TO EAT AND DRINK *Map, page 151*

Several of the hotels listed above can provide food to overnight guests, but the pleasant outdoor bar/restaurant at the Hotel SJV Groningen is the only one catering to a walk-in clientele. Other options include the following:

🍴 **River Breeze Restaurant**   With its superb riverfront location next to the jetty, this is the obvious place to eat or drink when it is open

(usually over w/ends, depending on proprietorial whim). It serves the usual local dishes for around SRD 12–15. **$**

top   The Fort Nieuw Amsterdam Open Air Museum houses displays on the history of the fort itself, as well as of the Commewijne plantations, the transatlantic slave trade and the Ashanti Kingdom (AZ) pages 127–8

above   Dating originally from 1640 and the oldest building in Paramaribo, Fort Zeelandia opened as the Suriname Museum in 1972, with excellent collections of pre-Columbian and Amerindian artefacts (AZ) pages 102–4

right   The Het Surinaamsch Rumhuis has several interesting displays about the history of rum production in the country (AZ) pages 114–15

above left   A local woman cleaning fish at a village in Upper Suriname (AZ)

above right   Children wearing traditional Amerindian dance costume (AZ)

left   Cassava bread, a traditional Amerindian and Marron staple, is a flat, hard loaf baked on a griddle (AZ) page 52

below   Handicrafts on sale at the Carbet du Souvenir in Galibi (AZ) page 146

above As part of an Amerindian cleansing ritual, individuals must drink *casiri* as a symbol of cleaning the body and soul (STF)

right Local women washing clothes in the Upper Suriname River (AZ)

below The thriving Nieuw Nickerie market is quieter after midday; on sale is a good range of fresh produce (AZ)
page 166

above   The South American coati, or ring-tailed coati (*Nasua nasua*), is known in Dutch as the *neusbeer* (nose bear) (AZ) page 24

below left   The South American tapir, or lowland tapir (*Tapirus terrestris*), is the largest native mammal in South America (AZ) page 27

below right   The giant otter (*Pteronura brasiliensis*) is often seen in groups of five or more (AZ) page 25

above left   Immature kinkajou (*Potos flavus*) in Galibi (AZ) page 24

above right   The black spider monkey (*Ateles paniscus*) is Suriname's largest monkey, with a small head and long gangly limbs (AZ) page 27

upper right   The giant anteater (*Myrmecophaga tridactyla*) moves with a shuffling gait or rolling gallop (AZ) page 30

lower right   The collared peccary (*Pecari tajacu*) has an odour not unlike dirty socks (AZ) page 28

below   Squirrel monkeys (*Saimiri sciureus*) can be seen in and around Paramaribo as well as in most forested areas throughout Suriname (AZ) page 25

above   The shell of the leatherback sea turtle (*Dermochelys coriacea*) can reach 2m in length (AZ) page 36

below   Red-footed tortoise (*Chelonoidis carbonaria*) in Lelydorp (AZ)

botom left   Black-throated mango (*Anthracothorax nigricollis*) spotted in District Sipaliwini (AZ)

bottom right   Frog (*Epipedobates trivittatus*) at Blanche Marie Falls (AZ)

above A king swallowtail (*Heraclides thoas*) resting on a leaf at the Neotropical Butterfly Park in Lelydorp (AZ) page 172

below left Almost anywhere outside central Paramaribo, visitors will encounter colourful parrots like the orange-winged Amazon parrot (*Amazona amazonica*) screeching overhead (AZ) page 33

below right Channel-billed toucan (*Ramphastos vitellinus*) (AZ) page 224

✕ Eethuis Chanté ⏰ lunch & early dinner. This clean Javan restaurant on Sidodadi Weg about 1km west of the town centre serves tasty *bami, nasi* & other typical Surinamese dishes for SRD 12–15. **$**

✕ Zeng Rui Fang Restaurant Situated about 2km along Sidodadi Weg, this informal eatery serves the usual local staples for SRD 15–20 as well as a selection of proper Chinese meals in the range of SRD 30–35. **$–$$**

✕ Smoking Pit Right opposite Zeng Rui Fang, this is mainly a bar but also doubles as an inexpensive BBQ selling grilled chicken & the like in the evening. **$**

OTHER PRACTICALITIES

Banking The only bank in town is the VCB on Sidodadi Weg. An ATM outside accepts international Master and Visa cards.

Internet There is no dedicated internet café but most of the hotels listed above have Wi-Fi.

Shopping The best of half a dozen supermarkets dotted around town are the Wan Lida and Yu Chen on Sidodadi Weg.

WHAT TO SEE AND DO

The town centre The focal point of Groningen is the riverside square in front of the police station. Here stands a cluster of monuments notable more for their quantity than quality. There are seven in total, erected to commemorate the indigenous people of Suriname, the centenary of the arrival of the Boeroes in 1845, the 19th-century Indian and Javan migrations, the centenary of the abolition of slavery in 1863, Surinamese independence in 1975 and the first anniversary of the 1980 revolution. The main square also once formed part of the now defunct Fort Groningen, and part of the floorplan of one of the bastions can be seen in the adjacent grounds of the District Commissioner's Residence, which started life as the home of the Boeroes leader Arend van den Brandhof. Another bastion has been discovered close to the stadium, and it is rumoured that more substantial excavations will take place soon.

The town centre is studded with attractive but largely undistinguished wooden buildings, the most interesting of which is the tall church of the Misericordia a few hundred metres south of the square. Those with a strong interest in local history should make contact with the Sukrupatu Resort, whose knowledgeable owner Roy conducts guided tours of the town for SRD 100 for up to ten people.

Boat trips An excellent and enjoyable way to see some of the wildlife associated with the Saramacca River and its forested banks is a boat trip on one of the two boats moored at Appartments Bloemendaal, 4km south of the town centre. The larger of these, used mainly for overnight group charters up the Saramacca and Coppename rivers, is *Mi Gudu* (literally 'My Sweetheart'), a tailor-built 28m cruise boat with six en-suite twin cabins below deck operated by Suriname Jungle Boats (✆ 327 097; www.surinamejungleboats.com). The more modestly proportioned *Pikin Gudu* ('Little Sweetheart') is a shaded boat used mainly for two-hour wildlife-viewing excursions that follow the river immediately upstream from Groningen and cost SRD 184 per party plus SRD 46 per person. Birds are plentiful along the river, and you can also be reasonably sure of seeing squirrel and brown capuchin monkeys. Sloth, manatee, giant otter and howler monkeys are also seen with some regularity. For bookings and further details, contact Appartments Bloemendaal (see opposite page) or visit the website www.surinamejungleboats.com.

Forest walks The plentiful forest around Groningen offers plenty of opportunity for casual rambling, birdwatching and monkey spotting. For those who prefer to join a guided excursion, a recommended option is the two-hour jungle walk offered by Hotel SJV Groningen for SRD 20 per person. These run through an overgrown former plantation on the east bank of the river opposite Groningen, and come with a good chance of spotting agouti, various monkeys and more occasionally sloths.

However, there is also plenty of scope for exploring under your own steam. The dirt road that runs north from opposite Sukrupatu Resort looks particularly promising: it follows the west bank of the Saramacca River for about 2km before veering slightly inland to join the main Paramaribo Road. Also worth exploring is Josikreek Weg, which branches northwest from the main road to Paramaribo about halfway between the traffic circle with Sidodadi Road and Saramacca Bridge, and passes through an area of lush vegetation studded with perhaps a dozen small lakes in the space of 3km.

LOWER COPPENAME RIVER

Some 50km west of Groningen by road, the west-flowing Saramacca and north-flowing Coppename River converge as they flow into the Atlantic about 5km north of the small village of Boskamp (Bush Camp). Built in 1999, the wide and rather murky Coppename River, which forms the border between the administrative districts of Saramacca and Coronie, is spanned by the impressive two-lane Coronie Bridge, the country's second-longest such construction, connecting Boskamp on the east bank to its notional west bank counterpart Jenny. Dolphins are often present in the area and commonly seen from boats.

Although no roads run upriver from the bridge, two sites of interest can be visited by boat. The first of these is the former Catholic leper colony at **Batavia** (see box, opposite page), which lies on the east bank of the Coppename about 10km south of Boskop, just past the confluence with the Coesewijne. Also on the east bank but another 5km further south, the magnificently isolated traditional Amerindian village of **Kalebaskreek** (Calabash Creek), surrounded by pristine jungle and home to around 180 people, is now the site of a little-known but worthwhile ecotourism project centred on a small guesthouse run communally by the local women.

For more adventurous travellers, the Lower Coppename can be explored on the no-frills post boat service (see opposite page) that runs from Paramaribo to the remote riverside village of Donderskamp (named after Father Petrus Donders) on the first Monday of the month.

GETTING THERE AND AWAY The easiest way to visit Batavia is on one of the monthly pilgrimages organised by the Roman Catholic Diocese in Paramaribo. These usually run on the last Saturday of any given month, departing from Paramaribo at 07.00, arriving at Boskamp at around 09.30 and then travelling by boat to Batavia, a trip that takes up to one hour. The cost is SRD 75 per person, inclusive of drinking water. For further information, contact the Diocese of Paramaribo at 14 Henck Arron Straat (✆ 426092; e secretariaat@ bisdomparamaribo.org; www.bisdomparamaribo.org).

Kalebaskreek is not really geared up to spontaneous independent visits. It is normally visited on a tour organised through Lodge Urana (see below), which can arrange boat transport from Boskamp for SRD 400 per party return. Day trippers could also head to Boskamp and arrange a boat there for around the same price (ideally including a stop at Batavia) but overnight visitors wouldn't save any money by doing this, and they would still need to make advance contact with the lodge to be sure of being accommodated.

The monthly post boat to Donderskamp sails from Paramaribo via the Saramacca Canal, Saramacca River and Coppename River, stopping at Uitkyk, Batavia and Kalebaskreek. Unfortunately, it had been suspended for a few months in early 2014, due to the silting up of the Saramacca Canal, but we are assured it will resume once dredging is complete. Depending slightly on the tides, it usually leaves from the SMS Jetty in Paramaribo at 07.00 on the first Monday of the month, arrives at Donderskamp at around the same time on Tuesday morning, and then starts the return journey in the afternoon, arriving back at Paramaribo lateish on Wednesday. The return fare is SRD 250 per person, and you can sleep on board (either bring a hammock or ask for one to be provided for a small fee). Food, drink and a cook can also be arranged on request, or you can bring all your own food. For further details, visit or contact the Pristine Tours office (*Ground floor of the SMS building on Waterkant;* 410281/479061; e *pristinetours@hotmail.com*).

FATHER PEERKE DONDERS AND BATAVIA

The leper colony at Batavia was established in the 1820s to isolate victims of a highly contagious disease that was first carried to Suriname in the 1760s and remained a severe problem until its virtual eradication in 1945. Most of the 500 inmates were former slaves and living conditions were harsh. One church delegate who visited in the early days described the colony as demonstrating 'leprosy in its greatest fury [emitting] a smell so terrible that some gentlemen of the committee fled away vomiting'.

Batavia is now strongly associated with the memory of Father Petrus (nicknamed Peerke) Donders, a Dutch clergyman who was born in Tilburg in 1809, accepted as a missionary in 1839 and who was transferred to Suriname in 1842, where he provided medical care to slaves as well as converting more than 1,000 people in his first eight years of service. In 1856, Donders volunteered to take charge of Batavia, where he dedicated the rest of his life to improving and then maintaining living conditions in the isolated colony. He often cleaned the wards himself, bathed and bandaged the inmates' rotting body parts, and often donated his own clothing and food to the neediest individuals. Nicknamed the Patron Saint of Lepers, Donders also had a famously strong constitution, seldom falling ill himself, despite his continuous exposure to all manner of tropical diseases and his habit of fasting three times a week. In his later years, he also undertook several expeditions from Batavia to bring the Catholic faith to remote Amerindian and Marron villages.

After 27 years running the leper colony, the 77-year-old Donders died of untreated kidney inflammation on 14 January 1887. He was buried at Batavia Cemetery the next day. Ten years later, the leper colony closed at the insistence of the colonial government after being razed by fire. In 1900, Donders's remains were exhumed and transferred to Paramaribo for reburial in the Saint Peter and Paul Cathedral. In 1982, he was beatified by Pope John Paul II, in recognition of his selfless service to the sick and to the church, and his feast day is 14 January. The old mission at Batavia has subsequently been restored using donor funds, and the Roman Catholic Diocese in Paramaribo conducts a monthly pilgrimage to it in Donders's memory.

Finally, the most luxurious way to explore the Lower Suriname would be to charter the cruise boat *Mi Gudu* from Suriname Jungle Boats in Groningen (see page 153).

🏠 WHERE TO STAY AND EAT

🏠 **Lodge Urana** (2 rooms) Kalebaskreek; m 8771998/8807653; www.facebook.com/pages/Kalebaskreek/147038185316262. Reached from the village via a patch of bamboo forest, this small community-run resthouse is the only accommodation we are aware of along the Lower Coppename. It comprises 2 rooms with 4 beds each, a recreation room, & a well-equipped kitchen. Meals & drinks can sometimes be bought at a local eatery & bar in the village, but it is advisable to bring all your food, drinking water & other refreshments with you. A cook can be provided on request. Booking is highly recommended as space is limited & you will probably need to arrange boat transport from Boskop in advance. SRD 45pp. **$**

CORONIE

Bordered by the Coppename, Wayambo and Nickerie rivers to the east, south and west respectively, Coronie is the least populated of Suriname's ten districts, supporting fewer than 3,500 people. Habitation is concentrated along the surfaced Paramaribo–Nickerie road, which runs through the narrow strip of dry land that separates the Atlantic coastline from the freshwater swamps that submerge the deeper interior. The local economy depends almost entirely on fishing and agriculture, with coconut palms all along the coastal belt and rice paddies dominating to the south of the main road. Several local place names such as Totness, Inverness, Clyde and Burnside date back to 1808, when a series of cotton plantations was established in the area by Scottish and English settlers.

TOTNESS AND AROUND Although Coronie doesn't offer much in the way of prescribed sightseeing, it's worth stopping briefly at its agreeably leafy but rather quirky administrative capital Totness, which sprawls along the main road towards Nickerie for some 2km. Totness is renowned for its colonial-era wooden buildings, which lend it a distinctive character, though nothing quite matches Paramaribo's finest

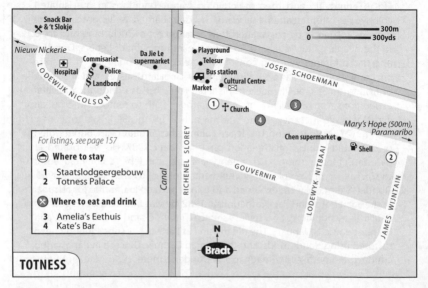

For listings, see page 157

🛏 **Where to stay**
1 Staatslodgeergebouw
2 Totness Palace

❌ **Where to eat and drink**
3 Amelia's Eethuis
4 Kate's Bar

TOTNESS

in terms of impact. Among the most impressive buildings in Totness is the partially restored old plantation house opposite the post office (now the Staatslodgeergebouw) and the nearby church and police headquarters. Totness is also surrounded by forest and wetland habitats that promise rewarding birding, and the village centre is only 1.5km from the Atlantic coastline. About 2km back along the Paramaribo Road is Mary's Hope, where an imposing church and several other tall wooden buildings form part of a still-active Catholic mission built in the late 19th century.

Getting there and away Totness flanks the surfaced road to Nickerie, around 135km west of Paramaribo and 50km past the Coronie Bridge. In a private car, having cleared the outskirts of Paramaribo and continued straight on at the traffic circle where a left turn would divert to Groningen, it would be exceptionally difficult to get lost – there really are no junctions of any significance along the way. There doesn't seem to be much in the way of direct public transport between Paramaribo and Totness, but any vehicle bound for Nickerie can drop you there. When you are ready to leave, buses and other transport heading in all directions stop at the main square next to the market.

Where to stay *Map, opposite*

Hotel Totness Palace (28 rooms)
m 8783909. Situated behind a Chinese supermarket at the junction of the Paramaribo road & James Wijntuin Weg, this clean but rather rundown & characterless lodge is Totness's only viable overnight option for the time being. All rooms have AC. SRD 70 dbl with shared bathroom; SRD 80–90 en-suite dbl. **$**

Staatslodgeergebouw
235129/235160 Magnificent 3-storey mansion opposite the post office that has been in the process of being restored as a municipal resthouse for 5 years now. While the cup-half-full contingent reckons it may open before the end of 2014, we wouldn't place much faith in it happening that quickly – shame, because it really does have enormous potential! Call the above numbers or visit the Commissariat (next to the police station) for details of progress and for room rates.

Where to eat and drink *Map, opposite*

Amelia's Eethuis This looks to be the pick of the few local eateries, offering a choice of indoor or outdoor seating, & serving a selection of typical Surinamese Javan dishes for about SRD 10–15. **$**

Kate's Bar Agreeable little bar serving the usual cold *djogos* & a limited selection of snacks.

Other practicalities

Banking There is an ATM outside the Commissariat and outside the Landboud Bank immediately behind it. Neither accepts Visa but you should be OK with a MasterCard.

Internet Although Totness is the landing station for the cable system connecting Surinam to Guyana and Trinidad, there is no dedicated internet café nor any hotel or restaurant likely to have Wi-Fi.

Shopping Several supermarkets are dotted around town, the largest and best-stocked is Da Jie Le, on the main road between the market and the police station. The market itself is very small and looked quite subdued when we were in town.

WAGENINGEN

The second-largest town in Nickerie District, with an estimated population of 4,200, Wageningen lies on the north bank of the Nickerie River about 50km west of Totness and 10km southwest of the bridge on the border with Coronie. The purpose-built town was established in 1949 to service a USA-funded mechanised rice production scheme that formed part of the post-war Marshall Plan to help rebuild politically sympathetic European economies and prevent the spread of communism. Some 6,000ha of Nickerie were cleared for rice production, and a massive factory and boat loading facility were built in the small town under the Dutch-managed Stichting Machinale Landbouw (SML; Foundation for Mechanised Agriculture), an innovative organisation that achieved an annual yield of more than five tonnes per hectare by breeding its rice to have a shorter growing season and better ears than other strains. Following independence in 1975, the SML was taken over by the state, which invoked an unmanageably bureaucratic infrastructure and diverted profits into its treasury, leading to the foundation's rapid decline and eventual collapse in the early 1980s. Subsistence rice farming is still practised in the area and the abandoned SML silos still dominate the urban landscape, but these days Wageningen feels like a town in terminal economic decline, salvaged only by its lovely setting on the forested banks of the Nickerie River.

GETTING THERE AND AWAY Coming from the direction of Paramaribo in your own vehicle, you'll cross a large bridge shortly after the border between Coronie and Nickerie districts. Then, after another 5km, you'll see Wageningen signposted to the left. The town centre starts about 2km down this side road.

Using public transport, two **buses** run between Paramaribo and Wageningen daily except Sundays and public holidays. These leave from Waaldijk Straat in Paramaribo at 05.50 and 13.00, and from Wageningen at the same times. The fare is SRD 8.50 and the trip takes up to three hours. A few light passenger vehicles run between Wageningen and Nieuw Nickerie daily.

WHERE TO STAY The **Hotel t'Wereld** (*15 rooms; Molen Straat*), is a relic of former boom days and is named after the hotel where the German capitulation in Dutch Wageningen was signed in 1945. It is in a lovely location between the park and the river, but it looked to be terminally closed in 2014. As far as we could ascertain, there is nowhere else to stay.

OTHER PRACTICALITIES There is no restaurant in Wageningen, but the Chinese supermarkets in the town centre stock all the ingredients you might need for a picnic lunch. The Hakrin Bank on Hoofd Pad has an ATM that accepts MasterCard but not Visa.

WHAT TO SEE The sprawling town centre is quite attractive in its low-key way, and like so many small settlements in Suriname it feels like an extension of the surrounding forest, teeming with avian activity. The obvious focal point is the small jetty, which overlooks the forest-fringed south bank of the Nickerie River. Overshadowing the river to the left of the jetty is the disused rice loading mechanism, a vast contraption now overgrown with lianas. For some mysterious reason, entrance to the grounds of the disused rice factory that once formed Wageningen's *raison d'être* is emphatically forbidden, but from the waterfront you can wander up Oost Einde Laan, running to the east of the factory, for a close-up look at the old silos. Wageningen's best-known landmark, the Misi Alida Monument (see box, page 160), stands at the junction of Oost Einde Laan and Hoofd Pad. Rather less memorable is a statue in the main park marking the 25th anniversary of independence.

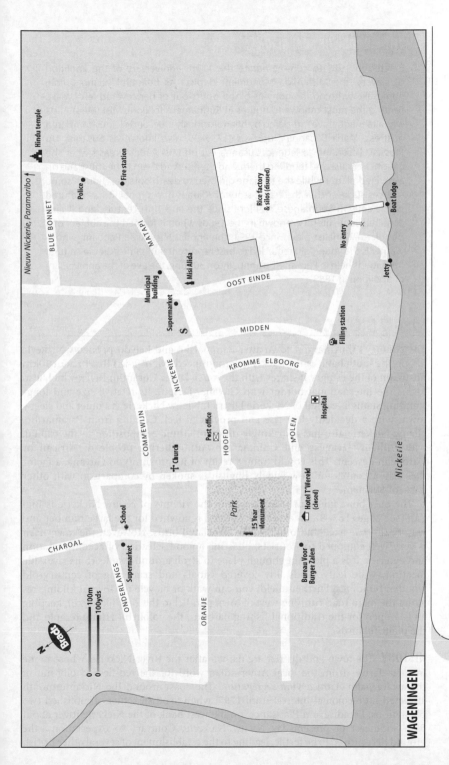

WAGENINGEN

Nieuw Nickerie, Paramaribo

Hindu temple

Police

Fire station

BLUE BONNET

MATAPI

Rice factory
& silos (disused)

Boat lodge

No entry

Jetty

Misi Alida

OOST EINDE

Municipal
building

Supermarket

$

MIDDEN

Filling station

KROMME ELBOORG

NICKERIE

Hospital

COMMEWIJN

Post office

HOOFD

MOLEN

Church

Nickerie

Park

Hotel T'Wereld
(diesel)

School

15 Year
Monument

CHAROAL

Supermarket

Bureau Voor
Burger Zalen

ONDERLANGS

ORANJE

N

Bradt

0   100m
0   100yds

Erected in 1973 to commemorate the 110th anniversary of the abolition of slavery, the Misi Alida Monument depicts its beautiful young Creole namesake writhing in agony as blood pours out of her severed left breast. Among the most renowned figures in Surinamese folklore, Misi (Miss) Alida was a teenage slave murdered by her notoriously cruel and vicious-tempered mistress, Maria Susanna Duplessis (1739–95, also known as Susanna Du Plessis). According to legend, Susanna cut off Misi Alida's breasts after she caught her husband fondling them, and then served them to her husband on a covered platter while the teenage girl bled to death outside. Though some sources suggest that the tragic story of Alida is apocryphal, it has featured persistently in Surinamese oral lore since the late 18th century, and it also acquired some literary renown in the 1960s when it formed the subject of a popular nationalist play. Since 1991, the annual Miss Alida Pageant, whose winner is the young girl regarded to best represent Suriname's Creole cultural heritage, is held in Paramaribo annually on 30 June, the eve of the anniversary of abolition in 1863.

NIEUW NICKERIE

The country's third-largest town after Paramaribo and Lelydorp, Nieuw Nickerie lies on the south bank of the Nickerie (pronounced 'Nie-kér-ie') River about 10km upstream of the estuary it shares with the much larger Corantijn River, which also forms the international border with Guyana. Despite its relative size and long-standing status as capital of Nickerie District, Nieuw Nickerie is a quiet and sleepy town, with a decidedly low-rise and provincial feel. Coming from Paramaribo, Nieuw Nickerie also has a strikingly different ethnic composition to the capital, with Indians, Javanese and Chinese far outnumbering people of African or European descent. This is said to be a result of its proximity to Guyana, a factor that also accounts for how widely English is spoken by comparison with other parts of Suriname.

The only bona fide tourist attraction in the vicinity of Nieuw Nickerie is Bigi Pan (see pages 167–8), an extensive wetland renowned for the large number and variety of its marine and other water-associated birds. However, the town itself is very well equipped for tourists, boasting a good selection of accommodation and eateries. It is a pleasant enough place to stroll around thanks to its riverside location, wide leafy roads, lily-covered canals and scattering of century-old wooden buildings. Further afield, you can walk or bicycle for several kilometres along the main road running west of town parallel to the Zeedijk (dyke), keeping an eye open for the traditional fishing harbour, the colourful Hindu temple and the plentiful birds.

HISTORY The town and district are named after the River Nickerie, whose name in turn derives from the local Amerindian word for the red-fleshed oily nut of the awara palm *Astrocaryum segregatum*. The coast around the Nickerie mouth attracted little colonial interest until 1797, when Scottish settlers established two plantations, Paradise and Plaissance, on the west bank of the Nickerie River about 5km southeast of present-day Nieuw Nickerie. Contrary to expectations, the ground here proved to be fertile, leading to the establishment of several other British cotton and coffee plantations in the early 19th century. Initially, the produce from these plantations, so remote from Paramaribo, was exported through present-day Guyana. That changed after 1820, when the port of Nieuw Rotterdam was founded on the north bank of Nickerie Point (the joint estuary with the Corantijn River). In 1834, Suriname was carved by Royal Decree into eight administrative divisions and two districts, and Nieuw Rotterdam was made the district capital of Nickerie.

By the 1850s, Nieuw Rotterdam, nicknamed the Smugglers' Eldorado, had grown to become a substantial trade centre. It housed a tall spired church, a stilted courthouse, military barracks, a few shops and a bakery. The constant breeze meant it was also regarded as one of the healthiest places in Suriname, and for that reason a convalescent home was built there. By 1863, however, it had become clear that much of the land drained to accommodate the expanding town was vulnerable to flooding and battering from the sea. An earthen dam was raised to protect it against the waves, but it wasn't enough to prevent the destructive flood that led to the official evacuation of Nieuw Rotterdam in 1866.

In the late 1860s, a new village was founded on the south side of the river, where land was drained to accommodate government buildings and private residences. By 1872, the old town was completely abandoned and its upstart south bank counterpart comprised around 400 buildings and twice as many residents. However, in 1875, the new location proved to be as vulnerable as its predecessor and disaster struck again in the form of a second flood. The colonial authorities toyed with the notion of constructing a dyke to protect the town, but daunted by the likely costs they decided to build Nieuw Nickerie at its present-day site on the former Margarethenburg and Waterloo plantations.

Nieuw Nickerie officially became the administrative headquarters of Nickerie District in 1879. Rice production started in the late 19th century, initially on a primarily subsistence level by Indian and Javan immigrants for whom it was the traditional staple. By 1922, the town was servicing a productive agricultural district with a cosmopolitan population of around 10,000 – Indian, Dutch, Javanese, Chinese, Creole and Amerindian. An important industry in the early to mid 20th century was the production of balatá, a water-resistant rubber-like gum (once used to make golf balls) manufactured from the latex of the tall massaranduba tree *Manilkara bidentata*.

In 1942, construction work started on the dyke that now stretches 8km west of the town centre to the old Corantijn Beach. Although balatá production ground to a standstill in the post war era, Nickerie District received a major economic boost in the late 1940s, when the paddies were expanded by thousands of hectares as part of a US initiative to make Wageningen the country's major rice growing area. Ever since, Nickerie has been the main rice supplier both for the domestic and export market, and much of the produce is shipped out of the port at Nieuw Nickerie. Another economic boost came in the 1960s, with the completion of the first road connecting Nickerie to the capital – prior to this, the only direct connection to Paramaribo was a 15-hour ferry ride. Nickerie is also an important source of export bananas and timber, and a major supplier of fish for the domestic market. Today, the town supports some 13,000 people, while Nickerie District – still largely agricultural – has a population of around 35,000.

GETTING THERE AND AWAY There are no scheduled **flights** to Nieuw Nickerie but any of the small airlines based at Paramaribo's Zorg en Hoop Airport can arrange a charter flight. Most operators based in Paramaribo offer overnight **tours** to Nickerie and Bigi Pan. This is a good option if you are pushed for time or don't feel

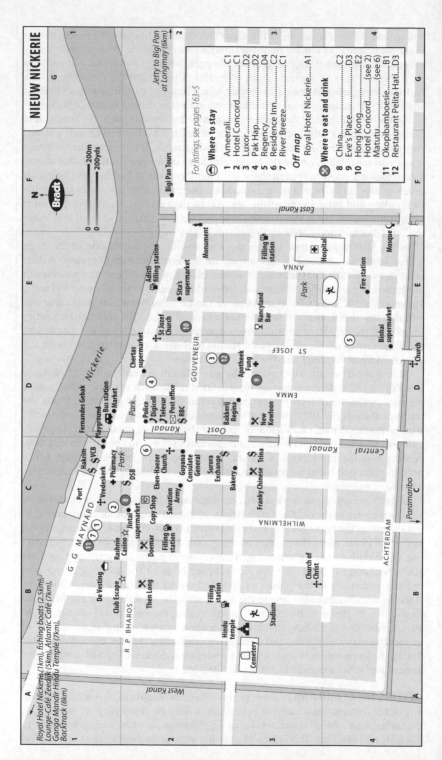

NIEUW NICKERIE

Jetty to Bigi Pan at Longmay (6km)

For listings, see pages 163–5

Where to stay

1	Ameerali	C1
2	Hotel Concord	C1
3	Luxor	D2
4	Pak Hap	D2
5	Regency	D4
6	Residence Inn	C2
7	River Breeze	C1

Off map
Royal Hotel Nickerie......A1

Where to eat and drink

8	China	C2
9	Eve's Place	D3
10	Hong Kong	E2
	Hotel Concord	(see 2)
	Matutu	(see 6)
11	Okopibamboesie	B1
12	Restaurant Pelita Hati	D3

Nickerie

Bigi Pan Tours

Royal Hotel Nickerie (1km), fishing boats (2.5km), Lounge-Café Zeedijk (5km), Atlantic Café (7km), Ganga Mandir Hindu Temple (7km), Backtrack (8km)

Adisti filling station

Sita's supermarket

Monument

Filling station

Hospital

Fire station

Mosque

St Jozef Church

Chertas supermarket

Nancyland Bar

Park

Binhai supermarket

Apotheek Fung

Fernandes Gebak

Market

Bus station

Playground

Police

Digicell

Telesur

Post office

RBC

Pharmacy

DSB

Vredeskerk

Hakrin

VCB

Eben-Haezer Church

Copy Shop

Salvation Army

Guyana Consulate General

Surora Exchange

Bakery

Franky Chinese

Bakkerij Regina

New Kowloon

Trina

Port

Rashnie

Casino

Jintai supermarket

Doemar

Filling station

Then Long

Club Escape

De Vesting

Church of Christ

Hindu temple

Stadium

Cemetery

Church

West Kanal

East Kanal

Central Kanal

Oost Kanal

Kanaal

MAYNARD

R P BHAROS

WILHELMINA

ACHTERDAM

Paramaribo

GOUVENEUR

ST JOSEF

EMMA

ANNA

Bradt

N

0   200m
0   200yds

like making your own way to Nickerie and arranging things on the ground. If you decide to do a tour out of Paramaribo, try and find one that overnights in the pan rather than visiting it as a day trip from Nieuw Nickerie.

By bus Two buses run in either direction between Paramaribo and Nieuw Nickerie daily except Sunday. They leave at 06.00 and 13.00, in both directions, and cost SRD 12.50 one-way, taking up to four hours. In addition, there are usually several private minibuses daily, charging around SRD 50 per person and leaving when full, while shared or private taxis cost around SRD 70 per person or SRD 350 for the whole vehicle. In addition, a bus runs twice daily between Wageningen and Nieuw Nickerie, leaving the former at 07.00 and 16.00 and the latter at 13.00 and 19.00, and taking up to 90 minutes one-way. All public transport leaves from and arrives at the bus station next to the market. Transport is often more difficult to find in the afternoon or at any time on Sundays.

By boat A more adventurous onward option would be to catch a boat travelling upriver on the Corantijn as far as Apoera (see page 226). One scheduled service operates on the river, leaving Nieuw Nickerie every Monday and Friday morning and Apoera every Tuesday and Saturday morning. It costs SRD 40 per person one-way and takes up to seven hours. Contact the captain, Arupa (m *8617713*), for further details. In addition, there has been some talk of the SMS post boat (see page 117) starting a regular run between Nickerie and Apoera. It may also be possible to grab a lift with a sand-dredger or cargo boat heading upriver. The best place to start asking around is the port, which is in the town centre opposite the Vredeskerk.

To Guyana Heading to Guyana, a ferry called the *Canawaima* travels twice a day between the Surinamese port of South Drain, about 45km from Nickerie, and its Guyanese counterpart Corriverton. Though timetables are not wholly reliable, the ferry usually leaves South Drain at 09.00 and 13.00 and Corriverton at 11.00 and 15.00. Shared taxis and minibuses connect the central bus station in Nieuw Nickerie to South Drain, taking up to one hour. There are also regular minibuses connecting Corriverton to the Guyanese capital Georgetown. Another option is to take one of the local boats that ply back and forth between Backtrack, a small harbour at the end of the Zeedijk 8km west of Nieuw Nickerie, and the Guyanese port of Springlands. Be warned, however, that these boats are a lot less safe than the large ferry. For further information about Guyana, contact the Guyana Consulate General in Nieuw Nickerie (see page 165).

⬆ **WHERE TO STAY** *Map, opposite*
Upmarket ($$$$)

🏠 **Residence Inn** (24 rooms) RP Bharos Straat; ☎ 210950; e info@resinn.com; www.resinn.com. This reasonably smart & modern hotel lies right in the heart of town, overlooking the main square & central canal. The clean motel-style rooms suffer from a distinct lack of character, but they are spacious enough, & come with tiled floor, 1 dbl & 1 sgl bed, satellite flat-screen TV, safe, AC, free Wi-Fi & en-suite hot shower. A good restaurant & street café are attached. It can also arrange bicycle hire & day trips to Bigi Pan. From SRD 215/250 sgl/dbl on w/days & SRD 228/270 at w/ends; all rates B&B.

Moderate ($$$)

🏠 ❋ **Pak Hap** (31 rooms) Emma Straat; ☎ 212381–2; e info@pakhap.com; www.pakhap.com. Though not exactly bursting with character, this clean, modern & central multi-storey hotel, overlooking the main square & the market, is easily one of the best deals in town. The smart rooms all sleep 2, & come with AC, satellite TV & en-suite bathroom with hot water.
A smaller dbl with dbl bed & shower costs SRD 120, while larger rooms with king-size or twin beds & combined tub/shower cost SRD 220. Suites are SRD 400. All rates B&B.

🛏 **Royal Hotel Nickerie** (14 rooms) Abdul Ghanie Weg; 📞231352; e reservations@ hotelroyalnickerie.com; www.hotelroyalnickerie. com. Boasting a great waterfront setting 2km west of the town centre, the Royal has the best location of any hotel in Nickerie, & other facilities include a tempting swimming pool, a breezy wooden deck above the river, a cosy restaurant serving a varied selection of international mains in the SRD 35–60 range, & free Wi-Fi. The en-suite rooms are adequate, & come with AC, satellite TV & en-suite hot shower, but they feel a little tired & overpriced in comparison with the competition. SRD 126/162 streetside/riverside dbl; suites & family rooms start at SRD 250.

🛏 **Regency Hotel & Casino** (17 rooms) Hendrik Straat; 📞211025/231389; e info@ regencynickerie.com; www.regencynickerie. com. Tucked away on the southern backstreets of Nickerie, this ostentatious hotel is a decent fall-back if the other options in this range are full, but it feels a bit rundown & the gaudy pink interiors could become wearing pretty quickly. Still, the en-suite rooms with queen-size bed, TV, AC & free Wi-Fi seem reasonable value, & there is a good restaurant & casino attached. SRD 116/172/209 sgl/dbl/trpl, rising to SRD 135/190/227 on Fri & Sat.

Budget ($$)

🛏 ✳ **Hotel Concord** (16 rooms) Wilhelmina Straat; 📞232345; m 8743517; e hotelconcordmhf@yahoo.com. Our favourite

hotel in Nickerie is a characterful 70-year-old colonial building where the ground floor is partially given over to a good Javan restaurant. If your budget runs to it, the very spacious but slightly pricier 1st-floor rooms, complete with creaky wooden floors, king-size bed, writing desk, AC, TV & en-suite hot shower, are worth the minor additional investment. The cheaper, smaller & dingier ground-floor rooms have similar facilities but lack the period charm, & come with cold water only. SRD 80/95 ground/1st-floor dbl B&B.

🛏 **Luxor** (30 rooms) St Jozef Straat; 📞231365. One of the better-value options in this range is this safe, quiet & central 3-storey hotel, which has clean & spacious rooms with en-suite hot shower. SRD 75 dbl with fan, SRD 100/215 dbl/ trpl with AC; all rates B&B.

🛏 **River Breeze** (15 rooms) GG Maynard Straat; 📞210926. This unexceptional central hotel next to Okopibamboesi Grill & Café offers clean but rather austere tiled rooms with AC, TV & en-suite hot shower. SRD 80/90 dbl/twin.

Shoestring ($)

🛏 **Ameerali** (10 rooms) GG Maynard Straat; 📞231212. Next to the River Breeze & considerably more rundown, the best feature of Nickerie's cheapest hotel is the breezy communal balcony offering a view of the river. The en-suite rooms, which come with creaky AC, TV & writing desk, are scruffy but reasonably clean. SRD 65 dbl or SRD 90 family room (sleeps 4).

🍴 **WHERE TO EAT AND DRINK** *Map, page 162*
Mid-range

🍴 **Hong Kong Restaurant** Gouveneur Straat; 📞231885; ⏱ 10.00–13.00 & 17.00–22.00 Mon–Sat. The top Chinese restaurant in town has a smart interior with comfortable seating & AC. There is also a varied menu with plenty of choice for vegetarians, as well as fish & meat dishes, & a well-stocked bar. Not to be confused with the lesser restaurant of the same name opposite Bakkerij Regina. Mains are mostly in the SRD 28–35 range, inclusive of rice. $$

🍴 **Matutu Restaurant** RP Bharos Straat; ⏱ 13.00–22.00 daily. Offering the choice of AC seating indoor or alfresco dining facing the lily-covered main canal, the ground-floor restaurant at the Residence Inn serves a varied selection of international dishes. Burgers & toasted sandwiches

are in the SRD 10–12 range & Surinamese Javan cuisine is SRD 20–25, while more exotic dishes such as grilled steak & Jamaica jerk chicken cost around SRD 40. It has the only free Wi-Fi in town. $$–$$$

Budget

🍴 **Okopibamboesi Grill & Cafe** GG Maynard Straat; 📞212111; e okopibamboesi@yahoo. com; ⏱ 16.00–23.00 Tue–Thu, 08.00–23.00 Fri–Sun. This pleasant Javan-owned restaurant is distinguished by its brightly painted walls adorned with jungle scenes, its comfortable cane furniture & the globetrotting menu. In addition to the usual Javan dishes, it serves international cuisine such as burgers, teriyaki chicken & pepper steaks, & it also has a well-stocked bar. Most dishes are in the

SRD 15–20 range but steaks are around SRD 40. $–$$$

✕ Hotel Concord Wilhelmina Straat; ⏲ noon–23.00 daily. The ground-floor restaurant at this time-worn hostelry (see opposite page) has low wooden ceilings & no-frills tables that evoke post-war Europe. It serves very good Javan food for around SRD 15 for a main. $

✕ Restaurant Pelita Hati St Jozef Straat; m 8712747; ⏲ 09.00–22.30 Mon–Sat. This spotless local-style eatery with blasting AC offers a variety of Javan dishes in the SRD 12–20 range. No alcohol served. $

✕ China Restaurant RP Bharos Straat; ☎ 212866; ⏲ 10.00–23.00 Mon–Sat. Though it's a bit of a hole in the wall & there's limited seating, this family-run place serves a varied selection of genuine Chinese dishes for around SRD 20–40, & there's a fridge stocked with cold beer. $–$$$

Bakeries

✕ Bakkerij Regina [162 D3] Emma Straat; ⏲ 08.00–14.00 & 17.00–22.00 Mon–Sat, 1700–23.00 Sun. This excellent bakery sells an incredible selection of sweet & savoury pastries, as well as fresh bread, rotisserie chicken, burgers, mini-pizzas, filled baguettes, cold drinks, & tea &

coffee. It's all very cheap & aimed mainly at the take-away market, but there are also a couple of tables where you can eat in. A good b/fast spot. $

✕ Fernandes Gebak [162 C1] GG Maynard Straat; ⏲ 08.00–14.00 & 17.00–20.00 Mon–Sat. This affordable bakery & confectionary next to the market sells fresh bread, cakes & pastries, as well as good ice cream. $

Bars

♀ Lounge-Café Zeedijk [off map, 162 A1] Abdul Ghanie Weg; m 8973035; e zeedijk@hotmail. com; www.cafezeedijk.com; ⏲ 18.00–01.00 Wed & Thu, 18.00–02.00 Fri & Sat, 16.00–01.00 Sun. Overlooking the Zeedijk about 3km west of the town centre, this contemporary new lounge bar is Nickerie's slickest nightspot, & the stylish 1st-floor balcony offers a good view over the dyke to the open sea. It serves a varied selection of cocktails & snacks, as well as inexpensive 'finger food' at w/ends.

✕ Eve's Place [162 D3] AK Doergasawh Straat; ☎ 210324; ⏲ 09.00–15.00 Mon–Wed, 09.00–late Thu–Sat. This pleasant outdoor spot is first & foremost a bar, but it also serves a dish of the day for around SRD 20 at lunchtime, & BBQ chicken & chips in the evenings. $

OTHER PRACTICALITIES

Banking Several banks with ATMs are scattered around the town centre. Most accept international MasterCard, among them the DSB on Landing Straat and Hakrin Bank on GG Maynard Straat. The only ATMs that accept Visa in addition to MasterCard can be found at the RCB on Oost Kanaal Straat and the VCB on GG Maynard Straat. For foreign exchange try Surora Exchange (m 8809097) on Oost Kanaal Straat.

Bicycle Rental Bicycles supplied by Fietse In Suriname (see page 78; m 8782220) can be rented from outside the Residence Inn for SRD 70 per day (plus a returnable deposit of SRD 200). Ask the Residence Inn reception for further details (see page 163).

Embassies The **Guyana Consulate General** [162 C2] (*Cnr Gouveneur & Oost Kanaal;* ☎ 210266/212080; ⏲ 07.30–14.00 Mon–Fri) issues visas overnight for SRD 125–250, depending on your nationality and planned number of entries. Note that no visa is currently required for British and most other EU passport-holders.

Internet Multi Colours Copy Shop [162 C2] (⏲ 08.00–19.00 Mon–Fri, 08.00–noon Sat) on RP Bharos Straat incorporates a small internet café charging SRD 1 per 15 minutes.

There's free Wi-Fi access in the rooms, restaurant and café at the Residence Inn (see page 163).

Medical The best hospital is the **Streekziekenhuis Nickerie** (*Anna Straat;* ✆ *231241; www.szn.sr*) on the east side of town. The central **Apotheek Fung** (*St Jozef Straat;* ✆ *211425;* ⊕ *08.00–13.00 Mon–Sat & 16.00–19.00 Mon–Fri*) is a very well-stocked pharmacy.

Shopping The lively **central market** is busiest from around 07.00 to noon daily but it's quiet in the afternoon. For those seeking a cheap breakfast, it has several stalls selling coffee and tea, freshly baked sandwiches, doughnuts and pastries, and there's plenty of fresh fruit available.

Numerous **supermarkets** are dotted around town. Two of the best are the Chertas Supermarket on GG Maynard Straat and the larger but less central Binhai Supermarket on Achterdam Weg.

WHAT TO SEE AND DO The most popular activity out of Nieuw-Nickerie is a day or overnight trip to Bigi Pan, which is covered under a separate heading below.

Around town It's worth dedicating an hour or so to a stroll around town. A good starting point is the neat central square in front of the Residence Inn, and the nearby municipal market, which is hemmed in by a couple of alleys that run down to the river and offer a view across to the mangrove-lined north bank. Elsewhere, the most attractive roads are those that follow the larger canals (the central Oost and Oost Kanaal, leading south from the market, and the more peripheral Achterdam, Waterloo and Margarethenburg), which generally support a cover of large-leaved water lilies and rows of tall palms, along with water-associated birds such as wattled jacana, great kiskadee and pied water tyrant. Most of the buildings are relatively new, given that the town only relocated to its present site in 1870, but there are some older wooden buildings in the centre, the most striking of which is the tall-spired **Moravian Vredeskerk** (Peace Church) on GG Maynard Straat and the Dutch Reformed **Eben-Haezer Church** on Oost Kanaal Straat. Other landmarks include **Winkel Elias**, on the corner of Emma and Gouveneur straats, which is the oldest shop in town, founded in 1911, and the monument on Waterloo Straat commemorating the centenary of the abolition of slavery.

The Backtrack road A pleasant longer excursion out of Nieuw Nickerie entails walking, or better cycling (bicycles can be rented outside the Residence Inn), west along Abdul Ghanie Weg, an extension of GG Maynard Straat that runs parallel to the Zeedijk, to the small harbour of Backtrack, about 8km out of town on the Corantijn-Nickerie estuary. For cyclists, several variations of the route are possible. The total distance for the shortest loop is around 15km, while the longest will be around 28km, and it is more-or-less flat all the way. On foot, you could walk as far as you want on Abdul Ghanie Weg, then pick up public transport back to town when you are ready to turn back. A good place to stop for a cold drink or light snack is the Atlantic Café, opposite the Ganga Mandir Hindu Temple, just before Backtrack.

As you leave Nieuw Nickerie, shortly before the start of the Zeedijk, you'll see a small fishing harbour (on your right) that reputedly sometimes gets busy at around 09.00, when the local fishing boats come in. The Zeedijk is a tall grass-topped dyke that runs between the main road and the rocky shore – you probably don't want to risk swimming in the choppy water here, but if you are on foot, you could walk along the top of the dyke, which offers a great vantage point over the surrounding suburbs and fields. About 7km past this, as the road veers southwest towards the end of the Zeedijk, the fabulous **Ganga Mandir Hindu Temple** is topped with three colourful bulbous domes that look rather like lilies. Several smaller statues adorn the temple, and it serves as an important place of cremation for Hindus from all over the country. After another 300m, the Zeedijk ends at the oddly named Backtrack, a small but often bustling harbour from where local boats run back and forth across the Corantijn River to the Guyanese port of Springlands.

From Backtrack, you can head back the way you came (if you are on foot, there are occasional minibuses) or take a 6km shortcut back to town along Rambaran Mishre Weg. Alternatively, energetic cyclists might want to extend the loop by continuing southwest for another 2–3km or so, passing Corantijn Beach to the right, before reaching a large tract of riverine forest that supports plenty of birds and also looks promising for monkeys. From here, you could cut back to town by turning left into Beatrix or Basti Weg, left again into Gemaal Weg, right into Delhi Weg (which becomes Cassava Weg) and then left into Walther Hewitt Straat following it all the way to Oost Kanaal Straat and the main square and market.

BIGI PAN

The most popular tourist attraction in Nickerie, Bigi Pan is a large nutrient-rich lagoon that forms the centrepiece of a sprawling and atmospheric 680km^2 network of estuarine wetlands separating the Atlantic Ocean from the Nickerie River. The area was set aside as the Bigi Pan Multiple Use Management Area (MUMA) in 1987 and is now earmarked to become Suriname's second Ramsar wetland site (www. ramsar.org). Vast black mangrove forests line the swampy coast, while the various rivers and creeks support smaller strips of red and white mangroves. These brooding, mosquito-plagued mangrove swamps serve an important role as breeding areas and nurseries for crabs, crustaceans and other small aquatic organisms inconspicuous to humans but integral to the coastal food chain. As a result, the MUMA is renowned for its vertebrate biodiversity, with a checklist of around 120 bird, 40 mammal and 30 fish species. Private fishing is still allowed in the MUMA, but commercial fishing is strictly regulated. The biggest threat to the area, however, comes from neighbouring agricultural areas, in the form of illegal expansion of rice fields, the inflow of toxic pesticides and fertilisers, and changes in salinity.

Particularly popular with birdwatchers, Bigi Pan is listed as an Important Bird Area (IBA), since it attracts seasonal aggregations of more than half a million shorebirds. Areas of open water, such as the 8km^2 main pan, are the best places to see spectacular shorebirds such as American flamingo, roseate spoonbill, wood stork, black skimmer and the somewhat less conspicuous semi-palmated sandpiper, semi-palmated plover and short-billed dowitcher. The MUMA also hosts the country's largest breeding colony of scarlet ibis, a stunning all-red shorebird whose range is more-or-less confined to the northeast coast of South America. Taken slowly, the mangrove-lined 8.5km channel connecting Bigi Pan to the Nickerie River also offers superb birding, and it hosts very different species to the main open water. It is here you are most likely to see three regional endemics associated with Bigi Pan, namely Guianan piculet, blood-coloured woodpecker and rufous crab-hawk. You may also spot the likes of three-coloured and little blue heron, various parrots and kingfishers, yellow-throated spinetail, carib grackle, yellow oriole and a variety of medium to large raptors. Birding is good throughout the year, but avian activity peaks between February and April, and again between August and November.

GETTING THERE AND AROUND Bigi Pan lies about 12km east of Nieuw Nickerie as the crow flies. Access is by boat only. The normal launching point for boats is at

Longmay (⊕N5 55.484 W56 56.707), which lies about 8km from the town centre and can be reached by following Friderici Weg southeast along the south bank of the Nickerie River. From Longmay, boats follow the river upstream for about 2km before taking a slipway into the artificial Jamaer Canal, which was dug by hand in 1953. It is about 8.5km from the start of the canal, which runs northeast through the mangroves, to the open waters of Bigi Pan.

Tours It isn't really possible to visit Bigi Pan independently and the cheapest option is a half-day trip from Nieuw Nickerie, which gets you to the pan and back, but doesn't really allow you much time to absorb the setting or to look for birds at the optimum time of day (early morning and late afternoon). Day trips can be organised through **Bigi Pan Adventures** (see below) for around SRD 280–350 for a group of up to five, inclusive of transport and guide. Alternatively, contact **Mr Kasadi** (either through the Residence Inn – see page 163 – or directly on m 8677289/8883236), who arranges day trips for around SRD 140 per person (minimum two people) inclusive of transport, drinks and lunch. In both cases, departure is usually at 08.00 and you should be back in Nieuw Nickerie by 14.00.

The best way to see the pan is to do an overnight trip from Nieuw Nickerie. For this, we strongly recommend Bigi Pan Adventures, which also operates Stephanie's EcoLodge (the only accommodation on the water) and runs one-/two-night trips for around SRD 350/595 all-inclusive per person, depending to some extent on group size. All tours with Bigi Pan Adventures are guided personally by its enthusiastic owner-manager Stephanie Kramawitana, who is very knowledgeable about the area's birds and other wildlife.

A cheaper alternative, particularly for larger groups and offering more basic overnight trips, is **Bigi Pan Tours** (*Friderici Weg, close to the junction with Wellington Straat;* m 8648244/8974429/8920773), which accommodates guests in hammocks or tents on a wooden deck, and charges SRD 850 per group (maximum seven) for a one-night stay including transport.

 WHERE TO STAY

 ✻ **Stephanie's EcoLodge** (10 rooms) m 8783651/8852471; e bigipan.adventure@ yahoo.com; www.stephanieslodge.com; www. facebook.com/BigiPanAdventures. The only lodge in Bigi Pan stands on an isolated stilted wooden platform on the 1st stretch of open water you reach coming from Longmay by boat. The twin rooms are all en suite, & have mosquito nets & a private balcony. There is also a public area where 3 meals are served daily & hammocks sway invitingly in the breeze (which also helps keeps the mosquitoes at bay). The lodge can be visited only as part of an all-inclusive tour run by Bigi Pan Adventures, & rates are inclusive of transport to & from Nieuw Nickerie, meals & soft drinks, & activities such as birdwatching by boat, kayaking, caiman spotting, fishing & anarchic mud baths in the mudflats. SRD 350pp for the 1st night & SRD 263 for additional nights all-inclusive. **$$$**

9

Wanica and Para

The southerly administrative districts of Wanica and Para can seem more like suburban extensions of Paramaribo than distinctive entities in their own right. This is particularly the case with the 443km² Wanica, which directly borders the capital to the south and west, and supports 120,000 people, making it both the second smallest of Suriname's administrative districts, and the second most populous. By contrast, Para, the country's third-largest district at 5,393km², supports a relatively modest population of 25,000, but it is home to the country's main port of entry in the form of the Johan Adolf Pengel International Airport at Zanderij.

Wanica District is bordered by the Saramacca River to the west and the Suriname River to the east. Both these rivers run through Para, but the district is actually named after the far smaller black-water Para River, which flows south from Zanderij to its confluence with the Suriname near Domburg. Wanica and Para are bisected by the two main roads to the interior: the westerly route to Apoera via Lelydorp, Onverwacht and Zanderij, and the asphalt road to Atjoni via Paranam and Brownsweg.

Wanica is of limited interest to tourists. Its one top-class attraction is the excellent Neotropical Butterfly Farm, which lies in the district capital Lelydorp, and is easily accessible by bus from Paramaribo. Other sites of interest are Domberg, a small town set on the west bank of the Suriname River about 30km south of Paramaribo, and the more remote Saamaka village of Santigron, which lies on the east bank of the Saramacca River west of Lelydorp.

The most significant historic attraction in Para is the ruined town of Jodensavanne ('Jewish Savannah'), which was founded by Sephardic Jews on the east bank of the Suriname River in the early 17th century. The district's largest towns are the capital Onverwacht and the nearby bauxite mining centre of Paranam, neither of which holds much of interest for visitors. Further south, in the vicinity of Zanderij, the Para River and its cola-coloured tributaries are studded with small jungle-fringed resorts that lure hordes of partying locals from the capital at weekends. Para is also home to White Beach, a popular swimming resort on the Suriname River just south of Domburg.

LELYDORP

The district capital of Wanica, Lelydorp is also the second-largest settlement in Suriname, though with a population of fewer than 20,000, it comes across more like a sprawling garden village than a city. In 1902, then known as Kofidjompo, it was selected as an important stop along the soon-to-be constructed railway inland to the goldfields at Lawa. Three years later, with the railway up and running, Kofidjompo was renamed in honour of Cornelis Lely, the civil engineer (and retiring governor of Suriname) largely responsible for the track being

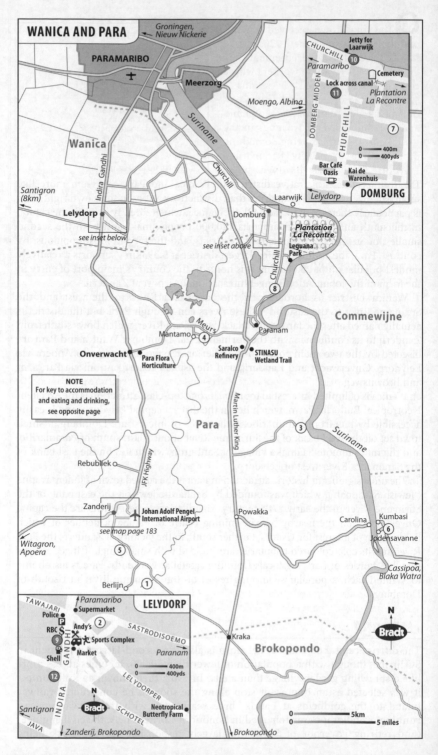

WANICA AND PARA

PARAMARIBO

Groningen,
Nieuw Nickerie

Meerzorg

Moengo, Albina

Wanica

Santigron
(8km)

Lelydorp

see inset below

Laarwijk

Domburg

see inset above

**Plantation
La Recontre**

Leguana
Park

Commewijne

Mantamo

Meurs

Paranam

Onverwacht

Para Flora
Horticulture

Saralco
Refinery

**STINASU
Wetland Trail**

NOTE
For key to accommodation
and eating and drinking,
see opposite page

Para

Rebubliek

Suriname

Powakka

Kumbasi

Carolina

Jodensavanne

Zanderij

**Johan Adolf Pengel
International Airport**

see map page 183

Witagron,
Apoera

Berlijn

*Cassipoa,
Blaka Watra*

Kraka

Brokopondo

N

Bradt

0 — 5km
0 — 5 miles

Inset: DOMBURG

CHURCHILL

**Jetty for
Laarwijk**

Paramaribo

Lock across canal

Cemetery

*Plantation
La Recontre*

DOMBERG MIDDEN

CHURCHILL

0 — 400m
0 — 400yds

**Bar Café
Oasis**

**Kai de
Warenhuis**

Lelydorp

DOMBURG

Inset: LELYDORP

TAWAJARI

Paramaribo

Supermarket

Police

RBC

Andy's

Sports Complex

Shell

Market

Neotropical
Butterfly Farm

Paranam

SASTRODISOEMO

LELYDORPER

SCHOTEL

INDIRA GANDHI

JAVA

Santigron

Zanderij, Brokopondo

LELYDORP

0 — 400m
0 — 400yds

N

Bradt

Brokopondo

laid. The small town received a major population boost in the 1920s, when it was selected as a resettlement area for immigrant Javanese workers whose contracts had expired. It retains a strong Javanese element to this day, one reflected in many of its road names and the abundance of warungs in the town centre. Despite being something of a satellite to nearby Paramaribo, Lelydorp today has its own hotel, medical facilities, waterworks, stadium, electricity plant and schools. Its premier tourist attraction is the excellent Neotropical Butterfly Farm about 1km east of the main square.

GETTING THERE AND AWAY Lelydorp is bisected by Indira Gandhi Weg (aka JFK Highway), the main road connecting central Paramaribo, 20km to the north, with Zanderij and Johan Adolf Pengel International Airport, 30km to the south. It's less than an hour's drive from the city centre or airport (unless traffic is unusually heavy) and a private taxi should cost around SRD 50 one-way. Alternatively, private Lijn PL (Paramaribo–Lelydorp) buses leave Paramaribo from Maagden Weg when full (typically every ten to 15 minutes), cost SRD 1.75, and take about one hour. Lijn PL buses headed in the opposite direction leave Lelydorp from in front of the market. Any shuttle from the airport could drop you in Lelydorp on request.

WHERE TO STAY Map, opposite

Lely Hills Hotel & Casino (32 rooms) 2–4 Sastrodisoemo Weg; 366289; e info@ lelyhillshotel.com; www.lelyhillshotel.com. This large & quite pleasant hotel lies in slightly rundown tree-shaded gardens & has a swimming pool & casino. It is perhaps 200m east of the central square & the market on Indira Gandhi Weg. Standard rooms come with queen-size bed, TV, fridge, free Wi-Fi, AC & en-suite bathroom. Larger moderate rooms overlook the gardens, & there are also self-catering rooms with kitchenette, & suites with king-size beds. It could be a useful alternative

WANICA AND PARA

For listings, see pages 171–2

Where to stay
1 Jungle Camp Carolina
2 Lely Hills
3 Overbridge River Resort
4 Parabello campsite
5 Pulula Camping
6 Redi Doti Camp
7 Surinat Vakantie Resort
8 White Beach Marina Resort

Where to eat and drink
Eethuis Rita (see 10)
Fessa's Fancy Food (see 10)
9 Grand Roopram Roti
Overbridge River Resort (see 3)
Pulula Camping (see 5)
Redi Doti Camp (see 6)
10 Warung Domburg
11 Warung Mit Shiv
12 Warung 'T Hoekje
White Beach Marina Resort (see 8)

KOFI JUMPS

Lelydorp was originally known as Kofidjompo ('Kofi jumps'), in memory of an escaped slave called Kofi – a name commonly given to boys born on a Friday, a tradition inherited from what is now Ghana (the birthplace, among many, of the former UN Secretary-General Kofi Annan, another Friday's child). One story has it that the nominate Kofi escaped his Dutch pursuers at Lelydorp by jumping over a creek to freedom. A less cheerful and more mystical tradition casts Kofi as an important Marron rebel leader who was captured and killed by the Dutch authorities. His body was decapitated and the severed head was placed on the end of a stick and paraded on a boat to warn other escapees of their likely fate if captured. Suddenly, however, when the boat reached the middle of the river, Kofi's head came back to life, jumped off and disappeared to freedom. The central square in Lelydorp was renamed Kofidjompo Plein in 1983.

base to Paramaribo itself, & seems pretty good value from that perspective. An adequate restaurant is attached, & there are plenty of other eateries within easy walking distance. From SRD 125 standard dbl to SRD 245 suite. **$$$**

✕ WHERE TO EAT AND DRINK Map, page 170

Lelydorp is well known for its many inexpensive Javanese eateries, and **Warung As-Sarinah** in the main cluster near the market and **Warung 'T Hoekje** on the main road a few hundred metres further south have both been recommended. In addition, a branch of the excellent **Grand Roopram Roti Shop** (*373 Indira Gandhi Weg;* ✆ *581432; www.grandroopramroti.com*) serves rotis and other Indian and Surinamese dishes next to the Shell filling station on the main square. In all cases, mains will be in the SRD 12–20 (**$**) range.

OTHER PRACTICALITIES There are several banks with ATMs that take MasterCard on and around the main square.

WHAT TO SEE AND DO

Neotropical Butterfly Park (*127 Lelydorper Weg;* ✆ *366525;* m *8892891;* e *info@butterflyparksuriname.com; www.butterflyparksuriname.com;* ⊕ *08.30–15.30 (last entry 14.00) Mon–Sat, 09.00–14.00 (last entry 13.00) Sun; entrance SRD 35pp*) Opened in July 2010, this world-class educational facility offers a thoroughly enjoyable introduction to the colourful tropical butterflies and other insects and creepy-crawlies that inhabit Suriname. It started life as (and still is) a working butterfly farm, established in 1996 by Ewout and Amira Eriks to breed various Surinamese species for export to butterfly parks in the USA and Europe. It now breeds more than 20 different butterfly species for export twice a week, and also has a plant nursery and breeding facilities for turtles and snakes. The educational facility includes a landscaped walk-in cage where visitors can see (and photograph) around a dozen colourful types of butterfly, each of which feeds on one specific plant, and also a highly informative insect museum containing some wonderful specimens, not only butterflies, but also giant stick insects, rhinoceros beetles and tarantulas. The entrance fee includes a fascinating 45–60-minute guided tour of the farm, conducted in Dutch or English, and there is also a pleasant little onsite café serving hot and cold drinks, as well as meals in the SRD 15–20 range (30 minutes preparation time required). The great gift shop stocks butterfly-related postcards, pendants, paintings and other souvenirs.

SANTIGRON

Situated about 17km west of Lelydorp, Santigron (literally 'Sandy ground') is probably the closest Saamaka village to Paramaribo. Founded in the 19th century, it is in a stunning location in the middle of the jungle, a few hundred metres inland of the east bank of the Saramacca River as it flows along the border between Wanica and Saramacca districts. Despite Santigron's proximity to the capital, its economic mainstay is agriculture, fishing and woodcarving, and many inhabitants still rely mainly on herbal medicines from the surrounding jungle and wear the traditional dress of a dyed cloth *kamisa* for men and a cloth *pangi* skirt for women. Though predominantly Christian, Santigron also boasts many of the traditional features mentioned in the box on pages 204–5, among them an *azan pau* as you enter the village from the river side, and an ancestral shrine or *faaka pau*. As a relatively large village (population 2,000), it is divided into seven parts, each with its own *kabiteni* (one of whom, unusually, is a woman), who form a village council recognised by central government. Since 2008, the village has been served by the community ecotourism venture Stichting Projecthulp & Toerisme Santigron (SPS), initiated and still managed by a Dutch volunteer who spent several months living there. SPS operates a guesthouse in Santigron and runs highly praised day and overnight tours there from Paramaribo. It is also technically possible to visit the Santigron independently, and to arrange a guide on the spot, but this isn't encouraged by SPS, and unguided visitors may well receive a frosty reception from locals.

GETTING THERE AND AWAY Santigron is about 40km from Paramaribo by road, and the most straightforward way to visit it is with an **official day or overnight tour** operated by SPS (contact details as for Santigron Eco-Resort below). These leave Paramaribo from the Torarica Hotel at 09.15 on Wednesday and Saturday, and include all transport, meals, beers, house wine and soft drinks, as well as guided tours of Lelydorp market and Santigron village. The overnight tour also includes accommodation at the Santigron Eco-Resort and a day hike through the jungle to Pikin Poika, a smaller Amerindian village found a short way inland of the river about 2km north of Santigron. Day tours cost SRD 365 and overnight tours SRD 730 per person.

By car For self-drivers, the road to Santigron is unsignposted and the village is quite difficult to locate based on all the printed maps we've seen. Coming from Paramaribo, first head to Lelydorp, then continue past the main intersection and market for about 500m, before turning right into Java Weg. After 8km, take the unsignposted road to the left (⊕N5 42.133 W55 17.106) about 100m past an electricity substation (on the right side of the road) and immediately before the Winkel GM Leter (on the left). After another 1km, where the road running straight ahead is unsurfaced, follow the asphalt as it curves to the right. After another 5km, again where the road running straight ahead is unsurfaced (and signposted for Pikin Poika), turn left, and then after another 2km branch right and you'll enter the village after a few hundred metres.

By bus The NVB operates two buses daily in either direction between Santigron and Heiligen Weg in Paramaribo. These leave at 05.30 and 15.00 Monday to Saturday and 08.00 and 15.00 Sunday, in both directions, and take around two hours. The fare is SRD 2.75 one-way.

WHERE TO STAY AND EAT

Santigron Eco-Resort (10 rooms) ☏366151; m 8728743; e info@santigron.com; www.santigron.com. Set in a palm-shaded forest clearing bordering the village, this attractive lodge consists of several wooden huts linked by wooden walkways, as well as a hammock house, dining area & bar stocked with wine, beers & soft drinks. The huts are all twin rooms & come with a tiled floor & en-suite hot shower. As far as we could ascertain, it is reserved for tours run by SPS, so there are no room rates as such, as these are incorporated into the price of tours. **$$**

DOMBURG

Perched on the west bank of the Suriname River south of Paramaribo, Domburg is a small town of around 5,500 residents, best known as the birthplace of President Dési Bouterse. Comprising a grid of partially forest-fringed roads running south from the main riverfront square, Domburg was divided between two colonial coffee, cocoa and citrus plantations from the early 18th to the mid 19th century:

La Rencontre to the east and Domburg to the west. In 1750, La Rencontre was inventoried as one of many plantations owned by Stephanus Neale, a wealthy and influential businessman who introduced coffee to Suriname, had a role in the appointment of several colonial governors and was nicknamed De Rijkste der Rijken (Richest of the Rich). The names of the two old plantations are preserved in those of the numbered *zijstraaten* (side streets) that flank Sir Winston Churchill Weg (the main thoroughfare) to the east and west.

GETTING THERE AND AWAY Domburg lies about 30km south of Paramaribo by road. Self-drivers should follow Zwartenhovenbrug then Van t'Hogerhuys Weg out of town until it becomes Martin Luther King Weg, and then keep heading south until they pass Rocky's Waterpark on their left. Immediately after this, take the first left (Domberg 12th Straat) and then the second right into Sir Winston Churchill Weg, and follow this to the waterfront. A taxi will cost around SRD 75 one-way. Using public transport, regular Lijn PPD (Paramaribo–Paranam–Domburg) buses leave central Paramaribo from Waaldijk Straat between 05.30 and 17.00, asking a fare of SRD 4. You could also presumably charter a boat from Paramaribo; there's a safe mooring in front of the square in Domburg.

🏠 **WHERE TO STAY**

🏠 ✳ **Surinat Vakantie Resort** (4 cottages & 1 studio) 234 La Rencontre 5e Zijstraat; ☏370048; m 8721504/8949505; e info@surinat.com; www.surinat.com. One of the nicest upmarket options in the vicinity of Paramaribo, this owner-managed, serviced-orientated lodge on the former La Rencontre plantation has large green grounds run through by an old canal & divided between a citrus orchard at the front & a wilder forest-fringed retreat at the back. It is an excellent base for birdwatchers, with nearly 200 species recorded, & monkeys also often pass through in the morning & evening. Accommodation is in spacious, comfortable & stylishly decorated open-plan self-catering cottages with king-size bed, sitting & dining areas, AC, kitchenette, en-suite bathroom, & a wide private veranda with seating & hammock. There is also a smaller studio apt with AC & kitchenette. Other facilities include a swimming pool, wellness centre, jacuzzi & free Wi-Fi. The multi-lingual Dutch owners create a real 'home away from home' feel & are very accommodating when it comes to things like check-in & check-out times, meal arrangements, etc. Particularly well suited to self-drivers, it makes an excellent & very peaceful rustic alternative to the city hotels if you're exploring the greater Paramaribo area. Cottages from SRD 520 dbl per night (with discounts for monthly stays); studio SRD 370 dbl per night. **$$$$**

✖ **WHERE TO EAT AND DRINK** There are several popular warungs on the waterfront main square, all selling decent Javan-Surinamese food for around SRD 12–15 (**$**). **Warung Domburg** boasts the best location, with seating facing the river, but **Eethuis Rita** and **Fessa's Fancy Food** have also been recommended. Probably the best eatery in Domburg, however, is the similarly priced **Warung Mit Shiv**, which is on Sir Winston Churchill Weg, about 1km from the Surinat Resort, and serves a varied selection of Javan-Surinamese and Indian dishes.

For self-caterers, the best supermarket is Kai de Warenhuis on Sir Winston Churchill Weg; it stocks a good selection of fruit, veggies, cold meat, cheese, wine and spirits, as well as the usual tinned meats and chilled local drinks.

WHAT TO SEE AND DO
Market square The centrepiece of Domberg today is the lovely old market square overlooking the tranquil Suriname River. Surrounded by low-key Javanese warungs, fruit stalls and a children's playground, the old square is shaded by tall

mahogany and almond trees, some of which were reputedly planted by Princess Juliana of the Netherlands during a royal visit in November 1943. The best day to visit it is Sunday, when locals come to gossip, eat, drink and enjoy the riverside location, giving it a quietly festive atmosphere. The square can be visited on any day of the week, however, though the choice of food might be more limited.

Plantation La Rencontre It is worth taking a relaxed stroll along the (mostly dirt) roads that run inland from the main square through the former La Rencontre Plantation. The lily-covered canals that served the plantation are still flowing, and there are several small stands of forest where monkeys are quite commonly seen and birdlife can be terrific, especially in the early morning and late evening cool. Even more alluring to birders is the roughly 6km² patch of uninterrupted rainforest running east from La Rencontre towards a wide 180° bend in the Suriname River. To get there from the main square, follow the riverfront La Rencontre Straat east for 500m, then inland for another 200m after it curves 90° to the south, then turn right to cross the canal via a historic lock, and follow La Rencontre 1ste Zijstraat east for another 500m (with the Suriname River about 100m to your left) until you cross a second canal and lock, from where a footpath leads into the forest proper.

Laarwijk Boasting an attractive location on the east bank of the Suriname River 2km upstream of Domburg, Laarwijk is a sprawling small settlement that started life as a sugar plantation back in the colonial era. After the plantation ceased operating in the wake of abolition, the owners divided the land into large rectangular plots and distributed it among the workers, whose descendents still live there today. Several prominent Surinamese have been associated with Laarwijk, among them Willem Campagne (one of the academics responsible for the formalisation of Sranan Tongo), who taught there in 1916–17, and the poet and playwright Eugène Drenthe, who was born there in 1925. Despite this, the former plantation retains a very rustic and anachronistic feel: there are no cars, electricity only came online as recently as 2010, most houses are still made of wood and the settlement is surrounded by forest or disused farmland on all terrestrial sides. It is, however, a very welcoming and relaxed place to explore. Plenty of interesting plants and birdlife can be seen from the almost 10km of narrow dirt roads that run between the individual plots and extensive fruit plantations, and along the main southward-flowing canal that empties into the Suriname River next to the mangrove-lined taxi-boat jetty. Facilities include a small warung and market next to the jetty, and a local farmer called Moen Poedan (m *8572727/8874855*) runs a weekend-only garden and fruit-tasting tour on demand.

Laarwijk technically lies in Commewijne District, but it is accessible only by water, and most easily reached from Domburg on the opposite bank. Motorised taxi-boats connect Domburg to Laarwijk between 07.00 and 17.00. The 2km trip takes about ten to 15 minutes and the fare is SRD 2.50. Crossings are infrequent, so it's worth calling ahead. The operators are Amer-Prem (m *8599261*) and Bandhoe (m *8562965*). Alternatively, you can just charter a whole boat, which costs SRD 25 per party one-way.

ONVERWACHT, PARANAM AND AROUND

Situated roughly 15km apart some 40km south of Paramaribo, the two principal towns of Para are both rather lacking in character and have little to offer tourists. The most surprising thing about Onverwacht is its name, which literally means

'Unexpected'. Otherwise, it is a rather nebulous town of around 2,000 that started life in the 17th century as a tobacco (and later timber) plantation, and grew organically in the early 20th century after it became a stop along the now defunct Lawa railway line. By contrast, Paranam is a customised deep-water port town built in 1938 on the Suriname River by Alcoa (now Suralco) to service a bauxite mine and refinery whose smelter produces more than 3,000 tonnes of alumina daily. The naturally marshy area between the two towns, currently Suriname's main source of bauxite, is studded with shallow lakes and sinkholes left behind by the mining operations. There is nowhere to stay in either town, but White Beach and Overbridge both offer moderate accommodation, and cheaper rooms can be found at Leguana Park and Parabello (all listed below).

GETTING THERE AND AROUND Paranam lies about 38km south of Paramaribo along Martin Luther King Weg. Onverwacht is a similar distance south of the capital along the JFK Highway (aka Indira Gandhi Road). In both cases, the road is surfaced all the way and the drive should take no longer than an hour, traffic permitting. To reach Paranam by public transport, you need to take the private Lijn PPD (Paramaribo–Paranam–Domburg) buses, which leave the capital from Waaldijk Straat. For Onverwacht, private Lijn PO (Paramaribo–Onverwacht) buses leave Paramaribo from the corner of Waaldijk and Dr Sophie Redmond Straat, while Lijn POZ (Paramaribo–Onverwacht–Zanderij) and Lijn PBO (Paramaribo–Billiton–Onverwacht) buses leave from a stand along Maagden Straat. The individual sites listed below can be reached by bicycle, private vehicle or taxi.

WHAT TO SEE AND DO
Leguana Park (*412 Koning's Laan;* m *8905184;* e *anuradha95@hotmail.com; www.leguanapark.nl/home.htm;* ⊕ *09.00–18.00 daily; entrance SRD 10/5 adult/ child*) Located on the west bank of the Suriname River about halfway between Domburg and Paranam, Leguana Park lies on the former Plantage Waterland, once one of the largest plantations in Suriname. Founded in the late 17th century, Waterland was at one point the property of Gerrit Hooft Junior, a poet and one-time mayor of Paramaribo. Today the plantation is a relaxed riverside resort, named after the large monitor lizards that frequent the property. You can swim, watch birds, chill out on the sandy beach or rent a kayak to explore the river. There's also good-value accommodation on offer in four traditional stilted wooden cottages (*SRD 100pp;* **$$**), each with twin or double beds, sitting room, kitchenette with hotplates and fridge, netting, fan and en-suite cold shower. The park sometimes opens by appointment only, so ring in advance.

White Beach Marina Resort (*213 Sir Winston Churchill Straat;* m *6808001;* e *info@whitebeachsuriname.com; www.whitebeachsuriname.com;* ⊕ *08.00–19.30 daily; entrance SRD 10pp*) The closest thing to a bona fide beach resort in the vicinity of Paramaribo, White Beach lies on the west bank of the Suriname River about 3km south of Leguana Park and 1km northeast of Paranam. It isn't quite as chic as the 'marina' epithet suggests, and indeed it comes across as rather down at heel, but it is a pleasant enough place to swim (on a securely netted stretch of river), soak up the sun and generally try and fool yourself into thinking that you're on a Caribbean island rather than riverside Suriname. It gets busy at weekends, when locals head out of the capital to lounge around in one of the hammock huts that line the beach (SRD 60–75 per unit) but it tends to be quite quiet on weekdays. Other facilities include a pier and jetty, a bar with a pool table and a restaurant serving chicken with chips or rice for around SRD 15 per plate. Those with an above average capacity for self-delusion and powerful shades might even want to spend a couple of nights at White Beach (*22 rooms; SRD 150 dbl; $$$*) living out a tropical island fantasy. The rooms are clean and spacious, with queen-size beds, air conditioning, fridge, satellite TV, en-suite hot shower and beach view and they seem pretty good value.

STINASU Wetland Trail Situated on the east side of Martin Luther King Weg, about 1km south of Paranam, directly opposite the Suralco Refinery, this trail was established by STINASU in collaboration with Suralco in 2007. It circles a 9ha area of mixed wetlands that includes patches of dense forest as well as half a dozen small expanses of open water. Unfortunately, the trail hasn't been maintained and it was all but unusable in 2014, but it is still a popular breakfast or lunch stop with tour groups heading towards Brownsberg or Atjoni, and plenty of birds can be seen from the car park. It is also the site of the excellent Warung Le Kasai (m *8155680;* ⏰ *07.00–17.00 Mon–Thu, 07.00–20.00 Fri & Sat*), which sells sandwiches for SRD 5 and full local meals (including very good *satao*) for around SRD 12–15.

Overbridge River Resort (*47 Oude Charlesburg Weg;* ✆ *422565–6;* m *7129899/8886604; www.overbridge.net; entrance SRD 15pp*) The smartest of Para's riverside resorts occupies the site of Suriname's first colonial settlement, Torarica, which was established by Sephardic Jews in 1629 but has long since vanished. It lies 20km southeast of Paranam by road, about one hour's drive from Paramaribo, on an isolated stretch of riverbank otherwise swathed in indigenous forest and wetland habitat. In addition to a large and well-wooded netted-off swimming beach, the resort has good facilities including kayak hire, beach volleyball, a pool table, a children's playground and hammock huts for day rental. The surrounding area is home to plenty of monkeys, and is a well-known birding hotspot, with some 230 species recorded, including 15 types of parrot and macaw. Other regular species of interest include least grebe, bat falcon, green-tailed jacamar, channel-billed toucan, black-necked aracari, boat-billed flycatcher and blue-black grassquit. The air-conditioned cocktail bar and restaurant (⏰ *08.30–10.00 & noon–20.00 daily*) serve the usual local dishes for around SRD 25 per plate. For those who want to stay overnight, there are 21 smart self-catering one- or two-bedroom wooden cabanas (*SRD 230/345/415 for 2/3/4 occupants Mon–Thu, the nicest time to be here, or SRD 303/445/515 Fri–Sun; discounts available for longer stays; $$$$*) available with air conditioning, fan, en-suite hot shower and self-catering kitchen. Each bedroom has one single and one double bed.

Para Flora Horticulture (*40 Meurs Weg;* ✆ *352031;* m *8803812;* e *paraflor@ sr.net; www.facebook.com/botanicalgarden.paraflor;* ⏰ *10.00–16.00 Tue–Sun; guided tours 10.00, noon & 14.00; entrance SRD 25 self-guided or SRD 45 guided tour including a drink*) Established in 2004, this family-run 3ha botanical garden, specialised in the cultivation of ginger, lies on the south side of Meurs Weg about 1km east of Onverwacht and the junction with Indira Gandhi Weg. Two-hour guided tours, conducted in Dutch or English, follow a circular footpath through the gardens, highlighting a variety of medicinal, flowering and edible plants, mostly from Suriname, though some exotics are also featured. The garden also hosts a rich birdlife, since it is surrounded by indigenous forest on two sides and a drainage line at the back. There is a small gift shop, and Green Fingers Bar (⏰ *10.00–18.00 Tue–Sun*) serves smoothies, frozen fruit cocktails and chilled beers.

To get there by public transport from Paramaribo, catch a Lijn PO bus to Onverwacht, then hop off at the junction of Meurs and India Gandhi Weg, from where it is a ten- to 15-minute walk to Para Flora.

Mantamo and Parabello Situated about 1km south of Meurs Weg, Mantamo is a small Amerindian village best known as the site of the **Pottenbakkerij (Pottery) Mantamo** (m *8515238;* ⊕ *09.00–19.00 Mon–Sat*) run by the Singa-Aloema family from their compound. The pottery is made in a traditional way, not with a turntable but by hand using clay extracted from nearby bauxite-mining sumps or rivers, and fired with quince tree bark in the open air. It mostly makes goods to order, but usually has a few trinkets for sale, too. There is no charge to look around, but photography costs SRD 5 and video filming SRD 20.

Around the corner from Mantamo, Parabello (m *7129731/8184125/8733012;* e *arjo-parabello@hotmail.com; www.webparabello.com;* ⊕ *08.30–18.00 daily; entrance SRD 9*) is a small hammock- and campsite overlooking a forest-fringed lake created as a result of bauxite extraction along the Para Creek. Though a little rundown, it is a peaceful spot for a picnic or swim, or even a relaxed overnight stay, and there is plenty of birdlife in the area, which can be explored via a short forest trail. The only facilities are a children's playground and hammock hut, which is rented out at SRD 25–45 per unit, depending on group size. Hammocks can be hired for SRD 7.50 per night, and kayaks are available for SRD 15 for 30 minutes. Unlike many of the swimming creeks around Zanderij, no music is permitted. Proper cabins are planned. All food and drink must be brought with you.

The two sites are both accessed via Stawel Weg, which runs south from the junction with Meurs Weg (⊕ N5 36.661 W55 08.943) about halfway between the JFK Highway (Onverwacht) and Martin Luther King Weg (Paranam). Follow this straight across a wide Suralco service road (access to which is for mining vehicles only) for about 600m until you reach a fork in the road where you need to branch left. After another 200m, you reach a junction where a left turn brings you to Parabello after around 400m and continuing straight on you reach Mantamo after a similar distance.

JODENSAVANNE AND THE EAST BANK

Arguably the most important and intriguing historical site in Suriname, the ruins of Jodensavanne ('Jewish Savannah') stand on the elevated east bank of the Suriname River some 50km upstream of Paramaribo. Now largely engulfed by jungle, this ruined town was Suriname's second-most important settlement from the late 17th century until its demise in the early 19th, and it is also a remote and poignant reminder of the South American exodus undertaken by some of the 800,000 Sephardic Jews expelled from the Iberian Peninsula by the Spanish Inquisition in the 1490s. Its most significant building is the ruin of the oldest brick synagogue constructed in the Americas, but the site also houses an extensive cemetery comprising 452 known graves marked with (mostly engraved) stones. The neglected and largely unexcavated site was placed on the World Monument Fund Watch List in 1996, and the Stichting Jodensavanne, Jodensavanne Foundation (JSF) has since helped to publicise its existence and to enhance visits with the provision of good onsite interpretative material. Jodensavanne was designated a national monument in 2009 and it is the only place in Suriname currently included on UNESCO's tentative list of proposed World Heritage Sites.

HISTORY The first Sephardic Jews, refugees from the inquisition in Spain and Portugal, arrived in Suriname in the 1630s, and were responsible for the foundation of the once important port town of Torarica on the west bank of Suriname close to the present-day Overbridge River Resort. The Sephardim settlers were joined in 1652 by an unknown number of English Jews, and then in 1664 by some 200 Dutch-Brazilian Jews forced out of the Brazilian town of Mauritsstad (now Recife) after its capture by the Portuguese. The administration at Willoughbyland (Paramaribo), keen to nurture this influx of mercantile and international trade experience, granted the Jewish community several special privileges, including freedom of religion and land ownership, and permission to observe the Saturday Sabbath and to work on Sundays.

In 1665, a second Jewish settlement was established on Cassipora Creek, along with a synagogue consecrated in 1671. After the Dutch captured Paramaribo in 1667, the privileges granted by the English were maintained and extended, attracting further Jewish settlement, and leading to the establishment of Jodensavanne in the 1670s. By 1684, Jodensavanne counted around 230 Sephardic inhabitants. In 1685, the massive synagogue Beraha ve Shalom was inaugurated at the centre of a 10ha plot donated by Samuel Nassi three years earlier. By this time, Jodensavanne was the second-largest colonial settlement in Suriname after Torarica, consisting of around 60 houses.

In 1691, the Dutch government donated another 40ha of land to the growing settlement and the Jewish population stood at 570. By 1694, the economic impetus for this growth was the export of sugar to Europe. Of the 400 plantations registered in Suriname by 1730, Sephardim owned around 30%, most of which were dedicated to sugarcane production, and sported names with Talmudic links such as Beersaba, Beit El, Hebron, Sara's Lust and Carmel. By 1737, Jodensavanne had expanded to a grid of four east–west and four north–south roads leading to the central square and synagogue. The Sephardic population numbered around 2,000, at least at weekends when farmers from the surrounding plantations congregated in the town, which also boasted a coffee shop, fire station, billiard hall and well-organised port.

From an 18th-century Jewish perspective, the Sephardim community centred on Jodensavanne enjoyed a level of political, religious and economic autonomy that was practically unique. Indeed, for the first century of its existence, Jodensavanne was not only the wealthiest and freest Jewish community in all the Americas, but also the cornerstone of the Surinamese economy. However, it should be noted that this booming economy – like most others in the Americas at the time – was based largely on slave ownership. At any given time, slaves would have represented at least 80% of the population of Jodensavanne. And the surrounding sugar and other plantations might typically have owned 200 slaves apiece. In other words, tens of thousands of slaves from West African, along with a small number of indigenous Amerindian descent, were held in bondage in and around Jodensavanne, where they were accorded none of the freedoms taken for granted by European settlers, whether Christian or Jewish.

The Jewish settlers didn't have it all their own way. Many plantations and merchants suffered heavy losses in 1712 as a result of a massive raid by a fleet of warships led by the notorious French buccaneer Jacques Cassard. Others were ruined by the 1773 collapse of several Amsterdam banking houses, most notably the one founded by Willem Deutz. In addition, the growth in production of sugar from beet extract, using a process pioneered in Berlin in 1747, started to undermine the European market for sugar, and the economic value of Suriname's most important export, towards the end of the 18th century. However, the biggest hazard faced by the Sephardim community in and around Jodensavanne was attacks by bands of escaped slaves, or Marrons, who waged an ongoing guerrilla war from the surrounding jungle against their reviled former masters. Despite the construction of two defensive bridle paths, the Oranjepad ('Orange Path') from Cassipora to the Post Rama military post in 1749, and the Cordonpad ('Cordon Path') from Jodensavanne to the Commewijne River in 1776, successful merchants and farmers started to abandon remote Jodensavanne or their beleaguered plantations for the safety of Paramaribo.

The above hardships notwithstanding, Jodensavanne retained a firm spiritual grip on Suriname's large and prosperous Jewish community. The official centenary of its synagogue, held on 12 October 1785, was among the grandest celebrations ever held in the colony, attracting more than 1,600 guests from Paramaribo, among them the governor and several other high ranking officials. And even in 1796, the village was still significant enough that one visitor, the Dutch officer JG Stedman, noted it had 'a beautiful synagogue' and was resided in by 'some very respectable Jewish families [who] possess particular rights and privileges ... I never knew Jews to possess in any other parts of the world'.

Nevertheless, the urban drain out of Jodensavanne continued, and by 1817 more than 80% of the colony's Sephardim lived in Paramaribo. This influx led to a growth in anti-Semitic sentiment in the capital, and eventually, in 1825, to the revocation of almost all the 'particular rights and privileges' enjoyed by Suriname's Jews since the 1660s. Within two years, the once prosperous settlement at Jodensavanne supported a mere eight Jewish families, who eked out a living by selling goods to soldiers protecting the Cordonpad. The final blow came in 1832, when a voracious fire swept through the already diminished town. Only three years later, MD Teenstra would describe Jodensavanne as 'an insignificant hamlet ... built upon a hill around a synagogue [whose] grave stillness arouses serious and reverential feeling'. Shortly afterwards, the town was abandoned entirely. Funds were raised to partially restore the cemetery and synagogue in 1906, but with limited and short-lived results. Ironically, Jodensavanne was last inhabited when it served as an internment camp for 139 Nazi sympathisers from the Dutch East Indies during World War II. The graveyard was once again cleared, only to be reclaimed by the jungle after the prisoners were released in 1946.

GETTING THERE AND AWAY Most people visit Jodensavanne on an organised bus, boat or combination **day tour** from Paramaribo. This can be organised through any local operator (see pages 78–9), with rates starting at around SRD 350 per person, including transport, guides and entrance fees. The acknowledged expert when it comes to Jodensavanne is **Tours with Flair** (℡ 498407; m 8749286; e flair@ tip-suriname.com; www.tip-suriname.com), whose enthusiastic and knowledgeable owner-guide Marina da Costa is a descendant of one of the earliest Jewish settlers there. Another option worth singling out is the twice-weekly post boat day tour that runs from Paramaribo in April, August and September (see page 117). More locally, Overbridge River Resort (see page 177) also operates boat tours to Jodensavanne on request; these are quite expensive at around SRD 575 for the first two passengers, but better value for larger groups at around SRD 170–230 per person depending on numbers.

By car Jodensavanne can also be visited independently. It used to be a straightforward 70km drive from Paramaribo, taking Martin Luther King Weg south for 50km, past Domburg and Paranam, and then turning left at Powakka and crossing the Suriname River along a bridge connecting the tiny west bank village of

Carolina to a dot on the map called Kumbasi. Unfortunately, however, this bridge has been inoperable since a drunken sand-barge captain rammed his vessel into it in November 2007, leaving a 50m gap in the middle. A vehicle ferry service has since started between Carolina and Kumbasi. This carries six vehicles, takes around five minutes to cross, and costs SRD 25 per vehicle and SRD 2 per foot passenger or cyclist. It runs from 08.00 to 18.00 Monday to Friday, and 07.00 to 18.00 on Saturday and Sunday. Arrive after 18.00 and you must either wait until the next day or pay SRD 250 for a special crossing. The ferry is not usually very busy, but vehicles may sometimes need to wait up to an hour to embark. Alternatively, given that it's only about 3km from Kumbasi to Jodensavanne, you could cross on foot and walk.

By bus Travelling by public transport, the NVB operates one bus between Paramaribo and Cassipora daily except Saturday, stopping at the entrance to Jodensavanne, Redi Dota and Blaka Watra. The bus leaves Paramaribo from Saramacca Straat at 08.30, takes two hours and costs SRD 7 per person. It starts the return trip at the same time, which means you would need to overnight on the east bank, or walk back to Kumbasi (allow 40 minutes), then take the ferry back across to Carolina and look for a lift back to Powakka and Martin Luther King Weg.

WHERE TO STAY AND EAT

Redi Doti Camp m 8518200. Less than 1km from Jodensavanne, Redi Doti (meaning 'Red Dirt') is a jungle-bound riverside village of around 100 predominantly Amerindian people whose agricultural economy has suffered as a result of the collapse of the only bridge linking it to the west bank. The only accommodation is this wooden hammock hut operated by a welcoming local couple, Anita & Eddy Stuger, who also own the village shop. Food can be arranged on request, & they also rent out hammocks. Facilities are limited to toilets & a shower at the back. You can swim in the nearby river. SRD 10pp. **$**

WHAT TO SEE AND DO

Jodensavanne ruins (\ 472817; m 8898982; www.jodensavanne.sr.org, ① 10.00–16.30 daily; entrance SRD 20pp) The entrance to Jodensavanne is clearly signposted on the right side of the main dirt road to Cassipora, less than 1km before the village of Redi Doti. From here, a wide footpath runs through the site for about 500m before emerging at a clearing alongside the river. Most of the old town has been reclaimed by the jungle, giving it a rather eerie but also very tranquil atmosphere, especially when (as is most often the case) no other visitors are present. The ongoing chattering of insects and the rustle of leaves is interrupted by regular explosions of birdsong and the creaking of tired epiphyte-laden boughs, while iridescent blue *Morpho* butterflies flit along the paths, and colourful lizards scuttle obliviously across the old graves and walls.

The first point of interest, to the right when coming from the entrance gate, is the so-called **Freeman's Cemetery**, which dates to the pre-abolition era and was used to bury free citizens of African or mixed descent rather than slaves. Dozens of wooden grave markers scatter the site, many adorned with an upside-down heart that bears a striking similarity to the *sankofa* symbol associated with the Akan people of Ghana. The sankofa loosely represents a return to the past or past values, so it's tempting to think that it reflected a widely held Afro-Surinamese belief that the dead return to the land of their ancestors, and would thus reclaim the African origin from which they had been separated by the slave trade. That said, the inverted heart might as easily be a variation on the *akoma* (symbolic of love, tolerance and goodwill) seen on many Sephardic tombstones in Paramaribo.

Located opposite the entrance to Jodensavanne is a cleared section of the Cordonpad, originally created in 1794 at the instruction of Governor Nepveu. It ran between Post Gelderland on the Suriname River opposite Jodensavanne, and Post Vredenburgh on the Atlantic coastline (close to the present-day border between Commewijne and Marowijne districts) via the upper reaches of the Commewijn and Cottica rivers. The path was 94km long, 10m wide and flanked on either side by 1.2m-deep drainage trenches. It was punctuated by lookout posts every 5km, and was guarded by more than 1,000 soldiers at any given time. The thinking behind its creation was to protect Jodensavanne and the plantations contained within from Marron attacks, whilst making it more difficult for slaves to escape into the jungle. How successful it was in achieving these goals is questionable. That no major military engagement with the Marron guerrillas ever took place along the Cordonpad could be taken as a sign of its effectiveness, but it might equally demonstrate how easy it was to bypass. If nothing else, however, it was the strong military presence at Post Gelderland, and the opportunity to trade with soldiers based there, that maintained the dwindling Sephardic population at Jodensavanne during the early 19th century.

A short distance further, the 4,000m² **Beth Hain Cemetery**, studded with palms but otherwise largely cleared of tall trees, contains 452 documented graves, most of them marked with inscribed marble or bluestone headstones imported from Italy. Although many of the texts are illegible, those that can be read are in Portuguese, Spanish, Hebrew and Dutch. Most are engraved with an 'S' or 'SA', an abbreviation of the Portuguese *sepultura*, meaning 'grave', and many with a symbol of the angel of death felling a tree, denoting an early death. The oldest legible headstone dates to 1683, the most recent to 1873, and it is clear that it was customary for family members to be buried close together in one plot. It seems likely that more than 452 people were buried here, many of them in unmarked graves.

The centrepiece of the riverside clearing is the **Synagogue Beraha ve Shalom** ('Blessing and Peace'), which has a ground plan of around 4,100m² and stood two stories high. Constructed with red bricks imported from Europe, it was designed by an unknown architect, probably of Dutch rather than Iberian origin since the layout of the interior strongly resembles its counterpart in Amsterdam. In keeping with Talmudic law, it was supposedly built at the highest point of the village and was the tallest building at around 10m high, with pointed gabled walls on its two narrower sides. In common with the synagogues in Paramaribo, and for the same reason (see page 110), it had a sandy floor. The Hechal, where the Torah was stored, was located on the east side, while the Tebah platform (where the prayers were read from) was on the west, and the interior was designed so the male congregation could see both. Women were seated in a gallery above the Tebah. The last time a service was held at the synagogue was in 1865, a full 1,800 years after its consecration. It is not known when the upper storey crumbled, reducing the building to little more than a ground plan, but it almost certainly occurred sometime before the first attempt at restoration work was undertaken in 1906.

Cassipora Cemetery Though less accessible and smaller than the ruins at Jodensavanne, the old Jewish settlement at Cassipora is survived by a partially cleared cemetery containing at least 200 marble and bluestone tombstones, several of which are engraved. The site lies in the forest next to Cassipora Creek, about 20 minutes' walk from the road to Blaka Watra and the modern Amerindian village of Cassipora. It can only be visited with a guide from Jodensavanne, which costs SRD 50 per party and might take an hour or so to organise.

Blaka Watra (⏱ *08.00–17.00 daily; entrance SRD 10pp*) Literally meaning black water, this is a bathing site on a short stretch of rapids along the eponymous cola-coloured creek about 10km southeast of Jodensavanne. The rapids give a pleasant bubble-bath effect, and the site is rather off the beaten track and little visited, but otherwise is it very similar in feel to the black-water creeks dotted around the Zanderij area. Day huts are available for SRD 30 per party.

ZANDERIJ AND AROUND

Located 50km south of Paramaribo, the village of Zanderij (meaning sandy ridge) is best known as the site of Johan Adolf Pengel International (JAPI) airport, the port of entry used by all KLM and other international flights to Suriname. It is also arguably the most important route focus in the interior, situated at the three-way junction of the JFK Highway north to Paramaribo, a recently surfaced 16-km road running southeast to Kraka (on the main road south to Brokopondo and Atjoni), and the unsurfaced trunk road connecting the rest of the country to more westerly sites such as Witagron (for Raleigh Falls), Blanche Marie and Apoera. Locally, Zanderij and its environs are well known for the half a dozen or so swimming resorts in the area that are associated with the Para River and its black-water tributaries. Most of these resorts are aimed mainly at the domestic market of Paramaribo, but the relatively upmarket Cola Creek and backpacker-friendly Pulula Camping are both well-managed and peaceful retreats situated less than ten minutes' drive from the airport. Also of interest is the small and characterful riverside village of Berlijn, about 7km south of Zanderij (see page 185). Altogether different from other attractions in the area is the Green Heritage Fund's Xenarthra Rehabilitation Centre, which is currently under construction at Cola Creek and set to open in 2015.

HISTORY In the 18th century the area around present-day Zanderij was carved up into colonial plantations, among the best known of which were Hanover, Vier Kinderen ('Four Children') and Republiek. In 1905, Zanderij (or more accurately nearby Republiek) and Berlijn opened as stations for the new railway line connecting Paramaribo to Lawa. The first airport was opened at Zanderij (then often known as Zandery) in the 1920s, as a stop for Pan American flights to South America. The celebrated aviatress Amelia Earhart landed her Lockheed Elektra at Zanderij in July 1937, only a month prior to her mysterious disappearance over the central Pacific. The airport was expanded by the USA during World War II, when it served as an important base for US troops, a stopover point for flights across the Atlantic to Sierra Leone and a launch base for aerial bombardments of German U-boats. Since the war, the airport has been greatly expanded to serve modern

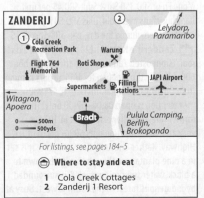

ZANDERIJ

② Lelydorp, Paramaribo
① Cola Creek Recreation Park
Warung
Flight 764 Memorial Roti Shop
Supermarkets Filling stations JAPI Airport
Witagron, Apoera
N
0 — 500m
0 — 500yds
Bradt
Pulula Camping, Berlijn, Brokopondo

For listings, see pages 184–5

🍴 **Where to stay and eat**
1 Cola Creek Cottages
2 Zanderij 1 Resort

airliners, and it now has a 3.5km runway. A US$70 million modernisation project that, among other things, aims to link the departure and arrival lounges with air bridges, is scheduled for completion in 2015.

GETTING THERE AND AWAY Zanderij lies 50km south of Paramaribo along the JFK Highway via Lelydorp and Onverwacht, a one- to two-hour drive depending on traffic. Shuttles between Paramaribo and JAPI airport cost around SRD 35–50 per person, and can be arranged by any hotel in the city. Private taxis cost SRD 125–175 one-way. The NVB operates four buses daily between Heiligen Weg (Paramaribo) and Zanderij, leaving in either direction at 05.30 (Monday to Saturday only), 06.30 (Sunday only), and 08.00, 15.30 and 17.00. More regular private Lijn POZ (Paramaribo–Onverwacht–Zanderij) buses leave Paramaribo from Maagden Straat. For further details see page 176.

⌂ WHERE TO STAY AND EAT *Map, page 183*
In Zanderij itself you will find several well-stocked supermarkets, some Javanese warungs and an Indian eatery.

⌂ ✳ **Pulula Camping** (2 hammock huts) 3km from Zanderij along the Kraka Road; m 8645223/8538676; e info@surinamecamping. com; www.surinamecamping.com. Set in a 24ha stand of white-sanded savannah forest, this wonderfully relaxed camp reflects the outdoor-orientated eco-friendly ethos of the Dutch-Surinamese owner-managers who live on site. The main clearing consists of 2 open-sided wooden hammock huts, a common shower & toilet, & a large well-equipped kitchen & dining area with solar- or gas-powered fridge & stove, & a full set of utensils. You can self-cater (it's only 3km to the warungs & supermarkets at the main junction in Zanderij) or ask them to provide food for you. The main attraction is the lovely natural swimming area in a metre-deep black-water creek just 5mins' walk from the main camp. There are also marked trails through the surrounding forest, which is home to several types of monkey, including the rather uncommon red-handed tamarin & white-faced saki, while giant anteater, three-toed sloth & ocelot have all been seen in the area. It also offers great birding, & is particularly strong on forest species associated with savannah forest, a localised habitat in Suriname. Also on offer are guided day walks through the jungle to Berlijn, night walks in search of nocturnal creatures, & 2-day bicycle tours operated in conjunction with Fietsen In Suriname (see page 78). Reservations are obligatory, since the camp sometimes hosts private groups, so do call in advance. Transport

from JAPI airport or the main junction in Zanderij can also be provided by arrangement. SRD 50/25 per adult/child (under 12) in own tent/hammock, plus SRD 20pp hammock hire; SRD 80 dbl tent hire; SRD 30pp stretcher hire. **$$**

⌂ **Cola Creek Cottages** (5 units) 3km west of the airport; ☎477088; m 6808188/6808283; e mets@sr.net; www.surinamevacations.com. Primarily a day facility (see opposite page), this large creek-side resort also offers secluded overnight accommodation in old-fashioned but comfortable houses that each sleep up to 7 people in 2 AC bedrooms (each with 1 dbl & 1 sgl bed), & also have a kitchenette with fridge, wide balcony with seating & fan, & free Wi-Fi. More basic hammock huts can also be rented overnight. Evening meals are available by prior arrangement with the restaurant. Try to be there during the week as it gets very busy at w/ends. SRD 295 per house Mon–Fri or SRD 350 Sat & Sun; SRD 45 per unit hammock huts overnight, plus SRD 60 if you want to retain them during the day, plus SRD 5pp. **$$$**

⌂ **Zanderij 1 Resort** (20 units) Along a dirt road (signposted Zanderij 1) on the right, about 600m before the junction for JAPI airport coming from Onverwacht or Paramaribo; ☎471980; ⊕ reception is open 08.00–17.00 only. This former forestry college, founded in 1974, has a very accessible location only 500m north of JFK Highway. Rather unusually for Suriname, it is set in a pine plantation, though this leads down to a black-water swimming creek & is surrounded by indigenous forest to the south & west. Busy at w/ends but very quiet during the week, it would make for an agreeable albeit rather budget retreat. All units are self-catering, & its proximity to the main road means that it is also within walking distance of a few warungs. SRD 30 dbl room or SRD 60 for a 4-bed house with shared bath & toilet; larger houses with en-suite baths from SRD 250 per unit. **$**

🏠 **Berlijn Cottage** (3 rooms) Lanpassi Road, Berlijn; 📞499902; m 8636429. In a compound next to the main creek & bridge in the village of Berlijn, this 3-bedroom self-catering house sleeps up to 8 & is usually rented out as 1 unit & guests must provide their own bedding. Rooms are simple but quite clean, & it has a well-equipped kitchen &

a bathroom with hot water. SRD 150/night for the whole house, making it great value for groups. **$$**

🏠 **Jungle Camp Carolina** (3 houses) 5km southeast of Pulula; m 8886659; entrance SRD 10pp. Carved into the forest on the west side of the Kraka road after it crosses Carolina Creek, this pleasant self-catering resort is centred on a 2m-deep swimming area in the black-water creek. It gets busy at w/ends but you'll most likely have the place to yourself during the week. Slightly rundown but adequately comfortable stilted wooden huts, sleeping up to 10 at a real push, cost SRD 150 per unit or you could rent a hammock hut for SRD 30 per unit. **$**

OTHER PRACTICALITIES There is a bank, an ATM and a Digicell shop in JAPI airport, along with several car-rental companies and places to eat. There is also a filling station in Zanderij. Travellers heading west by road towards Witagron, Raleigh Falls, Blanche Marie, Ananavero or Apoera should be aware that Zanderij's cluster of supermarkets and warungs is absolutely the last place to buy food or stock up on groceries and drinks until you reach Apoera, 300 very rough kilometres to the west.

WHAT TO SEE AND DO
Cola Creek Recreation Park (m *6808188/6808283; www.surinamevacations. com;* ⊕ *daily; entrance SRD 12.50pp Mon–Fri, SRD 15 Sat & Sun*) Established in the 1950s as a recreational facility for airforce personnel based at Zanderij, this rather quirky resort 3km west of JAPI airport is named for the cola-like colour of the black water creek that runs past it. The main activity here is swimming in the 780m length of creek that has been fenced off for that purpose, but the surrounding forest also offers excellent birding and it is also a very peaceful retreat from the capital on weekdays (though rather less so at weekends when it can attract several hundred visitors). The cafeteria (⊕ *09.00–17.30*) serves a good selection of local-style mains in the SRD 15.50–22.50 range, along with chilled beers and soft drinks, while open-sided hammock huts can be rented at SRD 60 per day plus SRD 5 per person. Overnight accommodation is also available (see opposite page).

Berlijn This one-street Marron village overlooks a large forest-fringed black-water pool on the Para River, 1km southwest of the Kraka road on a well-signposted side road about 2km past Pulula Camping. The village started life in the early 1760s as a timber and sugar plantation popularly known as Baroen or Borries. It was probably named Berlijn by Jan Schot, who arrived there from Philadelphia in 1768, constructed a water-driven sawmill and oversaw the growth of the plantation until it covered around 3,500ha by 1771. More recently, in 1940, Berlijn was the birthplace of the future politician and union leader Fred Derby. Today, this rather isolated village boasts some good examples of traditional stilted wooden houses and is also the site of an attractive old Moravian church and associated cemetery. The creek is safe for swimming, and a wooden footbridge runs across it into the forest. A footpath also connects Berlijn to Pulula Camping, which offers guided jungle walks there.

Flight 764 Memorial On 7 June 1989, Suriname Airways Flight 764, a McDonnell Douglas DC-8-62, crashed after it struck a 25m-high tree on approaching the airport, killing all but 11 of the 187 passengers and eight crew members on board. Among the fatalities were 15 members of the Kleurrijk Elftal ('Colourful Eleven'), a charitable exhibition football team composed of prominent professional Surinamese players based in the Netherlands. The only dog on board survived the crash and was given the name Lucky by the local police. A commemorative monument now stands at the crash site, immediately north of the Apoera road, 2km west of Zanderij.

Part Three

THE INTERIOR

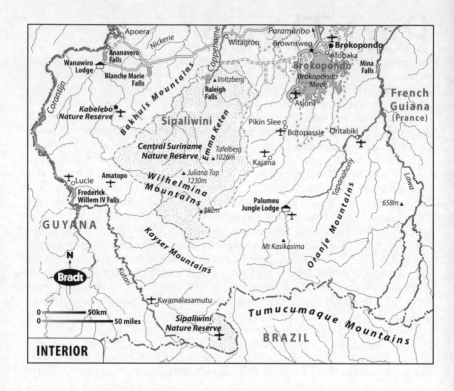

INTERIOR

The three chapters that follow cover the vast and thinly populated Surinamese interior, which for our purposes consists of the two southerly districts of Brokopondo and Sipaliwini (as well as the western part of Para). The immense tract of Amazonian rainforest protected within these two-and-a-bit districts accounts for more than 85% of Suriname's surface area yet supports fewer than 60,000 people, not even 10% of the national population. One of the world's greatest remaining wildernesses, this is an immensely exciting area to explore, traversed by only two roads of significance, a surfaced strip heading north to Afobaka Dam and Atjoni, and the rougher dirt road running west from Zanderij to Apoera. Indeed, much of the region is most easily explored by boat, with the Upper Suriname and Coppename rivers in particular forming wide rapid-strewn aquatic 'boat highways' navigable deep into the interior. Other places, such as Palumeu and Kabalebo, are strictly fly-in only.

Independent travel in the interior is at best challenging and at worst impossible. This means that most visitors experience the region by joining one or two organised round trips from Paramaribo to specific destinations. And in truth the experience offered by these different tours is to some extent interchangeable. Wherever you go, there will be forests, monkeys, parrots and toucans, there will be a river, some rapids or waterfalls, boats of one form or another, and opportunities to fish and swim. Equally, each of the various destinations covered in the next three chapters has its own individual attractions, as emphasised in the list of highlights below.

Bergendal should be the top choice for nervous jungle novices, Kabalebo is especially well suited to wildlife enthusiasts and birders with deep wallets and high expectations of service and comfort, and Palumeu is for well-heeled travellers with a strong interest in Amerindian cultures. More adventurously, Boven Coesewijne is the place for keen canoers, Central Suriname is for fit and flexible travellers seeking a packaged riverine adventure, and Brownsberg has something for everyone, as do the fascinating Marron villages of the Upper Suriname though the latter area is particularly suited to backpackers with time to spare and a tighter budget.

HIGHLIGHTS

(Normal duration of journey from Paramaribo given in parentheses)

BERGENDAL ECO-RESORT A recommended 'soft' introduction to the forests of the interior, this quality lodge also houses an adventure centre offering zipline cableway trips through the canopy, and kayaking on the Suriname River. See pages 193–4. (*1 or 2 nights, effectively tour only*)

BROWNSBERG NATURE PARK The top wildlife-viewing destination within day-tripping distance of Paramaribo will be doubly rewarding to unfussy travellers willing to put up with the basic overnight accommodation. See pages 196–8. (*Day or 1-night tour, 1 or better 2 nights independent*)

LODGE-HOPPING ON THE UPPER SURINAME Rather than single out one particular Saamaka village or lodge along this mesmerising river, adventurous travellers should allow a few days to lodge-hop all the way from Atjoni to Djumu. See pages 201–17. (*2- or 3-night tours, at least 3 nights independently*)

DANPAATI RIVER LODGE (Map, page 202) Arguably the pick of the few upmarket lodges along the Upper Suriname and Gran Rio rivers, Danpaati stands on a lovely forested island, at once very remote in feel but within easy day-tripping distance of the not-to-be-missed Saamaka Marron Museum in Pikin Slee. See pages 211–12. (*2- or 3-night tours*)

BOVEN COESEWIJNE NATURE RESERVE (Map, pages 66–7) At once adventurous and serene, canoeing trips into this otherwise inaccessible reserve also come with a good chance of spotting shy forest wildlife. See pages 219–21. (*Day or 1-night tour*)

CENTRAL SURINAME NATURE RESERVE Though much of this vast UNESCO World Heritage Site is inaccessible to tourists, Fungu Island – reached by a three-hour boat trip along the Coppename River – is an excellent base for climbing the iconic Voltzberg and spotting the country's most sought after bird, the spectacular Guianan cock-of-the-rock. See pages 221–4. (*3 nights, tour only*)

APOERA The most remote settlement of comparable substance in Suriname, this end-of-the-road town, carved into the jungle bordering the Corantijn River, offers little in the way of prescribed entertainment but might hold a certain appeal to backpackers wanting to get as far off the grid as public transport allows. See pages 226–9. (*1 night as part of a tour, allow at least 2 nights independent*)

KWAMALASAMUTU (Map, page 118) Impossibly remote and accessible by air only, this small Amerindian settlement lies within day-hiking distance of 300-plus ancient rock carvings that adorn the recently discovered Werehpai Petroglyph Site. See pages 230–1. (*Expedition-style tour only, at least 2 or 3 nights*)

KABALEBO NATURE RESERVE The top fly-in wildlife-viewing destination in the deep interior, this stylishly rustic upmarket resort also offers superb kayaking, birding and fishing opportunities. See pages 231–2. (*3 or 4 nights, tour only*)

MOUNT KASIKASIMA Set deep in the interior close to the Brazilian border, this multiple-peaked sacred granite sugarloaf is the goal of a week-long expedition starting at the Amerindian village of Palumeu. See page 234. (*7 nights, tour only*)

10

Brokopondo

The second largest of Suriname's administrative districts at 7,364km², Brokopondo is also the second least populous, supporting a mere 16,000 people in a few dispersed settlements including Brownsweg and the eponymous district capital. Protruding southward into the vast Sipaliwini District, which borders it on three sides, Brokopondo is typically hillier, more densely forested and wilder in feel than the districts to its north. Geographically, it is dominated by the 1,560km² Brokopondo Reservoir (which was created in the early 1960s when the Suriname River was dammed at Afobaka), accounts for around 1% of Suriname's surface area and produces enough hydro-electricity to meet around half the country's energy requirements. Economically, the district is somewhat stagnant, despite its vast timber resources and significant gold deposits. In terms of tourist development, it does boast two of the most popular destinations for day and overnight trips from Paramaribo. These are the hilly Brownsberg Nature Park, with its plentiful waterfalls, abundant wildlife and lovely views across the lake, and the upmarket Bergendal resort on the Suriname River downstream from the Afobaka Dam.

BERGENDAL ECO-RESORT AND AROUND

One of the most popular destinations for overnight trips from Paramaribo, Bergendal Eco-Resort opened in 2008 on a 24km² patch of forest that was formerly part of the Bergendal Plantation. Set on the west bank of the Suriname River, the resort provides a an excellent 'soft' introduction to the Surinamese interior, combining a genuinely wild setting and jungle feel with exceptionally comfortable upmarket accommodation and facilities. It is also easy to access along a good asphalt road that runs from Paramaribo to within 2km of the entrance gate. Bergendal is popular with outdoor lovers of a more active disposition, as a top-notch adventure centre that runs daily zipline cableway trips through the forest canopy, as well as day walks, kayaking and motorised boat trips can be found nearby. And while upmarket tourism is focused on the eco-resort, there is also more affordable accommodation on offer at the adventure centre. Not much further afield, agreeable budget accommodation, safe swimming and wonderful birding are available at the excellent New Babunhol River Resort, only 8km north of Bergendal. Those on a tighter budget can sling up a hammock at the low-key Bena Resort in the riverside transmigration village of Klaaskreek.

GETTING THERE AND AWAY Bergendal Eco-Resort lies about 85km south of Paramaribo by road, a drive of around two hours. Most people visit on a two-day, one-night or three-day, two-night **all-inclusive tour** from Paramaribo. These leave daily, irrespective of the number of people, and can be arranged

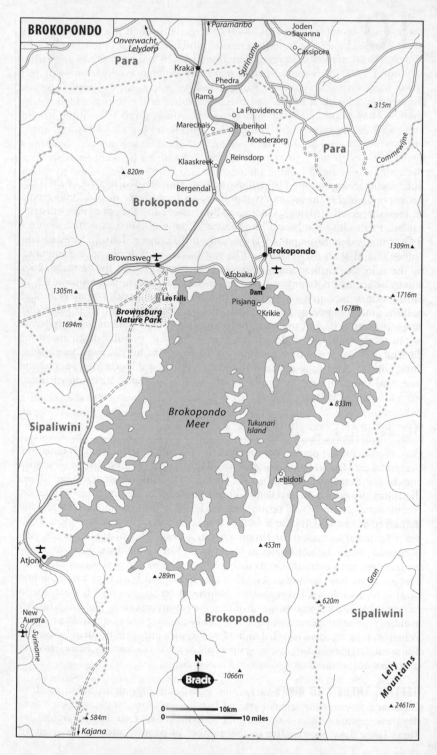

BROKOPONDO

Paramaribo

Joden
Savanna

*Onverwacht,
Lelydorp*

Para

Kraka

Cassipora

Phedra

Suriname

Rama

▲ *315m*

La Providence

Marechais

Bubenhol

Para

Moederzorg

Klaaskreek

Reinsdorp

Commewijne

▲ *820m*

Bergendal

Brokopondo

1309m▲

Brownsweg

Brokopondo

Afobaka

▲ *1716m*

1305m ▲

Leo Falls

Dam

Pisjang

*Brownsburg
Nature Park*

Krikie

▲ *1678m*

1694m ▲

Sipaliwini

*Brokopondo
Meer*

▲ *833m*

*Tukunari
Island*

Lebidoti

▲ *453m*

Atjoni

▲ *289m*

Gran

New
Aurora

▲ *620m*

Sipaliwini

Brokopondo

Suriname

N

*Lely
Mountains*

Bradt

1066m

0   10km

0   10 miles

▲ *584m*

▲ *2461m*

Kajana

through any operator (see pages 78–9) or directly through the resort. All tours use the same bus service from Paramaribo, which leaves from the Krasnapolsky Hotel at 10.00, arrives at Bergendal at around 12.30 and returns to Paramaribo at around 14.00. This means that it makes no difference which operator you travel with, so you may as well shop around for prices. Note also that the bus times don't gel with check-in and check-out times at the resort, which means that two-day tours can entail a disproportionate amount of waiting around and you'll get far more out of a three-day tour. Rates for a two-day, one-night visit start at around SRD 600 per person, but cheaper specials are sometimes available through the resort's own website. For those who want to experience the canopy trail and kayaking on an organised trip, but don't need to splash out on the accommodation, other options are the day tours offered by some budget operators for around SRD 370 per person, inclusive of transport and the aforementioned two activities, but not meals.

By car To get to Bergendal in a private vehicle, head out of the city along Martin Luther King Weg, passing Domburg and Paranam on the left and the Suralco Plant on the right. The main resort is signposted on your left about 50km south of the Suralco Plant, just before the junction for Brownsweg and Atjoni. The adventure centre is signposted to the left a few hundred metres after this junction. If you are heading to Babunhol or Klaaskreek, these junctions lie about 8km and 4km before Bergendal, respectively, and are clearly signposted on your left.

By bus If travelling by public transport, the NVB buses from Paramaribo to Brokopondo, Afobaka, Brownsweg and Atjoni all pass the junctions for Babunhol, Klaaskreek and Bergendal. They could drop you at any of these junctions, from where it would be about one-hour's walk to Babunhol, 20 minutes to the Bena Resort in Klaaskreek and 25 minutes along the forested drive to the Bergendal resort or adventure centre. There is also a direct daily bus from Paramaribo to Klaaskreek, leaving from Heiligen Weg at 08.30 and starting the return trip at the same time the following day. The trip costs SRD 7, takes two hours and the bus can drop you in Klaaskreek itself or at the junction for Babunhol. Alternatively, for those staying at the adventure centre, the resort operates a daily staff bus from Paramaribo, which costs SRD 25 per person for guests.

WHERE TO STAY AND EAT

⌂ ✳ **Bergendal Eco-Resort** (45 rooms) ☏ 475050 (head office); e info@bergendalresort. com; www.bergendalresort.com. The main resort at Bergendal ranks among the most aesthetically pleasing in Suriname, carved as it is into a tract of sloping riverine jungle. A clear effort has been made to preserve as much of the forest & undergrowth as possible, rather than chopping it down to make way for manicured lawns. About half the rooms run in 2 rows along the lengthy river frontage, & the large premier 'type A' rooms, directly on the riverfront, each have 2 dbl beds, & a sofa-bed in the lounge. The smaller 'type C' rooms have 1 large bed only & no lounge. The remainder of the rooms, mostly 'type B', have a king-size bed & lounge, are scattered along the forest paths & offer superb views into the canopy. All rooms have stylish contemporary fittings & furnishings, en-suite hot shower & toilet, AC, coffeemaker, fridge & safe. 'Type A' & 'type B' rooms also have a balcony. In addition to the activities offered by the adventure centre nearby, there is a large riverfront swimming pool, an attractive bar & lounge area overlooking the river, a restaurant serving adequate buffet meals (usually included in the room or package rate), a jetty with a view, a business centre & motorised transfers to & from your room as required. Dedicated birders could easily spend a few hours exploring the footpaths that run through the lush & shady grounds & the 2km stretch of forest-lined road leading back to the main road. Rates are usually incorporated into a package that includes accommodation, meals, transport from Paramaribo & also sometimes selected activities. It is worth checking the website for deals. $$$$$

🏠 ✳ **Bergendal Adventure Inn**
1km upriver from the eco-resort; 📞 325241/324133; m 8805061/8534697. Though primarily geared towards activities, the adventure centre is also home to the resort's staff quarters & a varying number of comfortable sgl rooms with AC, as well as a hammock hut. All have shared bathrooms. People staying at the adventure centre can eat staff meals for SRD 25pp for lunch or dinner, or wander up to the eco-resort to eat there for a heftier SRD 85pp. SRD 90 sgl room B&B inc day entrance fee; SRD 45 per unit for hammock huts, plus SRD 15 to rent a hammock. $$$

🏠 ✳ **New Babunhol River Resort**
(8 rooms, 2 houses & 11 hammock huts) 8km downriver from Bergendal, booking office 36 Watermolen Straat, Paramaribo; 📞 486889–90; m 8287809; e info@babunhol.com; www. babunhol.com; entrance SRD 12.50pp (w/days), SRD 25 (w/ends). This lovely self-catering resort, named after the red howler monkeys that still frequent the area, is reached along a 4km dirt road through grassy meadows & jungle patches signposted clearly from the left side of Martin Luther King Weg coming from Paramaribo. Catering mainly to a local clientele, it can be

quite busy at w/ends & public holidays, but is usually blissfully quiet in the week. Formerly a citrus plantation & cattle ranch, it now boasts a 200m-long beach covered in soft river sand, an arboretum with numbered trees (described in greater detail in a booklet available onsite) & an impressive checklist of 230 bird species including rarities such as the ornate hawk-eagle & the collared puffbird. Other facilities include affordable kayak hire & guided walks into the surrounding jungle. For those with their own transport, it also lies conveniently close to the Bergendal Adventure Centre – no more than 20mins' drive away. Best booked in advance, accommodation options include fully equipped houses sleeping up to 12, comfortable twin & dbl rooms set on a high rise above the beach, & hammock huts. SRD 70 dbl; houses from SRD 220–SRD 420 per unit; hammock huts from SRD 30 per unit, hammock hire from SRD 12.50pp; rates increase slightly at w/ends. $$

🏠 **Bena Resort** Klaaskreek;
m 8733609/8541535; entrance SRD 12.50pp. Located in the transmigration village of Klaaskreek, 4km downriver of Bergendal, this no-frills riverside camp consists of a few open-sided hammock huts running along a sandy swimming beach. As with Babunhol, it could be a useful base for the activity centre at Bergendal, & offers boat transfers there for SRD 20pp. No food is available, but there is a small supermarket in town & another at the filling station on the junction with Martin Luther King Weg. SRD 20 dbl hut; no hammocks provided. $

WHAT TO SEE AND DO

Berg en Dal Adventure Centre (📞 325241/324133; m 8805061/8534697; www. bergendalresort.com; ⊕ 08.30–17.30 daily; entrance free for overnight guests at the eco-resort or those staying at the adventure centre, SRD 24 for day visitors or hammock users) On a protected sandy swimming beach about 1km upstream from the eco-resort, this adventure centre is arguably the raison d'être of Bergendal and it offers a range of exciting activities to hotel guests and day visitors. The foremost attraction for adrenalin junkies is the 90-minute **canopy zipline cableway** (SRD 222pp for foreigners, SRD 96 for Suriname residents), which runs between seven wooden platforms high in the forest, including one with a 220m span and another that runs right across the river to its eastern bank. Other very popular activities are the **guided boat tour** downriver to Klaaskreek (SRD 80/60 for foreigners/residents), and the tranquil **kayaking excursion** to Mama Creek (SRD 120/36 for foreigners/ residents). Other guided walks and boat trips are also offered, as are day tours to Brokopondo Reservoir and Brownsberg (Thursdays only). A PDF with full list of activities, rates, departure times and minimum group sizes can be downloaded from the website.

The second most substantial town in Brokopondo, Brownsweg (literally Brown's Road) is also a route hub of sorts. It straddles the main tar road to Atjoni at the junctions for the popular Brownsberg Nature Park and Stoneiland Eco-Resort. Named after the late 19th-century gold prospector John Brown, it evidently started life as a mining camp, but was developed as a stop on the Lawa Railway from Paramaribo when the most southerly stretch was completed in 1913. The flooding of the Brokopondo Reservoir in the early 1960s had two important consequences for Brownsweg. The first was that it became the railway's most southerly terminus after the soon-to-be-submerged track to the river was ripped up. The second was that it was chosen as the site of a transmigration village for a dozen different Saamaka villages (each with its own *kabiteni*) along the affected part of the river. Today, Brownsweg supports a population of 2,200, and is characterised by high levels of unemployment, thanks to its remote location. Gold mining, both legal and illegal, is probably the most important economic activity in and around the small town. The main local attraction is Stoneiland, which lies on the west bank of the reservoir and is often used as an overnight base for tours to Brownsberg Nature Park.

GETTING THERE AND AWAY It is 106km from Paramaribo to Brownsweg along the recently surfaced road to Atjoni. Directions out of the city are as for Bergendal Eco-Resort (see pages 193–4), except that you need to continue past the resort for another 1km or so until you reach a prominent junction (⊕N5 08.354 W55 04.422) where you need to turn left. Brownsweg lies 18km along this road.

The NVB operates two buses daily in between Paramaribo and Brownsweg. These leave Paramaribo from Saramacca Straat, and run in both directions at 06.00 and 13.00 Monday to Saturday, and 06.00 and 13.30 on Sunday. The trip takes three hours and the fare is SRD 8.50. In addition, any buses or other vehicles travelling between Paramaribo and Atjoni can stop at Brownsweg, or pick up passengers there, space permitting.

The route to Stoneiland is clearly signposted at the northern entrance to Brownsweg. It's 4.5km of dirt road from this junction to the resort and it's quite hilly in parts, but those without private transport should be able to walk between the two in an hour or so.

WHERE TO STAY

Stoneiland Eco-Resort (10 huts & houses) On the shore of Brokopondo Reservoir, 4.5km southeast of Brownsweg, bookings at Body in Balance, 33 Frederick Derby Straat, Paramaribo; ☎424666; m 8753143. This agreeable budget resort offers accommodation in small waterfront huts & larger houses on a green wooded slope running down to a stony swimming beach. It is in a pretty location, with Brownsberg rising to the right, hundreds of dead trees periscoping out of the water, several green islands in view and a cooling breeze coming from the open water. The accommodation is quite cramped & basic but it's clean enough, with private balconies, & mattresses, nets & bedding are provided. There is a well-equipped kitchen, but no restaurant or shop, though they do sell a selection of chilled beers & soft drinks. Activities include swimming, kayaking (the latter rented out at SRD 50/day) & rambling along the nearby dirt road. The birdlife can be rewarding, with plenty of herons & kingfishers flapping over the lake, & parrots, woodpeckers & caciques calling from the trees. Management prefers visitors to book ahead & pay upfront in Paramaribo, so a 'penalty' of SRD 10pp is charged for walk-in guests. SRD 55 dbl with shared toilets & showers; SRD 205/260/315 sgl/dbl/trpl in en-suite cottage. **$$**

✕ WHERE TO EAT AND DRINK

🔺 **Fargo's Place** Brownsweg;
m 7151586/8683027. Almost all tours bound for
the Upper Suriname or Brownsberg stop at this
complex in central Brownsweg, which comprises
a filling station, a toilet, 2 quite well-stocked
supermarkets & a Chinese eatery selling the usual

Surinamese staples for around SRD 12–15 per
portion. It is the last place to buy food & drink
before you head out to Stoneiland, & also the last
opportunity to stock up for self-caterers heading to
Brownsberg Camp. $

BROWNSBERG NATURE PARK

(⊕ *daily; entrance SRD 20*) About 100km inland from Paramaribo as the crow flies,
and readily accessible by road, the scenic and wildlife-rich Brownsberg Nature Park
is one of the most popular destinations for organised day trips from the capital.
Created in 1969, the 112km² park protects the forested slopes of Brownsberg
('Brown's Mountain'), which rises to an altitude of 560m immediately east of the
Brokopondo Reservoir. Around 1,500 types of plant have been recorded in the
park, as have 410 bird species. It is also one of the most reliable sites in Suriname for
seeing large mammals, with red howler and black spider monkey both common in
the vicinity of the camp, along with several smaller monkey species and the twitchy
little agouti. The mountain, like nearby Brownsweg, is named after John Brown,
who worked the slopes in the late 19th century (some of his diggings can be seen
along the footpaths close to camp). Ironically, illegal gold mining is today probably
the biggest threat to the park's wildlife. In 2012, the WWF discovered 50 illegal
gold-mining sites in the vicinity of the park, which aside from contributing to
local deforestation, can result in increased subsistence hunting for bush meat and
also mercury contamination of the soil and water. The park receives an estimated
18,000 visitors annually, a high proportion of which are local weekenders from
Paramaribo, so it tends to be quietest on weekdays.

GETTING THERE AND AWAY By road, Brownsberg lies 120km south of Paramaribo,
a trip of up to three hours depending on traffic. Most people visit on an **organised
tour**, which can be arranged through any operator in Paramaribo (see pages 78–
9). The most popular and affordable option is a day tour, which is likely to cost
around SRD 250–300 per person, depending on the company you use and group
size. Alternatively, two-day, one-night tours, usually staying at either Stoneiland
or Brownsberg Camp, are in the SRD 370–690 range. Brownsberg Camp is less
comfortable and less favoured by tour operators, but it is the more alluring option
for anybody with a serious interest in wildlife. Day trips to Brownsberg can also
be undertaken in the far greater comfort from Berg en Dal (see page 194), which
is only 33km by surfaced road from Brownsweg and which runs a set trip every
Thursday. A more specialised option is the three-day, two-night mountain-bike
tours offered by Fietsen In Suriname (see page 78) for SRD 1,100 per person.

For self-drivers and other independent travellers visiting Brownsberg, first
head to Brownsweg (see page 195), which is 106km from Paramaribo on the
surfaced road to Atjoni. From Brownsweg, it's 13km along a signposted dirt road
to Brownsberg Camp, with the last few kilometres undulating uphill through lush
tropical jungle. This dirt road is usually well maintained, and should be manageable
in any car, but it may deteriorate after rain, in which case a 4x4 and an experienced
driver might be necessary (if in doubt, phone the camp to check). There is no public
transport to the park from Brownsweg, and the STINASU vehicles that used to
collect visitors by prior arrangement are no longer available. For travellers without

their own transport, this leaves two alternatives. For the fit and energetic, you could walk along the road through the forest, a thoroughly attractive prospect assuming that you are not too heavily laden with luggage. Allow yourself a good three hours to cover the ground. Otherwise, a taxi from Brownsweg will cost around SRD 300–350 one-way.

WHERE TO STAY Most tourist literature pertaining to Brownsberg states that accommodation *must* be booked and paid for in advance through the STINASU head office in Paramaribo. In practice, however, while advance booking and payment is the convention among tour operators, the camp is seldom very busy and (assuming availability) independent travellers can in fact be allocated rooms and pay on the spot. That said, before heading out to the reserve, it would be a good idea to call the camp to confirm availability using the direct line given below.

Brownsberg Camp (11 rooms in 3 houses, plus 2 hammock huts) ✆421683/476597; m (direct) 6808322; e stinasu@sr.net; www.stinasu.com. Boasting a stunning location on the Brownsberg plateau surrounded by forest & overlooking Brokopondo Reservoir, this potentially superb camp is now used infrequently by operators due to its limited facilities & rather rundown state. If you can live with that, however, it will be more than compensated for by the attractive setting & superb wildlife viewing & birding opportunities. The most affordable option for individuals & small groups is to hire a hammock & hang it in one of the 2 hammock huts (total capacity 22). For those who prefer a roof over their head, larger groups have the choice of the superbly located 8-bed Kapasi House, the 12-bed Kwatta House, & the 16-bed Tapir House, while for small groups the 4, 4-bed rooms in Tapir House can be rented out individually. SRD 345 for Kapasi House (up to 8 people), SRD 465 for Kwatta House (up to 12 people), SRD 600 for Tapir House (up to 16 people); the 4 individual rooms in Tapir House are charged pro rata (SRD 150/room, up to 4 people); SRD 50pp for hammock hut, hammock hire SRD 25. **$$**

WHERE TO EAT AND DRINK
Brownsberg Restaurant m 6806551/6808685; ☺ b/fast, lunch & dinner daily. This privately owned restaurant next to the reception kiosk is the social centre of Brownsberg Camp. It has covered open-air seating & a well-stocked bar, & serves typical local fare for around SRD 25 per plate. Groups or those who want food ready shortly after their arrival should call ahead to order. **$**

WHAT TO SEE AND DO The most popular activity in the park is the hike downhill to the Leo or Elena Falls, which are about 45 and 60 minutes from Brownsberg Camp respectively, and which tumble into small clear pools where you can swim. Elena Falls is the more spectacular of the two, and while the hike back up to the plateau is considerably longer and steeper than the one to Leo Falls, some guides will exaggerate its difficulty to encourage you to stick to the easier goal. Another worthwhile short hike leads to Masaroni Peak, the highest point on the mountain.

For wildlife viewing and birding, the best place to focus your attention is the forest fringing the Brownsberg Camp, which is home to plenty of red howler and black spider monkeys, along with lizards and agouti. The sprawling camp and surrounding roads generally offer more rewarding birding than the narrower footpaths through the forest interior. A speciality is the striking grey-winged trumpeter, an otherwise seldom-seen guineafowl lookalike that lurks around the forest floor in front of the restaurant. Among the many other alluring birds seen regularly at Brownsberg are the variegated tinamou, marail guan, black curassow, ornate hawk-eagle, green-backed trogon, white-throated toucan, Guianan tucanet, wedge-billed wood-creeper, white bellbird, thrush-like ant-pitta and purple honeycreeper. The checklist also includes 18 parrot and macaw, 38 ant-bird and 30 tanager species.

BROKOPONDO AND THE AFOBAKA DAM

Capital of the eponymous district, Brokopondo is a modestly proportioned town of around 2,500 people set on the west bank of the Suriname River, 100km south of Paramaribo. The town is an attractive enough place, boasting a sandy swimming beach, and it is unusually hilly for Suriname. The surrounding countryside is swathed in lush jungle, interspersed with marshes and small lakes, and rustling with birds and monkeys. The main local point of interest, about 8km further upstream, is Afobaka Dam, which hems in the vast Brokopondo Reservoir (see box, below). Afobaka is also the site of a small port bustling with *korjaal* dugouts that transport passengers and goods to and from various otherwise inaccessible lakeside villages, timber concessions and mining camps. Aside from a couple of

BROKOPONDO AND ITS RESERVOIR

The Suriname River upstream from Brokopondo town was one of the earliest parts of the interior to be settled by the Saamaka. Indeed, the confluence with Sara Creek, now the site of Afobaka Dam, is where the Dutch Crown and a dozen Saamaka leaders convened in 1762 to sign the historic Saramaka Peace Treaty (see box, pages 204–5). A century later, gold deposits were discovered immediately east of the Suriname River, opposite the present-day town and in the vicinity of Sara Creek, leading to an influx of prospectors. The name Brokopondo first appears as Broko Pondo, meaning 'Broken Pontoon or Boat', on an 1887 map of the Suriname River. Oddly, no oral tradition elaborating on the nature or fate of the nominal vessel has survived. However, since pontoons were used to transport freight across the river here, it seems likely the name was coined after one such boat crashed against submerged rocks and broke apart.

The turn-of-the-century discovery of fresh goldfields in the vicinity of the Lawa River was the impetus behind the construction of the *Lawaspoorweg* (Lawa Railway) between 1902 and 1913. The original intention was for the track to run all the way from Paramaribo to the Lawa River, on the border with French Guiana, a distance of around 350km. In the end though, construction was halted after gold production at Lawa proved to be disappointing. As a result, the railway terminated after 173km on the west bank of the Suriname River at a spot called Kabel (meaning Cable) east of Brownsweg and opposite Sarakreek (the name given to the east bank north of the confluence with Sara Creek). From Kabel, a 300m aerial cable track led across the river to Sarakreek.

The modern district of Brokopondo was created in 1958, the same year that the Surinamese Government and Alcoa (now Suralco) signed the Brokopondo Agreement, which provided for the creation of a hydro-electric dam on the Suriname River to supply the Paranam-based aluminium plant with power. Construction of the dam at Afobaka started in 1960, 8km upriver of Brokopondo town, and was complete by 1964. It is an embankment dam made of black rock, and stands 54m tall and is almost 2km long, supplemented by several secondary dams with a total length of 10km along the reservoir's margins. It supports a exclusive island camps (see *Where to stay and eat* below), tourist development in and around Brokopondo is rather limited. That said, provided you don't come here looking for prescribed entertainment, the area does possess a certain off-the-beaten-track appeal.

GETTING THERE AND AWAY Brokopondo and Afobaka are 106km and 110km south of Paramaribo by road, respectively. Directions are the same as for Bergendal (see pages 191–3), except that you need to continue straight past the resort, and also continue straight past the junction for Brownsweg shortly afterwards. About 12km past the junction for Brownsweg, a left turn takes you to Brokopondo after about 4km, whereas Afobaka lies about 8km straight ahead, crossing a bridge over the river right below the dam to reach the small port immediately to its east. NVB runs a separate bus service from Paramaribo to each of the villages, in both cases leaving from Saramacca Straat. Buses to/from Brokopondo leave at 07.00 and 13.30 Monday to Saturday and take up to four hours, and the fare is SRD 8.50. Buses to/from Afobaka leave at 06.00 and 13.00 Monday to Saturday and at 08.30 Sunday, take up to 3½ hours and the fare is SRD 7.50.

180MW power station, which went online in 1965 but only reached full operational capacity in 1971, when the reservoir behind it filled completely. Until 1999, about 75% of the hydro-electricity it generated was used by Suralco and its aluminium plant. Today, most of it helps power Paramaribo.

The reservoir behind Afobaka is officially named (in full) after Professor Doctor Ingenieur WJ van Blommestein, the Surakarta-born Dutch hydrological engineer who designed the dam. Quite reasonably, most people settle for calling it Brokopondo Meer ('Lake') instead. Brokopondo ranks among the world's 50 largest reservoirs in terms of surface area, extending over 1,560km^2, but it is very shallow, mostly less than 7m deep. It is so shallow that a 2003 World Bank report ranked it as the least efficient of 49 hydro-electric dams analysed worldwide in terms of hectares flooded per megawatt (5,333 ha/mw, almost four times less efficient than Burkina Faso's Kompienga Dam, ranked second-last on the same list).

When the dam was built, the large area flooded resulted in the displacement of around 5,000 Saamaka villagers, most of whom lived along the affected stretch of riverbank. The communities were relocated outside the area of flooding to so-called *transmigratiedorpen* (transmigration villages), the largest of which were Brownsweg and Klaaskreek.

The flooding also threatened the rich wildlife of the affected part of the Suriname Basin. As a result, the International Society for the Protection of Animals (ISPA) stepped in with a project called Operation Gwamba, which resulted in the rescue of around 10,000 medium to large mammals and their relocation to higher ground (locals claim that this is one of the reasons why nearby Brownsberg Nature Park hosts such a dense mammalian fauna). By contrast, it was deemed impractical and too expensive to clear the jungle before the floodwaters rose, hence the forest of dead trees that protrudes above the surface of all but the deepest parts of the reservoir. Since 2004, a scheme to harvest this deadwood from the lake has been under way. Most of the wood extracted is exported to the USA and Germany, where it is marketed as Stauseeholz (Reservoir Wood).

🏠 **WHERE TO STAY AND EAT** There don't appear to be any warungs or other eateries in Brokopondo town, but a trio of supermarkets sell a fair selection of fresh and packaged goods. There are also a few supermarkets at Afobaka, as well as a basic warung selling the usual inexpensive local fare.

🏠 **Brokopondo Staatslodgeergebouw** (19 rooms) m 7142692. The only non-island accommodation in the area is this good-value grey-blue state-owned resthouse, which stands prominently on a hill in Brokopondo town centre overlooking the forest-lined river & Ananie Strand. The dbl rooms all come with fan or AC, & there is a common kitchen you can use for SRD 50/day. There are plans to renovate in 2015, but it should stay open throughout. SRD 35 dbl with fan & shared bath; SRD 40/50 en-suite dbl with fan/AC. **$**

🏠 **Paradise Island** (3 lodges) ☎ 530203; m 8808030/8527740; e nhealy@galaxy.sr; www.facebook.com/paradise.islands.suriname. Spread across 2 isolated islands in the south of Brokopondo Reservoir, about 90mins by motorboat from Afobaka, this is one of the smartest & most stylish lodges in the interior, but it's geared mainly to large parties. There is an 8-bed, an 18-bed & an 26-bed lodge, & all 3 come with fully fitted & equipped kitchens, & comfortable bedding. Good facilities include a swimming pool, BBQ hut, kayaking, beach volleyball, nature walks, fishing (it's a good spot for peacock bass) & boat trips further afield, for instance to the villages on the Upper Suriname between the reservoir & Atjoni. Around SRD 700pp inc meals, activities & transport from Paramaribo. **$$$$$**

🏠 **Tonka Island** (4 houses) m 8899125/8604741; www.tonka-eiland.com. Another facility aimed mainly at large groups coming from Paramaribo, Tonka Island consists of 4 large lakeside houses, sleeping a max of between 15 & 40 people. All have cooking facilities, nets & generator power in the evenings. Houses range in price from SRD 450–700 per party on a self-catering basis, but a more viable option for tourists is an all-inclusive 3-day, 2-night package leaving Paramaribo every Fri at SRD 690pp. **$$$$**

WHAT TO SEE AND DO The only organised tourist facility in Brokopondo town is **Ananie Strand** (m 8676002; ⊕ 08.00–18.00 daily; entrance SRD 10pp), an agreeable swimming resort comprising a hammock hut (SRD 25/day) and a sandy beach facing a lushly forested island in the Suriname River. The town itself is attractive to walk around thanks to the luxuriant foliage, riverine views and plentiful birdlife. The dam at Afobaka lies about 8km away by road. No tours of the dam and hydro-electric plant are offered, but the port on the east bank is a busy and interesting spot.

Plenty of local cargo and taxi-boats run from Afobaka to the likes of Lebidoti, a remote transmigration village of around 1,000 people on the southern shore, and mining and timber camps of varying legality in the Sarakreek region. While these are not really suitable for travellers, unless they have an invitation to their chosen destination, it certainly wouldn't be a problem to charter a boat to explore the lake and visit its many forested islands. Expect to pay around SRD 400–500 for a full day out on the lake.

11

Upper Suriname

The most easily explored part of Suriname's interior comprises the Upper Suriname River, which stretches inland from the southern shore of Brokopondo Reservoir to the northern base of the remote Eilerts de Haan Mountains. Wild and largely untrammelled despite its relative accessibility, the Upper Suriname is lined with a few dozen small settlements and 20-odd island-bound or riverside lodges, all of which share a down-to-earth rustic feel in keeping with their jungle surrounds. It is also one of the most exciting parts of Suriname to visit, whether you opt to splash out on a fly-in package to the relatively upmarket Anaula, Danpaati or Awarradam, or to explore the river more whimsically, staying at budget lodges and using inexpensive taxi-boats to propel you slowly southwards.

A compelling feature of the Upper Suriname is its rich traditional culture. The only inhabitants of the region are the Saamaka, or Saramacca, descendants of escaped slaves who made the river their home several hundred years ago. The ancient African roots of the Saamaka are manifested vividly not only in the physical appearance of the people, but also in their social structure, in the organic wood and palm frond constructions that typify their smoky villages and in a traditional culture steeped in animism and ancestor worship. Every so often whilst on the river, a small dugout paddles past manned by two or three people off to visit a neighbouring village or go fishing for their evening meal, a scene that could come straight out of West or Central Africa. Indeed, though the Upper Suriname is part of South America, there is an oddly African quality to it.

Large wildlife is scarcer (or perhaps just shyer) here than it is along Suriname's less populated waterways, largely as a result of hunting. Still, it's not unusual to see squirrel monkeys as you cruise upriver, or to hear the eerie communal calls of distant howler monkeys. And birds are everywhere. Pairs of pied water-tyrant sit perkily on the rocks, often accompanied by cryptically camouflaged ladder-tailed nightjars and small flocks of white-banded swallow. Ringed and green kingfishers flash past a few metres above the water. The delicately marked striated heron is common, but you might also see the occasional (much larger) cocoi heron wading in the shallows, or a capped heron foraging below the rapids. Brightly marked parrots and toucans roost in riverside trees or flap noisily overhead, while raptors such as the dramatic swallow-tailed kite are mobbed by the ubiquitous greater kiskadee.

Ultimately, though, it is the mesmerising presence of the river that defines the Upper Suriname. Calm and blissfully tranquil for long stretches, but punctuated by dramatic rocky rapids that require great skill and years of practice to navigate, it is fringed by tall pristine rainforest throughout its length, except where occasional stands of palms or other fruiting trees mark the site of villages past and present. Capricious tropical storms explode out of nowhere and die down just as quickly, resulting in a few drenching minutes before the sun returns to dry things out. And as you plough further upriver, deeper and deeper into the interior, the lone ribbon

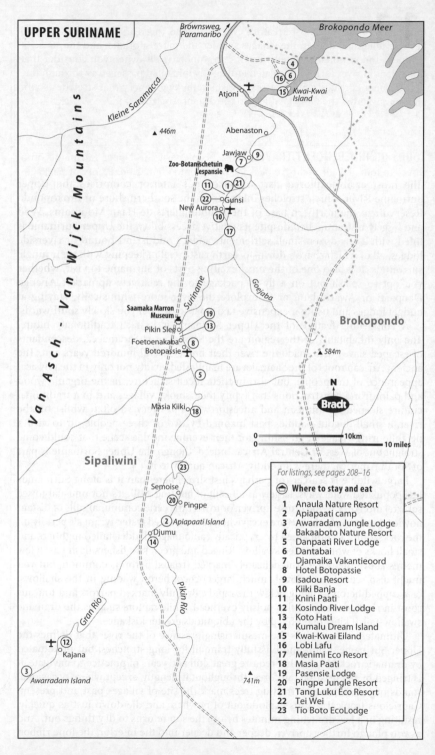

UPPER SURINAME

Brownsweg,
Paramaribo

Brokopondo Meer

Kleine Saramacca

▲ 446m

Atjoni

✈

4
6
16
15 Kwai-Kwai
Island

Abenaston

Jawjaw 9
7

Zoo-Botanischetuin
Lespansie

11 1 21

22 Gunsi
New Aurora
10

17

Suriname

Goejaba

Saamaka Marron
Museum

19
13

Pikin Slee
Foetoenakaba 8
Botopassie

5

▲ 584m

Brokopondo

Masia Kiiki 18

N

Bradt

0 ———————— 10km
0 ———————— 10 miles

Van Asch - Van Wijck Mountains

Sipaliwini

23

Semoise
20 Pingpe

2 Apiapaati Island
Djumu
14

Gran Rio

Pikin Rio

12
Kajana

3
Awarradam Island

▲ 741m

For listings, see pages 208–16

🛏 Where to stay and eat

1   Anaula Nature Resort
2   Apiapaati camp
3   Awarradam Jungle Lodge
4   Bakaaboto Nature Resort
5   Danpaati River Lodge
6   Dantabai
7   Djamaika Vakantieoord
8   Hotel Botopassie
9   Isadou Resort
10 Kiiki Banja
11 Knini Paati
12 Kosindo River Lodge
13 Koto Hati
14 Kumalu Dream Island
15 Kwai-Kwai Eiland
16 Lobi Lafu
17 Menimi Eco Resort
18 Masia Paati
19 Pasensie Lodge
20 Pingpe Jungle Resort
21 Tang Luku Eco Resort
22 Tei Wei
23 Tio Boto EcoLodge

of asphalt to Paramaribo retreating ever further to the rear, the forest seems to become taller and denser, the villages smaller and more sporadic, and the sense of wildness and remoteness intensifies. It's no wonder really, when you consider that this splendid river forms an isolated and lightly inhabited passageway through one of the planet's greatest wildernesses, a vast swathe of greenery that stretches south all the way across the Guiana Shield to the distant Amazon.

GETTING THERE AND AWAY

TOURS OR INDEPENDENT TRAVEL Most people visit the Upper Suriname on a three- to four-day all-inclusive package tour from Paramaribo. Plenty of packages of this sort are available, usually based at one lodge only, with the option of flying in and out of the nearest airstrip, or of travelling by asphalt road to the gateway village of Atjoni, then continuing by river to your lodge of choice. A package tour is undoubtedly the easiest, most hassle-free and a very popular way to see the Upper Suriname, but more adventurous travellers, or those on a tight budget, could also think about exploring the area independently, catching a bus from Paramaribo to Atjoni, then travelling upriver, possibly even hopping between a few lodges over several days, using inexpensive local taxi-boats. A useful resource for those planning to visit the area independently is the website of the Stichting Lodgeholders Boven Suriname (LBS; Association of Upper Suriname Lodgeholders; m *8664030; www.upper-suriname.com*), complete with a detailed downloadable brochure in English, Dutch and French.

OTHER PRACTICALITIES

COMMUNICATIONS There is mobile phone reception all along the river, but it tends to be intermittent and patchy, so it is worth carrying SIM cards from two different providers if you need to be in regular contact with the outside world. There is no mobile phone data connection, however, and to the best of our knowledge none of the lodges on the Upper Suriname has Wi-Fi or any other viable internet connection.

SHOPPING Shopping opportunities are limited except in Atjoni, where half a dozen well-stocked supermarkets line the short road to the slipway. These form the last opportunity for self-caterers to stock up on provisions before heading further upriver and also to buy bottled water, beer, wine and soft drinks at normal prices.

ACTIVITIES The remote back-to-basics feel associated with exploring this jungle-lined river is perhaps more of an attraction than any specific activity. Indeed, the Upper Suriname is an ideal place just to chill out and enjoy the natural surrounds. However, most camps offer facilities for fishing and swimming in the river (though you are advised to ask local advice about currents and piranha activity before taking the plunge), and they also offer other excursions such as guided bush walks, village visits and nocturnal caiman spotting. For those seeking a high level of cultural interaction, one of the handful of lodges based on the riverbank adjacent to a village is recommended. Also strongly recommended for those with an interest in local culture is a visit to the Marron Museum in Pikin Slee (see pages 212–13). Some lodges, such as Tei Wei, Pingpe and Kosindo, offer overnight excursions deeper into the jungle.

THE SAAMAKA OF UPPER SURINAME

The Saamaka, known to outsiders as the Saramacca or Saramaka, are the main inhabitants of the Upper Suriname region. They are descendants of Suriname's oldest community of so-called Marrons, former slaves who escaped from the plantations in the late 17th and early 18th centuries, and who fled into the rainforest along the Saramacca River, from where they waged regular attacks on plantations owned by their former European masters. On 19 September 1762, a century before the abolition of slavery, the Dutch Crown signed the Saramaka Peace Treaty, acknowledging the territorial rights and trading privileges of the Saamaka. It was not long after this that the first Saamaka offshoots relocated to the mid to upper reaches of the Suriname River, which they traditionally refer to as the Gaan Saamaka ('Big Saramacca'). Indeed, the Gaan Saamaka, including the area now flooded by Brokopondo Reservoir, eventually became the main numerical stronghold of the Saamaka people.

The Creole language Saamaka Tongo (literally Saamaka tongue) is quite closely related to, but also significantly different from, the coastal Sranan Tongo. In common with many African languages, it is strongly tonal and the grammar is clearly influenced by the Gbe and Fongbe languages of present-day Ghana and Benin. Unusually for a Creole language, the lexicon has two main sources, and several lesser ones, reflecting the region's turbulent early history. It is estimated that some 50% of Saamaka words have English roots, while another 35% are sourced from Portuguese, and the remainder from Dutch and various Amerindian and African languages. The Saamaka alphabet has no letter 'r', reflecting its speakers inability to enunciate this sound, hence the local preference for the spelling Saamaka as opposed to Saramacca.

Dominated politically by males, Saramaka society is otherwise relatively egalitarian. Based strongly on kinship, it places a high value on respect for the elders of a community, and doesn't recognise any rigid social classes or occupational castes. In common with Suriname's other five Marron communities, and many African societies, every village has a chief and assistant chief, known respectively as the *kabiteni* and *basiya*, all of whom are subservient to a paramount chief who is known as the *gaanman* ('Big Man') and is formally recognised by the central government of Suriname. It is some indication of the stability of Saamaka politics that it had only 12 paramount chiefs (average rule 20 years) between the signature of the 1762 treaty and the appointment of the incumbent Gaanman Belfon Aboikoni in 2005.

Despite the male political dominance, kinship is recognised along the line of the matrilineal clan or *lo*. Property ownership is based on claims staked out by the different *lo* in the 18th century. The inheritance of land, possessions and certain political offices is usually determined along matrilineal lines. And while an adult can choose to live in their father's village, or to settle elsewhere for that matter, the village of their mother is always considered to be their ancestral home, and is where

ATJONI

The twin Saamaka villages of Atjoni (sometimes spelled Atjonie) and Pokigron act as the gateway to the Upper Suriname and lie about 500m apart on the west bank of the Suriname River, approximately 20km upstream from the Brokopondo Reservoir and 150km south of Paramaribo as the crow flies. The most southerly they ought to be buried. Polygyny is widespread, in large part because a variety of historical circumstances, most recently the wholesale exodus of men in search of work, has repeatedly led to a gender imbalance favouring females. However, the Saamaka do not view marriage in the nuclear fashion of Western societies, and it would be unusual indeed for a man to permanently cohabit with his wife or wives, or even for them to spend extended periods at each other's homes.

The African roots of the Saamaka are particularly evident in their animist spiritual beliefs. Known as *Winti* (literally wind), the Saamaka religion centres on the idea of one creator God, and a pantheon of lesser deities and spirits, many of which are individually associated with one particular realm, such as the sky or water, and sometimes manifest in human, animal or floral form. Funereal rituals and ancestor worship also play an important role in Saamaka spiritual life. When an important elder dies, a series of complex rituals is conducted over several months, even a full year, culminating in the elevation of the deceased to a pantheon of ancestral spirits. Most villages possess several ancestral shrines, which are regarded to be a direct portal to the Winti spirits. The shrines are regularly consulted about village problems, and offerings are made at them when the spirits are required to intervene in earthly matters both important and mundane. However, not all ancestral sprits are perceived as benevolent. The *kunu* is a much feared avenging ancestral spirit dedicated to passing on diseases, madness and other torments to the close matrilineal kinsmen of those who did them wrong when they were alive. Today, something like 80% of Saamaka villages still adhere to traditional beliefs, with the remainder having switched over to Moravian, Roman Catholic or other Christian denominations.

Most traditional (ie: non-Christian) Saamaka villages have a similar layout. The entrance to the village is a goalpost-like *azan pau*, a wooden frame hung with palm fronds that wipe away bad spirits from the shoulders of visitors as they pass through. It is conventional for men to enter the frame on the left side and women on the right, in case they are menstruating. In most villages, the first building after the *azam pau* is the house of the *basiya* (assistant headman), who is charged with mediating between visitors and the *kabiteni*. The most important natural site in any traditional village will be the tallest *kankantri* (the local name for the tall buttressed kapok or silk cotton tree *Ceiba pentandra*), which is said to able to speak to the *Winti* gods due to its great height. Usually the area underneath this tree is left untended and overgrown, and many villages give an individual name to their main *kankantri*, just as they would to a person. The most important building is the *faaka pau*, which is usually situated at the place where, according to tradition, the village started. Both a meeting place and ancestral shrine, the *faaka paa* also serves a rather church-like function as the place where weddings and other ceremonies are conducted. In emergencies, the bell next to it is struck to call the villagers to assemble.

point in Suriname accessible by all-weather road, Atjoni is also the springboard for boat travel on the Upper Suriname River and to the two dozen lodges that line its banks and islands. Little is known about the origin of Atjoni, but oral tradition suggests that Pokigron was established by the Wepo family in 1880 or thereabouts. During the civil war in the 1980s, Ronnie Brunswick's Jungle Commando occupied Pokigron, leading to two controversial military attacks in late 1987 that laid waste to many of its buildings and resulted in an estimated 40 civilian deaths. Much reconstruction has occurred since then, but even so the combined population of Atjoni and Pokigron is fewer than 1,000 today.

GETTING THERE AND AWAY The section below is aimed at people making their own way to Atjoni. Most organised tours to the Upper Suriname also pass through Atjoni (the exception being fly-in packages) but in this case all transport between Paramaribo and your lodge of choice would be organised by the operator.

By road Atjoni lies roughly 190km south of Paramaribo via Paranam and Brownsweg. The once seasonally treacherous *poederweg* ('powder road') to Atjoni has recently been upgraded to a good surfaced road in its entirety. In a private vehicle, the drive should take around three to four hours, depending on traffic on the outskirts of Paramaribo. If you are heading upriver from Atjoni, it is advisable to park your car at the police station for safety.

Two NVB buses run daily from Paramaribo to Atjoni via Brownsweg, leaving from Saramacca Straat, opposite Jeruzalem Bazaar, at 08.30 and 11.00. In addition, up to ten private buses and trucks cover the same route daily, leaving from the same place, mostly between 08.00 and 09.00. The fare is SRD 20 one-way and the trip takes up to five hours. An early bus is strongly recommended for those planning to connect with boats heading to any of the various riverside camps and lodges the same day.

Returning to Paramaribo, the NVB buses leave Atjoni at 08.30 and 11.00. Some private buses leave the same day they arrive, usually between noon and 14.00, while others stay in Atjoni overnight and start the return trip between 09.00 and noon. This means it is pretty easy to locate buses heading to Paramaribo any time until around 14.00, but it may be difficult to find a lift north in the afternoon.

By boat Atjoni is the main transport hub serving the Upper Suriname and almost all taxi-boats travelling to other riverside villages leave from its slipway. Practically all taxi-boats take the form of the long traditional dugouts known locally as *korjalen* (see box, opposite page) and fall into two categories: *lantiboten* (subsidised government boats), which usually operate to fixed schedules and are relatively slow and inexpensive, and *lijnboten* (line-boats), which are privately operated, leave when full (or at the captain's whim) and tend to charge about double the fare.

Private *lijnboten* run south as far as Djumu (at the confluence of the Gran and Pikin Rio), while two government boats run weekly to Kajana on the Gran Rio. Most taxi-boats leave Atjoni between noon and 14.00, to tie in with the Paramaribo bus arrival times. *Lijnboten* fares start at around SRD 50 to Jawjaw or lodges downriver from Atjoni, and go up to SRD 100 to Djumu. *Lantiboten* fares range from SRD 15–25 to the lodges around Jawjaw, through to SRD 75 for trips all the way to Kajana. There is often an extra charge for luggage. For those who prefer not to use taxi-boats, it is possible to arrange a charter out of Atjoni at short notice; rates start at around SRD 500–800 for a ten-berth boat, depending on how far you want to travel.

If you arrive in Atjoni without a plan, the tourist office is very helpful when it comes to hooking travellers up with a suitable lodge and boat. But all things considered it is advisable to contact the lodge you intend to stay at in advance, as the owner or manager can find out which boats are heading in their direction on any given day. It is also worth asking about all-inclusive packages from Paramaribo, which tend to be more expensive but save you a lot of hassle. Further travel details for individual sites are included later in the chapter.

The characteristic boat of the Upper Suriname is known as a *korjaal* (plural *korjalen*), and despite its large dimensions, around 100cm wide and in some cases up to 15m long, it is essentially a giant dugout constructed by hand over the course of several months. The first stage in the process is to chop down a tree of suitable dimensions, then hollow it out using a combination of axes and fire. Once that is done, a series of beams is wedged into the hollow trunk, gradually widening it and flattening it until the proportions are correct. This distended trunk is to create a solid watertight hull, upon which the sides of the boat are built up using planks. A completed *korjaal* might fetch a price of up to SRD 10,000 depending on its size, and if you examine the boats used everywhere along the Upper Suriname, you will notice that no matter how long or short they are, the hull is always made of one solid dugout trunk.

TOURIST INFORMATION Since December 2012, the Suriname Tourism Foundation has operated a modern **tourist information centre** (m 7230290; ⊕ 08.00–16.00 *Mon–Fri*) in front of the slipway on the Atjoni riverfront. The office is stocked with brochures and pamphlets, and the staff are a good source of local information, as well as being very helpful when it comes to contacting lodges and boatmen. The office is closed at weekends, but if you call in advance they can still help make arrangements.

 WHERE TO STAY AND EAT For most visitors Atjoni is merely a springboard to lodges further upriver, and you should arrive early enough in the day so you can head straight to your lodge of choice by boat. Should you get stuck, however, the Woman's Foundation in Pokigron has a few rooms available for around SRD 30 per night – ask for details at the tourist information centre. A couple of warungs serving inexpensive local meals and cold beers overlook the jetty.

DOWNRIVER FROM ATJONI

Most of the Upper Suriname lodges are located upstream from Atjoni, but the most northerly cluster – comprising Bakaaboto, Dantabai, Lobi Lafu and Kwai-Kwai lies on the western bank and islands about 30 minutes boat ride downstream, in the direction of Brokopondo Reservoir. These lodges tend to be overlooked by tourists, probably because their location is not quite as tantalisingly remote as their upriver counterparts, and they mostly feel comparatively rundown. Nevertheless, for self-drivers, these lodges have the advantage of being directly accessible by road, and their proximity to Brokopondo Reservoir makes the otherwise inaccessible southern part of this vast island-studded water body a realistic target for a day excursion by boat.

GETTING THERE AND AWAY
By road The three west bank resorts that lie downriver of Atjoni can be reached directly by car, turning left into Weg naar Duwatra ('Road to Duwatra') at an unsignposted junction (⊕ N4 32.146 W55 22.776), 8km before you reach Atjoni. About 4km along this road you hit a Y-junction where sticking to the left takes you to Bakaaboto after about 2km, while a fork to the right takes you to the car parks for the Dantabai and Lobi Lafu lodges (the latter is another 20–30 minutes' walk away).

By boat Taxi-boats running north of Atjoni are scarce, but if you ask around, or better still phone ahead, it may be possible to catch a lift with a boat heading there anyway in which case the fare should be around SRD 50 per person. Otherwise, a return charter from Atjoni is likely to cost around SRD 400–600 per party.

WHERE TO STAY AND EAT *Map, page 202*

Bakaaboto Nature Resort (7 huts)
⊕ N4 31.276 W55 18.876; 582107;
m 8800157; e info@bakaabotonatureresort.com;
www.bakaabotonatureresort.com. On the west
bank of the river & directly accessible by road from
Paramaribo, this most northerly of the lodges stands
in large grassy grounds overlooking an impressive
set of rapids 15mins by motorboat from Brokopondo
Reservoir. The pick of the resorts downriver from
Atjoni, it is popular with self-catering groups from
Paramaribo, so is probably best avoided at w/ends.
However, it also offers FB packages to international
tourists. Accommodation is in simple wooden huts
sleeping 3–12 & using a shared kitchen. Activities
include boat trips to Brokopondo Reservoir &
Apeesina Waterfall, as well bush walks & village
tours. Bed-only rates are SRD 250/600/700/830
per night for 3-/8-/10-/12-bed hut. All-inclusive
packages cost around SRD 300–450pp/night,
depending on group size & duration of stay. **$$$**

Kwai-Kwai Eiland (8 huts) ⊕ N4 29.793
W55 19.845; m 8164420/8562187. Occupying a
wooded island more or less opposite Dantabai, this
well-run owner-managed camp has a vegetable
garden, as well as a patch of thick forest alive with
birds & monkeys. You can walk around the island in
15mins. The thatched wooden huts have mosquito
nets, & there is a large hammock hut overlooking
a flat stretch of river & the facing gallery forest.
Facilities include a kitchen, bar & well-maintained
communal showers & toilets. SRD 50pp bed only;
SRD 120 FB. **$$**

Dantabai (9 huts) ⊕ N4 30.095 W55
19.842; 475143; m 8871121; e wiwirie.tours@
hotmail.com; www.wiwirietours.com. Meaning
'Sound of the Rapids', Dantabai is one of the more
popular Upper Suriname lodges with operators,
thanks to its accessibility by road. It is in a great
location overlooking rapids that offer great rafting
opportunities. The huts are simple, but a little less
so than at some other places, with tiled floors, a
small balcony & access to a communal kitchen &
bathroom. 3 of the huts are on a stilted platform
on the riverbank, & there's a small island opposite
you can swim to & sunbathe on. SRD 60pp bed
only; SRD 120 FB. **$$**

Lobi Lafu (6 huts) ⊕ N4 30.409 W55
19.580; m 8180752/8509834/8898827;
e info@lobilafu.com; www.lobilafu.com. This
small riverside camp, accessible by road & then
a 25min walk, was looking quite neglected &
disorganised when we dropped by, possibly due
to changing management. Assuming that was
a temporary blip, it is a lovely & very affordable
lodge, offering accommodation in simple 4-bed
huts with bedding, netting & a communal toilet &
self-catering kitchen. It caters mainly to w/enders
from Suriname, so no food is available except by
prior arrangement. It has the only canopy zipline
on the Upper Suriname (SRD 100pp) & also offers
abseiling & a Tarzan swing, as well as village
& boat trips. SRD 50pp bed only; SRD 40 in a
hammock; add SRD 50pp/day for meals. **$$**

JAWJAW AND NEW AURORA

Heading south along the Upper Suriname from Atjoni, the first main cluster of accommodation starts about 15km further upstream, at the small village of Jawjaw (pronounced Yow-Yow, and also the name of the first rapids you encounter coming from Atjoni), and ends a few kilometres past the much larger village of New Aurora. It comprises eight lodges in total, half of which are clustered within an area of 1km² on the islands and west bank around the impressive Felulasi Rapids and the village of Gunsi. The lodges around Jawjaw and New Aurora are the most accessible upriver options from Atjoni, only about an hour away by boat, and the majority are in the shoestring and budget range, the most notable exception being Anaula Nature Resort, which vies with the more southerly Danpaati and Awarradam as the most upmarket address on the Upper Suriname. They mostly offer a fairly standard range of activities – swimming, fishing, bush walks and village tours – but it is worth taking the time to visit New Aurora, which is the second-largest village on the Upper Suriname.

GETTING THERE AND AWAY

By air It is possible to charter a flight from Zorg en Hoop to Laduani airstrip, which lies immediately inland of New Aurora, ten to 15 minutes by boat from any of the lodges listed below. Arrange an airstrip transfer in advance with your lodge.

By boat The lodges close to Jawjaw and New Aurora are accessible by boat from Atjoni, a 45–90-minute trip, depending on which lodge you are headed for and how powerful the boat's engine is. All the lodges offer all-inclusive packages from Paramaribo, including bus and boat transfers. Alternatively, a charter from Atjoni should cost around SRD 500–800 for the whole boat. Taxi-boats from Atjoni to any of these lodges usually ask SRD 50 per person, while government boats are about half the price and often charge a small surcharge for luggage. When you are ready to head back to Atjoni, or to travel further upriver, ask the lodge manager to phone around a day ahead. Boats to Atjoni usually leave in the morning. Boats heading upriver generally come past early to mid-afternoon, and charge SRD 25–30 per person to any of the lodges around Pikin Slee, or SRD 30–50 for lodges closer to Djumu.

WHERE TO STAY AND EAT *Map, page 202*

Anaula Nature Resort (17 rooms) ◈ N4 23.160 W55 23.289; ✆410700; m 8675501; e info@anaulanatureresort.com; www.anaulanatureresort.com. This smart new lodge occupies a lushly wooded island in the middle of the Felulasi Rapids, about 1km north of New Aurora. Facilities include a swimming pool, a restaurant & bar set on a raised wooden deck shaded by palms & surrounded by tall forest, & a children's playground & riverside hammock camp. The en-suite wooden cabins have 3 beds (sleeping up to 5), safe, standing fan & private balcony facing a narrow channel between 2 islands. From SRD 415pp/night including transport from Paramaribo, meals & excursions such as a visit to the Marron Museum in Pikin Slee, caiman spotting & bush walks. **$$$$**

Knini Paati (7 rooms, with plans for expansion) ◈ N4 22.984 W55 23.338; m 7132592/8859355; e nelson@kinini-island, tiapoe2@hotmail.com; www.knini-island.com. This new island-bound lodge next to Anaula is in a wonderful location overlooking the Felulasi Rapids & forested eastern riverbank, & has a friendly hands-on owner-manager who speaks excellent English. Accommodation is in comfortable en-suite stilted wooden huts with balconies, netting & 24hr solar heating. You can swim in the channels around the island, & other activities include boat trips to

the mainland, caiman spotting & bush walks. SRD 50pp bed only on a self-catering basis; all-inclusive 3-day, 2-night packages, including transport, meals, non-alcoholic drinks & activities cost SRD 500pp from Atjoni, SRD 920pp from Paramaribo. **$-$$**

Tei Wei (13 rooms) ◈ N4 23.284 W55 23.449; m 8561452/8828998; e bertajaiso@ gmail.com. Situated on a high rise on the west bank of the river alongside the traditional Saamaka village of Gunsi, this friendly community-owned lodge is one of the oldest in the region, built in 1991. It offers a great view over the verdant island-studded river a short distance upstream of New Aurora, and the manager speaks good English. The simple stilted wooden huts have nets & a small balcony, with shared toilet and shower, though there are plans to add some en-suite units soon. There is also a rather quirky cliffside honeymoon suite where the arrangement of 3 rooms, each with 3 beds, may or may not reflect polygamous local traditions. In addition to local day trips, the lodge offers an overnight jungle trail to a sleeping platform 3–4hrs away for SRD 500 per party. The lodge sells beers & cold drinks, & the village shop is right next door. SRD 35pp bed only; SRD 85 FB. **$**

Menimi Eco Resort (35 rooms) ◈ N4 21.133 W55 23.690; m 7222880/8884134; www. menimisurinamevakanties.com. Accommodating up to 150 people, this large resort, the most southerly in this cluster, is in a rather isolated location on the west bank about 5km upstream of New Aurora. Famed for its ebullient owner-manager, Menimi ('Remember Me' in the local tongue) is a very friendly & well-run set-up, catering mainly to a local clientele but equally welcoming to tourists. Accommodation is in en-suite dbl rooms or 4-bed wooden huts with shared bathrooms. Its central feature is a football pitch carved into a shady palm grove, while the adjacent wide stretch of river is good for fishing & swimming. Facilities include a kitchen, bar, restaurant, small grocery shop, bakery & souvenir shop. SRD 35pp bed only, plus SRD 50 per party per day for use of the kitchen; SRD 95 FB. **$$**

🏠 **Djamaika Vakantieoord** (22 rooms & huts) ✪ N4 25.560 W55 22.335; m 8636172/8811331. In the small Saamaka village of Jawjaw (population 500), next to the attractive rapids of the same name, Djamaika (pronounced 'Jamaica') is a low-key & very comfortable owner-managed lodge popular both with local holidaymakers & travellers. It offers the choice of an en-suite dbl room in a 2-storey wooden block, or a more isolated 4-bed en-suite thatched hut with a view directly onto the rapids. The lodge's proximity to a (predominantly Christian) village makes it particularly attractive to visitors seeking unforced interaction with locals. Food can be provided, or you can use the kitchen. There are 3 shops in the village. Activities such as bush walks, boat trips & caiman spotting are offered. SRD 50pp bed only; SRD 110 FB. **$$**

🏠 **Isadou Resort** (23 rooms & huts)

m 8703344/8979454; e info@isadou.com; www.isadou.com. Set on a substantial island in the middle of the Jawjaw Rapids, facing the jungle-lined east bank, this peaceful & well-equipped lodge caters mainly to large groups & has a total capacity of 144 guests. Set around a large green lawn, the brightly painted huts & houses are all en suite, with 4 ¾ beds apiece & a private balcony. Facilities include a bakery, restaurant, electricity in the evenings & safe swimming in the rapids. SRD 50pp bed only; SRD 450pp for a 3-day, 2-night stay including transport from Paramaribo, activities such as bush & village walks, & meals. **$$**

🏠 **Kiiki Banja** (5 rooms) ✪ N4 22.497 W55 24.011; m 8888146. The least resort-like accommodation on the Upper Suriname, this small guesthouse lies in a green compound next to the creek at the southern end of New Aurora. Rooms sharing a bathroom can be rented on a self-catering basis, but a cook can also be provided. There are 2 shops nearby. This is a good affordable option for those who want to experience a Saamaka village in an uncontrived manner. SRD 35pp bed only. **$**

🏠 **Tang Luku Eco Resort** (24 rooms) ✪ N4 22.902 W55 23.485; ☏ 402612; m 8799927; e info@tanglukuecoresort.com; www.tanglukuecoresort.com. This large but otherwise rather low-key resort is set on the south bank of a large leafy island overlooking the Felulasi Rapids a few hundred metres upstream from Knini Paati. The small wooden huts have nets but use a shared bathroom. SRD 35pp bed only; SRD 690pp for 3-day, 2-night stays including transport from Paramaribo, activities & meals. **$**

WHAT TO SEE AND DO

New Aurora The second-largest settlement on the Upper Suriname, New Aurora is a Saamaka village of around 2,000 inhabitants following Christian or traditional beliefs. Its central feature is a tall whitewashed Moravian church that looks to be of some antiquity and is rather reminiscent of Cape Dutch architecture in South Africa. The church is the focal point of the village on Sundays, when Christian villagers gather there for the 09.00 service dressed in their finest. In other respects, the village has a very African feel: children fish and cavort in the river alongside teenage girls doing the family laundry alfresco, while women walk past gossiping, seemingly unencumbered by the improbably heavy loads they carry on their head in traditional African style. Behind the church, a maze of narrow alleys is lined with stilted wooden palm-roofed houses, some of them still adorned with elaborate traditionally carved façades. It is fine to walk around the village alone, though some locals prefer you to do so with a familiar guide, but don't take photographs without permission, and better still not at all.

Zoo-Botanischetuin Lespansie (✦ *N4 24.880 W55 23.211*; m *8141918*; e *stgvjgeneratie@hotmail.com*) Located on the west bank close to the village of Lespansie, this well-signposted ecotourism site between the Jawjaw and Felulasi Rapids was earmarked for development in 2012 as a botanical garden, zoo, birdwatching facility and environmental education centre with overnight facilities. Despite the involvement of two reputable NGOs, the Small Grants Program and Suriname Conservation Foundation, development is currently limited to a few wooden platforms and the labelling of some trees with their Dutch and Latin names. Hopefully, further progress will be forthcoming.

PIKIN SLEE, BOTOPASSIE AND AROUND

For about 15km south of Menimi, boats follow a long, flat, tranquil stretch of river, lined with pristine forest and largely unpunctuated by rapids or settlements other than the small and rather isolated west bank village of Goejaba (aka Gulaba). The first riverside settlement after this, Pikin Slee, also on the west bank, is not only the largest village on the Upper Suriname but is also the site of the excellent Saamaka Marron Museum, which provides an informative overview of Saamaka history and traditions. Two other smaller villages, Foetoenakaba and Botopassie, also lie on the west bank and are within an hour's walk south of Pikin Slee, along a riverside footpath. The area supports a cluster of four lodges, including the highly regarded Hotel Botopassie and Pasensie Lodge, and the more remote island-bound Danpaati River Lodge, which is arguably the pick of the region's more upmarket accommodations.

GETTING THERE AND AWAY

By air A few flights weekly run on demand between Zorg en Hoop and Botopassie airstrip, which lies a few hundred metres from the river next to the eponymous village and opposite Hotel Botopassie. Flights are best booked in conjunction with your accommodation, and your lodge will arrange a boat transfer from the airstrip.

By boat The lodges around Pikin Slee are all accessible by boat from Atjoni, and can set up all-inclusive trips from Paramaribo, including bus and boat transfers. Alternatively, taxi-boats from Atjoni take around two to three hours, and the fare is SRD 50–70 per person, plus a small surcharge for luggage. Charters cost around SRD 600–800 one-way. Coming from a lodge near Jawjaw or New Aurora, the taxi-boat transfer should cost SRD 25–30. Heading upstream from any of the lodges around Pikin Slee, or if returning to Atjoni, ask your lodge manager to phone around to find a suitable ride. Boats to Atjoni usually leave in the morning, whereas boats heading upstream generally come past mid-afternoon and charge a fare of SRD 25–30 to any of the lodges *en route* to Djumu.

⌂ WHERE TO STAY AND EAT *Map, page 202*

⌂ ✳ **Danpaati River Lodge** (15 chalets) ✦N4 11.286 W55 26.041; ☎424522; m 8109727/8744499; e reservations@danpaati. net; www.danpaati.net. Our favourite upmarket lodge on the Upper Suriname, Danpaati lies on a substantial & lushly forested island surrounded by flat water about 3km upstream from Botopassie airstrip. The en-suite dbl or twin wood cabins have nets & a private balcony, while the larger luxury cabins, set in a separate clearing about 100m from the main camp, were being renovated in 2014. Facilities include a swimming pool on a large wooden deck, a small sandy swimming beach at the south end of the island, a yoga deck, a shady stilted wooden dining area with a *pinna* roof & generator electricity for about half the day. Activities include caiman spotting, visits to Pikin Slee & the Marron Museum, & an excursion to the Tapawutra Rapids at Djumu. SRD 345pp/ night including all meals & a daily bush walk; all-inclusive tours start from SRD 1,540pp for 3 days, 2 nights & leave Paramaribo on Mon, Wed & Fri. **$$$$**

🏠 ※ **Hotel Botopassie** (16 rooms) ✪ N4 13.454 W55 26.413; m 8659702/8126045/8607482; e corry_vonk@ hotmail.com; www.botopasi.com. On the east bank of the river opposite the village & airstrip of the same name, the relatively smart & stylish Hotel Botopassie (aka Botopasi) breaks the typical Upper Suriname jungle lodge mould, coming across more like a hybrid between a B&B & a superior backpackers. The central dbl-storey building has a ground-floor bar, a 1st-floor balcony & dining area with lovely views over the river, a TV room with a good DVD collection, a small library of novels & other books, & several neat, clean dbl rooms with shared bathroom with solar hot water. There is also a riverfront row of en-suite cabins with traditional *pinna* roofs, sleeping space for 3, & a private balcony. Other features of this very agreeable lodge, which was built by the Dutch-Surinamese owner-managers in 2000, are a small swimming beach, jungle & village walks, & overnight jungle stays. It seems very good value at SRD 115/160/180pp for hammock/room/cabin including all meals. **$$$**

🏠 ※ **Pasensie Lodge** (6 rooms) ✪ N4 14.848 W55 26.472; m 8665504; e pasensiepikinslee@gmail.com; www.pasensie. com. Located next to a forest-fringed coconut plantation on the southern edge of Pikin Slee, which is the largest village on the Upper Suriname & the site of the Marron Museum. This excellent small lodge offers the choice of a small but colourful twin room with nets in the colonial-style main house or a stilted *pinna*-roof cabin overlooking the river. The main building has a lovely wide balcony & dining area facing the river, a well-stocked bar, a TV, a selection of DVDs & a small library. Activities include a village walk & museum visit for SRD 30 per party, a short jungle walk for SRD 56 per party, & overnight jungle trips for SRD 23pp. Massages & workshops are also available. The lodge maintains a good relationship with the village, so it is a great option for those seeking to settle into village life for a few days. SRD 70pp bed only; SRD 140 FB. **$$**

🏠 **Koto Hati** (5 huts) ✪ N4 14.374 W55 26.678; m 8782879; www.kotohati.net. About halfway between Pikin Slee & Botopassie, alongside the jetty for the small Saamaka Christian village of Foetoenakaba, this simple lodge is in a pretty riverside setting. It offers 4-bed huts with clean shared bathrooms, & a 10-bed house with its own bathroom. There are a couple of shops in the nearby village which is a short walk inland. SRD 35pp bed only; relatively steep SRD 125 FB. **$**

WHAT TO SEE AND DO
Pikin Slee and the Saamaka Marron Museum Despite its name, which means 'Little Slee' (its larger counterpart lies further upriver), Pikin Slee is the largest settlement on the Upper Suriname and supports around 4,000 people. It is also possibly the largest traditional Saamaka village anywhere in the Guianas. Pikin Slee is well worth exploring on a guided tour (offered by Pasensie and several other lodges in the region), to see the massive and overgrown *kankantri*, as well as the open-air woodcarving workshop of the **Stichting Totomboti** (literally 'Foundation Woodpecker'; *www.totomboti.nl*; ⊕ *Mon–Fri*). It was established by a local Rastafarian group in the 1990s and produces a variety of innovative and beautiful carved wooden furniture.

Another worthwhile stop is **Marion's Winkel** (m *7248733*; ⊕ *daily*), which is named after its friendly owner and can be found on the opposite side of the football field to Pasensie Lodge. It stocks a range of inexpensive, locally produced goods, including coconut soap, maripa oil, an anti-itching concoction for insect bites and decorated calabash baskets and lampshades. It is also the only place in town to buy ice, should you or your drinks need cooling down.

The highlight of a visit to Pikin Slee is the impressive **Saamaka Marron Museum** (m *7161446/8291167*; e *saamakamuseum@gmail.com*; *www.saamakamarronmuseum. com*; ⊕ *10.00–15.00 Tue–Sun; entrance SRD 20pp; photography forbidden*), which is located on the edge of the village, about 2km from Pasensie. This impressive facility, which opened in 2010, is the only one of its sort in Upper Suriname. It lies in large grounds studded with carved artworks produced by members of the Stichting Totomboti, which is also responsible for the museum's existence. It consists of a large hall containing photographs, musical instruments, games and various other artefacts and displays relating to the history and culture of the Saamaka and other Marron peoples. The entry fee includes a highly informative guided tour, at present conducted only in Dutch. The museum also serves cold drinks and (by prior arrangement only) good local food in the SRD 10–25 range. It is a good idea to call in advance to let them know you're coming.

TOWARDS DJUMU

Less a cluster than a scattering, some five lodges line the long, remote and mostly smooth-flowing stretch of the Suriname River that divides Danpaati from the confluence of its two main tributaries, the Gran Rio and Pikin Rio (literally 'Big River' and 'Small River'). Situated at the confluence, Djumu (also spelled Djoemoe) is a substantial village with an airstrip and a well-known medical centre, and it enjoys a rather scenic setting facing the Tapawutra ('Top Water') Rapids, where the Gran Rio flows into the Suriname. Djumu is also something of a route focus, since those heading deeper into the south, along the Gran Rio, are required to porter boats and luggage over Tapawutra, which forms a far more significant obstacle than any rapids further downstream.

Most of the lodges along this stretch of river are in the moderate to shoestring range, with the busiest and arguably best being Pingpe Jungle Resort a few kilometres north of Djumu.

GETTING THERE AND AWAY
By air A few scheduled flights weekly run on demand between Zorg en Hoop and Djumu airstrip, which lies a few hundred metres south of the confluence of the Gran Rio and Pikin Rio. Flights are best booked in conjunction with your accommodation, and your lodge will also arrange a boat transfer from the airstrip.

By boat All of the lodges north of Djumu are accessible by boat from Atjoni. The trip takes up to five hours by taxi-boat, and these run every day except Sunday and will charge a fare of at least SRD 70 per person, plus a small surcharge for luggage. Charters will cost around SRD 800–1,000 one-way. If coming from a lodge further downriver, the taxi-boat transfer should cost SRD 30–50. Returning to Atjoni, boats usually leave at around 06.30 and arrive between 10.00 and 11.00. You will need to ask your lodge manager to phone around to find a suitable ride. For details of transport south to Kajana, see the Gran Rio section on pages 215–16.

WHERE TO STAY AND EAT *Map, page 202*
🏠 ✸ **Pingpe Jungle Resort** (6 huts)
✪ N4 02.436 W55 26.875; m 8768014/8234744;
e info@jungleresortpingpe.com;
www.jungleresortpingpe.com. About 4km downriver from Djumu on a forested island opposite the east bank village of Pingpe, this relatively new & busy resort is owned & managed by a hands-on former guide who hails from the village & speaks good English as well as Dutch. The dbl & 4-bed cabins are all en suite, & have nets, & a private balcony. Excursions include short walking tours of the village, home to around 200 traditional Saamaka, boat trips to Djumu Medical Centre & Tapawutra, & overnight jungle hikes. There is a well-stocked bar & a pleasant dining area where guests eat communally. SRD 120pp/night including meals;

SRD 1,315pp all-inclusive 3-day, 2-night packages from Paramaribo; SRD 2,880pp 5-day, 4-night packages, including an optional night in the jungle. See ad page 217. **$$$**

🏠 **Kumalu Dream Island** (10 rooms) ✪ N4 00.455 W55 28.330; opposite Djumu Medical Centre; \473322; m 8867059; e info@kumalu-dreamisland.com; www.kumalu-dreamisland.com. On a small beautiful island in the Pikin Rio, less than 1km upstream from its confluence with the Gran Rio, this newish lodge with 24hr solar power, has immense potential thanks to its lovely setting & unusually spacious, cool & solid rooms. All rooms have 2 beds with nets & small balcony, and some also have a clean en-suite bathroom. The lodge looked a bit neglected & dirty when we dropped by, but we are assured that this is not the case when guests are expected. It would be the obvious place to stay if you need to spend a night in Djumu waiting for transport up the Gran Rio. Excursions to Pineapple Mountain & Tapawutra are offered. SRD 40pp bed only & with shared bath; SRD 50 en suite; SRD 125 en suite inc meals; SRD 175 inc meals & activities. **$$**

🏠 **Apiapaati** (4 rooms) ✪ N4 01.569 W55 27.787; m 8157666/8948661; e info@

fredecotours.com; www.fredecotours.com. This small & quite popular island camp consists of 2 wooden huts each partitioned into 2 semi-private rooms with twin bed & nets. It also has a hammock hut. SRD 50pp bed only; SRD 100 FB; all-inclusive packages from Paramaribo start from SRD 1,035pp. **$**

🏠 **Masia Paati** (4 huts) ✪ N4 08.595 W55 26.074; m 8167319. One of the most low-key & little-visited lodges on the Upper Suriname, Masia Paati lies on the steep western bank of the eponymous island opposite the tiny village of Masia Kiiki. Situated about 6km upstream from Danpaati, it possesses a certain rustic, easy-going charm but the friendly owner speaks limited Dutch & no English whatsoever, so communicating could be interesting. SRD 35pp bed only; SRD 85 with meals. **$**

🏠 **Tio Boto EcoLodge** (6 huts) ✪ N4 05.593 W55 26.696; m 8617805/8365976/8144717; www.tioboto.webs.com. Another 5km or so upstream from Masia Paati, Tio Boto is a very rudimentary camp in a lovely riverside location ringed by forest, but it has quite a rundown and unattended feel. SRD 100pp inc meals. **$**

WHAT TO SEE AND DO

Pineapple Mountain Named after the spiky pineapples that grow wild on its upper slopes, Ananas Mountain is a modest granite dome whose bare summit, though only 220m high, offers splendid views across the surrounding forest. The dome is a couple of kilometres east of Djumu, a walk of up to an hour in either direction, and there is a chance of seeing monkeys on the way. A guide is mandatory and can be arranged through Kumalu Dream Island, Pingpe Jungle Resort or Apiapaati, all of which offer organised excursions to the peak.

KAJANA AND THE GRAN RIO

The very remote part of Saamaka upriver from Djumu is generally known as Langu. The Gran Rio (aka Gaanlio) flows through Langu, having come from the Guiana Highlands near the border with Brazil to form the larger of the two main tributaries feeding the Suriname River. Far less accessible than the Upper Suriname itself, Langu supports a total human population of perhaps 1,000, spread across seven villages, of which the largest is Kajana (pronounced Kayana, and sometimes spelled Cajana). All but the solitary Christian settlement of Ligolio follow traditional beliefs. Only two lodges service this remote and alluring area, neither of them suited to tight budgets. These are the upmarket island-bound Awarradam Jungle Lodge, which celebrated 21 years of service in 2014, and the more low-key owner-managed Kosindo River Lodge on the riverfront next to Kajana village (see page 216). Both lodges also act as springboards for an overnight boat trip deeper into the interior to the unpopulated stretch of river at Sintiadam.

GETTING THERE AND AWAY In practice, the only way to visit Awarradam is on a **pre-booked fly-in package** from Paramaribo, landing at Kajana, from where you'll be ferried the last 10km to the lodge itself by motorboat. Most visitors to Kosindo also fly to Kajana, which is right opposite the lodge, but it can also be reached by boat. Indeed, a popular option for Kosindo is to fly one way and take a boat the other way. If you do this, best to arrive by air and leave by boat, as the boat trip downriver is far quicker (what's more, if you are using public transport, it is far easier to get through from Kajana to Paramaribo in one day than to travel in the opposite direction). The various options and associated costs are covered in detail on Kosindo Lodge's website.

RAPIDS ON THE GRAN RIO

All the rapids on the Upper Suriname between Brokopondo Reservoir and Djumu can be traversed or bypassed in normal conditions by a boat steered by a skilled and experienced local skipper (a qualification process which, incidentally, requires at least five years' apprenticeship). This is not the case, however, for the two largest rapids on the Gran Rio between Djumu and Kajana, both of which must usually be navigated by portage, though many tour operators, lodges and even taxi-boats get around this by arranging for a different boat to meet their passengers on the other side and carrying all the luggage between the two boats.

The first rapid that you'll come to when travelling upriver from Djumu is Tapawutra (literally 'Top Water'; ⊕ N4 00.873 W55 28.698), which lies directly opposite the village and is where the Gran Rio flows into the Suriname. Formed by a 4m-high granitic ridge with a large crack in the middle, this natural dyke is usually portaged, which involves hauling the boat across a patch of relatively flat water and ideally carrying all valuables or non-waterproof luggage around by land. There are two portage sites. The southeastern one (to your left when approaching the confluence from the Suriname River) is regarded as safe, but the northwesterly one (to the right) is studded with potentially treacherous submerged pits whose location will not be apparent to visitors, so it is advisable to walk around with the luggage. Note, too, that skippers heading downriver occasionally try to take their boat through the cataract-like central channel, an option they might get away with more often than not, but still a very risky one – neither you nor your luggage want to be in any boat attempting this!

The second rapid, about 8km upriver from Tapawutra, is Gaandam (literally 'Big Dyke'; ⊕ N3 58.379 W55 30.831), the name given to the largest fall in a long, labyrinthine network of channels, rapids and islets whose hydrology and appearance vary greatly depending on the water level. Most people change boat here. Failing that, boats need to be hauled across the rapids in all seasons, though the best route varies depending on the water level. The narrow stair-like channel known as Kimbotobasu is the quickest and most popular route when the water is high, but it's tricky and possibly dangerous for tourists who don't know where the footholds are and can't speak the language. By contrast, when the water level is low, the boat may need to be hauled a full 400m along a shallow side channel running to the right of Kimbotobasu when coming from Tapawutra. Either way, you know you are through when you reach a bus stop-like shelter, complete with a map of the river as far as Kajana, at the top of the rapids.

By air A few weekly scheduled flights connect Zorg en Hoop and Kajana airstrip, usually tying in with the Monday and Friday fly-in packages at Awarradam. Flights take one hour and should be booked in conjunction with accommodation. Your lodge will also arrange a boat transfer from the airstrip.

By boat A twice-weekly *lantiboten* service connects Atjoni and Kajana, charging SRD 75 per person one-way. It leaves Kajana at 07.00 on Monday and Friday, and usually arrives at Atjoni around five hours later, in time to connect with buses to Paramaribo. The *lantiboten* usually starts the return trip from Atjoni before 13.00 on Monday and Friday, but it cannot reach Kajana the same day, since it's going against the current. This enforces an overnight stop in Djumu, before travelling on to Kajana the next morning (ie: Tuesday or Saturday). In Djumu, you can either arrange to sleep over at Kumalu Dream Island or Apiapaati (see page 214), or else join the locals and crash in a hammock in the village. The alternative to the *lantiboten* is to arrange a private charter with Kosindo River Lodge. This costs around SRD 575 per boat one-way between Kajana and Djumu, or SRD 1,150 all the way between Kajana and Atjoni.

 WHERE TO STAY AND EAT *Map, page 202*

🏠 **Awarradam Jungle Lodge** (13 chalets)
✆N3 50.700 W55 36.744; ✆477088; e mets@
sr.net; www.surinamevacations.com. Established
in 1993 & operated by METS Travel & Tours (see
page 78) in collaboration with local Saamaka
communities, this legendary lodge in a seriously
remote location, is about 10km upstream from
Kajana airstrip. It is on a lovely forested 200m-long
island & the rapids known variously as Awarradam
(after the *awarra* palm fruit) or Makakuzedi
(Monkey's Head) sweep past. It offers the best
accommodation on the river, in spacious stilted
wooden chalets each with 1 dbl & 1 sgl bed, a wide
balcony looking through the canopy to the river
& en-suite bathroom. Instead of a pool, there's a
lovely swimming spot close to the rapids, & other
facilities include a spa & large stilted dining area
with a view over the rapids. Activities include
kayaking, guided bush & village walks, & various
longer excursions. It can be visited only on 5-day,
4-night fly-in tours starting on Mon or 4-day,
3-night fly-in tours starting on Fri. Around SRD
2,460pp for the package, though you may find
cheaper rates by booking through other operators.
$$$$

🏠 **Kosindo River Lodge** (6 huts)
✆ N3 54.098 W55 34.446; m 8841273; e info@
surinamelodge.nl; www.surinamelodge.nl.
Situated on the steep east bank of the Gran Rio,
adjacent to the village of Kajana & opposite the
eponymous airstrip, this long-serving owner-
managed lodge lies on neat riverside grounds
studded with palms & other trees. Accommodation
is in river-facing huts with 2 or 4 beds with
framed nets, 24hr solar power, tiled floors, private
balconies & en-suite showers. Meals are served
in a stilted riverfront summerhouse & there is a
reasonably well-stocked shop & bar in the main
building. Activities include a guided village walk,
night trips to look for caimans, a 5hr round hike to
a 400m-high granite dome known as Okkoberg, a
wide variety of local cultural activities (for instance
woodcarving, calabash-making or cooking lessons)
& overnight boat trips to Sintiadam (see below).
SRD 170pp/night including all meals: all inclusive
5-day, 4-night packages from Paramaribo start
from around SRD 1,100pp depending on group size
& whether you travel by boat, air or a combination
of both. See ad, opposite page. **$$$**

WHAT TO SEE AND DO

Sintiadam The most remote yet accessible point along the river, the Sintiadam Rapids are about four hours upstream from Kajana, in an area with no permanent settlements and a fair amount of wildlife. The rapids can be visited by boat on a day trip from Kosindo or Awarradam, but there is a great camping area at the site, and you will get far more out of the trip by staying there overnight. Monkeys and birds are plentiful in the area, and larger species such as tapir and jaguar are seen very occasionally. Fishing is also rewarding. The return boat trip should cost around SRD 1,100, irrespective of the number of passengers, and Kosindo Lodge charges the same to sleep there (hammock and net; **$$**) as it does to stay at the lodge.

12

The Deep Interior

The most alluring region of Suriname, the deep interior – a term that embraces the entire country bar the coastal belt and area flanking the surfaced road between Paramaribo and Brokopondo – is also the most difficult to explore independently. Much of the region's limited tourist development is focused along the Upper Suriname (an area covered in the previous chapter), while the remainder is scattered across an area so vast it accounts for perhaps 80% of the country's total surface area.

The only road worth talking about in the western interior is the 300km tract of rock and dirt running west from Zanderij to the border town of Apoera. Poor though it is, this road offers access to several key tourist sites. The most popular of these, accessible by boat along the wide Coppename River, is Raleigh Falls, centrepiece of the vast and wildlife-rich Central Suriname Nature Reserve and a base for day hikes to the summit of the iconic Voltzberg. Other sites of interest close to the Apoera road are the Boven Coesewijne Nature Reserve, where regular canoeing trips are run on the river for which it is named, the island camp and Amerindian petroglyphs at Avanavero, and the pretty forest-ringed Blanche Marie Falls.

This long road west ends on the Guyana border, at the improbably remote town of Apoera, which scarcely qualifies as a prescribed tourist site, but does possess a certain off-the beaten-track appeal, thanks to its jungle-bound location alongside the Corantijn River. For hardy backpackers, Apoera is one of the few places in the deep interior accessible on public transport, and it can also be visited as part of a tour.

Untrammelled by roads and too far inland to be a realistic goal by boat, the far south is studded with a handful of upmarket riverside lodges that can be visited only on a fly-in package. Although relatively pricey, these lodges provide more adventurous visitors with a genuine jungle experience very different from the 'soft' introduction associated with the likes of Bergendal, but they are generally a lot less basic than the facilities at Blanche Marie or Raleigh Falls. The pick of these lodges, especially for wildlife enthusiasts, is Kabalebo Nature Reserve, which offers some of the best mammal and bird viewing in the country, as well as top-notch accommodation. The two other genuinely upmarket facilities in the deep interior are Palumeu, where the main attraction is the opportunity to interact with local Amerindians, and chilled-out Arapahu Island. Should these all sound too tame for your tastes, however, there's always the possibility of a week-long river expedition to Mount Kasikasima, or – for those with the money to throw at it – to the peerless field of ancient rock engravings discovered near Kwamalasamutu in 2004.

BOVEN COESEWIJNE NATURE RESERVE

Accessible only by boat, the little-known and untrammelled Boven ('Upper') Coesewijne Nature Reserve extends over 270km² to the south of the bauxite road connecting Zanderij to Apoera. As its name suggests, it protects the upper reaches

OPERATION GRASSHOPPER AND THE WEST SURINAME PLAN

What little infrastructure exists in the Surinamese interior is mostly associated with two landmark schemes hatched by Frank Essed, Minister of Development from 1958 to 1974. The first of these, initiated in 1959, was Operation Grasshopper, which entailed the cutting of grass airstrips at Tafelberg, Palumeu, Kabalebo and four other sites inaccessible by road, to be used as bases from which to map the interior's largely unexplored natural resources from the air. The second, a direct result of Operation Grasshopper, was the West Suriname Plan (WSP), the main impetus for which was the 1963 discovery of immense bauxite reserves in the remote Bakhuis Mountains, a short distance north of Blanche Marie Falls. ('Bakhuis', in case you were wondering, translates as 'Bakery', but has no significance beyond being the surname of the military officer who led a pioneering expedition to the mountains in 1901.)

Over the course of the late 1970s, Apoera, located on the east bank of the Corantijn River, was developed as a port to service the planned bauxite mine at Bakhuis, a venture funded largely by the Dutch government. This was also when the 300km dirt road running west of Zanderij was laid, along with an 80km railway line connecting Apoera directly to the foot of the Bakhuis Hills. Other long-term plans included the construction of a hydro-electric dam similar to Afobaka on the Kabalebo River, and the development of Apoera as a district capital and export harbour with its own aluminium smelter and housing capacity for 50,000 people.

In the wake of the 1980 coup, all Dutch development funds to Suriname were frozen. Furthermore, the declining market price of bauxite in the mid-1980s raised doubts about the economic feasibility of the WPS. As a result, the project ground to a halt, and subsequent attempts to revive it have yet to amount to much more than talk. So it is that for the time being, the bauxite resources at Bakhuis remain unexploited, the railway line constructed in the late 1970s has yet to see service and Apoera itself has the decidedly unfinished look of an urban planner's unrealised gleam in the eye.

of the Coesewijne River as it runs through the remote marshes and jungles of western Para to its coastal confluence with the Coppename. The nearby village of Bigi Poika holds the traditional rights over the reserve, whose diversity of habitats protects most wildlife associated with the coastal forests and rivers of Suriname, from jaguars, sloths and several species of monkey to manatee, giant river otter and spectacled caiman. Listed as an Important Bird Area, it protects a wide variety of forest and wetland species and it is one of the best places to search for the massive harpy eagle.

Among the most exciting and adventurous excursions offered from Paramaribo, a canoe trip along the Upper Coesewijne is also particularly rewarding for wildlife enthusiasts. As far as we are aware, the only operator currently running trips of this sort is Fietsen In Suriname (see page 78), which offers a one-day option, as well as an overnight trip lasting two days, bookable through most agents in Paramaribo. The starting point is 70km from Zanderij along the Witagron–Apoera road, about three hours' drive from Paramaribo, and the collection point is the village of Pakoeli (or Pakuli), which was at one point earmarked as a tourist centre by STINASU but remains totally undeveloped at the time of writing. The trip is suitable for

As visually inconspicuous as it is aurally dominant in the forest interior, the screaming piha (*Lipaugus vociferans*) is a smallish, dull grey-brown bird that tends to stick to the upper canopy. Here, it divides its time between eating fruit and emitting what must surely be the most characteristic sound of the Surinamese rainforest: a piercing, liquid and very loud three-note whistle reflected in several local Amerindian names for the bird, such as *pwe-pwe-yoh* and *kwow-kwee-yo*. In Suriname, this highly territorial bird is often referred to as the *bospolitie* ('bush police'), due to the siren-like nature of its call. Unsurprisingly, the screaming piha's is also one of the bird calls that features in the popular computer game 'Angry Birds Rio'. Nevertheless, despite its ubiquitous aural presence on forest walks in Suriname, seeing a screaming piha requires some luck and patience. Indeed, so little is known about its habits that only one sighting of a nesting bird has ever been recorded in Suriname.

beginners as well as experienced kayakers, covers 20km of smooth water per day and it is relatively undemanding as you are travelling downriver most of the way. The one-day trip costs SRD 345 per person and the overnight trip SRD 805 per person, including guide, tent or hammock, meals, transportation, boats, camping equipment and kayak equipment. The minimum group size is four.

CENTRAL SURINAME NATURE RESERVE (CSNR)

Suriname's most important conservation area, the CSNR accounts for almost 10% of the country's surface, extending over 16,000km² of untrammelled lowland and montane forest. It was created in 1998 following the amalgamation of three smaller nature reserves designated in the 1960s (namely the 780km² Raleigh Falls, 2,200km² Eilerts de Haan Mountains and 1,400km² Tafelberg Nature Reserve) with the vast corridor of forest that links them. Declared a UNESCO World Heritage Site in 1990, the CSNR is not only the largest reserve in Suriname but also the fifth-largest terrestrial protected area anywhere in South America. The CSNR incorporates Suriname's tallest mountain, the 1,280m Juliana Top in the Wilhelmina Range, along with the 1,026m Tafelberg ('Table Mountain') and many smaller granite domes of which the best known and most accessible is the 245m Voltzberg. It is bisected by the Coppename River, which forms part of the western boundary and is also the usual access point for tourists. It also incorporates important headwaters of the Suriname, Saramacca, Kabalebo and Corantijn rivers. The reserve is an important stronghold for large mammals such as jaguar, puma, ocelot, tapir, giant river otter, and it harbours all eight primate species recorded in Suriname.

It is a measure of the CSNR's remote and pristine character that, despite its vast area, no roads run close to it and the only area developed for tourism is Fungu Island on the Raleigh Falls, which can be accessed by air or by boat along the Coppename River. A major attraction of the Fungu area is its abundant wildlife, which tends to be far more conspicuous than in populated areas such as the Upper Suriname. Fungu is also within day-hiking distance of the Voltzberg, an iconic granite formation depicted on SRD 20 bank notes. The area is of great interest to birdwatchers, with almost 500 species recorded in the vicinity of Raleigh Falls alone, and Voltzberg is the best place in the country (if not anywhere) to tick off the splendid Guianan cock-of-the-rock. Other attractions include fishing in the river, swimming in the pools below camp and a boat trip to the Moeder Vallen ('Mother Falls'), a set of rapids that offers particularly enjoyable swimming.

GETTING THERE AND AWAY The main tourist focus is Fungu Island, which is accessible only by light aircraft or by boat from Witagron (aka Bitagron), on the east bank of the Coppename River where it is bridged by the Apoera road. **Charter flights** to the grassy airstrip on the south side on the island can be arranged through Blue Wing (see page 74) and other airlines operating out of Zorg en Hoop Airport in Paramaribo. It is more normal, however, to join an **organised four-day, three-night tour** and travel by road and then boat from Paramaribo. Small-group rates, sleeping in hammocks, are typically around SRD 1,400–1,600 all inclusive, but larger groups should be able to negotiate a better price.

It is difficult to visit the reserve affordably under your own steam, but direct buses do connect Paramaribo with Witagron on Fridays and Sundays, leaving from Saramacca Straat at 08.00 and Witagron at 15.00. The journey takes around five hours and costs SRD 20 per person one-way. Any transport heading to Apoera could also drop you at Witagron. However, boat hire starts at around SRD 1,000 for a small group and foreigners who arrive without a guide are likely to be asked a lot more. This is one instance where we would recommend that even the most independently minded of travellers join an organised tour.

 WHERE TO STAY AND EAT

 Fungu Island Lodge (16-bed house, 12 rooms, unlimited hammock space) ☏421683/476597; e stinasu@sr.net. Funded by Conservation International (CI) to help promote ecotourism to CSNR but handed over to STINASU before it was fully complete, this sprawling all-wood self-catering lodge is on the rocky southwest shore of the 2km-long Fungu Island overlooking the Raleigh Falls. The lodge lies on what used to be a Kwinti Marron village before the residents relocated to Witagron on the Apoera road, so the gardens are studded with mango, cashew, coconut palm & other fruiting trees, though the rest of the island supports a dense cover of indigenous forest. The pick of the accommodation is Gonini River Lodge, which contains a dozen private en-suite rooms each with electric lighting, twin beds & a balcony overlooking the river. Cheaper beds are available in the 16-bunk Tamanua Lodge, which is effectively an open-sided dormitory with shared facilities. Finally, the stunning 3-storey main building overlooking the river, originally intended to be a restaurant & visitor centre, now operates as a massive hammock hut that could easily accommodate 50-odd visitors, & there are other buildings available to handle any overspill. The lodge is entirely self-catering & there is no official shop, but the staff sell overpriced beers & a few other goods from their houses. In addition to a shared ablution block, you can swim & wash in a series of calm pools around the rapids (ideally using biodegradable soap, though you'd probably be the 1st person ever to do so here!). The lodge is visited regularly by a semi-tame troop of squirrel monkeys, & the birdlife is superb, especially along the airstrip & the short path connecting it to the lodge. It is rumoured that CI might soon resume construction & complete what it started with fresh funding. SRD 210/270 en-suite dbl/trpl in Gonini Lodge; SRD 60pp/night in Tamanua Lodge, with preference given to larger groups; SRD 50pp/night to hang a hammock; a one-off nature fee of SRD 30pp is also levied. **$–$$**

WHAT TO SEE AND DO

Voltzberg hike The most popular day trip from Fungu is the long and quite challenging 14km round trip to the top of the Voltzberg, which usually takes the best part of a day at a leisurely pace with a few breaks, though fit travellers could probably make it there and back in four hours. Departing from the east bank of the river a short boat ride upstream from the lodge, the first 5km run through the

A 1.1km-long sugarloaf rising roughly 150m above the forest canopy, the Voltzberg is a monolithic granite dome with two bare peaks separated by a giant fissure. The taller of the two peaks, ascendable from the east along a steep and largely unshaded footpath, attains an altitude of 245m and terminates in a tall cliff offering immense views over the surrounding forest to distant mountains. As with other inselbergs in the Suriname interior, the Voltzberg comprises an outcrop of two-billion-year-old biotitic granite that has over the years proved to be more resistant to glacial and other weathering than the surrounding bedrock. Though much of the mountain is bare, a few hardy xerophytic plants, including several orchid and grass species, are adapted to its hot, rocky and relatively dry slopes.

The first outsiders known to reach and ascend the Voltzberg were members of the 1901 Coppename Expedition led by the Dutch military officer Major LA Bakhuis (for whom the bauxite-bearing mountains further west are named). Voltzberg was named 20 years earlier by Professor K Martin, who saw the dome from a distance whilst navigating Raleigh Falls on his Coppename Expedition of 1881. Martin named it after the German geologist Dr Franz Voltz, who had travelled along the Coppename River in 1855 but died that same year after his return to Paramaribo, without fully documenting his journey. It is known that Voltz saw the dome that would later bear his name, but it seems unlikely he approached it, as he mistook it for a chalkstone formation, which would be feasible only from a distance. The 1901 Bakhuis Expedition is credited with the discovery of two other nearby domes, the 362m Van Stockum Berg (named after the expedition member who first ascended it) and the 453m Van de Vijck Top (named after the then chairman of the Royal Netherlands Geographic Society). Today, the peak is studded with cairns and plaques commemorating subsequent ascents, the earliest one by Governor Aarnoud van Heemstra in 1923.

forest, crossing a few streams along the way, but are otherwise quite flat underfoot and shady all the way. Squirrel monkeys are the most conspicuous primates seen *en route*, but brown capuchin and black spider monkeys are also frequently spotted. About 1km before reaching the base of the inselberg, you cross a low sparsely vegetated granite rock offering great view to the Voltzberg. Then it is back into the forest until you reach the rock base, from where it a steep 20–40-minute scramble to the top, first through a ravine with good handholds, then on an exposed slope that has a reassuringly coarse texture except after rain, when multiple streams make the slope treacherously slippery and climbing is forbidden. The stunning views from the top of the Voltzberg stretch more than 50km south to the Wilhelmina Range and Tafelberg. Unless you are prepared to drink stream water along the way, you need to carry your own liquid – at least two litres in this sweaty climate – and you might also want to carry a few snacks.

Cock-of-the-rock lek The ultimate must-see for most serious birders visiting Raleigh falls is the Guianan cock-of-the-rock (see box, page 224), which can be observed with reasonable ease at a lek (communal display and breeding ground) near the base of the Voltzberg. If you want to look for this stunning bird, you'll need to make special arrangements with your guide, as it entails a side excursion of roughly 30 minutes from the main trail to reach the lek. It used to be possible to stay overnight at a basic hammock camp at a research station close to the lek, which greatly increased your chance of a good cock-of-the-rock sighting, but this facility has been closed to tourists since 2013 and it is unclear when or whether it will reopen. Until it does, your best chance of sighting would be to get away from Fungu Island Lodge as early as possible (fit walkers could probably cover the ground in two hours in either direction) and allow yourself at least two hours at the site.

Other birding The Raleigh Falls area ranks among the country's top ornithological hotspots, and at least 480 species have been recorded there. The relatively open gardens of Fungu Island Lodge are a good place for South American birding novices to get started, with some of the more conspicuous species being white-throated and channel-billed toucan, green-backed trogon, black nunbird, green oropendola and various tanagers. It is also worth standing vigil along the river with binoculars, keeping watch for pairs of the stunning scarlet, red-and-green and blue-and-yellow macaws, which regularly cross between the banks in the early morning or late afternoon. Herons, egrets, kingfishers and even green ibis are also often seen along the river, while a variety of raptors – sometimes including the eagerly-sought-after king vulture and harpy eagle – might be seen soaring overhead. Also very rewarding is the airstrip a few hundred metres from camp, since it offers clearer views into the forest canopy than you will get on a walking trail, and a good chance of spotting the likes of green and black-necked aracaris, lineated woodpecker, red-fan parrot, crimson topaz, white-tailed trogon and little chachalaca.

Birding along the Voltzberg trail is tougher, thanks to the density of the forest, but it is also more likely to throw up good forest interior species such as the white bellbird, white-headed piping guan, yellow-throated woodpecker, great jacamar, rufous-throated ant-bird and ochre-bellied flycatcher.

GUIANAN COCK-OF-THE-ROCK

A Guianan endemic associated with the rocky outcrops on whose walls it nests, the Guianan cock-of-the-rock (*Rupicola rupicola*) ranks as one of the most beautiful, eagerly sought after and easily identifiable of the Neotropical birds. This is thanks to the male's brilliant orange feathering complete with a Mohawk-like black-rimmed crest. A substantial bird, measuring up to 30cm long, it is not particularly shy or rare, but it is very localised and difficult to see casually due to the relatively inaccessible nature of its preferred habitat. If you know where to look, however, it is actually quite an easy bird to locate due to the male's highly competitive and complex courting displays, which take place at communal leks, where all the birds sharing a cluster of territories usually gather a few times a day. The best known of these is the lek used by a community of around 50 males on the lower slopes of the Voltzberg. Leks are most active during the mating season, which is during the first few months of the year, and in the early morning (before 09.00) and late afternoon (after 16.00), when the males call, fluff up their feathers and dance to attract the attention of the females. With patience though, you're likely to see a couple of male cock-of-the-rocks at the lek below the Voltzberg at any time of the day or year.

This pretty waterfall on the Nickerie River lies in the Bakhuis foothills, about 15km north of the main road between Zanderij and Apoera. At around 100m wide, this waterfall is one of the most impressive cascades in Suriname, not so much because of its height but because of the sheer volume of water that tumbles over it in the rainy season.

The first outsider to reach this site was Lieutenant Van Drimmelen, then the District Commissioner of Nickerie, who visited in 1897 and named the falls after his wife Blanche Marie. Situated on private property, the waterfall became a popular tourist attraction following the construction of the Apoera road in the late 1970s, when the Guesthouse Dubois, then with a bed capacity of more than 140, attracted Paramaribo weekenders in droves. It has since fallen out of vogue, partly due to the deterioration of the road and partly because of a gradual decline in accommodation standards and facilities. Nevertheless, Blanche Marie still ranks among the most alluring sites in the interior. It is one of the few Surinamese waterfalls worthy of the name, as opposed to being glorified rapids. In addition, the remote location more than 50km from the nearest human habitation, is a good spot for wildlife spotting. All eight of the country's monkey species are present in the area, along with a varied and vociferous assemblage of colourful forest birds.

GETTING THERE AND AWAY Blanche Marie Falls are about 315km from Paramaribo by road. Follow the Apoera road west from Zanderij via Witagron, then continue westward for another 120km to the junction (✪ N4 50.794 W56 52.280), where you need to turn left along a road marked by a small and easily missed red signpost. About 4km along this road, turn left again at another small red signpost, from where it's another 10km or so to the lodge along a very rough and in parts muddy 4x4 track that passes through several deep but firm-based pools, and is often obstructed by fallen trees. The falls are not accessible by public transport and most people visit as part of an organised tour. Operators running regular departures to Blanche Marie include All Suriname Tours, Jenny Tours and Orange Travel (see page 78). Rates start at around SRD 1,150 per person for a four-day, three-night tour, and a visit to the falls is usually twinned with a stop in Apoera.

🏠 WHERE TO STAY AND EAT

🏠 **Guesthouse Dubois** m 8776700. Boasting a wonderful location on a grassy rise overlooking a pretty forest-lined stretch of the Nickerie River, Guesthouse Dubois was the largest & most popular accommodation facility in the Surinamese interior in its 1990s heyday. More recently, following the death of its eponymous owner, it has undergone a gradual decline, but things have picked up slightly in the last couple of years under new management. Only 1 of the 6 riverside houses, comprising 5 rooms with 12 beds, is properly functional at the moment, but there are plans to revive & redecorate some of the others soon. Meanwhile, most of the former public areas, such as the bar & dance floor, now function as hammock huts used by group tours. The once excellent facilities are now limited to a row of flush toilets & showers in cubicles in the main building. You can also swim & wash in the river below the lodge. It is normally self-catering only, & no drinks are for sale, but with some notice, ideally around a week, meals can be provided & drinks brought in. There is no telephone reception, so if you cannot get through to the manager's number provided above, then contact Tant Annie in Apoera (see page 228) & she will get a message through. SRD 75pp bed only; SRD 60 to camp or hang a hammock. **$**

WHAT TO SEE AND DO The main attraction at Blanche Marie is the actual waterfall, which lies about 20 minutes' walk upriver along a wide and well-marked track through the forest. The waterfall is most impressive during the rainy season, but dry season visitors can usually swim in the frothing pelled-like pool below the main fall as compensation. The footpath there, best taken slowly and quietly, is an excellent place to look for squirrel monkeys and capuchins, along with birds of the forest interior, colourful painted frogs and other small wildlife. The stretch of river immediately below the guesthouse is home to giant river otters, while jaguars and pumas are very occasionally seen in the area. The park-like grounds of the guesthouse and surrounding gallery forest offer very rewarding birding, with plenty of parrots, hummingbirds, toucans and raptors conspicuous, especially in the early morning. Time permitting, you can also walk an hour upriver (or, when the river is high, take a boat) to the smaller but very pretty Eldorado Falls.

APOERA

Despite being the largest town in Suriname's most expansive administrative district, Apoera (sometimes spelled Apura) is by any other standards a tiny place, supporting a total population of around 3,000 people, including a significant proportion of Amerindians. Set alongside the Corantijn River on the border with Guyana, Apoera is essentially a relic of the West Suriname Plan (see box, page 220) wherein it was envisaged as a future district capital and bauxite export centre supporting a population of around 50,000. The town centre was laid out in the late 1970s and some 80 stilted timber houses were constructed, along with a government guesthouse, swimming pool and other sporting facilities. The harbour, about 1.5km south of the town centre, was built at the same time, and doubled as the terminus of an 80km railway line to the proposed mine at Bakhuis. After the West Suriname Plan fell through, however, many moveable assets associated with its projected urban hub were sold or relocated by the government, and the local economy stagnated. Today, the biggest business in Apoera is the riverfront Greenheart Sawmill, which processes and exports timber for the international forestry company of the same name.

From a visitor's perspective, Apoera's main points of interest are the Corantijn River, the Amerindian village of Klein ('Little') Kwamalasamutu south of the harbour and the town centre itself, where a scattering of wooden houses and other buildings are interspersed with several substantial forest patches. For independent travellers using public transport, a visit to remote Apoera might fairly be characterised as travel for its own sake, but the town also forms part of long travel loop through western Suriname Apoera, linked as it is to Nieuw Nickerie by a twice weekly boat service.

GETTING THERE AND AWAY A night in Apoera is often included on the itinerary of organised tours from Paramaribo to Blanche Marie Falls or Avanavero. It can also be visited independently, although there is no formal public transport from Paramaribo. A few private minivans cover the route weekly, however, usually with room for up to 15 passengers. They leave from Dr Sophie Redmond Straat close to the US Embassy, the fare is SRD 150 per person and you will need to pay the same for your luggage if it occupies a seat. There are no fixed departure days or times, so you will need to check what's going and book a seat in advance. Either call Tant Annie (see below) or one of the following individual drivers: Baby (m 8760700), Terry (m 8593769) or Tony (m 8677475).

A scheduled boat service connects Nieuw Nickerie to Apoera. It leaves Nieuw Nickerie every Monday and Friday morning, and Apoera every Tuesday and Saturday morning. It costs SRD 40 per person one-way and takes up to seven hours. You can contact Captain Arupa (m 8617713) for further details.

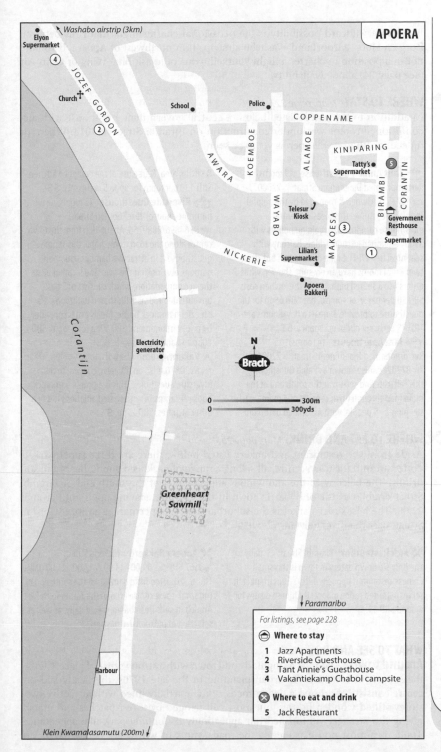

APOERA

Washabo airstrip (3km)

Elyon
Supermarket

(4)

J O Z E F   G O R D O N

Church ✝

(2)

School ●

Police ●

C O P P E N A M E

K O E M B O E

A L A M O E

K I N I P A R I N G

Tatty's
Supermarket ●

(5)

B I R A M B I

C O R A N T I N

A W A R A

W A Y A B O

Telesur
Kiosk

M A K O E S A

(3)

Government
Resthouse

Supermarket

(1)

N I C K E R I E

Lilian's
Supermarket ●

Apoera
Bakkerij ●

C o r a n t i j n

Electricity
generator ●

N

Bradt

0 ————————— 300m
0 ————————— 300yds

Greenheart
Sawmill

Paramaribo

For listings, see page 228

⬠ **Where to stay**

1 Jazz Apartments
2 Riverside Guesthouse
3 Tant Annie's Guesthouse
4 Vakantiekamp Chabol campsite

✖ **Where to eat and drink**

5 Jack Restaurant

Harbour

Klein Kwamalasamutu (200m) ↓

The Deep Interior   APOERA

12

A more wildcard possibility is the occasional charter flight that runs between Zorg en Hoop Airport and Washabo airstrip, 4km northwest of Apoera. If you are not in a position to charter a flight yourself, you could ask Blue Wing or Gum Air (see page 74) about availability.

⌂ WHERE TO STAY *Map, page 227*

In addition to the places listed below, a central government guesthouse with air-conditioned rooms was under construction on Birambi Street in 2014. When, or indeed whether, it will open is yet to be seen.

⌂ **Tant Annie's Guesthouse** (9 rooms) Kertomohamed Djoeminem Straat; ✆220007; m 8672538. Owned & managed by the helpful Tant ('Aunt') Annie, this pleasant central guesthouse comprises 2 adjoining houses with a fully equipped kitchen, fridge, balcony with seating & free Wi-Fi. Some of the small but clean twin & dbl rooms have an en-suite shower, while others use a shared bath. Use of the kitchen costs SRD 50 per party, or you can pay SRD 65pp for the guesthouse to provide 3 meals a day. Rooms are SRD 75 each, sgl or dbl occupancy. **$$**

⌂ **Jazz Apartments** (4 rooms) Kertomohamed Djoeminem Straat; ✆220014; m 8770284. Also known as Paul's Guesthouse, this self-catering set-up at the south end of the main road through town consists of 4 rooms, each sleeping 2–5 people, with AC, shared bathroom

& sitting area, & free use of the equipped kitchen. SRD 130 per room for up to 5 occupants. **$$**

⌂ **Riverside Guesthouse** (2 rooms, hammock house) Jozef Gordon Straat; m 8764896/8889256. About 1km from the town centre along the road to Washabo, this simple guesthouse is in attractive bamboo-clumped gardens overlooking the river. The location beats the accommodation, which consists of 2 basic unventilated rooms with shared bathroom, & a breezier hammock house. Meals can be provided by prior arrangement. SRD 50pp for a room; SRD 40pp to hang a hammock. **$**

⋏ **Vakantiekamp Chabol** Jozef Gordon Straat; m 8920876. Also on the river, *en route* to the Riverside Guesthouse, this is a simple hammock house & campsite with shared ablutions but few other facilities. SRD 25pp. **$**

✕ WHERE TO EAT AND DRINK *Map, page 227*

Aside from the restaurant and bakery listed below, there are three supermarkets dotted around the town centre, all selling a range of packaged goods, beers and soft drinks. The balcony of the anonymous supermarket at the south end of Birambi Straat doubles as the only bar in town in the evening, staying open until around 22.00. The best supermarket is the suburban Elyon Supermarket on Jozef Gordon Straat, past the Riverside Guesthouse.

✕ **Jack Restaurant** Birambi Straat; ⊕ daily. The only sit-down eatery in town is this small Chinese restaurant opposite Tatty's Supermarket. It serves a limited range of local & Chinese dishes for around SRD 15. **$**

✕ **Apoera Bakkerij** Nickerie Straat; ✆8667118; ⊕ 09.00–13.30 & 17.00–21.00 daily. This unexpected little gem lies at the south end of the small town centre around the corner from Tant Annie's. It sells fresh bread, baked daily, as well as a selection of inexpensive pastries. **$**

WHAT TO SEE AND DO

Around town Apoera is a singularly odd town with a strong sense of place. Clearly the subject of considerable urban planning in the late 1970s, the neatly laid-out centre consists of around a dozen roads, some partially lined with attractive two-storey stilted wooden houses, but most still fringed by forest patches and marsh, giving it a strangely unfinished but appealingly *au naturel* park-like appearance. Traffic is almost non-existent, so the roads, most of which are neatly paved, are great for cycling or jogging, while the forest patches support a wealth of birds you'd expect to see in a jungle or nature reserve rather than in a town centre. There's plenty more accessible forest immediately to the north and south of town too, and doubtless a good chance of encountering monkeys and other forest mammals. Another option, aside from the sites mentioned below, would be to walk north along Jozef Gordon Straat for around 4km, with the Corantijn River on your left, until you reach Washabo, a smaller Amerindian village that houses the main clinic and airstrip servicing Apoera, as well as a worthwhile Sunday market (busiest in the morning) on the right side of the main road next to the football field.

Greenheart Sawmill and Apoera Harbour About 20 minutes' walk south of the town centre along Jozef Gordon Straat, Apoera Harbour was developed in the 1970s as the terminus of the Bakhuis Railway. On the way there, you pass the Greenheart Sawmill, which stands on the left side of the road, along with piles and piles of massive ancient tree trunks, felled for export. It's rather a sad sight – the forest equivalent of a mortuary – even though it is all sourced from a legitimate concession at ostensibly sustainable rates. Much of this timber leaves Apoera on the back of a truck, but the harbour itself is clearly used to shift large amounts of granite rock, quarried near Blanche Marie and transported by boat to Nieuw Nickerie and Paramaribo, where it is used for construction. At the end of the unused railway line in the harbour, a solitary red-and-yellow carriage stands abandoned and overgrown with vines.

Klein Kwamalasamutu Set alongside the Corantijn River, a few hundred metres south of the harbour and easily visited in conjunction with it, this settlement of stilted wooden homesteads is inhabited by around 200 Amerindians who originate from the Tiriyó village of Kwamalasamutu in the deep south. Not as traditional as some tour operators might have you believe, Klein ('Little') Kwamalasamutu it is a friendly enough place, and there is no restriction on walking around unguided, though it would be something of a protocol breach to take photographs. You'll certainly win friends if you splash out on some of the inexpensive traditional jewellery made from fruit pits and other organic materials, sold by several of the local women.

Semi-traditional dances are put on by the village children under the auspices of the We Sarwatho Adatokoto (literally 'We are the Beautiful Flowers') Troupe, which was established in 2012. Usually held at dusk, the performance costs around SRD 250 per party and is best booked at least 24 hours in advance through the (English-speaking) troupe leader Gwendolyn (m 8611436).

AVANAVERO FALLS

Situated on the Kabalebo River, a 375km drive southwest of Paramaribo, the pretty Avanavero Falls was earmarked as the site of a hydro-electric dam in the late 1970s, one designed to power the proposed bauxite mine at Bakhuis and aluminium processing plant at Apoera. The dam never happened of course, but a road was cut all the way there and the village built in anticipation of the dam construction still features on some maps of Suriname, even though its inhabitants abandoned it in favour of Apoera in the early 1980s. Today, Avanavero is a peaceful end-of-the-road kind of place, boasting a lovely island lodge flanked by two waterfalls. It also lies within easy walking distance of the most accessible of several ancient Amerindian petroglyph (rock engraving) sites in the Corantijn Basin. The petroglyph in question is engraved onto a rock next to a small stream, and depicts a squat humanlike form. Because it is quite remote from human settlements, Avanavero is also very good for wildlife, protecting a similar selection of species to Blanche Marie and Raleigh Falls. Other attractions include swimming in the rapids and hiking in the Wanawiro Hills south of the river.

GETTING THERE AND AWAY The most westerly terminus of the road constructed to service the West Suriname Project, Avanavero lies around 90km west of the road junction south to Apoera. The road is in variable condition and usually requires a 4x4. Unless you are kitted up in full-on expedition mode, the area can only realistically be visited with a tour operator. The main road runs through the abandoned village of Avanavero, from where Wanawiro Lodge is signposted to the right. It is then a 15-minute boat ride from the launch site to the lodge. A good contact for four- to five-day trips to Avanavero from Paramaribo is All Suriname Tours (see page 78).

 WHERE TO STAY AND EAT

Wanawiro Lodge (2 huts) m 6803173. On a forested island a short boat ride from Avanavero, this remote owner-managed lodge set in an area teeming with monkeys & birds provides comfortable accommodation in a 10-bed wooden cabin. There is also room for 10 more people in a hammock hut. Catering mainly to tour groups, it usually only takes 1 self-catering party at a time. To contact the manager, leave a message at the number above & he will get back to you. SRD 160pp inc boat transfers to/from the mainland. **$$**

ARAPAHU ISLAND

This remote island in the Corantijn, almost 300km upstream from the river mouth, is the site of a small and little-known upmarket camp offering access to the attractive Frederik Willem IV Falls, the King George Falls, and an ancient petroglyph site. The surrounding area is practically uninhabited so it is also home to plenty of monkeys and other large mammals, as well as an impressive avifauna. Access is by air only, with the closest airstrip being Amatopo, a 75-minute flight from Zorg en Hoop Airport. From Amatopo, it's a ten-minute walk through the jungle to the river, then 30 minutes by boat to the camp. Accommodation (**$$$$**) is in en-suite thatched cottages with private balconies, and there is also a communal lounge, hammock hut, restaurant and bar. Three-day, two-night tours start at around SRD 3,700 per person including flights, accommodation, meals and activities.

KWAMALASAMUTU

The most southerly destination in Suriname, Kwamalasamutu is a legendarily remote Amerindian village set on the banks of the Sipaliwini River, close to its confluence with the Corantijn. It is home to around 1,000 predominantly Tiriyó inhabitants, who were first exposed to the outside world in 1960 as a result of Operation Grasshopper (see box, page 220), and have since been heavily influenced by the teachings of Baptist missionaries.

The main attraction of the region is the elaborate petroglyphs engraved into the walls of the Werehpai Caves, which lie about two hours' walk from the village along a rough jungle path. Discovered by outsiders in 2004, Werehpai is a formation of gigantic boulders and overhangs that extends across a couple of hectares, and is decorated with at least 350 ancient rock carvings, the greatest concentration in the Amazon region. Depicting humanoid forms, animals and abstract patterns, the richly symbolic petroglyphs are almost impossible to date, but are probably more than 4,000 years old, the work of unknown forest dwellers presumably ancestral to the Amerindians that inhabit the region today. The rocks are also a nesting site for the Guianan cock-of-the-rock.

Following the discovery of the Werehpai engravings, Conservation International attempted to develop community-based tourism at Kwamalasamutu, most notably with the construction of the Iwana Samu Rainforest Lodge on the river 15 minutes by boat from the airstrip. Unfortunately, this facility is now more or less defunct and few operators run tours to Kwamalasamutu. An exception is Access Suriname ↘ 424522; m 8862406; e info@surinametravel.com; www.surinametravel.com), which will set up a four-day, three-night fly-in camping expedition to the village and petroglyph site for around SRD 6,000 per person.

KABALEBO NATURE RESERVE

The closest thing in the Surinamese interior to a genuinely world-class eco-lodge, the private Kabalebo Nature Reserve also provides some of the region's finest wildlife viewing and birding, thanks to its isolated location in a region with no permanent villages. The reserve was established in 2004 when the dynamic owner-managers built Main Lodge next to Kabalebo airstrip (cut in 1962 and a relic of Operation Grasshopper), around 150km from the closest road. Today, the reserve supports three different lodges overlooking the Kabalebo River (a tributary of the Corantijn) and the forested Misty Mountain, which rises to around 250m on the opposite bank. As with many other sites in the interior, the reserve supports a varied birdlife (around 300 species have been recorded) along with conspicuous populations of several monkey species, but it is also perhaps the best place to seek out more elusive medium to large mammals. The lowland tapir is often seen crossing the airstrip, the peculiar capybara and giant river otter are frequently encountered on boat trips, the beautiful ocelot often visits the camp at night and jaguars are observed in the vicinity from time to time. Activities on offer include guided walks, kayaking, swimming in the various rapids and waterfalls, game fishing, birdwatching and night walks. Facilities include a wide wooden balcony where you can relax on a hammock, a large swimming pool surrounded by a varnished wooden deck and shady sunbeds and a well-stocked honesty bar. Also impressive are the friendly English-speaking staff, the relatively high standard of guiding and the unusually varied buffet-style meals.

GETTING THERE AND AWAY Kabalebo Nature Reserve is accessible only by air from Zorg en Hoop Airport, and the flight takes around an hour. Taking one of the scheduled flights on Tuesday or Saturday, a return ticket costs around SRD 1,300 per person, but charter flights can also be arranged for other days and these are usually more expensive.

WHERE TO STAY AND EAT Note that all accommodation can be booked together with flights as one package directly through Kabalebo's head office (↘ 426532; m 8201902; e info@kabalebo.com; www.kabalebo.com), or through most other upmarket operators in Paramaribo (see pages 78–9). Low season discounts are available in January, April, May, June and December.

⌂ ❋ **River Cabins** (3 rooms) Though not as smart as Inspiration Point, this trio of tall stilted cabins set in a riverside clearing surrounded by pristine jungle is ideal for those seeking peace & quiet, as well as for keen wildlife enthusiasts. Its isolation might not suit nervous travellers though who are experiencing the jungle for the first time. Each cabin has a bedroom with AC, en-suite hot shower, minibar & a balcony overlooking the river & forest on the opposite bank. At the opposite end of the airstrip, it is a 15min walk or 5min drive to Main Lodge (where meals are eaten & and most activities start) in the resort's golf cart. SRD 880/1435 sgl/dbl inc meals, soft drinks & activities. **$$$$$**

🏠 ✳ **Main Lodge** (10 rooms) The oldest structure at Kabalebo, Main Lodge is a large stilted wooden building with a wide communal balcony facing Misty Mountain & a central dining area & honesty bar. The en-suite rooms are small &

uncluttered but very comfortable, & come with twin beds, hot shower, fan & AC. SRD 543/900 sgl/dbl inc meals, soft drinks & activities. **$$$$**

🏠 **Inspiration Point** (6 rooms) The newest & smartest lodge on the property lies in an orchard overlooking the swimming pool, perhaps 200m from Main Lodge. The en-suite wooden rooms all have stylish wooden furnishings, hot shower, fan, AC, private rear balcony facing the forest, & front balcony offering a view towards Misty Mountain. Meals are served in Main Lodge. SRD 720/1240 sgl/dbl inc meals, soft drinks & activities. **$$$$$**

ACTIVITIES
Misty Mountain hike The popular hike to the top of Misty Mountain, which lies on the south bank of the river opposite the resort, is usually undertaken on the first full day in Kabalebo. Depending on your fitness level, the ascent, which is quite steep towards the end, might take anywhere from 1½ to 2½ hours, and there's a good chance of spotting black spider, squirrel and other monkeys on the way up. You can swim in the Charlie Waterfall on the return trip. A less strenuous variation on this walk involves visiting the waterfall but not climbing the mountain.

Fishing Though more popular with locals than tourists, fishing on the Kabalebo River is excellent, with some of the more desirable species being Anjoemara, catfish, pakoe, toekoenari, wolf fish and various types of piranha. The largest fish caught on the river to date was clocked in at 130kg.

Kayaking A highlight for wildlife enthusiasts is the two-hour kayaking trips that run from the lodge to a set of rapids about 12km downriver. Moving more quietly and slowly than motorised boats, these offer a good chance of spotting wildlife including capybara and otter, as well as aquatic and forest birds. Look out for the spectacular rufescent tiger heron, which is often seen sitting unobtrusively on overhanging branches along the river.

Birdwatching Kabalebo must rank as one of the country's top birding sites, not least because it is one of the few places in the country where the guides all have some basic identification skills. Around 280 species have been recorded to date, with some of the more alluring being harpy eagle, king vulture, blue-headed parrot, black skimmer and buff-throated saltator. The area around the lodge is especially good for tanagers and hummingbirds (the latter are attracted by feeding devices close to the main building), while a slow walk along the airstrip is likely to yield several types of parrot, toucan and other forest species. Serious birders should think about pre-booking the services of the resort's specialist birding guide, which costs SRD 210 per day for up to three people.

PALUMEU AND MOUNT KASIKASIMA

Situated on a bend in the Tapanahony River, a tributary of the Marowijne, Palumeu Jungle Lodge is a small but comfortable community-run lodge at the confluence with the Palumeu (also spelled Paloemeu), deep in the western interior around 250km south of Paramaribo. Surrounded by jungle on all sides, the lodge lies alongside the eponymous village, a remote community of around 300 Amerindians. Palumeu Lodge is managed by villagers in collaboration with the Paramaribo-based tour operator METS, and it is particularly suited to those with an interest in Amerindian culture. Attractions include day hikes, boat trips, swimming in the rapids, birdwatching and wildlife viewing, though mammals are less conspicuous than in places such as Kabalebo or Raleigh Falls, as subsistence hunting is still practised in the area. Palumeu is also a springboard for longer expeditions, also operated by METS, to the utterly remote and very beautiful Kasikasima Mountain, which rises to an altitude of 780m from the west bank of the Palumeu River, 70km further towards the border with Brazil.

GETTING THERE AND AWAY The only realistic way to get to Palumeu is by air from Paramaribo's Zorg en Hoop Airport, a fantastic flight over the endless swathe of multi-hued broccoli-textured green rainforest that runs towards and beyond the Brazilian border. The lodge and village both lie alongside Palumeu airstrip, which is also known as Vincent Fajks airstrip in memory of a Polish pilot killed when his plane carrying building materials crashed during the construction. Almost everybody visits Palumeu on one of two standard packages offered by METS, a four-day, three-night tour starting on Friday or a five-day, four-night tour starting on Monday. Rates for these packages start at SRD 2,450 per person sharing, including flights, accommodation, meals and activities, and can be booked at the same price through any operator in Paramaribo (see pages 78–9). Kasikasima can be visited only on eight-day, seven-night packages, which usually start on Mondays or Fridays to tie in with flights to Palumeu, and cost SRD 3,250 per person all-inclusive, with a minimum group size of four. It would, of course, be possible to arrange Palumeu or Kasikasima trips of other durations or with other starting days, but this would entail chartering a flight from Zorg en Hoop.

🏠 **WHERE TO STAY AND EAT**

🏠 **Palumeu Jungle Lodge** (10 rooms) ☎ 477088; e mets@sr.net; www.surinamevacations. com. Comprising 5 thatched wooden houses spread out along a rise overlooking the jungle-fringed river, the spacious semi-detached rooms here all come with twin or dbl bed with nets, a neat tiled en-suite bathroom, & a private balcony with seating & a view. This is where all guests booked on a Palumeu package stay. **$$$$**

🏠 **Kasikasima Lodge** (5 rooms) ☎ 477088; e mets@sr.net; www.surinamevacations.com. Right next to Palumeu Jungle Lodge but run under a different name, this more modest lodge caters exclusively to guests on a Kasikasima package. It occupies the top floor of a 2-storey wooden house & consists of 5 small dbl or twin rooms sharing a lounge & bathroom. **$$$**

WHAT TO SEE AND DO

Palumeu village Packages normally start with a guided afternoon tour of Palumeu village, which was established in the 1960s when the residents of several smaller and even more remote riverside settlements – Tiriyó, Wajana and Akurio – relocated to the confluence following the establishment here of Vincent Fajks airstrip. The village consists of a few dozen stilted wooden houses scattered around two important communal congregation points: the traditional thatched circular meeting place and an open-side Baptist church. Its residents mostly wear modern Western dress, but still indulge in traditional subsistence occupations such as cultivation, hunting and baking flat round cassava loaves. Surprisingly, given that Palumeu Jungle Lodge is ostensibly a community-based concern, it is forbidden to walk around the village without a guide, creating a rather contrived feel to any interaction between tourists and locals, and photography of people is generally not allowed unless you pay a fee. At some point during your stay, you will probably also be taken to the forest to be taught local bow-and-arrow techniques.

Short excursions A popular half-day excursion, usually undertaken on your first morning at the lodge, is the ascent of a relatively bare 235m granite outcrop called Poti Hill. It's a six-hour round trip by boat and on foot, breakfasting along the way, and you should see plenty of birds and possibly a few monkeys from the river. The walking component of the excursion is not particularly demanding, taking around 30 minutes in either direction, and it yields a good view over the surrounding jungle. Also popular is a full-day excursion to the Mabuka Rapids, about two hours away by boat. You can swim in the sauna-like waters, and the excursion includes a barbecue lunch.

Visiting Mount Kasikasima Remote, even by Surinamese interior standards, Kasikasima can be visited only as part of an extended seven-night tour involving a night at Palumeu's Kasikasima Lodge at the start and end, a night in a temporary camp at Kamakabari *en route*, and then four nights at the semi-permanent Kasikasima Camp near the base of the mountain. The main attraction in the area, aside from the total remoteness, Mount Kasikasima is a magnificent granite sugarloaf comprising a dozen separate peaks, the tallest of which rises to around 780m and whose forested side can be ascended via a steep footpath to an altitude of around 500m, from where it offers views across the rainforest all the way to the Brazilian border. Held as sacred by locals (its name reputedly translates as 'House of the Ruler'), the mountain is also home to plenty of birds and several bird species rare at lower altitudes, including the iconic Guianan cock-of-the-rock.

UPPER MAROWIJNE

Remote and seldom visited by tourists, the island-studded and forest-fringed Upper Marowijne is renowned for its many rapids, which are typically wilder than their counterparts on the Upper Suriname. The river not only runs along the border with French Guiana, but is also the eastern border of Tapanahony, the largest of Suriname's 62 administrative *resorts*. (Indeed, with a surface area of 42,000km², Tapanahony accounts for slightly more than a quarter of the country's surface area, yet it is populated by a mere 15,000 people). The main inhabitants of the Upper Marowijne are the Paramacca, a Marron people numbering around 1,000 whose unique language incorporates many English and Portuguese words. The Paramacca leader or Gran Man is based at Lange Tabiki ('Long Island'), which lies about 80km upriver of Albina, facing the most southerly road head anywhere along the river. About a two-hour motorboat ride further south, Grankreek ('Big Creek') is graced by the small but attractive Mina Falls, which lie two hours' hike into the jungle. Further south still, Stoelman's Island, also known as Stoeli, can be found at the confluence of the Marowijne's two main tributaries, the Tapanahony and Lawa. The island's strategic position means it has regularly served as a military post. It is named after a colonial officer who led an 18th-century campaign against the Marron leader Boni, and it also served as the headquarters of Ronnie Brunswijk's 'Jungle Commando' for a period during the late 1980s.

GETTING THERE AND AWAY Realistically, the only affordable way to explore this remote area is on an **organised tour**, and these are few and far between. A recommended budget-ish option is the fixed-departure four-day trip to Mina Falls offered by **Blue Frog Travel** (`\`*420808;* `e` *info@bluefrogtravel.eu; www.bluefrogtravel. eu*), which involves a road transfer to Lange Tabiki, then a boat trip upriver to a hammock camp on an uninhabited island in the shadow of the Nassau Mountains, as well as the hike to the waterfall and a visit to the traditional Paramacca village of Loka Loka. Alternatively, for those without budgetary restrictions, more upmarket operators in Paramaribo should be able to organise a trip flying in and out from the airstrips at Lange Tabiki and/or Stoelman's Island.

12

Appendix 1

FURTHER INFORMATION

Note that the lists below only include books published in English. A much larger body of Dutch-language literature covers almost all aspects of Suriname, and a comprehensive selection is stocked at the Vaco Book Shop in Paramaribo (see page 98).

GENERAL HISTORY AND BACKGROUND

Balai, Leo *Slave Ship Leusden: A Story of Mutiny, Shipwreck and Murder* Kindle Edition, 2014. This self-published and inexpensive book, downloadable from amazon.com, provides a detailed account of the sinking of the *Leusden* and the massacre of its human cargo on New Year's Day 1738.

Carlin, Eithne & Diederik Van Goethem *In the Shadow of the Tiger: The Amerindians in Suriname* KIT Publishers, 2009. This fascinating study of Suriname's last indigenous peoples is largely pictorial, but also includes some illuminating text.

Gimlette, John *Wild Coast: Travels on South America's Untamed Edge* Profile Books, 2012. This highly praised contemporary travelogue covering a chaotic trip along the wild coast of Guyana, Suriname and French Guiana provides a gripping and approachable pre-travel introduction to this little-known region.

McLeod, Cynthia *The Cost of Sugar* Waterfront Publishers, 2007. The best known of several worthwhile historical novels by Suriname's pre-eminent writer explores the 18th-century plantation society and repression in Jodensavonne through the eyes of two Jewish stepsisters. It was recently made into a movie that opened the 2013 Netherlands Film Festival.

McLeod, Cynthia *The Free Negress Elisabeth* Arcadia Books, 2008. Fascinating semi-biographical novel documenting the life of Elisabeth Samson, the first free black woman in Suriname, based on five years of historical research.

Versteeg, Aad *Suriname before Columbus* Libri Musei Surinamensis, 2003. This lavish and beautifully illustrated overview of archaeological finds associated with pre-Columbian Suriname is sold at the museum shop in Paramaribo's Fort Zeelandia.

Westoll, Andrew *The Riverbones: Stumbling after Eden in the Jungles of Suriname* McClelland & Stewart, 2008. Written by a primatologist who spent five months studying monkeys in Central Suriname Nature Reserve, and also published under the name *Surinam*, this enjoyable introduction to the natural and human geography of the interior reads like a travelogue.

NATURAL HISTORY
Birds

Haverschmidt, Francois *Birds of Suriname* Vaco, 1995. This comprehensive and authoritative reference work illustrates and describes all species recorded in

Suriname prior to 1995, but is a little dated taxonomically and is also far too bulky for field use. Most websites list it as out of print but it can still be bought (for a price) at the Vaco Book Shop in Paramaribo.

Ottema, Otto *Wild Birds of Paramaribo* STINASU, 2007. Aimed at casual birders based in the capital, this inexpensive and portable book illustrates and describes 100 species commonly seen in and around Paramaribo.

Ottema, Otte H, Jan Heim JM Ribot & Arie L Spaans *Annotated Checklist of the Birds of Suriname* WWF Guianas, 2009. This excellent small book, sold cheaply at several outlets in Paramaribo including the STINASU headquarters, is the ideal companion to volume 2 of the regional Helm Field Guide listed below, and contains plenty of local information useful for narrowing down identification.

Restall, Robin, Clemencia Rodner & Miguel Lentino *Birds of Northern South America: An Identification Guide, Volume 1: Species Accounts* Helm Field Guides, 2007. Probably too bulky and detailed for one-off visitors to the region, this is nevertheless a superb companion to the second and more portable volume 2 (Plates and Maps) recommended below.

Restall, Robin, Clemencia Rodner & Miguel Lentino *Birds of Northern South America: An Identification Guide, Volume 2: Plates and Maps* Helm Field Guides, 2007. This excellent and reasonably practical field guide is a must-buy for serious birders. It illustrates and shows the distribution of all species found in Suriname (along with many that aren't). For the sake of portability, full species accounts are included in a separate volume (see above), but the short notes on the plates, ideally used in conjunction with the *Annotated Checklist* (see above) are enough to allow for identification of all but the most tricky species.

Spaans, Arie *Coastal Birds of Suriname* STINASU, 2003. A very handy volume for casual birders or those sticking to the coast, this inexpensive and portable book illustrates and describes 100 common species, and also has plenty of other interesting background information.

Other wildlife

Boinski, Sue *Monkeys of Suriname* STINASU, 2002. This handy 64-page book is a must for primate enthusiasts. It has excellent text and good pictures covering all eight monkey species known in Suriname.

Eisenberg, John *Mammals of the Neotropics, Volume 1: The Northern Neotropics* University Of Chicago Press, 1989. Too bulky for field use, this rather academic work is nevertheless the only book to include comprehensive coverage of all mammals, terrestrial and marine, found in Suriname.

Gernaat, Hajo *Butterflies of Suriname: A Natural History* KIT Publishers, 2012. This bulky but authoritative introduction to the butterflies of Suriname includes 600 illustrations and accounts of 150 of the more common and interesting species.

Kricher, John *A Neotropical Companion* Princeton University Press, 1999. This readable and broad-based stalwart remains perhaps the finest available introduction to the natural history of the tropical Americas.

Lowen, James *Pantanal Wildlife* Bradt, 2010. This useful and well-illustrated one-volume guide to the wildlife of Brazil's largest wetland has plenty of overlap with Suriname, especially as its coverage of more localised taxa is generally not focused on individual species.

WEBSITES

www-01.sil.org/americas/suriname/Sranan/English/SrananEngDictIndex.html
Very useful online Sranan Tongo–English dictionary

www.consulaatsuriname.nl The website of the Surinamese Consulate in Amsterdam is an invaluable reference point for information about visas, embassies in other countries, and other related matters

www.jodensavanne.sr.org Fascinating website of the Jodensavanne Foundation

www.planktonik.com/birdingsuriname Very useful resource for birders

www.stinasu.sr The authority responsible for nature reserves and conservation in Suriname

www.surinaamsmuseum.net Website of the Suriname Museum Foundation

www.surinamebirds.nl Detailed coverage of Suriname's avifauna with useful checklists for a dozen hotspots

www.surinametourism.sr The official website of the Suriname Tourism Foundation contains plenty of useful travel information

www.surinamyp.com Suriname's Yellow Pages website

www.vaco.sr Website of Suriname's leading bookshop and publisher of local interest books

Appendix 2

LANGUAGE

Written by Ariadne Van Zandbergen, based partly on the equivalent section in Emma Thomson's Bradt Guide to Flanders.

English is widely spoken in Suriname, many signposts are bilingual and most of the time you will have little problem communicating with people involved in any service industry. However, it can be useful to speak a few words of Dutch, even if correct pronunciation can be tricky for the uninitiated thanks to its characteristic strings of running consonants, conjugated vowels and complex array of growls, slurs and throat-clearing sounds. Still, as a general rule, most Dutch speakers are quite used to the sound of spoken English, and vowel pronunciation in both languages is broadly similar, so communication is not as daunting as it would be in, say, French or Spanish. Some rules of thumb are to try and place stress at the beginning of a word, to devoice any consonants at the end of a word and to listen to native speakers and follow their vocalisations as far as possible.

Getting to grips with Suriname's unofficial street language Sranan Tongo would be an ambitious task for the average tourist, especially as Dutch is so widely spoken throughout the country. Nevertheless, Sranan Tongo is an interesting language, not least because so much of the vocabulary derives rather quirkily from English. A comprehensive two-way Sranan Tongo–English dictionary, complete with pronunciation tips and a bit of linguistic background, can be downloaded at www-01.sil.org/americas/suriname/Sranan/STEng.pdf.

DUTCH BASICS Dutch is littered with diphthongs (double sounds) that involve complicated contortions of the mouth and tongue; it's nearly impossible to find the proper equivalent sounds in English, but here are the fundamentals:

Vowels

a like 'a' in 'allotment'
aa like 'ar' in 'arrow'
ae like 'ar' in 'cart'
au like 'ow' in 'cow'
ee like 'ai' in 'sail'
ei like 'ay' in 'way'
eie like 'ay' in 'hay'
eu like 'err' in 'herring'
eeu pronounced ay-ooh

ie like 'ee' in 'free'
ieu pronounced ee-oo
ij like 'ei' – see above
oe like 'oo' in 'stool'
oo like 'oa' in 'coat'
ou like 'ou' in ' about'
ui like 'ui' in 'alleluia'
uu like ' oo' in 'soot'

Consonants

ch like 'ch' in 'chip'
kh like 'ch' in Scottish 'loch'
g like 'g' in 'grow'
j like 'y' in 'yes'
ng like 'ng' in 'string'
nj like 'nio' in 'onion'
v like 'f' in 'follow'
w like 'v' in 'vacuum'
sch like the 'sk' in English 'skip' – 's' is soft, but 'k' is pronounced with throat-clearing as if you're about to spit.

ENGLISH Essentials	DUTCH
Hello	Hallo
Goodbye	Tot ziens
Good morning	Goedemorgen
Good afternoon	Goedemiddag
Good evening	Goedenavond
Good night	Goedenacht
My name is …	Mijn naam is …
I am from …	Ik ben van …
How are you?	Hoe gaat het?
Very well, thank you	Goed, dank u wel
And you?	En met u?
Nice to meet you	Aangenaam kennis te maken
See you later	Tot straks
Thank you	Dank u wel
What's your name?	Wat is u naam?
I don't understand	Ik begrijp het niet
Do you speak English?	Spreekt u engels?
I don't speak Dutch	Ik spreek geen Nederlands
Could you speak more slowly please?	Kunt u wat langzamer praten?
What is this called?	Hoe noemt dit?
What is that?	Wat is dat?
Could you write it down?	Kunt u het opschrijven?
Yes	Ja
No	Nee
No, thank you	Nee, dank u
Please	Alstublieft (a.u.b.)
You're welcome	Graag gedaan
Excuse me	Pardon
I'm sorry	Sorry het spijt me
I don't like …	Ik hou niet van …
Cheers!	Proost!

Requests	
I would like …	Ik wil …
Can I have …?	Kan ik …. krijgen, a.u.b.?
Where is …?	Waar is …?
Where are …?	Waar zijn …?

When do you ...?	Wanneer gaat u...?
I like ...	Ik hou ...

Time

today	vandaag
tonight	vanavond
tomorrow	morgen
yesterday	gisteren
morning	de morgen
afternoon	de middag
evening	de avond
night	de nacht
now	nu
next	volgende
early	vroeg
late	laat
later	later
What time is it?	Hoe laat is het?
When do you close?	Wanneer sluit u?
When do you open?	Wanneer opent u?
one minute	een minuut
one hour	een uur
half an hour	een half uur
a day	een dag
a week	een week
a month	een maand
a year	een jaar

Numbers

0 nul	14 veertien	90 negentig
1 een	15 vijftien	100 honderd
2 twee	16 zestien	1,000 duizend
3 drie	17 zeventien	
4 vier	18 achttien	first eerste
5 vijf	19 negentien	second tweede
6 zes	20 twintig	third derde
7 zeven	21 eenentwintig	fourth vierde
8 acht	30 dertig	fifth vijfde
9 negen	40 veertig	sixth zesde
10 tien	50 vijftig	seventh zevende
11 elf	60 zestig	eighth achtste
12 twaalf	70 zeventig	ninth negende
13 dertien	80 tachtig	tenth tiende

Days of the week

Monday	maandag	Friday	vrijdag
Tuesday	dinsdag	Saturday	zaterdag
Wednesday	woensdag	Sunday	zondag
Thursday	donderdag		

Family

mother	moeder	boyfriend	vriend/lief
father	vader	girlfriend	vriendin/liefje
sister	zus	I am single	Ik ben vrijgezel
brother	broer	I am married	Ik ben getrouwd
grandmother	grootmoeder	friend	vriend
grandfather	grootvader		

Transport

I would like a ticket to …	Ik zou graag een ticket naar …
single	enkel
a return	heen en terug
How much is it?	Hoeveel kost het?
What time does the … leave?	Om welk uur vertrekt de …?
get off?	ik mag uitstappen?
from	van
to	naar
How far is …?	Hoe ver is …?
How do I get to …?	Hoe kom ik naar …?
Where is the …?	Waar is de …?
Is it near?	Is het kort bij?
bus station	busstation
airport	luchthaven
port	haven
bus	bus
plane	vliegtuig
boat	boot
ferry	ferryboot
taxi	taxi
arrivals	aankomst
departures	vertrek
Where is the nearest …	Waar is het dichst bijzijnde …
service station?	benzine station?
diesel	diesel
unleaded petrol	loodvrijë benzine
car	auto
motorbike	moto
bicycle	fiets

Directions

Is this the road to …?	Is dit de weg naar …?
Where is it?	Waar is het?
straight ahead	rechtdoor
right	rechts
left	links
north	noord
south	zuid
west	west
east	oost
behind	achter
in front of	tegenover

| near | dichtbij |
| opposite | tegengesteld |

Signs

entrance	ingang	open	open
exit	uitgang	closed	gesloten
push	duwen	toilets	toiletten/wc
pull	trekken	information	informatie

Accommodation

Where is a cheap/good hotel?	Waar is een goedkoop/goed hotel?
Do you have any rooms available?	Heeft u nog kamers vrij?
I'd like ...	Ik zou graag ...
a single room	enkele kamer
a double room	dubbele kamer
a room with two beds	een kamer met twee bedden
a room with an en-suite bathroom /shower	een slaapkamer met badkamer/douche

Food and drink
Eating out

breakfast	ontbijt
lunch	middagmaal
dinner	diner
I am a vegetarian	Ik ben vegetarisch
soup	soep
main course	hoofdgerecht
dessert	nagerecht
Please may I have ... ?	Kan ik ... krijgen, a.u.b.?
glass	glas
cup	kop/tas
knife	mes
fork	vork
spoon	lepel
plate	bord
menu	kaart
the wine list	de wijn kaart
Where are the toilets?	Waar zijn de toiletten?
It's delicious	Het is heel lekker
Enjoy your meal	Smakelijk
Please may I have the bill	De rekening, alstublieft
tip	drinkgeld/fooi

Basics

bread	brood	sugar	suiker
butter	boter	vinegar	azijn
olive oil	olijfolie	cheese	kaas
pepper	peper	egg	ei
salt	zout	jam	konfituur

Preparation

boiled	gekookt	smoked	gerookt
stewed	gestoofd	grilled	gegrild
fried	gebakken		

Fruit

fruit	vruchten	lemon	citroen
apple	appel	orange	sinaasappel
banana	banaan	pineapple	ananas
grapes	druiven		

Vegetables

vegetables	groenten	mushroom	champignon
beans	bonen/haricots	onion	ui
cabbage	witte kool	peas	erwten
carrot	wortel	potato	aardappel
chips	frieten	rice	rijst
garlic	knoflook	spinach	spinazie
lettuce	sla	tomatoes	tomaat

Fish

fish	vis	lobster	kreeft
seafood	schaaldieren	prawns	garnalen
cod	kabeljauw	squid	inktvis
crab	krab	tuna	tonijn

Meat

meat	vlees	lamb	lam
beef	rundvlees	liver	lever
chicken	kip	pork	varkensvlees
duck	eend	sausage	worst
ham	ham/hesp	venison	wildbraad
kidney	nier		

Drinks

drinks	drankjes
a bottle of red/white wine	een fles rode/witte wijn
still water	platwater
sparkling water	bruiswater
beer	bier
coffee	koffie
tea	thee
milk	melk
ice	ijs

Shopping and practicalities

How much does this cost?	Hoeveel kost dit?
Do you have …?	Heeft u …?
Do you have this in …?	Heeft u dit in …?
chemist/pharmacist	apotheek
market	markt

newsagents	nieuwsagentschap
bookshop	boekhandel
bakery	bakkerij
grocers	kruidenierswinkel
clothes shop	kledingwinkel
I am looking for a …	Ik zoek een …
post office	postkantoor
embassy	ambassade
currency exchange office	cambio/geldwisselkantoor
internet café	internet café

Colours

black	zwart	orange	oranje
blue	blauw	red	rood
brown	bruin	white	wit
green	groen	yellow	geel

Adjectives

cheap	goedkoop	big	groot
expensive	duur	bigger	groter
ugly	lelijk	small	klein
beautiful	mooi	hot	heet
bad	slecht	cold	koud
good	goed	slow	langzaam
difficult	moeilijk	quick	snel
easy	makkelijk	empty	leeg
old	oud	full	vol
new	nieuw		

Index

Page numbers in **bold** indicate major entries; those in *italic* indicate maps

INDEX OF ADVERTISERS